DEMOCRACY IN CHAINS

DEMOCRACY IN CHAINS

THE DEEP HISTORY OF THE RADICAL RIGHT'S STEALTH PLAN FOR AMERICA

NANCY MacLEAN

SCRIBE
Melbourne • London

Scribe Publications
2 John Street, Clerkenwell, London, WC1N 2ES, United Kingdom
18–20 Edward St, Brunswick, Victoria 3056, Australia

This edition published by arrangement with Viking,
an imprint of Penguin Random House LLC, New York

Published by Scribe 2017
Reprinted 2017 (twice), 2018, 2022

Set in Minion Pro

Printed and bound in the UK by CPI Group (UK) Ltd, Croydon CR0 4YY

Scribe Publications is committed to the sustainable use of natural resources and the use of paper products made responsibly from those resources.

978 1 911344 68 1 (UK edition)
978 1 925322 58 3 (Australian edition)
978 1 925548 53 2 (ebook)

Catalogue records for this book are available from the National Library of Australia and the British Library.

scribepublications.co.uk
scribepublications.com.au

ALSO BY NANCY MacLEAN

Freedom Is Not Enough
Behind the Mask of Chivalry

For my teachers

The public choice revolution rings the death knell of the political "we."

—PIERRE LEMIEUX[1]

CONTENTS

INTRODUCTION

A QUIET DEAL IN DIXIE

As 1956 drew to a close, Colgate Whitehead Darden Jr., the president of the University of Virginia, feared for the future of his beloved state. The previous year, the U.S. Supreme Court had issued its second *Brown v. Board of Education* ruling, calling for the dismantling of segregation in public schools with "all deliberate speed." In Virginia, outraged state officials responded with legislation to force the closure of any school that planned to comply. Some extremists called for ending public education entirely. Darden, who earlier in his career had been the governor, could barely stand to contemplate the damage such a rash move would inflict. Even the name of this plan, "massive resistance," made his gentlemanly Virginia sound like Mississippi.

On his desk was a proposal, written by the man he had recently appointed chair of the economics department at UVA. Thirty-seven-year-old James McGill Buchanan liked to call himself a Tennessee country boy. But Darden knew better. No less a figure than Milton Friedman had extolled Buchanan's potential. As Darden reviewed the document, he might have wondered if the newly hired economist had read his mind. For without mentioning the crisis at hand, Buchanan's proposal put in writing what Darden was thinking: Virginia needed to find a better way to deal with the incursion on states' rights represented by *Brown*.

To most Americans living in the North, *Brown* was a ruling to end segregated schools—nothing more, nothing less. And Virginia's response was about race. But to men like Darden and Buchanan, two well-educated sons of the South who were deeply committed to its model of political economy, *Brown* boded a sea change on much more.

At a minimum, the federal courts could no longer be counted on to defer reflexively to states' rights arguments. More concerning was the likelihood that the high court would be more willing to intervene when presented with compelling evidence that a state action was in violation of the Fourteenth Amendment's guarantee of "equal protection" under the law. States' rights, in effect, were yielding in preeminence to individual rights. It was not difficult for either Darden or Buchanan to imagine how a court might now rule if presented with evidence of the state of Virginia's archaic labor relations, its measures to suppress voting, or its efforts to buttress the power of reactionary rural whites by underrepresenting the moderate voters of the cities and suburbs of Northern Virginia. Federal meddling could rise to levels once unimaginable.

James McGill Buchanan was not a member of the Virginia elite. Nor is there any explicit evidence to suggest that for a white southerner of his day, he was uniquely racist or insensitive to the concept of equal treatment. And yet, somehow, all he saw in the *Brown* decision was coercion. And not just in the abstract. What the court ruling represented to him was personal. Northern liberals—the very people who looked down upon southern whites like him, he was sure—were now going to tell his people how to run their society. And to add insult to injury, he and people like him with property were no doubt going to be taxed more to pay for all the improvements that were now deemed necessary and proper for the state to make. What about his rights? Where did the federal government get the authority to engineer society to its liking and then send him and those like him the bill? Who represented their interests in all of this? *I can fight this,* he concluded. *I want to fight this.*

Find the resources, he proposed to Darden, *for me to create a new center on the campus of the University of Virginia, and I will use this center to create a new school of political economy and social philosophy.* It would be an academic center, rigorously so, but one with a quiet political agenda: to defeat the "perverted form" of liberalism that sought to destroy their way of life, "a social order," as he described it, "built on individual liberty," a term with its own coded meaning but one that Darden surely understood. The center, Buchanan promised, would train "a line of new thinkers" in how to argue against those seeking to impose an "increasing role of government in economic and social life."[1]

He could win this war, and he would do it with ideas.

While it is hard for most of us today to imagine how Buchanan or Darden or any other reasonable, rational human being saw the racially segregated Virginia of the 1950s as a society built on "the rights of the individual," no matter how that term was defined, it is not hard to see why the *Brown* decision created a sense of grave risk among those who did.[2] Buchanan fully understood the scale of the challenge he was undertaking and promised no immediate results. But he made clear that he would devote himself passionately to this cause.

Some may argue that while Darden fulfilled his part—he found the money to establish this center—he never got much in return. Buchanan's team had no discernible success in decreasing the federal government's pressure on the South all the way through the 1960s and '70s. But take a longer view—follow the story forward to the second decade of the twenty-first century—and a different picture emerges, one that is both a testament to Buchanan's intellectual powers and, at the same time, the utterly chilling story of the ideological origins of the single most powerful and least understood threat to democracy today: the attempt by the billionaire-backed radical right to undo democratic governance.

For what becomes clear as the story moves forward decade by decade is that a quest that began as a quiet attempt to prevent the state of Virginia from having to meet national democratic standards of fair treatment and equal protection under the law would, some sixty years later, become the veritable opposite of itself: a stealth bid to reverse-engineer all of America, at both the state and the national levels, back to the political economy and oligarchic governance of midcentury Virginia, minus the segregation.

Alas, it wasn't until the early 2010s that the rest of us began to sense that something extraordinarily troubling had somehow entered American politics. All anyone was really sure of was that every so often, but with growing frequency and in far-flung locations, an action would be taken by governmental figures on the radical right that went well beyond typical party politics, beyond even the extreme partisanship that has marked the United States over the past few decades. These actions seemed intended in one way or another to reduce the authority and reach of government or to diminish the power and standing of those calling on government to protect their rights or to provide for them in one way or another.

Some pointed to what happened in Wisconsin in 2011. The newly elected governor, Scott Walker, put forth legislation to strip public employees of nearly all their collective bargaining rights, by way of a series of new rules aimed at decimating their membership. These rules were more devilishly lethal in their cumulative impact than anything the antiunion cause had theretofore produced. What also troubled many people was that these unions had already expressed a readiness to make concessions to help the state solve its financial troubles. Why respond with all-out war?

Over in New Jersey, where Governor Chris Christie started attacking teachers in startlingly vitriolic terms, one headline captured the same sense of bewilderment among those targeted: "Teachers Wonder, Why the Heapings of Scorn?"[3] Why indeed?

Equally mysterious were the moves by several GOP-controlled state legislatures to inflict flesh-wounding cuts in public education, while rushing through laws to enable unregulated charter schools and provide tax subsidies for private education. In Wisconsin, North Carolina, Louisiana, Mississippi, and Iowa, these same GOP-controlled legislatures also took aim at state universities and colleges, which had long been integral components of state economic development efforts—and bipartisan sources of pride. Chancellors who dared to resist their agenda were summarily removed.[4]

Then came a surge of synchronized proposals to suppress voter turnout. In 2011 and 2012, legislators in forty-one states introduced more than 180 bills to restrict who could vote and how. Most of these bills seemed aimed at low-income voters, particularly minority voters, and at young people and the less mobile elderly. As one investigation put it, "the country hadn't seen anything like it since the end of Reconstruction, when every southern state placed severe limits on the franchise."[5]

The movement went national with its all-out campaign to defeat the Obama administration's Affordable Care Act. Hoping to achieve consensus, the White House had worked from a plan suggested by a conservative think tank and tested by Republican Mitt Romney when he was governor of Massachusetts. Yet when the plan was presented to Congress, opponents on the right almost immediately denounced it as "socialism." When they could not prevent its passage, they shut down the government for sixteen days in 2013 in an attempt to defund it.

Numerous independent observers described such stonewalling, vicious partisanship, and attempts to bring the normal functioning of government to a halt as "unprecedented." When the Republicans would not agree to conduct hearings to consider the president's nominee to fill the Supreme Court seat left vacant after Justice Antonin Scalia died in early 2016, even the usually reticent Supreme Court justice Clarence Thomas spoke out. "At some point," he told the Heritage Foundation, a conservative think tank, "we are going to have to recognize that we are destroying our institutions."[6]

But what if the goal of all these actions *was* to destroy our institutions, or at least change them so radically that they became shadows of their former selves?

Many people tried to get a better handle on what exactly was driving this sortie from the right. For example, William Cronon, a University of Wisconsin historian and the incoming president of the American Historical Association, did some digging after Governor Walker's attack on public employee unions in Wisconsin. His investigations convinced him that what had happened in Wisconsin did not begin in the state. "What we've witnessed," he said, is part of a "well-planned and well-coordinated *national* campaign" (italics added). Presciently, he suggested that others look into the funding and activities of a then little-known organization that referred to itself as the American Legislative Exchange Council (ALEC) and kept its elected members a secret from outsiders. It was producing hundreds of "model laws" each year for Republican legislators to bring home to enact in their states—and nearly 20 percent were going through. Alongside laws to devastate labor unions were others that would rewrite tax codes, undo environmental protections, privatize many public resources, and require police to take action against undocumented immigrants.[7] What was going on?

In 2010, the brilliant investigative journalist Jane Mayer alerted Americans to the fact that two billionaire brothers, Charles and David Koch, had poured more than a hundred million dollars into a "war against Obama." She went on to research and document how the Kochs and other rich right-wing donors were providing vast quantities of "dark money" (political spending that, by law, had become untraceable) to groups and candidates whose missions, if successful, would hobble unions, limit voting, deregulate corporations, shift taxes to the less well-off, and even deny climate change.[8] But still missing from this exquisitely detailed examination of the money trail was any clear sense of the master plan behind all these assaults, some sense of when and why this cause started, what defined victory, and, most of all, where that victory would leave the rest of us.

In an attempt to find that master plan, to understand whose ideas were guiding this militant new approach, others attempted to link what was happening to the ideas of the celebrity intellectuals of the so-called neoliberal right (neoliberal because they identify with the eighteenth- and nineteenth-century pro-market liberalism of thinkers such as Adam Smith)—especially such avid promoters as Milton Friedman, Ayn Rand, and Friedrich A. Hayek.[9] But such inquiries ran aground, because none of the usual suspects had sired this campaign. The missing piece of the puzzle was James McGill Buchanan.

This, then, is the true origin story of today's well-heeled radical right, told through the intellectual arguments, goals, and actions of the man without whom this movement would represent yet another dead-end fantasy of the far right, incapable of doing serious damage to American society.

I discovered Buchanan's formative role in the rise of this distinctive strand of the radical right by sheer serendipity, not intentional pursuit. I am a historian of American social movements and their impact on public policy. About ten years ago, I became interested in Virginia's decision to issue state-subsidized education vouchers to fund enrollment in all-white private schools in the aftermath of *Brown*. The thinker most associated with vouchers at that time was Milton Friedman, so I began to read his work and examine his papers. Twice, though, I came across a footnote pointing to another economist named James McGill Buchanan, who had founded what some called the Virginia school of political economy. Although I had not previously heard of him, he seemed to be someone with big ideas that somehow differed from Friedman's, even as they played on the same team.[10] Given the Virginia connection, I thought I should know more about him and began to read his work, too. When I learned of an unlisted archive located at George Mason University's Fairfax, Virginia, campus that held his papers, I decided to pay it a visit in 2013, after Buchanan's death earlier that year.[11]

Most archives house the papers of dozens, if not hundreds, of different individuals and organizations. There is invariably a full staff of trained archivists and various assistants who work tirelessly to collect, process, and make available to scholars their holdings. "Buchanan House" was different. It turned out to be an old clapboard mansion on the grounds of George Mason University's main campus, where this once revered figure and his colleagues had worked. Now it is all but deserted. Rooms that had once served as seminar spaces and sitting areas for meeting with visitors and donors were now filled with boxes of unsorted material from the dead man's home. There were file cabinets everywhere—even, I soon learned, in a closet under a stairwell.

When I entered Buchanan's personal office, part of a stately second-floor suite, I felt overwhelmed. There were papers stacked everywhere, in no discernible order. Not knowing where to begin, I decided to proceed clockwise, starting with a pile of correspondence that was resting, helter-skelter, on a chair to the left of the door. I picked it up and began to read. It contained confidential letters from 1997 and 1998 concerning Charles Koch's investment of millions of dollars in Buchanan's Center for Study of Public Choice and a flare-up that followed. Catching my breath, I pulled up an empty chair and set to work.

It took me time—a great deal of time—to piece together what these documents were telling me. They revealed how the program Buchanan had first established at the University of Virginia in 1956 and later relocated to George Mason University, the one meant to train a new generation of thinkers to push back against *Brown* and the changes in constitutional thought and federal policy that had enabled it, had become the research-and-design center for a much more audacious project, one that was national in scope. This project was no longer simply about training intellectuals for a battle of ideas; it was training operatives to staff the far-flung and purportedly separate, yet intricately connected, institutions funded by the Koch brothers and their now large network of fellow wealthy donors. These included the Cato Institute, the Heritage Foundation, Citizens for a Sound Economy, Americans for Prosperity, FreedomWorks, the Club for Growth, the State Policy Network, the Competitive Enterprise Institute, the Tax Foundation, the Reason Foundation, the Leadership Institute, and more, to say nothing of the Charles Koch Foundation and Koch Industries itself. Others were being hired and trained here to transform legal understanding and practice on matters from health policy to gun rights to public sector employment. Still others were taking what they learned here to advise leading Republicans and their staffs, from Virginia governors to presidential candidates. The current vice president, Mike Pence, a case in point, has worked with many of these organizations over the years and shares their agenda.[12]

With these records, combined with those I found elsewhere, I started piecing together the first detailed picture of how this movement began and, more important, how it evolved over time, both in its goals and in its strategy. I learned how and why Charles Koch first became interested in Buchanan's work in the early 1970s, called on his help with what became the Cato Institute, and worked with his team in various organizations. What became clear is that by the late 1990s, Koch had concluded that he'd finally found the set of ideas he had been seeking for at least a quarter century by then—ideas so groundbreaking, so thoroughly thought-out, so rigorously tight, that once put into operation, they could secure the transformation in American governance he wanted. From then on, Koch contributed generously to turning those ideas into his personal operational strategy to, as the team saw it, save capitalism from democracy—permanently.

These papers revealed something else as well: how and why stealth became so intrinsic to this movement. Buchanan had realized the value of stealth long ago, while still trying to influence Virginia politicians. But it was Koch who institutionalized this policy. In his first big gift to Buchanan's program, Charles Koch signaled his desire for the work he funded to be conducted behind the backs of the majority. "Since we are greatly outnumbered," Koch conceded to the assembled team, the movement could not win simply by persuasion. Instead, the cause's insiders had to use their knowledge of "the rules of the game"—that game being how modern democratic governance works—"to create winning strategies." A brilliant engineer with three degrees from MIT, Koch warned, "The failure to use our superior technology ensures failure." Translation: the American people would not support their plans, so to win they had to work behind the scenes, using a covert strategy instead of open declaration of what they really wanted.[13]

The irony haunted me as I systematically worked my way through the piles of papers in Buchanan's personal office and then moved on to the cabinets filled with documents that revealed virtually every step in the evolution of his ideas and associations. I was able to do so because Koch's team had since moved on to a vast new command-and-control facility at George Mason called the Mercatus Center, leaving Buchanan House largely untended. Future-oriented, Koch's men (and they are, overwhelmingly, men) gave no thought to the fate of the historical trail they left unguarded. And thus, a movement that prided itself, even congratulated itself, on its ability to carry out a revolution below the radar of prying eyes (especially those of reporters) had failed to lock one crucial door: the front door to a house that let an academic archive rat like me, operating on a vague hunch, into the mind of the man who started it all.

James Buchanan did not start out as a shill for billionaires. For one thing, there were no billionaires in the United States in 1956—only the oil magnate J. Paul Getty even came close.[14] In an age when even kindred economists like Milton Friedman were producing ever more specialized and technical scholarship, Buchanan was a throwback to another time. His dream was to become a political economist in the classical mode, like Adam Smith, a veritable social philosopher. But instead of studying the things others in the discipline did, Buchanan wanted to use an economic definition of incentives to examine government behavior, in the hope of returning America to "the free society" it had once been, only some of whose lineaments the Virginia of the 1950s had managed to preserve.

So what exactly constituted that "free society" where the "liberty of the individual" was preserved? Buchanan found it in an earlier time when government was usually weak. There were, consequently, few rules to constrain how a man might get wealthy, and great restraints on the government in asking for some part of that wealth, other than for the maintenance of order and military defense.

What animated Buchanan, what became the laser focus of his deeply analytic mind, was the seemingly unfettered ability of an increasingly more powerful federal government to force individuals with wealth to pay for an increasing number of public goods and social programs they had had no personal say in approving. Better schools, newer textbooks, and more courses for black students might help the children, for example, but whose responsibility was it to pay for these improvements? The parents of these students? Others who wished voluntarily to help out? Or people like himself, compelled through increasing taxation to contribute to projects they did not wish to support? To Buchanan, what others described as taxation to advance social justice or the common good was nothing more than a modern version of mob attempts to take by force what the takers had no moral right to: the fruits of another person's efforts. In his mind, to protect wealth was to protect the individual against a form of legally sanctioned gangsterism.

Where did this gangsterism begin? Not in the way we might have expected him to explain it to Darden: with do-good politicians, aspiring attorneys seeking to make a name for themselves in constitutional law, or even activist judges. It began before that: with individuals, powerless on their own, who had figured out that if they joined together to form social movements, they could use their strength in numbers to move government officials to hear their concerns and act upon them.

The most powerful social movement back then was what Buchanan's proposal referred to as "the labor monopoly movement," or what most of us would today call organized labor. But other movements, also injurious in his mind, were on the horizon, including the increasingly influential civil rights movement and a resumed push by elderly citizens to organize as they had not since the Great Depression. From his vantage point, it did not matter whether the movement in question consisted of union members, civil rights activists, or aging women and men fearful of ending their lives in poverty. Nor did the justness of the cause they advocated, the pain of their present condition, or the duration of the injustice they were attempting to reverse move him in any way. The only fact that registered in his mind was the "collective" source of their power—and that, once formed, such movements tended to stick around, keeping tabs on government officials and sometimes using their numbers to vote out those who stopped responding to their needs. How was this fair to other individuals? How was this American?

Buchanan believed with every fiber of his being that if what a group of people wanted from government could not, on its own merits, win the freely given backing of each individual citizen, including the very wealthiest among us, any attempt by that group to use its numbers to get what it wanted constituted not persuasion of the majority but coercion of the minority, a violation of the liberty of individual taxpayers.

To end the coercion, he counseled, one had to stop "government corruption." By that he meant the quiet quid pro quo reached between government officials and organized groups that keeps these officials reflexively attuned and responsive to the demands of such groups in exchange for their votes.[15] At first he thought he could explain to government officials how wrong it was for them to accede to this arrangement; even under Keynesian economic theory, popular since the Great Depression, government was only meant to spend more than it took in during recessions. But he soon learned that even in antidemocratic 1950s Virginia, few politicians would follow his recommended courses of action if doing so jeopardized their own reelections.

UVA in the 1950s was not a top research institution, but it was a venerable one, so Buchanan understood that asking Darden to fund what was in essence a political center at a nonprofit of higher learning was highly inappropriate. To avoid criticism that "an organization with extreme views, or a propagandizing agency" was being established on campus, he recommended that the center should *not* have the words "economic liberty" in its name, even if this phrase captured "the real purpose of the program."[16]

He displayed the same canniness in the names he gave to various elements of his economic theory—the Virginia school of political economy, as it came to be known. His study of how government officials make decisions became "public choice economics"; his analysis of how the rules of government might be altered so officials could not act on the will of the majority became "constitutional economics." The enemy became "the collective order," a code phrase for organized social and political groups that looked to government.

Jargon aside, Buchanan used his center to refine his research program over the years while also figuring out how to develop a sophisticated strategy to implement his vision. The intellectual and the activist in him worked side by side, but one had enormous success while the other did not appear to be making much headway.

Buchanan's penetrating analyses of how incentives guide government action would be awarded the Nobel Prize in Economic Sciences in 1986. That award was the supreme vindication of his intellectual achievement. But the other Buchanan, the deeply political foot soldier of the right, experienced mounting despair. His attempts to win passage of radical proposals in Virginia in the late 1950s failed miserably, because legislators understood what at first he did not: the unpopularity of his political-economic vision.

Buchanan's hopes were lifted with the presidential run of Barry Goldwater in 1964. But when the candidate conveyed to voters his desire to end Social Security as we know it, to disallow the Civil Rights Act under the combined rubric of property rights and states' rights, to create a flat tax system, and to undercut public education, he lost every state in the union except his home state of Arizona and those of the Deep South.[17]

Even when conservatives later gained the upper hand in American politics, Buchanan saw his idea of economic liberty pushed aside. Richard Nixon expanded government more than his predecessors had, with costly new agencies and regulations, among them a vast new Environmental Protection Agency. George Wallace, a candidate strongly identified with the South and with the right, nonetheless supported public spending that helped white people. Ronald Reagan talked the talk of small government, but in the end, the deficit ballooned during his eight years in office. When the Cold War suddenly came to an end in 1989, social movement organizations began sharing ideas about how to apply what came to be called "the peace dividend," each with its own proposals for domestic betterment. Compounding the problems Buchanan faced of elected officials who seemed like allies but, once in power, failed to walk the walk was the passage of the National Voter Registration Act of 1993. It began drawing into the electorate more poor people who, in Buchanan's eyes, were likely to support proposals for programs that cost yet more money. Moreover, as the 1990s went on, environmentalists pushed climate change into the national discussion. Their calls for bold new government action looked likely to succeed, because so many citizens identified as environmentalists by then. It was hard for Buchanan not to become pessimistic.

Had there not been someone else as deeply frustrated as Buchanan, as determined to fight the uphill fight, but in his case with much keener organizational acumen, the story this book tells would no doubt have been very different. But there was. His name was Charles Koch. An entrepreneurial genius who had multiplied the earnings of the corporation he inherited by a factor of at least one thousand, he, too, had an unrealized dream of liberty, of a capitalism all but free of governmental interference and, at least in his mind, thus able to achieve the prosperity and peace that only this form of capitalism could produce. The puzzle that preoccupied him was how to achieve this in a democracy where most people did not want what he did.

The Libertarian Party he funded to run against Ronald Reagan in 1980, with his brother David on the ticket, had proven a joke, hardly worth the investment, save for its attraction of new recruits to the cause. The Cato Institute, which he founded and funded, had not proven much more effective in its advocacy. Politicians might be persuaded to spout such Cato slogans as "the ownership society," but when push came to shove, they were unwilling to inflict radical changes of the magnitude his team sought. Ordinary electoral politics would never get Koch what he wanted.

Passionate about ideas to the point of obsession, Charles Koch had worked for three decades to identify and groom the most promising libertarian thinkers in hopes of somehow finding a way to break the impasse. He subsidized and at one point even ran an obscure academic outfit called the Institute for Humane Studies in that quest. "I have supported so many hundreds of scholars" over the years, he once explained, "because, to me, this is an experimental process to find the best people and strategies."[18]

Koch first learned of Buchanan in the early 1970s, the moment when the economist shifted from analysis of the seeming inability of government officials to say no when deficits were allowed to crafting the playbook for radical change—change so radical he referred to it as revolutionary. The goal of the cause, Buchanan announced to his associates, should no longer be to influence *who* makes the rules, to vest hopes in one party or candidate. The focus must shift from *who* rules to changing *the* rules. For liberty to thrive, Buchanan now argued, the cause must figure out how to put legal—indeed, constitutional—shackles on public officials, shackles so powerful that no matter how sympathetic these officials might be to the will of majorities, no matter how concerned they were with their own re-elections, they would no longer have the ability to respond to those who used their numbers to get government to do their bidding. There was a second, more diabolical aspect to the solution Buchanan proposed, one that we can now see influenced Koch's own thinking. Once these shackles were put in place, they had to be binding and permanent. The only way to ensure that the will of the majority could no longer influence representative government on core matters of political economy was through what he called "constitutional revolution."[19]

This was Buchanan's parting gift to the cause he had sired—the insistence that majority rule, under modern conditions, had created such systemic corruption, at such risk to capitalism, that "no existing political constitution contains sufficient constraints or limits" on government. "In this sense, all existing constitutions are failures," he stated repeatedly to operatives of the right that his team trained, as well as to corporate sponsors. So, too, had been "almost all proposals for reform."[20]

By the late 1990s, Charles Koch realized that the thinker he was looking for, the one who understood how government became so powerful in the first place and how to take it down in order to free up capitalism—the one who grasped the need for stealth because only piecemeal, yet mutually reinforcing, assaults on the system would survive the prying eyes of the media—was James Buchanan. For a brief moment in time it seemed as if Buchanan and Koch would lead the revolution together. But men like James Buchanan and Charles Koch do not share power, and in a competition between the two, who would win was a forgone conclusion. Choosing to slide into effective retirement, Buchanan would live to see Charles Koch and his inner circle turn the ideas into a revolutionary plan of action with frightening speed and success.

Koch never lied to himself about what he was doing. While some others in the movement called themselves conservatives, he knew exactly how radical his cause was. Informed early on by one of his grantees that the playbook on revolutionary organization had been written by Vladimir Lenin, Koch dutifully cultivated a trusted "cadre" of high-level operatives, just as Lenin had done, to build a movement that refused compromise as it devised savvy maneuvers to alter the political math in its favor.

But no war is won with all generals and no infantry. The cause also needed a popular base to succeed, one beyond the libertarians of the right, who were kindred in conviction but few in number. Camouflaging its more radical intentions, the cadre over time reached out and pulled in the vast and active conservative grassroots base by identifying points of common cause.[21] Indeed, after 2008, the cadre more and more adopted the mantle of conservatism, knowing full well that the last thing they wanted was to conserve, but seeing advantages in doing so.

A similar cynicism ruled Koch's decision to make peace—at least in the short term—with the religious right, despite the fact that so many libertarian thinkers, Buchanan included, were atheists who looked down on those who believed in God. But the organizers who mobilized white evangelicals for political action—men such as Reverend Jerry Falwell and Ralph Reed and Tim Phillips—were entrepreneurs in their own right, so common cause could be made. The religious entrepreneurs were happy to sell libertarian economics to their flocks—above all, opposition to public schooling and calls for reliance on family provision or charity in place of government assistance.[22] So, too, did the Koch team learn how to leverage wider corporate backing, despite its opposition to the fruits of corporate lobbying of government—from farm subsidies and targeted tax breaks to protection of particular industries from foreign competition.[23]

The Koch team's most important stealth move, and the one that proved most critical to success, was to wrest control over the machinery of the Republican Party, beginning in the late 1990s and with sharply escalating determination after 2008. From there it was just a short step to lay claim to being the true representatives of the party, declaring all others RINOS—Republicans in name only. But while these radicals of the right operate *within* the Republican Party and use that party as a delivery vehicle, make no mistake about it: the cadre's loyalty is not to the Grand Old Party or its traditions or standard-bearers. Their loyalty is to their revolutionary cause.

Republican Party veterans who believed they would be treated fairly because of their longtime service soon learned that, to their new masters, their history of dedication to Republicanism meant nothing. The new men in the wings respect only compliance; if they fail to get it, they respond with swift vengeance. The cadre targets for removal any old-time Republicans deemed a problem, throwing big money into their next primary race to unseat them and replace them with the cause's more "conservative" choices—or at least to teach them to heel.

U.S. senator Arlen Specter, of Pennsylvania, one of the first longtime Republicans to lose his seat for his failure to obey, referred to those who undermined him as "cannibals" who seek "the end of governing as we know it." Others learned from experience how to survive. The Reagan Republican and six-term U.S. senator Orrin Hatch of Utah exploded after being targeted by a challenger from his own party in 2012: "These people are not conservatives. They're not Republicans. They're radical libertarians. . . . I despise these people." He was right that they were not what they said they were, but the scare taught him to stop bucking and comply to keep his job. And, of course, there is John Boehner, the former House Speaker, who in 2015 finally gave up and walked out, calling one of the leaders of this cause inside the Capitol, Ted Cruz, "Lucifer in the flesh."[24]

These are not words people use for their trusted teammates in a partisan program.

Our trouble in grasping what has happened comes, in part, from our inherited way of seeing the political divide. Americans have been told for so long, from so many quarters, that political debate can be broken down into conservative versus liberal, pro-market versus pro-government, Republican versus Democrat, that it is hard to recognize that something more confounding is afoot, a shrewd long game blocked from our sight by these stale classifications.

We don't understand that the old Republican Party, the one my own father voted for during most of his life, exists no more. Many do grasp that the body with that name has somehow become hard-line and disciplined to a degree never before seen in an American major party; yet, not having words to fit what it has become, we assume that what we are seeing is just very ugly partisanship, perhaps made worse by social media.[25] But it is more than that. The Republican Party is now in the control of a group of true believers for whom compromise is a dirty word.

Their cause, they say, is liberty. But by that they mean the insulation of private property rights from the reach of government—and the takeover of what was long public (schools, prisons, western lands, and much more) by corporations, a system that would radically reduce the freedom of the many.[26] In a nutshell, they aim to hollow out democratic resistance. And by its own lights, the cause is nearing success.[27]

The 2016 election looked likely to bring a big presidential win with across-the-board benefits. The donor network had so much money and power at its disposal as the primary season began that every single Republican presidential front-runner was bowing to its agenda. Not a one would admit that climate change was a real problem or that guns weren't good—and the more widely distributed, the better. Every one of them attacked public education and teachers' unions and advocated more charter schools and even tax subsidies for religious schools. All called for radical changes in taxation and government spending. Each one claimed that Social Security and Medicare were in mortal crisis and that individual retirement and health savings accounts, presumably to be invested with Wall Street firms, were the best solution. Jeb Bush went so far as to coauthor a book with a perennial Koch favorite, Clint Bolick, urging immigration reform on terms that suited their vision.[28]

But then something unexpected happened. Donald Trump, a real estate mogul and television celebrity who did not need the Koch donor network's money to run, who seemed to have little grasp of the goals of this movement, entered the race. More than that, to get ahead, Trump was able to successfully mock the candidates they had already cowed as "puppets." And he offered a different economic vision. He loved capitalism, to be sure, but he was not a libertarian by any stretch. Like Bill Clinton before him, he claimed to feel his audience's pain. He promised to stanch it with curbs on the very agenda the party's front-runners were promoting: no more free-trade deals that shuttered American factories, no cuts to Social Security or Medicare, and no more penny-pinching while the nation's infrastructure crumbled. He went so far as to pledge to build a costly wall to stop immigrants from coming to take the jobs U.S. companies offered them because they could hire desperate, rightless workers for less. He said and did a lot more, too, much that was ugly and incendiary. And in November, he shocked the world by winning the Electoral College vote.

Although Trump himself may not fully understand what his victory signaled, it put him between two fundamentally different, and opposed, approaches to political economy, with real-life consequences for us all. One was in its heyday when Buchanan set to work. In economics, its standard-bearer was John Maynard Keynes, who believed that for a modern capitalist democracy to flourish, all must have a share in the economy's benefits and in its governance. Markets had great virtues, Keynes knew—but also significant built-in flaws that only government had the capacity to correct. I am not an economist, and I hold no special brief for Keynes; I leave it to others to debate the details of his views. But as a historian, I know that his way of thinking, as implemented by elected officials during the Great Depression, saved liberal democracy in the United States from the rival challenges of fascism and Communism in the face of capitalism's most cataclysmic collapse. And that it went on to shape a postwar order whose operating framework yielded ever more universal hope that, by acting together and levying taxes to support shared goals, life could be made better for all.[29]

The most starkly opposed vision is that of Buchanan's Virginia school. It teaches that all such talk of the common good has been a smoke screen for "takers" to exploit "makers," in the language now current, using political coalitions to "vote themselves a living" instead of earning it by the sweat of their brows. Where Milton Friedman and F. A. Hayek allowed that public officials were earnestly trying to do right by the citizenry, even as they disputed the methods, Buchanan believed that government failed because of bad faith: because activists, voters, and officials alike used talk of the public interest to mask the pursuit of their own personal self-interest at others' expense.[30] His was a cynicism so toxic that, if widely believed, it could eat like acid at the foundations of civic life.[31] And he went further by the 1970s, insisting that the people and their representatives must be permanently prevented from using public power as they had for so long. Manacles, as it were, must be put on their grasping hands.

In writing this book, in telling the story of Buchanan and his progeny from 1956 to the present, I have found myself more and more fixated on one gnawing question. Is what we are dealing with merely a social movement of the right whose radical ideas must eventually face public scrutiny and rise or fall on their merits? Or is this the story of something quite different, something never before seen in American history? Could it be—and I use these words quite hesitantly and carefully—a fifth-column assault on American democratic governance?

The phrase originated in the Spanish Civil War, when one of Francisco Franco's subgenerals in the military rebellion against the elected government, according to the contemporaneous *New York Times* report, "stated that he was counting on four columns of troops outside Madrid and another column of persons hiding within the city who would join the invaders as soon as they entered the capital."[32] Since then, the term "fifth column" has been applied to stealth supporters of an enemy who assist by engaging in propaganda and even sabotage to prepare the way for its conquest. It is a fraught term among scholars, not least because the specter of a secretive, infiltrative fifth column has been used in instrumental ways by the powerful—such as in the Red Scare of the Cold War era—to conjure fear and lead citizens and government to close ranks against dissent, with grave costs for civil liberties.[33] That, obviously, is not my intent in using the term. I believe we have an urgent need for more open and probing discussion, not silencing.

Yet, imperfect though it may be, the concept of a fifth column does seem to be the best one available for capturing what is distinctive in a few key dimensions about this quest to ensure the supremacy of capital. For a movement that knows it can never win majority support is not a classic social movement. Throughout our history America has been changed, mostly for the better, by social movements, some of them quite radical—the abolition movement, above all. Our national experience over the past two and a half centuries has demonstrated time and again that the citizenry can learn and grow from social movements, sifting through their claims to adopt and reject as we see fit. Where movement activists win over majorities, they make headway; when they fail to, they in time falter.

This cause is different. Pushed by relatively small numbers of radical-right billionaires and millionaires who have become profoundly hostile to America's modern system of government, an apparatus decades in the making, funded by those same billionaires and millionaires, has been working to undermine the normal governance of our democracy. Indeed, one such manifesto calls for a "hostile takeover" of Washington, D.C.[34]

That hostile takeover maneuvers very much like a fifth column, operating in a highly calculated fashion, more akin to an occupying force than to an open group engaged in the usual give-and-take of politics. The size of this force is enormous. The social scientists who have led scholars in researching the Koch network write that it "operates on the scale of a national U.S. political party" and employs more than three times as many people as the Republican committees had on their payrolls in 2015. This points to another characteristic associated with a fifth column: the tactic of overwhelming the normal political process with schemes to disrupt its functioning. Indeed, this massive and well-funded force is turning the party it has occupied toward ends that most Republican voters do not want, such as the privatization of Social Security, Medicare, and education.[35]

Again, this program is distinct from social movements that build on the basis of candor about their ultimate aims in order to win over majorities. Certainly, the people who created and back this program have every right to fight hard for what they believe in. But they should do it honestly and openly—in all their operations. Rather than subverting democratic processes, they should fully inform the American public of their real goals and leave the decision to the people, once the people have been told the whole truth.

The dream of this movement, its leaders will tell you, is liberty. "I want a society where nobody has power over the other," Buchanan told an interviewer early in the new century. "I don't want to control you and I don't want to be controlled by you."[36] It sounds so reasonable, fair, and appealing. But the story told here will show that the last part of that statement is by far the most telling. This cause defines the "you" its members do not want to be controlled by as the majority of the American people. And its architects have never recognized economic power as a potential tool of domination: to them, unrestrained capitalism *is* freedom.

For all its fine phrases, what this cause really seeks is a return to oligarchy, to a world in which both economic and effective political power are to be concentrated in the hands of a few. It would like to reinstate the kind of political economy that prevailed in America at the opening of the twentieth century, when the mass disfranchisement of voters and the legal treatment of labor unions as illegitimate enabled large corporations and wealthy individuals to dominate Congress and most state governments alike, and to feel secure that the nation's courts would not interfere with their reign.

The first step toward understanding what this cause actually wants is to identify the deep lineage of its core ideas. And although its spokespersons would like you to believe they are disciples of James Madison, the leading architect of the U.S. Constitution, it is not true.[37] Their intellectual lodestar is John C. Calhoun. He developed his radical critique of democracy a generation after the nation's founding, as the brutal economy of chattel slavery became entrenched in the South—and his vision horrified Madison.

DEMOCRACY IN CHAINS

PROLOGUE

THE MARX OF THE MASTER CLASS

Those who are leading today's push to upend the political system are heirs to a set of ideas that goes back almost two centuries: the push-back of imperious property against democracy. Its earliest coherent expression in America came in the late 1820s and '30s, from South Carolina's John C. Calhoun, a strategist of ruling-class power so shrewd that the acclaimed historian Richard Hofstadter dubbed him "the Marx of the master class."[1] Hofstadter's label gestured, with his signature sense of irony, to the revolutionary nature of Calhoun's strategy for how the wealthiest one percent (actually, far fewer) of his day could wield outsize power in a constitutional republic. A former vice president and, at the time he devised his plan, a U.S. senator, Calhoun was America's first tactician of tax revolt, and arguably the nation's most influential extremist.

It's not a secret legacy. Some of James M. Buchanan's intellectual heirs have remarked on how closely his school of political economy mirrors that of John C. Calhoun's. Alexander Tabarrok and Tyler Cowen, two economics professors at the core of the operation funded and overseen by Charles Koch at George Mason University, Buchanan's last home, have called the antebellum South Carolina senator "a precursor of modern public choice theory," another name for the stream of thought pioneered by Buchanan. Both Buchanan and Calhoun, the coauthors observe, were concerned with the "failure of democracy to preserve liberty." In particular, Buchanan and Calhoun both alleged a kind of class conflict between "tax producers and tax consumers." Both depicted politics as a realm of exploitation and coercion, but the economy as a realm of free exchange. And both designed inventive ways to safeguard minority rights that went beyond the many protections already enshrined in the Constitution.[2] Calhoun and Buchanan both devised constitutional mechanisms to protect an elite economic minority against "exploitation" by majorities of their fellow citizens, and advocated a minority veto power that, as the acolytes note, had "the same purpose and effect."[3] Both thinkers sought ways to restrict what voters could achieve together in a democracy to what the wealthiest among them would agree to.[4]

Appreciation for John C. Calhoun turns out to be not an aberration but a recurrent theme in the brain trust the Kansas-based billionaire Charles Koch has funded over the years. What is so valuable to them in Calhoun's antidemocratic theorizing, notably in his *Disquisition on Government* and in his long magnum opus, *A Discourse on the Constitution and Government of the United States*?[5]

One of the first scholars subsidized by Koch, the Austrian economist Murray Rothbard, spoke openly of the cause's debt to Calhoun, crediting his class analysis of taxation as foundational to the libertarian cause. "Calhoun's insight," Rothbard explained, was "that it was the intervention of the State that *in itself* created the classes and the conflict," not the labor relations of the economy, as previous thinkers believed. Calhoun saw "that some people in the community must be net payers of tax funds, while others are net recipients." (In today's parlance, makers and takers.) By his theory, the net gainers of tax monies were "the 'ruling class' of the exploiters"; the net losers of tax funds were "the 'ruled' or the exploited." Most crucially, Calhoun and Rothbard inverted how most people would construe who had power over whom. A man whose wealth came from slavery was a victim of government tax collectors, and poorer voters were the exploiters to watch out for. "Calhoun was quite right," Rothbard instructed, "in focusing on taxes and fiscal policy as the keystone" of democracy's threat to economic liberty.[6] To see how Calhoun's project unfolded in his day is to better understand the stealth plan for transformation under way in our own.

By 1860, two of every three of the relatively few Americans whose wealth surpassed $100,000 lived below the Mason-Dixon Line. New York at that time had fewer millionaires per capita than Mississippi. South Carolina was the richest state in the Union. The source of southern wealth was staple crops—particularly cotton—produced by enslaved men, women, and children for world markets. So matchless were the profits that more money was invested in slaves than in industry and railroads.[7]

And no one thought harder about how to safeguard those investments than John C. Calhoun. One female contemporary referred to him as "the cast-iron man," in reference to his hammering manner. With blazing eyes and a raw-boned face, he had a countenance as stern as that of the militant abolitionist John Brown, but with a mission fully opposite. In his day—indeed, for more than a century thereafter—Calhoun had no rival in the sheer wizardry of what one famous political scientist called the "set of constitutional gadgets" that Calhoun engineered to constrict the operations of democratic government.[8]

Calhoun had enjoyed the kind of education available to only a sliver of the elite in early America, including an undergraduate degree at Yale and legal training. He enlisted that education to advance what he took to be the interests of his peculiar class, a richer one than the world had ever known, and one whose interests were not adequately protected, Calhoun believed, by the Constitution as then understood.

There was something alarming, even to his allies, in the monomania with which Calhoun conducted ideological warfare against the political liberalism of his day. He wore people out with his certainty that "the force of destiny" guided him, his relentless reductionist logic, and the nakedly instrumental manner with which he approached human relationships. Compassion, patience, and humor all seemed as foreign to him as the notion that the people he owned had intellects and dreams of their own. President Andrew Jackson, the leader of Calhoun's political party, suggested that the man be hung for treason. That was imprudent. But there was a logic to it, and not only because Calhoun was so unlikable. His ideas about government broke sharply from the vision of the nation's founders and the Constitution's drafters, and even from that of his own party. He wanted one class—his own class of plantation owners—to overpower the others, despite its obvious numerical minority.[9]

Calhoun and his modern understudies are not wrong: there *is* a conflict between their vision of economic liberty and political democracy. Where they are allowed to, majorities will use the political process to improve their situations, and that can result in taxes being imposed on those with the wealth to pay them. The American people have used their power to do many significant things that required tax revenues: provide public education, develop manufacturing, build roads and bridges, create land-grant universities, protect the safety of food and drugs, enable workers to speak as one through unions, prevent old-age poverty, fight discrimination, assure the right to vote, and clean up our air and water, to name a few. These are achievements in which most citizens have taken pride.[10]

But they all came about through means that have become anathema to the militant economic libertarians among today's donor class. They, like Calhoun, believe that Madison's Constitution was flawed by its failure to fully hamstring the people's ability to act "collectively." All the government policies just named came about through group action, after all. The groups persuaded government to act in ways that necessarily limited the freedom of a minority of citizens: those who wanted to go on in the old way.

And that is why Calhoun concluded that if something must be sacrificed to square the circle between economic liberty and political liberty, it was political liberty. The planters' will must prevail. Their property rights should trump all else. The southern delegates to America's founding Constitutional Convention had built numerous protections for property owners, including slave owners, into the document. But that was inadequate in Calhoun's view. He also advocated that states be able to pass whatever laws they saw fit to ensure "their internal peace and security"—in particular, "all such laws as may be necessary to maintain the existing relation between master and slaves." That included measures to outlaw the circulation of antislavery literature. In the name of secure property, he called on the federal government to use its control of the Postal Service to enforce such prohibitions on others' First Amendment freedom to publish and read what they liked.[11]

Note the emerging pattern, which we will see again: while criticizing government action that threatened his own liberty as a property owner, Calhoun saw nothing untoward in calling on the federal government to use its police powers to help his class stifle debate about its practices. That sleight of hand—denying the legitimacy of government power to act for the common good while using government power to suppress others—appears repeatedly in the pages that follow. Indeed, like Calhoun, the members of the team now applying Buchanan's thought are interested not so much in fighting big government, per se, as in elevating that branch of government they can best control in a given situation.

After all, government, for someone like Calhoun, was there to protect property rights, even at the expense of the rights of others to freedom of speech and movement. He opposed allowing popular sovereignty to decide whether slavery should be legal in new states entering the Union.[12] Similarly, in 1847, he warned a free abolitionist of African descent that he would be "turned out of town" if he dared come to Charleston. On what grounds? If "free blacks were allowed to come here," Calhoun noted, "they might excite their fellow Africans to insurrection."[13]

Calhoun's yen for repression appeared in another way that is also revealing for our present situation—and for the history recounted in this book. While he waxed eloquent on the threat of a strong federal state, do not imagine that he preferred local government to state government as a more authentic expression of the people's will. On the contrary, Calhoun led a campaign in the early republic that, in the name of property and individual rights, took powers away from local authorities, on whom ordinary people had more influence, and shifted them to central state governments. Why? State government was the level that men like him could most easily control. In South Carolina, he implemented a new style of state government with centralized power that, the legal historian Laura Edwards explained, was "a radical departure from the past." Under his leadership, South Carolina became the one state in antebellum America furthest from the ideal of government of, by, and for the people. Another leading southerner judged it a "despot's democracy."[14] Far from expressing the original intentions of the Constitution's framers, then, Calhoun and his allies conceived a novel reshuffling of authority in the pursuit of more power for their class.

That pattern of newly power-hungry state governments treading on the time-honored powers of local communities is reappearing in red-state America today, along with the revival of Calhoun-like moves in the nation's capital.[15] Slavery is a moot point now, of course, but the quest to shore up the desires of the most aggressive few over the collective rights of the many is not. Where they have achieved control of state governments since

2010, the ardent advocates of liberty from the federal government have been overturning the accustomed rights of local governments and rushing through radical alterations of established law, as this book's final chapter will show.

The revival of such tactics points to a core theme of this book. What we are seeing today is a new iteration of that very old impulse in America: the quest of some of the propertied (always, it bears noting, a particularly ideologically extreme—and some would say greedy—subsection of the propertied) to restrict the promise of democracy for the many, acting in the knowledge that the majority would choose other policies if it could.

Interestingly, in light of the role of the Tea Party in shaking up American politics after 2009 and the role of U.S. manufacturing's decline in the face of foreign competition in the presidential election of 2016, it was complaints about taxes to help infant industries that first induced Calhoun to advocate extremist measures—and to make his own original contributions to what he called "political science" to justify what he advocated.[16]

Outraged southern planters dubbed the 1828 federal tariff on imported manufactured goods the Tariff of Abominations. Designed to help the infant industries of the United States grow after the War of 1812 with Britain, a war that had exposed America's grave economic weakness, the protective tariff most benefited the region interested in nurturing manufacturing: the free states of the Northeast. The tax disproportionately pinched the export-oriented cotton-growing South, whose most powerful citizens, owing to the profitability of slave-based production, had little concern for economic diversification. Calhoun cried foul. "We are the serfs of the system," he fulminated. Rage over what he viewed as discriminatory taxation led him to radical positions that could all but undermine the effective framework of government that the Constitution's authors had crafted only a generation earlier. A "government based in the naked principle that the majority ought to govern," Calhoun warned, was sure to filch other men's property and violate their "liberty."[17]

Stepping up to lead the first regionwide tax rebellion in U.S. history, Calhoun was also moving, willy-nilly, to question representative government itself. It may surprise today's readers to know that in those days, Calhoun and like-minded large slave owners found themselves to be very much alone in their questioning of the legitimacy of taxation to advance public purposes. Such concerns did not arise where slavery was absent, the historian Robin Einhorn has shown, in the first careful study to examine state and local tax practices in early America. Einhorn found that where they were free to do so, voters regularly called on their governments to perform services they valued and elected candidates who pledged to provide them. They believed, as Oliver Wendell Holmes Jr. later put it, that taxes are "the price we pay for civilization."[18]

What early free-state American voters liked about tax policy in their self-governing republic was that they, the people, decided by majority rule what they wanted their elected officials to do and how to tax for it. For these citizens, liberty meant having a say in questions of governance, being able to enter the public debate about the best way forward. Tracing such debates from the Colonial Era to the Civil War, Einhorn concluded, "American governments were more democratic, stronger, and more competent" where slavery was negligible or nonexistent. They were "more aristocratic, weaker, and less competent" where slavery dominated, as well as more likely to be captured by the wealthy few, who turned them to their own ends. Voters in free states wanted active government: they taxed themselves for public schools, roads to travel from place to place, canals to move their goods, and more. In the southern states, the yeomen of the backcountry, where slaves were fewer, often tried to get their governments to take up their concerns but found that "planters saw threats to their 'property' in any political action they did not control, even if the yeomen actually were demanding roads, schools, and other mundane services." The irony of all this is vast, as Einhorn points out: "The anti-government rhetoric that continues to saturate our political life is rooted in [support for] slavery rather than liberty." The paralyzing suspicion of government so much on display today, that is to say, came originally not from average people but from elite extremists such as Calhoun who saw federal power as a menace to their system of racial slavery.[19]

More than that, to stop what he imagined to be the exploitation of men like himself, Calhoun set out to alter understanding of the U.S. Constitution. The system that James Madison and the other framers had devised for the protection of property rights did not go far enough, according to the South's most self-seeking capitalist. It did not shackle the people's power sufficiently—even though one of the main goals of the U.S. Constitution's famed checks and balances was precisely to keep sudden swings of public opinion from undermining political institutions, particularly those that protected property. But the Constitution no longer seemed enough.

To grasp the scale of Calhoun's departure from the vision of the founders, it bears remembering that neither Madison nor his colleagues had been fans of pure democracy. As the main architect of the Constitution and a slave master of great wealth himself, Madison thought long and hard about how to protect minority rights in a government based on sovereignty of the people, a people then understood to be white men of property. He and his fellow framers built numerous protections of minority rights and property rights into the document, among them the Electoral College and the Senate, with their systems of representation that favored less populous states. They also safeguarded slavery, the most well known example being the clause of Article I, Section 2, that counted "all other Persons" other than "free Persons" and Indians as "three fifths" of a person in apportioning representation and taxes. Still, Madison, Jefferson, and other statesmen of the founding era were sufficiently ashamed of slavery that they never mentioned it by name in the document. They anticipated that their system of human bondage would and should wither away.[20]

Not so Calhoun. Not of the revolutionary generation himself, he had none of the founders' embarrassment over "the peculiar institution" of chattel slavery. His was the cohort of the cotton gin, the technological innovation that turned plantation slavery into the most profitable capitalist enterprise the world had yet seen. Calhoun made slavery a point of pride, going so far as to announce from the Senate floor that it was "a positive good." It was good, Calhoun asserted, for the masters of the South, good for the capitalists of the North (because it made the South "the great conservative power" able to protect the interests of property nationwide against any rebellion from free labor), and good even for the enslaved, who, according to Calhoun, could count on food and shelter where the free wage earners of the North could not.[21]

Calhoun, the precocious political scientist, began making his aggressive case for slavery's superiority just as the free-labor North was outstripping the South in population and its political institutions were becoming more inclusive of working people (rather akin to the changes in demography and voting rights in the early twenty-first century that alarmed some billionaires). Calhoun was not about to forgo the riches King Cotton augured for men like him just because some escaped slaves, free blacks, and born-again white abolitionists had started campaigning against slavery as an affront to God that desecrated the teaching of Jesus and despoiled the Declaration of Independence. Being a shrewd man, Calhoun could see the arithmetic of national politics changing. If something was not done, slave masters would lose the sway they had enjoyed at the founding, when the regions were more evenly matched in population. "The South," Calhoun warned in 1831, was already "a hopeless minority."[22]

The South Carolina statesman left no stone unturned in his quest to make his region's labor system appear acceptable. Nature decreed, he avowed, that those of different races "cannot live together in peace, or harmony, or their mutual advantage," unless one dominated the other, as whites did blacks in the South. Slavery was the proper condition for those not of European descent.[23] And had not the Bible condoned enslavement? As Calhoun once summarized his case, "Slavery is an institution ordained by Providence, honored by time, sanctioned by the Gospel, and especially favorable to personal and national liberty."[24]

Slavery favorable to liberty? For all their invocations of the Bible and the era's pseudoscience of race, Calhoun and his peers knew the cold reality that they were practicing a type of capitalism that would not pass democratic scrutiny much longer if majority opinion was allowed to prevail in Washington. Even if those outside the South were not prepared to abolish slavery outright, let alone grant its victims civil and political equality, they were increasingly inclined to see the institution as an affront to the nation's founding principles—and a mortal threat to their own economic and political future. The cry "free soil, free labor, free men" captured their hopes and fears.[25]

To Calhoun, by contrast, freedom above all concerned the free use and enjoyment of one's productive property, without any impingement by others. If he deemed it necessary to punish one of his workers with "30 lashes well laid on" and a diet of "bread and water," as he did a young runaway slave named Aleck, such was his prerogative as an owner. How he disciplined his labor force to keep his enterprise profitable should be no one else's business.[26] Such practices fell under the heading of the property rights that Calhoun was trying to make absolute in a society that, in point of fact, had always regulated property rights in all kinds of ways, albeit then mainly at the state and local level.[27]

Where the economy should be the realm of total liberty for the owning class in Calhoun's interpretation, government—particularly the federal government—was the realm of potential abuse, such that men of property must ever guard against the certainty of "oppression" if that government came under the control of the majority. As his class's interests increasingly diverged from those of other citizens', Calhoun more and more identified the federal government as a menace to liberty. Scared of what democracy in the nation's capital portended for the security of slavery in his region, Calhoun became almost hysterical in his denial that such a "community ever existed as the people of the United States." No, he railed, all "sovereignty" was vested "in the people of the several states" that consented to the federal Union—"not a particle resides . . . in the American people collectively."[28]

What exactly did Calhoun so fear coming from "the American people collectively"? He feared, as his successors today do, a government that his band of like-minded property supremacists could not control. It is unlikely that many of his current heirs have read Calhoun in the original. Rather, they have learned the ideas from modern-day libertarians who exhumed Calhoun's analysis to address matters that troubled them, too.

Indeed, the path to the present of advocacy for the rights of the radical rich minority has been not continuous, but broken for long stretches.[29] Calhoun's ideas went into abeyance for almost a century after the surrender of General Robert E. Lee and his Army of Northern Virginia at Appomattox in April 1865. Yet their value remained understood by some in the South's educated elite, those who cherished a mythical version of the War Between the States (as they called the Civil War) and portrayed it more as a quest to preserve liberty than a defense of slavery. The South as Calhoun and such admirers imagined it was not the actual South, with its biracial population and millions of low-income and middle-class whites who have benefited greatly from the public resources that taxes enable in democracies.

Rather, among the white elite in America's most history-minded region, a refusal to acknowledge the danger of extreme wealth and inequality went hand in hand with antidemocratic and racist strategies of rule. Propertied southerners took the lead in devising schemes to subdue democracy because of their determination to safeguard the distinctive race-based, hyperexploitative regional political economy that Calhoun and his fellow planters did so much to shape, one based first on chattel slavery and later on disenfranchised low-wage labor, racial segregation, and a starved public sector.[30] In no other part of America has the divergence been starker between the affirmations of the Declaration of Independence and the realities of economic and political power.

The only force strong enough to stop the injustice was the federal government, when pushed to act against the violation of widely shared ideals. As a result, nowhere were elites more self-conscious and strategic in thinking about how to preserve their domination over those they bent to their will—and how to hamstring national democracy. Central to their efforts was a self-serving yet astute interpretation of the Constitution that emphasized states' rights, buttressed by a battery of other rules to subdue the people, black and white. A case in point: to suppress a biracial movement of the region's farmers at the turn of the century without running afoul of the Fourteenth Amendment, white elites in state after southern state devised new laws that decimated black voter turnout without ever mentioning race. Those rules held down everyone but the most wealthy for generations, but they hurt racial minorities most, because they needed the federal government to preserve their rights in the face of abusive employers and state authorities. They still do. And from the start, as Calhoun's calculations illustrate, the notion of unwarranted federal intervention has been inseparable from a desire to maintain white racial as well as class dominance. Not surprisingly, then, but with devastating consequences all around, attacks on federal power pitched to nonelites have almost always tapped white racial anxiety, whether overtly or with coded language.[31]

By the 1950s, the nation's premier workshop for the shrewd construction of elaborate rules to ensure the minority elite's power over the majority was the state of Virginia. The Old Dominion had a venerable tradition of political leadership, as the birthplace of four of the nation's first five presidents, the capital of the Confederacy, and the veritable fiefdom of Senator Harry F. Byrd Sr., the archnemesis of Franklin Delano Roosevelt and the New Deal. Byrd presided over midcentury Virginia like a lord over his manor. Dr. James Buchanan arrived at the state's flagship university just as Senator Byrd's allies were exhuming Calhoun's theories of government for the battle against *Brown v. Board of Education.*

CHAPTER 1

THERE WAS NO STOPPING US

Virginia had become a defendant in one of the five cases folded into *Brown v. Board of Education* owing to the determination of one teenager who had had enough. Tired of taking classes in "tar paper shacks" in an overcrowded "hand-me-down" high school in Prince Edward County, one of the state's former plantation communities, Barbara Rose Johns led a two-week-long strike by her fellow high school students—some 450 in all—to demand a better school. The niece of the Reverend Vernon Johns, the radical minister who later mentored the Reverend Martin Luther King Jr., Barbara Johns never consulted her Montgomery uncle about the strike she was planning.[1]

Instead, the studious girl with sparkling eyes and a luminous smile looked to her favorite teacher, Miss Inez Davenport. The students in Miss Davenport's afternoon class regularly complained that "it wasn't fair" that they attended classes in jury-rigged structures without indoor plumbing that passersby imagined to be chicken coops. Students contended with leaky roofs, woodstoves, rickety furnishings, and cast-off textbooks from white schools. The white students attended a new high school, replete with science labs, indoor plumbing, steam heat, and a well-stocked library and gym. One day in the fall of 1950, when her students were again bemoaning the miserable state of their school, Davenport shared with them a news article about some Massachusetts students who had gone on strike and won over an issue that concerned them. "If they could do that, so could you," she said. Intrigued, Barbara stayed after class to ask whether her teacher really meant what she had said. Strikes were often in the news then, bringing American workers better wages and new powers. But Barbara had never imagined that students might strike, too.[2]

That afternoon exchange was the beginning of a secret student-teacher collaboration that shook Virginia's Jim Crow system as nothing else had before. The black parents in the PTA had again and again visited the superintendent of schools and the school board in their quest for school improvements. A 1947 state Board of Education survey supported their case, finding Robert Russa Moton High School "inadequate," especially with enrollments sure to rise now that the postwar baby boom was under way. The petitioners could at least get a hearing now, because thanks to a push by the National Association for the Advancement of Colored People (NAACP) for "equalization" of black and white schooling, southern officials knew that federal courts were beginning to look askance at their claims to provide "separate but equal" education.[3]

But winning upgrades was another matter, because Virginia's poll tax made it hard for low-income parents to hold elected officials accountable for neglect of their children. Like many other southern states, Virginia required voters to pay a tax to participate in the political process, and it was one of the states that also made that tax cumulative, so that if, say, two elections had not featured candidates who interested you but the third one did, you would have to pay all three years' taxes to vote. In areas like Prince Edward County, which had large numbers of impoverished black farmworkers, the poll tax had proven an effective way to keep them from influencing policy. So the parents had to beg. And county leaders were not persuaded that black students' education merited raising more money.[4]

In self-justification, the officials "would always talk about the Negro tax contribution being so low," only about one-tenth of the county's total revenue from property taxes, said M. Boyd Jones, Moton's principal. "They expected us to raise our incomes without improving education."[5] A better black high school would require either tax increases or a bond issue, neither of which white voters would support, because their children were well provided for in their own schools. Anyway, officials reasoned, why do more for "colored kids" capable only of work in the fields, kitchens, or factories?[6] The white folks making these judgments sought no understanding of the kids whose futures they were so casually writing off.

Collective organization, including strikes, was how the disempowered became strong enough to right the balance against the elites who lorded over them in those days, as an avid reader like Barbara knew. So the seed planted by Miss Davenport grew. As a member of the chorus, the debating team, the drama club, and the student council, Barbara traveled the state and saw enough of other schools to believe it was worth a try. Miss Davenport's vision was straightforward: "If the kids went on strike, the school board would get the message—these kids are serious; let's build them a better school." But she also knew that a strike could put her own and perhaps others' jobs at risk—teachers had no union protection then against retaliatory firing—so she told Barbara that they could no longer be seen talking one-on-one. They must communicate in writing, through notes placed in a music book on Miss Davenport's desk. It was all so unheard of and daring—and therefore dangerous in Jim Crow Virginia—that they destroyed the notes after reading them. Absolute secrecy was essential, Miss Davenport insisted from the outset, as was "orderly and respectful" conduct of the strike.[7]

Miss Davenport instructed Barbara to work slowly and carefully, by recruiting as co-organizers a few strong students who were already popular leaders and who came from respected Prince Edward families that could not be intimidated by employers. Barbara worked methodically, "like a Sidewinder missile locked on its target," in the telling of her first recruit. John Stokes was class president, a top student, a member of the track and debate teams, and the elected statewide president of New Farmers of America, an organization that helped rural young black men develop their leadership abilities. John's younger sister Carrie was president of Moton's student council, created by the principal to enable the students to experience a kind of democracy denied them in real life. Even the local white newspaper recognized the Stokes family as "outstanding" people. The parents were educated, landowning farmers whose three older sons had served as noncommissioned officers in the Army and whose eldest daughter worked for the U.S. Marine Corps; they were also trusted advisers to the black farmers in their part of the county. Barbara summoned John and Carrie to a secret meeting out on the cinder-block bleachers by the school's playing field.[8]

The three dubbed their plan the "Manhattan Project," taking the code name of the World War II mission that produced the first atomic bomb.

Emphasizing "character and leadership skills," they recruited additional leaders to form "the core strike force" of twenty. The plan was straightforward: At an assembly, Barbara "would give a speech stating our dissatisfaction." Carrying picket signs, as other strikers did, the students would then march into town so "people would hear us and see us and understand our difficulty." Student pickets "just outside the high school grounds" would stop any potential strikebreakers from entering Moton.[9]

"We planned this thing to a gnat's eyebrow," John Stokes recalled.[10] For six months, they prepared until "D-Day" arrived, on April 23, 1951. To protect the principal from being held responsible for the strike, a few students lured him away from campus just before 11 A.M. for a fictitious emergency, while the others called a school assembly. The strike committee took the stage. John Stokes led the students in the Lord's Prayer. Teachers were exiled from the auditorium so they wouldn't be fired for collaborating. The organizing committee arrayed behind her on the stage like a Greek chorus, Barbara delivered her speech. With controlled fire she laid out what every student knew—all the problems of their broken-down, overstuffed school, how they were denied resources that every high school student should have to promote learning, not just the white kids. Nothing would change, she told her rapt listeners, unless they joined together and demanded a new school facility.[11]

"Man, you talk about rocking," Stokes would reminisce; amid all the clapping and stomping, "no one was seated." The students rose and walked out en masse, some carrying picket signs made days earlier and hidden for this moment. Heads held high, they marched into town to see the white superintendent of schools. Speaking for the full committee that crowded into his office, Barbara told him that the students were living in "a modern world, and we would appreciate growing with it." His threats of expulsion made no impression. His warning that the students' parents would be jailed unless they desisted got more attention—until someone observed that the town jail was far too small to hold them all. "After that," Stokes said, "there was no stopping us."[12]

With the help of another local adult, the Reverend L. Francis Griffin, Barbara Johns and Carrie Stokes obtained contact information for the state NAACP.[13] Two Richmond-based NAACP attorneys, Spottswood W.

Robinson and Oliver Hill, agreed to come to Farmville to meet with the strikers and their parents. They told them that they would take on the case only if the plaintiffs would go beyond asking for equal facilities and contest segregation itself as inherently unequal. Although neither Johns nor Stokes knew this before they approached the lawyers, the NAACP had just come to an important decision. A team led by the brilliant Charles Hamilton Houston, the dean of Howard University School of Law, had moved beyond its earlier litigation strategy of demanding that separate schools be made truly equal. While they had won improved salaries for black teachers and new black schools in many counties, their campaign required endless one-off battles—with seventy-five school districts in Virginia alone. Taking on Jim Crow itself seemed a surer remedy, if harder to achieve.[14]

The lawyers also insisted on something else: backing for the strike from 95 percent of the black parents.[15] With Reverend Griffin's help, the students signed up parents throughout the far-flung rural county. Even farm tenants and wage laborers who stood to lose their livelihoods if their bosses retaliated signed on. No one was willing to see the new light in their children's eyes extinguished.[16]

On May 3, the NAACP attorneys filed a petition with the Prince Edward County School Board to end separate and inferior education. That night, another mass meeting at First Baptist Church was "jam-packed." Many adults spoke. But the voice that everyone remembered was that of Barbara Johns. "We are depending on you," she told the assembled parents and grandparents, to tears and resounding applause. Reverend Griffin closed the meeting. "Anybody who would not back these children after they stepped out on a limb is not a man," he said.[17]

And that was it: the strike was over. The 450 teenagers, who had maintained complete solidarity, with not a single student returning to school until they all agreed to, pledged to resume classes on Monday, May 7. That was the day their attorneys brought their lawsuit to federal court: *Davis v. County School Board of Prince Edward County,* named for the ninth grader, Dorothy Davis, whose name headed the list of 117 students and 67 parents.[18]

The lawsuit astounded the white elite. Its members could not believe that "their" Negroes would show such ingratitude. After the filing of the lawsuit, they searched for scapegoats and took revenge. County officials refused to renew the principal's contract. Blacklisted throughout the state, Principal Jones and his new wife, Inez Davenport Jones, the teacher who had secretly advised Barbara Johns, moved to Montgomery, Alabama, where they found new jobs and joined Reverend Vernon Johns's congregation. Parents who signed on to the lawsuit and whose names were published in the *Farmville Herald* incurred economic retaliation. Even self-employed farmers, thought safe, could no longer find local buyers for their crops or secure bank loans to get them through to harvest time. What with the menace in the air, Robert and Violet Johns sent their daughter Barbara to live with her uncle Vernon's family in Montgomery, where she could finish high school in safety. John Stokes's family "kept five loaded guns ready" in case they were needed for self-defense; other black households stocked up on shotgun shells to be prepared if trouble came.[19]

In the end, no vigilante violence occurred. Virginia was not Georgia or Mississippi or Alabama, where politicians placated lawbreakers; this was a place where gentlemen ruled, and applauded themselves for well-managed race relations.[20] But they would not concede. And the state court backed them, forcing the aggrieved to appeal.

When *Davis v. County School Board of Prince Edward County* reached the U.S. Supreme Court, as one of the five cases folded into *Brown v. Board of Education,* the state of Virginia intervened on behalf of the county school board and superintendent. "Virginia attacked the psychological evidence introduced by the NAACP," noted the historian James H. Hershman Jr., "and countered with its own expert witnesses who contended that blacks were inferior in mental development."[21] The state attorney general brought in the Virginia-born chairman of Columbia University's psychology department to be the "star witness" for the defense. Dr. Henry Garrett testified that segregation was simply "common sense," and in the best interests of all students. Seeking to rebut the testimony of his former doctoral students Dr. Kenneth Clark and Dr. Mamie Phipps Clark, whose research supported the plaintiffs, Professor Garrett maintained that racial segregation could be stigma free.[22] That argument, like the others, failed to persuade the court.

In May 1954, the justices announced their verdict in *Brown v. Board of Education*. Lost to all but the scholarly literature is the fact that most of Virginia's white citizens were inclined to accept it. Hardly any liked it, but it was the unanimous decision of the highest court in the land, after all. More than a few knew, too, deep down, that the system had been grossly unfair; seeing the latest ruling as definitive, they took the end of segregation to be beyond their control. For a time, calm prevailed.[23]

But the state's governing elite, which was led by the Byrd Organization and based in the former plantation, black-majority communities of the state's Southside, like Prince Edward County, viewed the Supreme Court decision as but the latest and most shocking in a string of federal incursions on their right to rule, a string that had begun with the policies of the later New Deal. As important to them, segregation was bound up in a complex of institutions that sustained the rigid social order and culture they were determined to hold in place—what they liked to call "our way of life."[24]

How could defenders of the old order fight *Brown* lawfully? Into the breach stepped a young Oklahoma-born journalist named James Jackson Kilpatrick, who recently had been promoted to editor of the *Richmond News Leader*, one of the state's leading daily newspapers. His mentor at the paper, John Dana Wise, a learned conservative, was fond of quoting John Randolph of Roanoke, the scion of one of Virginia's esteemed First Families, who had proclaimed, "I am an aristocrat. I love liberty; I hate equality." Kilpatrick recalled of his first years at the paper that "every time I let a liberal impulse escape in print, [Wise] summoned me into his office" for a "line-by-line" takedown. The paper's owners, as one contemporary noted, took as a given that society separated itself into "those who ride and those who are the donkeys to be ridden."[25]

Kilpatrick wanted to be a rider. He had issued a startling suggestion when the students filed their lawsuit in 1951. It might soon be time, he announced, to "abandon tax-supported public education altogether."[26] In November 1955, in the wake of the Supreme Court's *Brown II*, the implementation decree, Kilpatrick followed that call to privatize education with a crusade against federal "dictation."[27] Kilpatrick began agitating in earnest on November 21, 1955; from then until January 1956, his daily column pounded home the case that no ground whatsoever should be ceded to a federal government trying to dictate how Virginia should conduct its affairs. His mallet was the constitutional theory developed by John C. Calhoun, the antebellum South Carolina U.S. senator who sought to conjure a militant south.

To protect his region's distinctive political economy, anchored in the treatment of black people as property, Calhoun had argued that state governments had the right to refuse to abide by those federal laws that they found odious. He based his case on the Tenth Amendment to the Constitution, which specifies that "the powers not delegated to the United States by the Constitution, nor prohibited by it to the States, are reserved to the States respectively, or to the people." Fearing a rising national antislavery majority in the North and the West, Calhoun insisted that the authority for the U.S. Constitution came not from the American people collectively but from the states that consented to the Union. Therefore, he deduced, state leaders had the right to "interpose" their authority between their residents and Washington.[28]

Most Americans who thought about such matters at all assumed that the Union victory in the Civil War had settled the question. A national Union "of the people, by the people, and for the people" had defeated the planter class's bid to insulate its power from the collective will of the majority from whom federal authority flowed. But as Kilpatrick looked for a respectable way to fight *Brown,* to lift the cause above "the sometimes sordid level of race," Calhoun's theory of states' rights seemed his only option.[29] The *Washington Post* came to call him the "apostle" of interposition, training the whole region in its intricacies.[30]

Working as many as fourteen hours a day, he composed one opinion piece after another for six weeks running to persuade fellow white southerners that they had a constitutional right to reject the federal mandate to end Jim Crow schools—and that honor required it. The imposing display of arcana served a purpose: to persuade readers that the "naked and arrogant declaration of nine men" in *Brown* constituted a "rape of the Constitution." Kilpatrick's passion, as much as his purpose, commanded attention. "When people bought the *News Leader* on the stand" during this period, "they would turn to the editorial page the first thing," recalled a local newsman. "You had to see that with your own eyes to believe it."[31]

What so alarmed Kilpatrick was that Virginia was about to accede not to the spirit of the decision, with a plan for genuinely integrating its schools, but to its letter, with token concessions. A commission appointed by the governor had accepted some of the proposals of the diehard segregationists—above all, tax-subsidized tuition grants. These vouchers, to use today's language, would enable diehard white parents who could not stand the idea of integration to send their children to segregated private schools, something only the richest could do without such financial help. But the Gray Commission, named for its appointed chair, State Senator Garland Gray, was also recommending a local option: individual school districts faced with court orders would be able to decide for themselves whether to obey, albeit in a way limited by a state-controlled pupil placement plan designed to radically restrict desegregation in those communities willing to allow any.[32]

When the Arlington County School Board announced its plan to comply with the courts, a Kilpatrick ally demanded of fellow legislators that if some communities "won't stand with us then I say make them"—by shutting down their schools if they planned to admit any black students.[33]

As Kilpatrick considered his next move, no one loomed larger in his calculations than Virginia's senior U.S. senator, Harry Flood Byrd Sr. At sixty-eight, Byrd had lost some of his hair but none of the vigor that had made him one of the most formidable men in Washington—and the most powerful man back home, bar none. Those aspiring to influence in mid-century Virginia had to ask of any issue: What would Harry say? For Harry Byrd was the sun and the moon; those who found places in the firmament were there on the sufferance of the Byrd Organization, as participants referred to it (or the Byrd machine, to use the phrase critics preferred).

Senator Byrd was "an authentic aristocrat," *Time* magazine observed. But as an ABC News investigative report in the 1950s revealed, he had become a very rich one in part by importing "cheap labor from the Caribbean" to work his land, despite "considerable local unemployment." One federal official depicted aspects of the program "at worst as a modern counterpart to the slave trade, [and] at best as a system of indentured servants." With no rights in America, the guest workers could be paid "$60 or less for a 60-hour week"—with transportation and other expenses deducted from their wages. Those from the Bahamas, like Senator Byrd's workers, "suffer the worst exploitation of all."[34]

But exploitation was a matter of perspective. For Byrd, a property rights enthusiast, this was just the free market at work: abundant labor sellers willing to contract for less pay with an employer who could thus maximize his operation's profitability. Such imported workers were desirable to big growers precisely because their employment was not subject to irritating "federal standards of living or working conditions." By midcentury Byrd had become "the world's largest individual apple orchard owner." He looked down upon his "200,000 trees in rows up to two miles long" from a white-columned mansion whose grandeur rivaled that of Mount Vernon and Monticello. Byrd saw himself as a free-enterprise success story, enabled by personal liberty backed by states' rights protections from intrusive federal power.[35]

No single man has ever dominated a state so completely for so many years, albeit with studied courtliness. He presided as governor for most of the 1920s and as U.S. senator from 1933 until his retirement in 1965, acquiring a power that would have awed Calhoun. But Harry Byrd's Organization bore no resemblance to the machines of northern cities, with their abundant services to attract the loyalties of motley low-income electorates. It was their veritable opposite: "the united establishment of Virginia," one authority on Virginia politics has observed, over which "Byrd functioned as chairman." Its aim was to insulate government from citizen pressure for public spending or other reform. It did that by punishing dissent. Because the Organization's enforcers could be found in every county courthouse, if they put out "the word" on someone, that was enough to shutter a business or halt a career.[36]

Harry Byrd wielded his vast power to protect liberty—but as he understood it. He represented the state that had produced more of the Constitution's framers than any other, and he was determined to enforce what he took to be their intentions. One liberal scold called the senator "a steadfast opponent of most of the twentieth century," but Byrd wore his antiprogress politics as a badge of pride. A colleague said that as chair of the all-powerful

Senate Finance Committee, Byrd "measured his success as a senator not by what he passed, but what he stopped from passing." In his view, if liberty was to be preserved, the federal government should provide for the national defense and law enforcement, and little else.[37]

Because the Byrd Organization favored policies that were against the majority's interests, it was preoccupied with manipulating the rules for voting and representation. Among its tried-and-true tools was a poll tax that effectively kept most whites as well as nearly all blacks away at election time. The black electorate had plummeted to one-seventh of its earlier strength after the 1902 constitutional provisions aimed at it, but the provisions took out others, too. "20 percent of the electorate rules—20 percent at the maximum," railed a Richmond editor about *white* participation in city politics in the 1920s. "And it is called democracy!" Another key technique was malapportionment of the General Assembly to overrepresent more conservative rural residents and underrepresent more moderate city and suburban residents, a practice used since the Colonial Era. Indeed, "when the Virginia legislature voted in 1956 to close public schools rather than integrate," explains the historian J. Douglas Smith, "the twenty-one senators who voted in favor of the action represented fewer Virginians than did the seventeen senators who opposed it."[38]

For forty years, in fact, the Byrd Organization had to win only about 10 percent of the potential electorate to hold on to power. "Of all the American states, Virginia can lay claim to the most thorough control by an oligarchy," the political scientist V. O. Key Jr. observed in his classic study of southern politics. Key went on to quip that, compared with Virginia, "Mississippi is a hotbed of democracy."[39]

Virginia's oligarchs maintained their control not with night rides but with carefully designed rules. They showed little tolerance for the vigilantism freely practiced in the Deep South. In fact, when Byrd was governor, the state effectively outlawed the Ku Klux Klan and all but ended lynching.[40] The rulers understood, better than others, how clever legal rules could keep the state's voter participation among the lowest in the nation relative to population, and its taxes among the lowest in the nation relative to wealth. Above all, the rules served to hold in check the collective power of those who might want their democracy to do more.[41]

A case in point: Virginia was among the first states in the nation to outlaw the closed shop—that is, to outlaw contracts that required union membership of employees. Months before a conservative Congress passed the 1947 Taft-Hartley Act, called "the Slave Labor Act" by critics and passed over President Harry Truman's veto, the state's governor had signed a pioneering "right-to-work" law to weaken labor unions.[42] If, in the face of this snare of shrewd restraints to keep them from influencing government, some citizens still managed to come together to seek change, the daily press could simply overlook it. That, too, was part of "the Virginia Way." If collective action could not be wholly stopped, at least news of it could be buried.[43]

That was the system of liberty that so urgently needed defense, in the eyes of those who upheld it. Kilpatrick hit the mark in his campaign against compromise with *Brown:* the most powerful man in state history was elated. "I read carefully every one of your editorials," Byrd said in praising his ally's "brilliant" writing. Senator James Eastland of Mississippi likewise rejoiced, calling Byrd to exult that Kilpatrick's "plan was gaining great popularity all through the South" in the run-up to Christmas of 1955. To ensure that no southern senators "compromise our convictions" by accepting *Brown,* Byrd invited Kilpatrick to Washington to strategize with a group of them about how his case could provide the "foundation stone" for "a united front of 11 states." It was all but a second coming of Calhoun.[44]

Following Virginia's example, by late 1956 the legislatures of eleven southern states had passed interposition and pro–massive resistance measures of their own—106, all told. Their representatives in Congress backed the militancy back home with a joint resolution that came to be known as the Southern Manifesto. "You would think today Calhoun was walking and speaking on the floor of the Senate," commented a senator from Oregon about its reading. Every member of Congress from Virginia, and a total of 101 from the old Confederacy, signed the rebuke of the Supreme Court decision as an "unwarranted" deviation from the intentions of "the Founding Fathers."[45]

In August, licensed by the interposition resolution to defy the federal government, a special session of the Virginia General Assembly convened to pass a suite of massive resistance measures—a "legislative hurricane," as one dazed state senator called it. One feature eliminated local control of education; it compelled the governor to close and cut off funds to any school that planned to desegregate under federal court order. That meant white students would go without education if local officials conceded to the courts, because it was the white schools that faced lawsuits. Another law authorized tax-funded tuition grants to enable white parents to send their children to private schools to evade the Supreme Court ruling. As intended, this made viable the establishment of segregation academies. An additional seven laws set out to debilitate the NAACP so that it could no longer protest the injustices of the system. Indeed, the civil rights group lost one of every three members of the once thriving Virginia conference in a single year, owing to what an American Jewish Committee study found to be the South's "most elaborate, systematic and sophisticated attempt to frustrate NAACP activity."[46]

The rashness of it all worried Colgate Whitehead Darden Jr.[47] He was a leading member of the state's tight-knit white elite, anchored by the landed rich yet inclusive of corporate leaders. He had been elected to Congress and then backed as governor because he stood on the right side of every issue related to employers' power, states' rights, and racial segregation. He owed his appointment as president of the university to his old mentor Harry Byrd and others who stood to his right and were still well represented on the university's Board of Visitors. Darden knew that they expected every decision he made to reflect that awareness. But the Columbia Law School– and Oxford University–trained attorney also knew that the massive resistance laws were doomed. Meanwhile, the forced shutdown of any school that desegregated would batter an already weak public school system and damage economic development in the state.[48]

The days were past, Darden could see, when emotional agitation, backed by rash appeals to Calhoun's theories, could move the country. Virginia's best chance to find its footing once again might just be the newcomer, James Buchanan.

PART I

THE IDEAS TAKE SHAPE

CHAPTER 2

A COUNTRY BOY GOES TO THE WINDY CITY

The village of Gum, Tennessee, where Jim Buchanan was born in 1919, lies along the Dixie Highway, about an hour southeast of Nashville. Like the rest of the state, it was a place without airs, very unlike Virginia. Buchanan grew up at a time when Model T Fords shared the roads with horse-drawn wagons. No one in the countryside had indoor plumbing, heating, or electricity; the outdoor "privy" was a fact of life. Those who wanted to read in the evening did so by kerosene lamps. Located between the plantation culture of West Tennessee, home to Memphis, and the mountain culture of East Tennessee, home to Knoxville, Middle Tennessee, where the Buchanans lived, was the most middle-class part of the state, known for fertile land and midsize farms that gave way to meadows of bluegrass edged by groves of evergreen cedar.[1]

"My family was poor," Buchanan told all who would listen in his later years, and, indeed, agriculture was one of the sick industries of the 1920s that augured the Great Depression ahead. But poverty is relative, he himself would teach, and compared with most of their fellow Tennesseans, even his family's own neighbors, the Buchanans had it very good. Their home, perched atop a hill, overlooked a spread of several hundred acres in Rutherford County, home to the most productive dairy farms in the state. They had a large herd of registered Jersey dairy cattle, whose butterfat-rich milk could be sold to the new Carnation Milk plant nearby, and unlike most residents, they owned the land, rather than working it as tenants, sharecroppers, or day laborers. While the house itself may have been "in varying states of disrepair" and was often in need of a fresh coat of paint, it must have seemed like a mansion to others, with its fourteen rooms and ten fireplaces to heat them.[2]

Both the family's relative comfort and "pure Scotch-Irish" lineage no doubt stamped young Jim's sense of the world. Though he never mentioned it, the census of 1920 shows that when Jim was a baby, his parents had a live-in servant and farm laborer, a black man named Foster Garner, who was twenty-one years old. In 1940, a family of black sharecroppers worked Buchanan land. Where the owners' home was then valued at $2,000 and their 255 acres of land valued at $6,300, their black laborers were the truly poor, renting at $4 a month, to be paid at harvest time.[3]

The Buchanans also had a proud lineage. The public school that Jim and his two sisters attended was named after his father's father, John P. Buchanan. Grandfather Buchanan had been a Populist, elected as the candidate of the Tennessee Farmers' Alliance and Laborers' Union to the governorship in 1890. There weren't many manufacturing workers in the South then, but there were lots of coal miners, and in Tennessee the miners and the farmers had some common enemies, especially the big railroad corporations that gouged farmers and hired convict labor. Alliance members shared a burning conviction that a government of, by, and for the people, as a historian of this struggle writes, "had a solemn obligation to maintain fairness in the industrial economy." Those they called "monopolists" should not receive "special privileges." No man should be allowed to impose "degrading" work on another through sheer private economic power, nor should any lender crush an honest farmer with debt. Government should serve all citizens, not act at the behest of "arrogant" would-be "aristocrats."[4] It was a stirring campaign that gave thousands new hope.

In narrating his own life story in later years, the grandson laid claim to his grandfather's tradition, presenting himself as an ally of those who worked hard, only to be set upon by claims from grasping "special interests." He told of spending many hours as a youth reading in the old man's vast book-and-pamphlet collection.[5] Yet the grandson never mentioned the events that had made John Buchanan a one-term governor. It was a curious omission, because the cause of his downfall was one of the most spectacular rebellions in the Gilded Age South against collusion between state governments and corporations. It may also help explain some of the later economist's animus against organized workers.

Locals called the yearlong struggle that swept five counties from East to Middle Tennessee the "convict wars." The coalition of farmers and miners that elected John Buchanan governor wanted one thing above all: the end of the system of coerced private prison labor whereby Tennessee's state government helped mining magnates secure cheap labor and fat profits at the expense of innocent miners trying to earn enough to feed their families. The widely reviled system, so redolent of slavery, created a perverse incentive to lock men up for petty offenses so the state could rent them out to coal companies as dirt-cheap labor to take the jobs of free miners, who had organized the United Mine Workers of America to demand living wages and decent treatment. The miners had tried everything: persuasion, publicity, lobbying, and legal challenges. But each successive official ignored their pleas, because he had "corporation cotton" in his ears, in the words of one state legislator. When John Buchanan failed to shut down the system after his election, his earlier supporters turned to direct action. More than a thousand miners marched on the hated Tennessee Coal, Iron and Railroad Company (TCIR); farmers, local merchants, professionals, and like-minded women joined them along the way. The exasperated citizens wrecked the TCIR's stockades and liberated the black and white convicts held in them. They even supplied changes of clothes so the abused prisoners could avoid recapture. But Governor Buchanan, instead of ending the accursed system, called out the state militia in support of the company and against those to whom he had broken his promise. As a pitched battle claimed lives, the miners lost, convict labor lingered, and the voters ended a once promising political career with a thrashing in the next election.[6]

Grandfather Buchanan never got over his loss; his grandson described him as "psychologically tarnished" by his defeat, which led him back to the repressive Democratic Party he had earlier denounced.[7] Something else perhaps gnawed at Grandfather Buchanan that may have helped sour his grandson on how democracy worked: the way the sheriffs refused to carry out his unpopular orders against the rebellious miners because they wanted to keep their jobs come election time, knowing as they did that the protest had wide popular backing. His defeat left Buchanan convinced that too large an electorate was a problem for the white, property-owning class of men like himself. He raged against a Republican bill that would have allowed Washington to protect popular voting rights in the South. He warned that it would put "colored heels upon white necks" and create "negro supremacy." And he backed a higher poll tax to keep those he viewed as riffraff from voting.[8]

Lila Scott Buchanan, Jim's mother, also had a more lace-curtain lineage than her neighbors. She came from a long line of rural "deputy sheriffs and Presbyterian preachers." A former teacher who lamented the local school's failure to offer Latin, Mrs. Buchanan tutored Jim so well that he skipped two grades. She seemed determined to ensure that her only son would *not* follow the example of her husband, a man whose good looks and charm were never matched by steadiness as a provider, let alone ambition. The son's later training in economics would help him explain all this in ways that buttressed his own commitments. Because the title of the vast "Buchanan estate" left by his grandfather to his many children dispersed responsibility along with rewards, Jim maintained, "my father had no incentive for effective maintenance." Why should he care if the paint peeled on the house, or the barn grew shabby, if he was not the sole owner? Whatever the reason, James Sr. seemed unworthy of acknowledgment by his son, who dropped the suffix "Jr." in his own career.[9]

The whole family had high hopes that the bright young Jim would go into politics, as his grandfather had done, and perhaps reclaim the governorship someday. But he lacked the winning charm of his father. More simply put, Jim did not enjoy other people—or they him—in the way that those who succeed in politics do. His bearing was "austere," a later colleague explained; while he was "a good person"—a man of integrity—he was also "one of the coldest people I have ever met." A solitary child in his formative years, he would describe himself, toward the end of his life, as "always an outsider." At his memorial service, in 2013, a friend of thirty years was asked how he had gotten to know Buchanan. "Did I?" he responded.[10]

What no one questioned, including Buchanan himself, was that he had an unusually keen mind, and a hunger for a future beyond farming. Vanderbilt University, in Nashville, loomed large in the family's vision for

Jim's future, its stature as the state's top private university no doubt a draw. Vanderbilt was also the site of a cultural project that attracted James Buchanan—one that stamped his vision of the good society and the just state. The university was the home of the Southern Agrarians, the literary men who in 1930 published a manifesto for southern rural life, *I'll Take My Stand*. The "Twelve Southerners," the collective authors on the spine, were mainly literary men, novelists and poets, remembered still for their call to preserve humane rural values from corruption by creeping industrialism and materialism. But their version of those values was racially exclusive, and their mission was profoundly political. Taking their title from a lyric in "Dixie," they set out to redeem the southern "agrarian tradition" from the disrepute into which it had fallen.[11]

The Nashville Agrarians concluded that the best defense of their region's established ways was a strong ideological offense. They set out to burnish the South's reputation by transforming understanding of the conflict that had given its white governing class a bad name: the War Between the States. Resurrecting "Jefferson's ideal polity of yeoman farmers," as Buchanan later put it, they also cultivated an image of the South as having been victimized by northeastern elites, such that the militant white former Confederates who had used violence to drive black voters from the polls were merely engaging in reasonable self-defense. They would ennoble the scorned Confederate cause even if, as their correspondence reveals, it took willful blindness, outright falsification, and the highly strategic demeaning of African Americans to achieve it.[12]

The Nashville writer who seemed most decisive in Jim Buchanan's emerging intellectual system was Donald Davidson, the Agrarians' ringleader, who portrayed the growth of the federal government since the Progressive Era as a move toward "the totalitarian state" that was destroying regional folkways. It was Davidson who also named the enemy: Leviathan. First used in the Old Testament for a monstrous sea creature whom God would destroy at the end of time, it then served as the title and metaphor for the seventeenth-century treatise of Thomas Hobbes on the origins of government. But Davidson used "Leviathan" in a new and distinctive way: to evoke an evil national government, enlarged by northeasterners who acted selfishly and in bad faith, first by setting the abolition wind blowing and later by pushing workers' rights and federal regulation. Such ideas could never arise from American soil, Davidson insisted. They were "alien" European imports brought by baleful characters. Leviathan was "the subtlest and most dangerous foe of humanity—the tyranny that wears the mask of humanitarianism and benevolence."[13] Buchanan would devote the first part of his career to tearing off what he called the "romantic" mask, and the last part to enchaining the beast behind it.

In the end, owing to the Depression, Buchanan never made it to Vanderbilt. Instead he attended Middle Tennessee State Teachers College, in Murfreesboro, which was cheaper and closer to home. He could milk the cows every morning and night to pay his tuition and costs and catch rides with an itinerant Methodist minister who commuted to his various churches. Buchanan triple-majored, in English, math, and economics, and won a scholarship to attend graduate school at the University of Tennessee, where he earned an M.A. in economics. But he never got over the way others, more privileged in their schooling, seemed to sniff at his alma mater.[14]

When he left Tennessee for New York to do his military service in 1941, the new graduate seemed to see through lenses wholly crafted by Donald Davidson. New York City was to the Nashville writer a veritable cussword, a synecdoche for all that was wrong with reform-minded modern America.[15] "I felt I was in enemy territory," Buchanan said of his first encounter with America's leading city, surrounded by "strange beings."[16]

Still, the Gotham stopover proved priceless, in that it supplied him with a personal reason for hostility to a specific elite he was already predisposed to dislike: the "eastern establishment." Again and again in his later years, Buchanan told a story of how flint had lodged in his soul in the New York City Naval Reserve Officer Training Corps. "I was subjected to overt discrimination based on favoritism for products of eastern establishment universities," he recounted. In the initial appointment of cadet officers, he was passed over, and not simply for Ivy League graduates, but for a Rockefeller; it was, he said, "blatant discrimination." The episode fortified his "populist preconceptions," his conviction that northeastern elites gained at the expense of "southerners, midwesterners, and westerners." Few would argue that meritocracy prevailed at this moment. Yet what is notable in Buchanan's formulation is the Davidson-like framing of the problem in regional terms that missed the most egregious impact of bigotry: on Catholics, Jews, Mexican Americans, working-class white men, and, above all, African Americans.[17]

Indeed, rather than sympathize with the plight of black Americans, Buchanan later argued that the failure of the black community to thrive after emancipation was not the result of the barriers put in their way, but rather proof that "the thirst for freedom, and responsibility, is perhaps not nearly so universal as so many post-Enlightenment philosophers have assumed."[18] It was a breathtakingly ignorant claim, a sign of a willful failure to see what his paradigm would not allow him to. Both Koch and Buchanan would make similarly blind and insulting claims about others who did not do well in the labor market these men chose to believe was free and fair.

It was uncanny how well young Jim Buchanan's notions of individual efficacy, group power, and government overreach fit with the teachings of the economics faculty of the University of Chicago. The school had been founded at the turn of the century by the oil industry magnate John D. Rockefeller and in its early years earned renown as a laboratory for social science in the service of progressive reform. But by 1946, when a twenty-seven-year-old Buchanan enrolled, the school's president boasted to donors of having "the most conservative economics department in the world."[19]

Buchanan's choice of Chicago was not an ideological one; knowing little of institutions outside the South, he went on the advice of a professor at Tennessee who had earned a political science degree at the university and who presented a "near-idyllic sketch" of its singular "intellectual ferment." Buchanan enrolled there for doctoral study after service in the U.S. Navy. He was accompanied by his wife, Ann Bakke, a North Dakotan nurse ten years his senior, whom he met on a base in Oahu. She took to the attractive young noncommissioned officer, and after they met again at war's end in San Francisco, they married a month later. As he set out to become a professional economist at the University of Chicago, she took jobs to pay their living expenses. In Buchanan's telling, he used the tuition subsidy that came to him from the G.I. Bill and "a new wife for partial support" in graduate school.[20]

Today, when talk turns to the Chicago school of economics, most people think of Milton Friedman. But when Buchanan arrived, Professor Frank Hyneman Knight was widely viewed as the star, so much so that there was a saying among the student vanguard: "There is no God, but Frank Knight is his prophet." It was he whom Buchanan credited for his own conversion to a "born-again economist."[21]

Knight was as much a social philosopher as an economist; he wanted his students to think hard about "the ethical nature of a good society." A rebel against the "prairie evangelism" of his youth, Knight felt "revulsion" for "dogma" of any kind; he pushed his charges to question every claim, especially those most taken for granted in their day—which happened to be Rooseveltian liberalism and Keynesian economics. Buchanan appreciated, too, what he saw as Knight's midwestern humility, so unlike "the more sophisticated, sometimes effete, culture of the eastern seaboard" that he saw in other faculty. A fellow country boy, albeit from rural Illinois, Knight, too, had attended college in Tennessee. He reached out to the newly discharged veteran, whose soft drawl was perhaps hard to hear among his cocksure peers. In one of their unhurried conversations, Knight shared his mantra that an academic career was "better than plowing." Having cut furrows beyond number behind a mule named Rhoda, Buchanan needed no persuasion.[22]

After some six weeks of Knight's course, Buchanan, by his own telling, "converted into a zealous advocate of the market order." Whether it was the cogency of Knight's teaching or the upheaval on Chicago's South Side as steel and meatpacking workers downed tools in the most massive strike wave in America's history was not clear. But Chicago price theory provided a science to support his existing "antigovernment" feelings. Buchanan took from Chicago school economics a conviction that socialism in any form—that is, any group or government meddling with the market—was a sentimental and dangerous error. For the newly minted libertarian economist, far-reaching individual marketplace freedom was the fairest and surest route to prosperity. Each person should be allowed to pursue his or her self-interest without interference from those with different values and goals and without direction by governing elites who flattered themselves that they knew what was in others' best interests.[23]

That fall, conservatives swept what one pundit dubbed the "beefsteak elections" because of the role of the meat producers and butcher shops, who held back their wares to protest continuing price controls during reconversion. The new Republican majority in Congress used its power to end the controls and to stymie the ambitions of the Congress of Industrial Organizations (CIO), among them the unionization and democratization of the South, by passing the Taft-Hartley Act of 1947.[24]

The lineaments of a long battle were being drawn: collective security versus individual liberty.

In fact, that very spring, Frank Knight and some other University of Chicago faculty members headed to Switzerland to strategize for the fight. They came home having created what they called the Mont Pelerin Society. Answering a call from the Austrian polymath Friedrich A. Hayek, whose postgraduate training encompassed law, political science, and economics, some three dozen men and a few women traveled to a site high in the Alps, with panoramic views of the only nation on the continent not devastated by the world war just past: neutral Switzerland. Traveling in the days before low-cost air travel, the Americans came by ocean liner to meet with European counterparts who journeyed by train from war-ravaged countries like England, France, and Germany. They converged at the Hôtel du Parc, an elegant Belle Époque mansion in the mountains near Vevey.

The attendees feared for the very survival of Western civilization as they understood it: for the endurance of self-governing nations of freely associating individuals and of the market capitalism that by the turn of the twentieth century had made Europe and America into powerhouses of production and culture. The rise of first Communism, after 1917, and then fascism appalled them. The global conflict whose toll was still being reckoned showed how vulnerable modern societies were to self-destruction. And still there was no peace. Most of Europe was devastated by bombing; with food rationing in place and black markets rife, its political future was in question. Greece and Italy were leaning left—just the previous month, President Harry Truman had announced the costly Truman Doctrine, in fear of what such a tilt portended. The thirty-eight assembled scholars, journalists, foundation officials, and businessmen at the mountain meeting shared ten days of intense discussion, meeting "morning, afternoon, and night." Their concern was how they might, together, shift the tide of history away from what they called "statism," or what we might call a strong role for government.[25]

The man who convened the meeting of like-thinking friends was himself a refugee, who had dropped the aristocratic "von" from his family name in the revolutionary year of 1919.[26] Tall and lean, with a tightly trimmed mustache, rimless round spectacles, and gracious Old World manners, F. A. Hayek had been worrying since the early 1930s about the growing appeal of social democracy in particular. He was concerned about the model of government that so many organized citizens of Europe and the United States were seeking, based on labor unionism, a welfare state, and government intervention for economic security. He opened conversations with others who shared his unease and might contribute to what came to be understood as "an intellectual counterrevolution." But what most built his worldwide reputation was a 1944 book that divided political thought in the stark manner Buchanan was learning in his Ph.D. program at Chicago.[27]

Three American publishing houses rejected *The Road to Serfdom*, largely because they disagreed with its premise. It took the intercession of the Chicago legal scholar Aaron Director with the University of Chicago Press to get it into print. But someone at *Reader's Digest* saw something in the book he thought would resonate with its million subscribers. Indeed, it did. "Imagine my surprise," the reserved professor reported, when he found himself in an overflow hall with more than three thousand listeners in New York, faced with a "battery of microphones and a veritable sea of expectant faces." As a story in the May 1945 *Saturday Review* observed, "Seldom have an economist and a nonfiction book reached such popularity in so short a time."[28]

The Road to Serfdom was a clarion call. Hayek argued that "the rise of fascism and Nazism was not a reaction against the socialist trends of the preceding period but a necessary outcome of these tendencies." In his view, their distinguishing and shared feature was reliance on the central state; their people's break with individual self-reliance was the germ that caused the disease.[29] Millions who hated Nazism, he wrote, "work at the same time for ideals whose realization would lead straight to the abhorred tyranny."[30]

Here was the rub: "It is because nearly everybody wants it that we are moving in this direction." Everywhere, people were deluding themselves "that socialism and freedom can be combined" when in fact they were dire enemies. The growth of government, he argued, would in time undermine all freedom and usher in totalitarian states.[31]

If the road to serfdom was reliance on government, the detour to salvation was resuscitation of classical liberalism, what Hayek called "the abandoned road." To save itself from doom, the Western world must regain reverence for individual liberty, particularly economic liberty. Hayek took pains to persuade readers that the free market was not simply an efficient way of producing economic progress. Rather, the price signals of supply and demand provided the only means yet discovered of coordinating the desires and actions of millions of freely acting individuals, without government compulsion, in what Hayek called a "spontaneous order." Without "freedom in economic affairs" there could be no lasting "personal and political freedom." There was no other choice, then: "socialism means slavery."[32]

Hayek's book, not surprisingly, spoke powerfully to right-wing American businessmen still smarting from the loss of time-honored prerogatives of the propertied class, who now were told that they had to negotiate with unions and meet new regulatory agency rules and standards. To them, the reforms of the Depression and World War II constituted an illegitimate "revolution." The New Deal was "nothing more or less than the Socialistic doctrine called by another name," in the summary of one of the men who founded the American Liberty League to combat it.[33]

Enraged by their losses, recalcitrant businessmen set up institutions to fight the new order. The one with the greatest long-term impact was the William Volker Fund. Its president, Harold Luhnow, became Hayek's American patron, paying for his national tour and subsidizing his salary at the University of Chicago for ten years—as well as that of Aaron Director, also at the University of Chicago, and Ludwig von Mises, the leader of the Austrian school, at New York University. It was Volker Fund money that sent Frank Knight and the rest of the American delegates to the conference in Switzerland in that summer of 1947.[34]

Hayek was vague about where and how "to draw the line" he said must be drawn—this was the core weakness of his book in the view of his friend and intellectual nemesis John Maynard Keynes—but at this point he maintained that a return to Gilded Age laissez-faire was undesirable. Similarly, he and the other founding scholars of the society bristled at being labeled conservative. "We must have the courage to make a new start" for "a better world," *The Road to Serfdom* concluded.[35]

From their ten-day gathering in Switzerland came an enduring transnational, invitation-only network that linked scholars with like-minded journalists and appreciative businessmen and foundation officials. Putting the intellectuals in the lead, the society set out to shift the tide of history—to ensure lasting peace and prosperity by freeing markets worldwide from the collective action and government planning that its members believed so perilous.[36]

James Buchanan's mentor Frank Knight enjoyed such regard that he was the only U.S.-born scholar among the three named cofounders of the society. Like Buchanan, and unlike cofounders F. A. Hayek and Ludwig von Mises, Knight had a populist streak. When the Europeans proposed to name the group after Lord Acton and Alexis de Tocqueville, Knight blocked them. Absolutely not, he said. No organization to advance "the free society" and individual liberty should be named after "Roman Catholic aristocrats." It was because of Knight's opposition to the Austrians' suggestions that the group took as its name the Mont Pelerin Society, from the mountain where they met. As Milton Friedman later noted, the name "was selected only because it did not offend anyone, as every other proposed name had."[37]

Even as James Buchanan took inspiration from his mentor and committed to the transnational battle of ideas Knight helped to set off, he was finding his own distinctive voice, in part through wariness about the younger generation of the Chicago school, particularly Milton Friedman, whom he experienced more as an irritant than as a muse. Where the "lovable" Knight fostered others' growth, Buchanan said, Friedman shamed students with his "dominating intellectual brilliance." Beneath the personality clash, and perhaps some residual distrust of a Brooklyn-born know-it-all, was an emerging split over what the field should do. Friedman's avowed approach, if honored in the breach, was toward "positive" economics. Scholars should not make normative judgments in their work, he taught, but instead should develop a "science" through the mathematical testing of refutable hypotheses. As Friedman eclipsed Knight, whose production had stalled by his sixth decade, the new Chicago school became known for its technical proficiency.[38]

Buchanan, by contrast, felt drawn to an older style of political economy that was concerned more with the social contract and governance of the economy than with mathematical derring-do. By his last year in the program, he was flatly annoyed with the fixation on mathematical "technique." He mourned the parting of economics from its origins in "a comprehensive moral philosophy" like that of Adam Smith. He dreamed of someday building a program to battle collectivism in a bolder way.

In his last year of graduate school in 1948, in a chance conversation with fellow doctoral student G. Warren Nutter, Buchanan learned that he was not alone. A World War II veteran like himself and a kindred spirit in his politics, Nutter shared his distaste for the prevailing focus in the discipline on mathematical technique and empirical work, even at Chicago. They talked about the contribution that economists of their bent might make if they turned their focus to understanding the big political economic questions of their world.[39] Perhaps, someday, they would have a chance to.

Like the Austrians Hayek and von Mises, Buchanan in particular wanted to help others see that the market could coordinate millions of individual projects far better than government could. The market was simply the most efficient means of allocating goods and services but also the best social decision-maker, one that might allow escape from the contentious political realm. To look to politics to promote one's interpretation of fairness, Buchanan came to argue, was to enable an establishment-controlled economy and coerce others.[40] But how to spread that view in an era in which Americans—indeed, people the world over—distrusted markets after the Great Depression and the global conflagration it set off, and found government protection beneficial for more and more?

Buchanan chose an area of economics not surprising for a libertarian seeking a job in a southern public university: public finance, which focuses on the proper role of government in the economy. It encompasses taxation, government spending, and the relationship between the public and private sectors, matters on which southern officials had firm convictions.[41] When he set to work, the primary focus of scholars in this area was "market failure": situations in which for-profit enterprises failed to allocate goods or services efficiently or fairly, thus requiring government action to correct the problem.

He chose to build a career by turning a critical eye the other way: identifying and analyzing perceived "government failure," so as to make the case that it should not be relied on by default without a sophisticated evaluation of its drawbacks. That was an innovative approach at the time and, on the face of it, a sensible one. Why simply assume government could do better? Yet empirical comparison never interested Buchanan or the school he founded. Where his interest and genius lay—even if you call it an evil genius—was in his intuitive grasp of the importance of trust in political life. If only one could break down the trust that now existed between governed and governing, even those who supported liberal objectives would lose confidence in government solutions.[42]

Having developed a reading knowledge of German, French, and Italian, Buchanan reached overseas for new ideas and tools in what he knew would be a major political struggle. One day in 1948, while roaming the stacks of the University of Chicago's well-stocked library, Buchanan found a half-century-old dissertation written in German by a nineteenth-century Swedish political economist named Knut Wicksell. Economists, Wicksell argued, should stop offering up policy advice to leaders they imagined as "benevolent despots" who could act on behalf of the public good. Instead, scholars should assume that public officials had the same self-interested motives as other economic actors and go on to scrutinize the actual operational rules, practices, and incentives that created the framework of government and bureaucratic decision-making. Buchanan came to call the approach he derived from Wicksell "politics without romance." It was a career-making find, he would later say, because most of his own contributions were "reiterations, elaborations, and extensions" of what Wicksell had first identified.[43]

This may in fact be true. For example, Wicksell articulated the notion that tax policy ought to be arrived at through unanimous consent. "It would seem to be a blatant injustice," he wrote, "if someone should be forced to contribute toward the costs of some activity which does not further his interests or may even be diametrically opposed to them."[44] In Harry Truman's Fair Deal America, marginal tax rates on higher incomes were creeping upward, and—aside from the emerging Cold War, which accounted for a goodly share of the budget—that revenue paid for projects the wealthiest were less likely than other citizens to support, from the Tennessee Valley Authority, which brought electricity to the rural poor, to factory inspectors to ensure fair labor standards. Buchanan found a way of thinking about fairness in Wicksell's work that matched his own inclination as a man of the midcentury right (which was ironic, because Wicksell was a man of the left who had in mind disenfranchised wage earners who were being taxed for the projects of a monarchical government in which they had no vote). Wicksell's ideas, Buchanan later said, "seemed to correspond precisely with those I already had in my head" but "would not have dared to express in the public-finance mindset of the time."[45]

Among Europeans, he was finding career-making support for other ideas he already had. For the 1955–56 academic year, Buchanan secured a Fulbright Fellowship to Italy, where he studied the works of a public finance tradition suspicious of—indeed, hostile to—central government and taxation, owing to a long history of corruption. Living in Rome and Perugia, he steeped himself in Italian theories of the state and the processes of political decision-making that determined taxation. By year's end, he said, he "suddenly 'saw the light.'" The new light notably resembled the old dogma of the southern-state "Redeemer" governments that had put an end to Reconstruction, although Buchanan did not comment on the similarity, whether or not he perceived it. He had found theoretical anchors for both sides of his fiscal inclinations: to curtail taxation and contain government spending. "Pay as you go" was both economically wise and morally just, Buchanan concluded in his first book. He took his stand alongside "the much-maligned man in the street," who compared national budgets to household ledgers and abhorred red ink in either. A government forced to balance its books every year, he believed, would act more like the nineteenth-century federal government and the southern states whose ongoing tightfisted policies he equated with economic liberty.[46]

Left unspoken was how that framework appealed to the more right-wing members of the propertied class by keeping their taxes low and denying basic services—schools, roads, and sanitation—to those who could not pay for them. After early jobs at the University of Tennessee and then at Florida State University, Buchanan got the break of his career in 1956: a post at the University of Virginia, as the new chairman of the economics department. To his delight, the department also hired Warren Nutter, the fellow graduate student with whom he had talked about setting up a philosophically grounded program almost a decade before. With the help of Nutter and a steadily growing number of others at UVA, Buchanan would be able to turn a regional libertarian creed into a national counterrevolution.

CHAPTER 3

THE REAL PURPOSE OF THE PROGRAM

It was the chance of a lifetime. The university founded by Thomas Jefferson himself was giving the new chair of the economics department "full rein" to create a kind of program that existed nowhere else. At a time when the discipline of economics, in James Buchanan's words, "threatened to become extremely boring," his new employer entrusted him and Warren Nutter to chart a new course.[1]

The private mission statement for the Thomas Jefferson Center for Political Economy and Social Philosophy that Buchanan submitted to university president Colgate Darden in December 1956 made a lot of promises. It promised to be guided by two traditions: that of the "old-fashioned libertarians" whose ideas encouraged laissez-faire economic policies in nineteenth-century England and America, and that of "the Western conservatives," who feared the "revolt of the masses," as the title of one text put it, and sought new ways to ensure "social order." The document also made clear who would "not be allowed to participate": anyone who, even inadvertently, would value "security"—the New Deal's mantra—above liberty, and who would "replace the role of the individual and of voluntary association by the coercive powers of the collective order." The latter would include supporters of industrial unions and government intervention in the economy. Buchanan, by contrast, pledged to train "social philosophers," men (for the university admitted only men then) ready to put into effect a society based on liberty. With a hint of defensiveness, knowing that such exclusiveness was, indeed, unusual in an academic enterprise, he assured: "To start in a small way to produce such a line of new thinkers is an eminently legitimate endeavor for a great university." The center's members, Buchanan vowed, would take up such matters of concern to Virginia's governing elite as the growing power of labor unions; the correct relationship between the federal government and the states (made all the more urgent by Supreme Court decisions such as *Brown*); what he depicted as the "problems of equalitarianism" (among them "income redistribution," "the welfare state," and "the tax structure," his archaic way of speaking of egalitarianism an indicator of how his program would approach them); and "the social security system and [its threat to] individual initiative."[2]

More specifically, the center aimed to combat what its founders referred to as "social engineering" by changing the way people thought. They hoped to break "the powerful grip that collectivist ideology already had on the minds of intellectuals," as Buchanan later put it.[3] Almost all professional economists then accepted the pump-priming doctrines of Keynes to ensure demand to keep the economy growing. Nearly everyone, even as they differed on the particulars, believed that in the age of the giant corporation, America needed what the liberal economist John Kenneth Galbraith had recently termed "countervailing power": organized workers and consumers. The federal government must also put its weight on the other side of the scale to ensure fair play and economic stability. Put simply, most Americans then trusted their government. In such an era, Buchanan said, "our purpose was indeed *subversive*."[4]

Darden knew precisely what Buchanan meant by "collectivist" solutions to social problems. His father-in-law was Irénée du Pont, the former president of the DuPont Company and one of the nation's wealthiest men. He was also among the most right-wing of the rich. Du Pont so hated FDR that he had helped found the American Liberty League, in hopes of restoring an "employers' paradise" by nipping the New Deal in the bud. But he and his corporate colleagues had muffed the job. Their arguments were so crude and self-interested that their mobilization redounded to the president's advantage, enabling him to denounce the millionaires as "economic royalists" bent on keeping others down.[5]

Colgate Darden was less vocally right-wing than his father-in-law, but he shared his new hire's disdain for how powerful labor unions, civil rights organizations, and others were looking to the federal government to bring about what they depicted as social justice. As a congressman, Darden himself had voted against a core component of "collectivism": the Social Security Act.[6] Darden understood—indeed, could recite chapter and verse of—the mantra of right-leaning business leaders regarding the encroachments of the federal government into their private business affairs. To their minds, they, not the federal government or their employees, had made the U.S. economy into a world powerhouse. It made them irate to be taxed—at higher rates than others, no less—for programs they viewed not only as bad for the economy but also as infringements on their personal liberty. How dare federal officials tell them how to manage their employees? Why should they pay into unemployment and retirement funds to support those who failed to save in personal accounts? Such matters should not be the business of the federal government. They were for men of property to decide as they saw fit.[7]

But unlike the aging du Pont, Darden had been exposed to the often brilliant arguments for the other side while earning his J.D. in the early 1920s at Columbia Law School in New York City. There, northern legal scholars were systematically and thoughtfully undercutting the radical free-market doctrines espoused by elite-dominated courts after the defeat of Reconstruction, while laying the conceptual foundations for the judiciary's acceptance of new federal powers in response to the Great Depression. "All realists shared one basic premise—that the law had come to be out of touch with reality," writes their leading historian. In the age of the large corporation, the notion that the economy was a realm of freedom, whereas government action was intolerable coercion, simply no longer corresponded to the facts of American life. Massive struggles on the part of workers and farmers had repeatedly belied that stark opposition, and the new century's leading thinkers in the social sciences and history had refuted the Gilded Age ideology that unalloyed property rights and freedom of contract could ensure liberty and justice for all.[8]

By the time Buchanan arrived in Virginia in the mid-1950s, this breaking with the past to master a new reality, this refutation of the late-nineteenth century ideology of the sanctity of private property rights and the concomitant embrace of an affirmative role for organized citizens and their government as the counterbalance to corporate power, had become the new stance of virtually every Western democracy. Faculty at institutions such as Columbia, the University of Wisconsin, and Harvard produced a steady stream of sophisticated and densely empirical arguments to construct the intellectual foundations upon which modern liberalism in all its forms would depend. Such university-based researchers had urged, and sometimes even helped design, policies ranging from the New Deal's requirement that employers bargain in good faith with duly chosen representatives of their workers to the creation of Social Security and unemployment compensation and, most recently, the court's ruling that segregated public schools were "inherently unequal" and thus a violation of the equal protection clause of the Fourteenth Amendment to the Constitution.[9]

Buchanan understood the authority and commitment of those whose arguments he set out to counter. But having had his fill of Ivy League northerners in the Navy, he was unafraid. He relished the opportunity to build a team of intellectuals who would develop political-economic arguments to "preserve a social order based on individual liberty" and thereby lay the groundwork for an intelligent pushback against federal power. The economist's vision meshed almost perfectly with what Virginia's elite sought, while avoiding the pitfalls. Buchanan never mentioned race in outlining his program, for example. He named his center the Thomas Jefferson Center for Studies in Political Economy and Social Philosophy, after UVA's founder, noting privately in his précis to the president that the venture needed an innocuous name that would not draw attention to its members' "extreme views . . . no matter how relevant they might be to the real purpose of the program."[10]

To boost his department's reputation, he planned to bring to Charlottesville, as scholars in residence, such international free-market figures as the Austrian F. A. Hayek; Peter T. Bauer, of Cambridge University; Bruno Leoni, of the University of Pavia; W. H. Hutt, of the University of Cape Town; and, of course, distinguished economists from Buchanan's alma mater, the University of Chicago.[11]

The William Volker Fund was already on Darden's radar as a source of possible funding for the kind of special program Buchanan proposed to create. Its president was a vehement opponent of the New Deal, but someone who understood that the fight to defeat it would require the cultivation of scholars. Perhaps he might be interested in establishing a southern outpost of the cause. The Volker Fund was, indeed, quite interested; it pledged five-year start-up funding of $145,000 for Buchanan's center (about $1.2 million in 2016 dollars).[12]

All major commitments, such as the proposed Thomas Jefferson Center, needed approval by the university's Board of Visitors, but that would be no problem. It featured longtime Harry Byrd allies, among them representative Howard W. Smith, an architect of the conservative coalition of southern segregationist Democrats and northern business Republicans in Congress.[13] Such men were sure to be enthusiastic about the program Buchanan proposed. That same year the Board of Visitors also awarded James Jackson Kilpatrick a gold medal in journalism for his interposition editorials.[14] And it granted the School of Education's request to hire Dr. Henry Garrett, the "star witness" for the state's defense of segregated education in the *Brown* case.[15] When a later president worried about the overt ideological mission of the leaders of the Department of Economics, the dean who had hired Buchanan rightly reassured him, "I feel sure that their position will do you more good in Virginia than harm."[16]

Indeed, while there is no evidence that Buchanan and Senator Harry F. Byrd ever met, the two men were soul mates when it came to fiscal policy and social reform. As the chairman of the Senate Finance Committee, Byrd was the premier debt hawk in Washington, a man for whom a belief in the essential immorality of debt fused with an approach to the economy and government that would later be called supply-side economics. In Byrd's view, government must defer entirely to business owners to run the economy while balancing its own budgets like a prudent household. His mantra was "pay as you go": no public investments that would incur debt, no matter how great the promised payoff might be. He would have applauded the book on public debt that Buchanan was writing at the time of his hire, as he would Buchanan's admission to the Mont Pelerin Society. Among Senator Byrd's favorite books in these years was *The Road to Serfdom* by the Austrian economist F. A. Hayek, with its bracing case against collectivism.[17]

Meanwhile, the state of Virginia had done nothing to integrate its public schools; instead, its officials continued to bluster, with massive resistance as their official reply to the Supreme Court. The militant standoff was also buying time to set up a new infrastructure of private academies that, being private, had no obligation to integrate under *Brown*. And while liberals all over the country, north and south, east and west, continued to see the issue at stake as one of race and equal treatment under the law, not to mention finally giving African Americans a chance at the American dream, pioneering northern libertarians—a term then just coming into use—all but lined up to show their support for the Virginia elite. Eschewing overt racial appeals, but not at all concerned with the impact on black citizens, they framed the South's fight as resistance to federal coercion in a noble quest to preserve states' rights and economic liberty. Nothing energized this backwater movement like *Brown*.

Who exactly were these libertarians and what so excited them? For New Yorker Frank Chodorov, the founder of the cause's first publication, *The Freeman*, and an inspiration to many, it was the opportunity the resistance to *Brown* presented to finally do away with the "public school system," and see its buildings "leased off to individual groups of citizens and operated on a private basis."[18] For the Southern California–based Robert LeFevre, whose soon-to-be-founded Freedom School would attract nearly all the leading thinkers of the cause as well as the wealthy entrepreneurs who subsidized dissemination of their ideas, it was the belief he expressed to Jack Kilpatrick that "the segregation decision" was a step too far that could lead to a "political realignment." LeFevre predicted that "an aroused and embittered South" would find allies among northerners who wanted to fight federal overreach.[19]

Brown so energized this ragtag collection of outraged radicals of the right that some were no longer happy calling themselves "libertarian." The name had no passion and fire; with its seven Latinate syllables, it could never become a household word. Some wanted to call themselves what they were: "radicals" of the right. Others understandably feared that any name with the word "radical" in it might turn off the wealthy men of affairs who would be needed to fund the cause, and so opted for "conservative" as interchangeable with "libertarian." Yet while "conservative" might help in attracting powerful allies, that name understated the demolition-minded nature of their vision.[20]

Members of the Mont Pelerin Society initially chose to refer to themselves as "neoliberals," to signal the way they were retooling nineteenth-century pro-market ideas; it's the name applied to them today by critics of the policies they advocated. But the word "neoliberal" confused Americans because Democrats in the Roosevelt mold now had such a hammerlock on the word "liberal." So some called themselves "classical liberals," or "eighteenth- and nineteenth-century liberals." But that had problems as well because they parted with classical liberals such as Adam Smith and John Stuart Mill on so much—not least, enthusiasm for public education. One thing all advocates of economic liberty agreed on, at least, was that they were "the right," or the "right wing," and against "the left" and anything "left wing." In the split inherited from the French Revolution, in which the left upheld popular participation and equality, and the right upheld private property rights and order, those coming together in the 1950s stood on the right—and proudly.

No cause that seeks to change the world can make headway without a propaganda arm, and that's where Chicagoan Henry Regnery came in. An early Mont Pelerin Society member, Regnery had launched a publishing company upon the founding of the society in order to disseminate these ideas of the right.[21] Now it was time to build up the publication list. After James Kilpatrick, the Richmond editor, wrote the piece heralding public school closures in any district in Virginia that agreed to integrate, Regnery urged him to write a full-length book on the topic.[22]

The book that resulted in early 1957, *The Sovereign States,* drew plaudits from advocates of economic liberty on both sides of the Mason-Dixon Line. In it, Kilpatrick blended his Calhounian case for states' "right of interposition"—or "veto" of federal action—to protect their peculiar interests with an argument that the high court's current interpretation of the Constitution's Commerce Clause, which since 1937 had enabled all federal regulation, was a departure from the original intent of the founders. By his lights, the Wagner Act, the Social Security Act, and the Fair Labor Standards Act were as unlawful as *Brown.*[23]

Long recognized as a segregationist tract, the book thus also spoke powerfully to those who yearned for the kind of arch economic liberty that prevailed in the early twentieth century. Donald Davidson, the Vanderbilt professor who led the Southern Agrarians in the 1930s, exulted that Kilpatrick had "opened the way" for a South-led "battle of the nation" to arrest "the drift" toward "centralized, one-state, socialist government of the European type."[24]

The William Volker Fund, which subsidized so much of the early free-market cause, underwrote bulk purchases of *The Sovereign States* to distribute, free of charge, to some 1,200 college libraries and 260 private schools, and planned an educational outreach "program for selected editors." Indeed, national coverage of the southern civil rights struggle had led many on the right to complain about "the liberal press." They argued that something must be done to combat the kind of reporters who made southern state officials, to say nothing of liberty-minded employers, look bad.[25]

Kilpatrick's book was a beacon of sorts for Americans like these who were sorely disappointed that the election of the first Republican president in twenty years, war hero Dwight Eisenhower, had not led to a sharper turn to the right. Unlike the centrist majority of Republican voters, they somehow expected a man who had no connection with their movement and no reason to be particularly sympathetic to its aims to pursue their agenda. To the contrary, believing that capital and labor must cooperate to ensure stability and prosperity, Eisenhower accepted the New Deal welfare state and mass unions of working people with political influence, to say nothing of Soviet power in Eastern Europe, as settled matters. He conserved, as it were. He even secured the expansion of Social Security to cover more people and asked Congress to include the "millions of low-paid workers now exempted" from the minimum wage. If all that were not enough, it was Eisenhower who earlier had appointed as chief justice of the U.S. Supreme Court Earl Warren, who issued the *Brown* decision. From the perspective of the far right, perhaps most galling was Eisenhower's characterization of his administration and its approach to problem solving as "modern Republicanism"—with the not-so-subtle implication that those who upheld pre-Great Depression ideas of economic liberty at any cost were obsolete relics.[26]

It is said that nothing stirs a social movement like hopes raised and then dashed; that was true here. Virginia's fight against federal power excited those on the right who had come to feel they had no real home in the Democratic or Republican parties of the 1950s. "We [voters] really have only one party now," a New Jersey businessman complained to Jack Kilpatrick: "the New Deal Party!" He suggested that "a new party, headed by a conservative Southern Democrat but welcoming a conservative Republican" would have "a fair chance of succeeding in 1956."[27]

Harry Byrd's friend T. Coleman Andrews had come to the same conclusion. He ran for president on a States' Rights ticket in 1956, attracting support from top leaders of the new libertarian cause. What was needed was a "political realignment," he said, based on "a clear fight over the fundamental issue of our time": "collectivism and slavery versus capitalism and freedom."[28] Black southerners' claim to equal schooling when they did not pay equal taxes and their calling in of the federal government to help them get it was a prime example of the collectivist menace to liberty. It was part of the "dangerous trend toward socialism" the candidate pledged to fight.[29]

A proud "tax rebellion leader," the Richmond resident and certified public accountant had quit his position as Eisenhower's commissioner of the Internal Revenue Service in 1955 to stay true to his beliefs. Andrews said that he could no longer stay on because he had become convinced that the graduated income tax was a "devouring evil," tantamount to "slavery." Its problems were many, in his estimation, but his main complaint was "the ideological objection" from a libertarian perspective. "The 'soak the rich' purpose" of graduated taxes was "discriminatory," Andrews announced. For government to be "confiscating property" from citizens on "the principle of the capacity to pay," he said in an interview with *U.S. News & World Report*: "That's socialism."[30]

Andrews's candidacy attracted not only segregationists from the white Citizens' Councils of the Deep South but also other critics of what they called collectivism. In truth, the causes were hard to distinguish below the Mason-Dixon Line. Those who were interested were largely businessmen and professionals who considered themselves "the forgotten white majority . . . fighting for their life and liberty" against "the Socialistic trend," in the words of Virginia's J. Addison Hagan. He complained that leaders of both major parties had "been playing to the minorities such as Farmers, Unions, Negroes, and Jews" at the expense of "the white majority" whose "forebears made this country."[31] Other arch advocates of economic liberty beyond Dixie viewed the situation similarly and rallied to support the Virginian's protest candidacy. Among them was Robert Welch, who two years later would recruit Andrews and others among his free-market backers, including the Notre Dame legal scholar and right-wing radio host Clarence Manion, to form the John Birch Society.[32]

In the end, the only presidency Andrews won was that of the Richmond Chamber of Commerce. He won a majority of voters in only one county in the country: Virginia's Prince Edward County, where Barbara Johns and her fellow student strikers had started the fight for equal education that led to *Brown*.[33]

The autumn after T. Coleman Andrews ran, another stand against the federal government followed. In September 1957, Arkansas governor Orval Faubus summoned his state's National Guard to prevent Central High School, in Little Rock, from admitting, under federal court order, nine African American students. As fifteen-year-old Elizabeth Eckford approached the line of troops massed outside the school, they sent her back toward a shouting crowd that was holding up a Confederate flag and a placard reading NIGGER GO HOME. Seeking safety, she turned back to the National Guardsmen, but they again ignored her pleas: they were there on the governor's orders to keep blacks like her away. Thrilled by this application of interposition, Jack Kilpatrick advised from his editorial page, "the Governor has a strong hand. He ought not to pitch in his cards now."[34] Faubus did not fold. So what if the nine boys and girls were outstanding students who had volunteered and trained to make the transition as easy as possible for the school of two thousand students? So what if the plan to phase in a modest amount of integration a little bit at a time had been three years in the making?[35] It was fighting Washington that mattered.

President Eisenhower was not particularly interested in assisting integration, as he more than once made clear, but he worried that he could not maintain face as the leader of the free world if he ignored this affront to the nation's legal system, one the Soviet Union was broadcasting to the world. The commander in chief had held back for more than two weeks when, on a Friday, a federal judge ordered Faubus's National Guard to stand down. As the students were being admitted the following Monday, the several hundred white protesters who had amassed to stop them turned violent, punching four black reporters, kicking a man who'd been knocked to the ground, threatening lynching, and more. No one intervened to stop the mayhem. "We're close to a reign of terror," the *Washington Post*'s publisher called the U.S. deputy attorney general to say. "The police have been routed, the mob is in the street." What exactly was the president waiting for? he asked. With the whole world now following the news from Little Rock, President Eisenhower that night informed the nation—with two of every three television sets in America tuned in to the broadcast—that he was sending the Army's 101st Airborne Division to Arkansas to enforce the law. In addition, he federalized the state's National Guardsmen and sent them back to Central High School, this time to defend the students.[36]

Now it was not just southern firebreathers like Kilpatrick suggesting that "blood may flow ankle-deep in the gutters."[37] *National Review* editor William F. Buckley Jr. defended the governor's actions, telling his readers that Faubus had been merely "interposing" his authority against the Supreme Court's "tyranny." Buckley condemned "the shameful spectacle of heavily armed troops patrolling . . . once tranquil towns." The nine justices of the Supreme Court had created a situation that could "be settled only by violence and the threat of force." And besides, Buckley said, the NAACP was exaggerating the mistreatment of the black students. What were "ugly epithets," spitting, and being "pushed around" compared with "the picket-line practices of monolithic labor unions"?[38] The "line of bayonets in Little Rock," intoned Buckley, was what had always been hidden under "the maternal skirts" of "Mother Welfare State." What civil rights, labor unions, and social insurance came down to in the end, Buckley warned, was the "army of occupation . . . enforcing unconditional surrender."[39]

Back in Virginia that September, James Buchanan, fresh from the recent Switzerland meeting of the Mont Pelerin Society, privately called Eisenhower's "dispatching of troops" to Little Rock a terrible mistake. "The whole mess" of school segregation versus desegregation, he argued, should have been "worked out gradually and in accordance with local sentiment."[40] He never acknowledged that this is exactly what the school board of Little Rock and those in three districts in Virginia that wanted to admit some black students to white schools had tried to do, only to be overruled by the power elites of their states.

Instead, he focused on the task at hand: building the center he headed into the force for change he had promised to make it. And in that he left no stone unturned. Buchanan worked tirelessly to make it a magnet for idealistic young men of the right. Its student participants—"our boys," as he referred to them privately—became, said one, "disciples in the best sense." They felt part of a project to change the world. "Buchanan changed my life," said another. "He asked us to join him in a journey of intellectual exploration and conquest—that never leaves you." The conquest would take time, but the mission was there from the start. Just as the social milieu of Cambridge University had stamped the Keynesian world-making of the 1930s, so that of Charlottesville molded the nascent counterrevolution of the late 1950s against government action in answer to collective citizen demand. Its economics department was one of the few at the University of Virginia at the time that ranked among the nation's top fifteen graduate programs. Under Buchanan's leadership, a sharp shift occurred in the program, as together participants invented a new school of thought.[41] The Virginia school of political economy, as it came to be known, never lost the stamp of its origins.

In the foothills of the Blue Ridge Mountains, Buchanan later reminisced, "there was sufficient isolation from mainstream pressure to lend confidence to the unorthodox."[42] Daily collaboration made the center—which occupied a fine building along the yard designed by Jefferson, one that Buchanan called "the most beautiful enclosure of space in the world"—a hive of creativity and common purpose. Eschewing formal titles and simply addressing one another as "Mr.," as all the scholars at Mr. Jefferson's university then did, the faculty and students shared a "moral commitment to individual liberty" and to scholarly innovation.[43]

It was a time of passionate intensity. "We were collaborators in the process of rediscovering political economy," recalled William Breit. Deep devotion to their shared project made for unusual mutual loyalty. Nearly all the men came to the office every day. At exactly 12:30, they headed off to the university cafeteria for a meal that might be mistaken for a seminar as they critiqued one another's research and dissected journal articles. Jim Buchanan set the standard. His "door was always open." If someone asked him to read a paper, he did it so quickly and helpfully that bets could be won on his speed. Unlike Friedman, when faced with a vulnerable student, Buchanan took care "never to disgrace or disparage them," as one grateful alumnus said years later. It was a movement culture in the making, one of mutual commitment.[44]

Women were not admitted to the university until 1970 (and only after suing in federal court to gain access), yet the cause depended on one woman in particular. Buchanan's secretary became a lifelong loyalist, staying with him for nearly fifty years as his "gal Friday" and the Virginia school's "First Lady." Betty Hall Tillman was the soul of the center—and the sole female employee. Newly divorced after twelve years as a homemaker, she was happy to find a full-time job—even if the $200-a-month starting salary meant that to support her three children she had to live with her mother and sister and rely on them to care for her infant son while she worked. Mrs. Tillman's honey-coated use of "darling" and "sweetheart" to address center members knit the men into closer communion as her daily kindnesses advanced their work. There was almost nothing the economists did not count on Tillman to do, including, for one returning from leave, moving his furniture from apartment to apartment, unpacking his kitchen and books, setting up his phone service, washing his floors, and giving his old "shower curtain a good cleaning."[45]

Over time, the center's faculty and students began to see themselves as heroic figures fighting the good fight, a notion they could maintain and embellish because there were so few on campus who might raise difficult questions about whose liberty was being saved, and at what cost to others. Few working-class men attended the University of Virginia then. If a hardy soul somehow scraped together tuition (financial aid was scarcely a priority for the nation's worst-funded public university, relative to population and wealth), the closed country-club culture created a chilly climate. Until

1953, the dean had been a biologist who provided the "scientific rationale" for the state's "racial integrity" laws of the 1920s. For twenty years, Dean Ivey Lewis held sway over faculty hiring and the curriculum, without fail rejecting "applicants who might critically examine southern traditions, advocate environmental interventions to social problems, or otherwise disconcert the flourishing community of eugenicists he had installed at the university." An example of his intellectual regime: correcting one student's "sap-headed thinking . . . that all men are brothers."[46]

African Americans endured the brunt of such attitudes. Not until the fall of 1950 was the first black student admitted, and then only because of litigation by the NAACP that persuaded the Supreme Court to rule, in *Sweatt v. Painter,* that graduate and professional programs must be opened to all who met the requirements for admission. And so Gregory Swanson was able to enroll in the law school, the first black person besides a menial worker to gain official access to the university in 125 years. He experienced little hostile behavior in the classroom, but there was muttered ugliness outside of it, to say nothing of lit cigarettes tossed at him. When Swanson tried to attend a campus dance, he was informed by the university administration that the fraternities holding them were "private organizations" that had the right to discriminate. Their right to exclude was steadfastly upheld by the editors of both the student newspaper and the Charlottesville *Daily Progress.* To the great relief of the administration, Swanson withdrew at year's end.[47]

Buchanan and Nutter were not just big men on the campus; they were up-and-coming players in the free-enterprise cause. When they invited F. A. Hayek to their "new Jefferson Center" in Charlottesville, he not only came but was so impressed that he immediately invited the two to join the Mont Pelerin Society, securing travel subsidies for them to attend the annual meetings in Europe. The stream of visits added to the frisson of innovation: leading lights of the cause came often, usually staying for a good while thanks to the generosity of the program's right-wing donors, and thus more tightly connecting the center's participants to the greater cause.[48] As Buchanan concentrated on building up the economics department and the Jefferson Center, Nutter helped William Baroody Sr. to transform the

American Enterprise Institute from a squawker on the sidelines into a leading public policy institution.[49]

The visiting celebrities helped give new luster to a favored project of the state's most powerful men: the use of right-to-work legislation to hamper workers' ability to build strong unions. The AFL-CIO was a thorn in the side of the Byrd Organization, what with its push to bring some democracy to workplaces and its fights against the poll tax and massive resistance. Heretofore, the right-to-work cause had been on the defensive as the United States, long the holdout against labor unions in the developed capitalist world, brought wage earners into the world of rights protection through the New Deal's Wagner Act. By the early 1950s it seemed that only domineering businessmen and Dixiecrat politicians objected to working people being allowed a countervailing voice to that of corporations.[50]

Yet through the Jefferson Center, European economists were visiting Charlottesville to say that the South's state officials were right about the labor movement. Hayek, already a favorite thinker of Harry Byrd's, visited to address a spring 1958 conference on "The Public Stake in Union Power." Hayek delivered a biting critique of labor unions in general and in particular of Walter Reuther, president of the progressive United Auto Workers Union, as agents of "coercion" that ought not to be "allowed to continue." After Hayek came another foreign-born member of the Mont Pelerin Society, W. H. Hutt, this time as a long-term visitor. The pro–economic liberty Relm Foundation covered most of the cost, which was not surprising, in that Hutt's 1954 *Theory of Collective Bargaining* had won the acclaim of the grandfather of the cause, Ludwig von Mises.[51]

Buchanan carried the anti-organized-labor message into his classes, teaching his students that the Wagner Act had licensed "union monopolies" that distorted the wage structure. He used an example involving the state's labor market, blaming the United Mine Workers of America for the rising unemployment of coal valleys. With unemployment came worsening poverty in Appalachia. Buchanan's lecture notes were firm on this, too: "But should government intervene? No."[52]

Buchanan took pride in what he called his academic entrepreneurship. Contributions from corporations such as General Electric and several oil companies and right-wing individuals flowed in, as anti–New Deal foundations provided funds to lure promising graduate students.[53] Before long, the cofounders of the center were able to seize an opportunity to prove their enterprise's value to the Byrd Organization on the issue that mattered most to its stalwarts in these years: the future of the public schools.

CHAPTER 4

LETTING THE CHIPS FALL WHERE THEY MAY

James Buchanan and Warren Nutter did not put forward their proposed solution to the school crisis until early 1959. When they did, it was as if they had pulled down the shades on every window, cancelled their subscriptions to all the newspapers, and plugged their ears to a new set of voices in Harry Byrd's Virginia. The economists and their allies had steadfastly maintained that the state's fight was against the federal government, against coercion from outsiders, in a stand for liberty. They ignored the overt racism and turned a blind eye to the chronic violations of black citizens' liberty and constitutional rights that led to the federal intervention, true. But the voices of 1958 and early 1959 defied even their narrow and exclusionary framing of the conflict, because they came from white, middle-class Virginians, from parents, in particular, who were shocked at the actions of their state officials and determined to resist. Most were moderate Republicans and Democrats of the expanding suburbs and cities of Northern Virginia. And they spoke powerfully enough over a six-month period to move Buchanan and Nutter to explain publicly what their vision of liberty would mean in practice on the most pressing matter of the day.[1]

In the summer of 1958, three very different communities—the port city of Norfolk, home to a U.S. Navy base; Charlottesville, home to the University of Virginia; and the textile mill town of Front Royal, in the Shenandoah Valley—announced their intentions to admit a few black students to some previously white schools the following September. They were moved to do so not because the white townspeople or their school boards suddenly converted to equal rights under the law. No doubt a few did. But most, having been reared since infancy in the culture of Jim Crow, did not.[2] Still, many did see themselves as patriotic, law-abiding citizens, and so were unwilling to defy a court ruling, even on the matter of race. Federal courts had instructed their communities to desegregate, without further delay, particularly schools that had been the focus of NAACP lawsuits, and they planned to comply. Those local plans triggered the implementation of the 1956 state massive resistance legislation empowering the governor to close any white school that planned to admit any black students. His act would deny public education to some thirteen thousand white students, all told, from first graders to high school seniors. (No whites were suing to enter black schools, so they were unaffected by the closures).[3]

In July of 1958, the week after Governor J. Lindsay Almond Jr. announced he would close these schools come September, a Virginia country doctor, who before this time had paid little attention to state politics, announced that she would run for the U.S. Senate seat held by Harry Byrd. Her name was Louise Wensel. Dr. Wensel minced no words in explaining why she was running: because Senator Byrd's "massive resistance program is designed to close our schools, thus hurting our Virginia children more than any other group."[4] That was the horror that moved her, as a mother of five, to run.

But she didn't stop there. The problem was not just whether local communities should be allowed to decide to admit black children to formerly white schools. Virginia's coming generation, she argued, black and white, needed more and better schooling, period. And that was just the beginning of the changes she was campaigning for. With the demand for agricultural labor shrinking, she announced, the state should cease being so tightfisted and spend money on public works projects to combat unemployment. It should also pay more attention to the health of its people. The doctor told newspaper reporters of regularly visiting elderly patients in her rural county "who live in cardboard houses without heat, or doors and windows that close in winter." How was it, she asked, that Virginia, among the wealthiest states in the South, "gives the lowest old-age assistance allowances of any state in the nation except Mississippi[?] . . . I do not believe that saving money is more important than saving human lives and relieving human suffering."[5] Franklin Delano Roosevelt could not have said it better.

Wensel was fearless in shaming Byrd for presiding over an electoral system rigged to keep most citizens from the ballot box. "I believe that people everywhere," she said, "in Virginia as well as in Russia, should have a chance to vote for a candidate who opposes the political machine that oppresses them." Whose liberty was the Byrd Organization protecting? She noted that in the U.S. Senate, Byrd was among "the most outspoken opponents of centralization in government." Yet "his political machine has been gradually depriving our counties and cities of their rights," now even dictating to school boards what they can and cannot do. Her campaign motto was Virginia's own: *Sic semper tyrannis.* "Thus always to tyrants." It was time, prescribed Dr. Wensel, for the state's citizens to "resist tyranny."[6]

The state's labor movement threw its support behind Wensel. Indeed, it was the president of the Virginia AFL-CIO, Harold M. Boyd, who persuaded her to run after she sent a letter to the editor of a major daily condemning the threat to the schools. Unions distributed tens of thousands of pamphlets calling on Virginia's "moderate" majority to "speak up" and "organize" to stave off a "schoolless" future.[7] So, too, did a number of mainline Protestant religious leaders and churchgoers who believed in the Golden Rule. They had been the first white Virginians to organize for peaceful school desegregation.[8]

But the biggest problem the Byrd machine faced was the white mothers and fathers of children confronting the prospect of padlocked schools. On the eve of the September closures, the moderate white Virginia journalist Benjamin Muse bewailed, "It is a monstrous, uncivilized thing to close a public school—to lock the door and turn children and teachers away, to halt the process of education in the modern world."[9]

Affected children and their parents, in large numbers, agreed. Families scrambled to cope. In Charlottesville, home to UVA, ten elementary school PTA mothers had formed the Parents' Committee for Emergency Schooling, cobbling together temporary schooling in church basements, home family rooms, and clubhouses, so as to avoid a mass rush to private schooling. The mothers differed on some questions, one explained, "but the one point on which we all agree is balking at the idea of doing away with the public school system." The "tense air" in town marked a change "from the usual tranquility of Albemarle County," noted the University of Virginia student newspaper.[10]

In Front Royal, seventy-five miles away from Charlottesville, some teenagers complained to a journalist, "We're losing our education" because of the shutdown. "They wanted to go to school," he wrote; "they didn't want to risk their future over whether a few Negro kids came to their classes." Norfolk, where nearly ten thousand white youth found themselves shut out of high school on September 27, became the site of the most avid organizing by parents, students, and teachers. At a rally there, one high school student's sign read 2-4-6-8, WHEN DO WE GRADUATE?[11] Here in "Virginia's most cosmopolitan and racially moderate city," as one writer described it, owing in no small part to the large U.S. Navy presence, public school educators refused to cooperate with the privatization campaign. As an alternative, they provided tutoring to four thousand students, reaching less than half of the shut-out youth, but sixteen times more than those who enrolled in the segregation academy.[12]

The grassroots organizing to reopen the schools and save public education from massive resistance continued throughout the fall, as Wensel helped get the message into the news. Taking time from her busy medical practice, she stumped the state in her old green station wagon, her eldest son, Bert, at the wheel, in what was truly, said a nearby newspaper editor, "a battle of David against Goliath." All Virginians "should be grateful," the editor said, for her determination to promote a vital debate "that would never have existed without opposition for the office."[13]

When Election Day came, Byrd still won, and easily so.[14] But Wensel attracted "more voters than any previous opposition candidates in [Senator] Byrd's five elections," despite lacking any political party's backing. And in a sharply restricted electorate that deterred most blacks and many whites, over 120,000 voters—about one-third of the turnout—chose a vision of the common good based on the preservation of public schools. And more: they voted for a vision of Virginia in which the wealthy and propertied class were taxed something more than a pittance, so the state's people could have better schools, better health, better roads—more opportunity to build better lives.[15]

As important, the people Dr. Wensel had energized did not go quietly away after an election whose outcome was assured by disenfranchisement. Instead, they continued working on the still unresolved schools crisis. Fifteen "open-schools" committees joined together in December, with backing from the state teachers' association and the PTA, to form the statewide Virginia Committee for Public Schools (VCPS). Some twenty-five thousand Virginians joined, twice as many as the pro–massive resistance Defenders of State Sovereignty and Individual Liberty claimed at their peak.[16]

And behind the scenes, their organizing action forced the state's business elite, until now inaudible, to stir. Scrambling to catch up with public opinion in the parts of the state most promising for economic development, some corporate leaders opened back-channel conversations with the governor's office and the legislature about the perils of massive resistance.[17] The Richmond-based Virginia Industrialization Group (VIG), most of whose members were from the state's largest banks, retail operations, and new industries, warned the governor that public school closures were "an obstacle" to industrial recruitment and a sword hanging over Norfolk, where so many jobs depended on the federal government. They also pointed out that while it was one thing for the state to create new private schools in rural, black-majority Southside communities to serve the minority white population, "the abandonment or emasculation of the public school system" statewide was quite another. That would be a "calamity."[18]

In January of 1959, the courts put an end to the uncertainty. Two sets of judges—federal and state—ruled the school closure laws unconstitutional. As long as public schools operated in any locality of the state, they found, it was a violation of the guarantee of equal protection to shut them down in another. Conceding that his state must, finally, obey the courts, the governor convened an emergency session of the state legislature to revoke the school closure legislation and form a commission to propose a new course of action.[19]

While the state legislature began to work out a new plan, Buchanan and Nutter put the finishing touches on their own plan. On February 10, eight days after Norfolk reopened its schools, they sent a "private" report to all the members of the new commission. The economists made their case in the race-neutral, value-free language of their discipline, offering what they depicted as a strictly economic argument—on "matters of fact, not of values." Yet they were, in effect, urging the state to ignore its concerned white parents and continue to stonewall the African Americans seeking equal schooling. And they knew it, which is why they noted that by intervening, they were "letting the chips fall where they may."[20]

While most Virginians now assumed that the path forward would include gradual integration in most parts of the state, albeit with mechanisms holding it to a minimum, Professors Buchanan and Nutter made the case for the very opposite: unlimited privatization of education. As believers in individual liberty, they said, they approved of neither "involuntary (or coercive) segregation" nor "involuntary integration."[21] Tax-funded private schools were the answer.

They offered a plan they believed could salvage what remained of massive resistance while surviving court review. How? Privatize education, but do so on the basis of strictly economic arguments. First and foremost, they contended that public schools, which they insisted on referring to as "state-run schools," had an effective "monopoly." They lacked adequate competition, because on their own, few parents could afford alternatives. As a result, like all monopolies, state-run schools had no incentive to improve. "Privately operated schools," by contrast, would have to compete for students, so they would have a strong incentive to try out a "diversity" of curricula, not only encouraging experimentation but meeting different tastes. In essence, "every parent could cast his vote in the [educational] marketplace and have it count." To foster this system, Virginia should provide a tax-subsidized voucher to any parent who wished to send a child to a private school for any reason. Those schools, being private, would enjoy autonomy, admitting or rejecting students as they chose to, without government interference.[22]

The importance of the economists' case rested less on what they proposed than on how their proposals were framed to undercut the arguments of the parents and others who were saying that Virginia simply could not afford to subsidize private schools to salvage segregation.[23] Not so, the Chicago-trained scholars countered: those who argued this way were making an accounting error by failing to consider the significant dollar value of existing school facilities. If authorities "sold all the buildings and equipment to private owners," that would equalize the operating costs of the two systems, and the private schools would prove their inherent superiority. They assured those charged with recommending a court-proof approach that fears that "industry will leave Virginia unless we keep the traditional system of public schools" were groundless. Corporations would not care who ran the schools, they said, as long as good education was available. "All that matters" for the economy, the two scholars maintained, was that the state government support *some* school system "cheaply and efficiently." How that schooling was provided was immaterial.[24]

It was a radical proposal, no question about it, the work of ideologues so committed to their own postulates that they disdained evidence to the contrary, including the cries of colleagues outside economics. Indeed, about ten days before they reached out to the state legislators, over one hundred and fifty moderate local professors had released a petition urging "respect for law and order"; that is, compliance with the federal courts. The scholars described "the maintenance of an efficient system of public education" as the foundation of "our democratic system of self-government." In a state that denied black citizens political representation, the signers pointedly urged that "all the races . . . be respectfully consulted" and involved "in seeking a satisfactory solution" to the crisis. "We emphatically believe, in keeping with basic democratic principles," they concluded, that local people have the right to "solve our school problems ourselves," an implicit reproach of the state government closing schools in local communities that wanted to obey the courts, such as Charlottesville.[25]

Buchanan and Nutter disagreed: to them, as to Kilpatrick, that would be bowing to federal coercion. It was the team's first intervention on a public policy issue in their adopted state and they wanted to get it right, so Nutter asked his mentor at the University of Chicago to review their statement on the "ticklish situation." After all, their arguments were in line with Milton Friedman's own 1955 article making the case for just such action, which he had written as news of segregationist public officials' threats to close public education garnered national media attention.[26]

Friedman found the 1959 Buchanan-Nutter report "admirable." He urged them to "circulate it widely privately and also seriously consider its publication." And then he admitted that he "would go much farther than you [have]. . . . In principle the full burden of education should be borne by the parents of children," not paid by the state. Why, you may wonder, did Friedman want the government out of schooling? That would promote personal responsibility—through birth control. If parents had to bear the full cost of educating their children, he believed they would have "the appropriate number of children."[27]

Antigovernment economists had already been worrying about the tax consequences of the then near-hegemonic commitment to public education. Buchanan, together with a like-minded economist, Roger A. Freeman, had served on the National Tax Association's Committee on the Financing of Public Education, where the two men flagged the growing public school spending of the baby boom era as a "pork barrel" problem and a threat to states' rights, because with federal investment in education would come regulations concerning how it was to be spent. "Who is going to pay the taxes needed to finance the ambitious programs which are being proposed?" Freeman demanded in a publication issued by the American Enterprise Institute.[28] "No nation," he said in reference to compulsory high school, "has ever attempted to keep so many children in school so long." It was an excess of democracy to try to educate so many, he suggested, and it would cost taxpayers too much money.[29]

Professor Freeman also warned the Volker Fund, the foundation that funded Buchanan's center and most libertarian endeavors, that those calling for more spending on schooling were not just "well organized throughout the country." They were doing first-rate research and "an extremely effective job of disseminating" their findings. By contrast, "action to offset this propaganda has been negligible," because the foes of government spending were "largely unorganized."[30] The southern schools fight was changing that, however, opening new hope to the property rights supremacists associated with the Volker Fund.

That hope depended on indifference, at best, to the harm being inflicted on African Americans. To a person, after all, the southerners clamoring for state subsidies for private schooling were whites who wanted to maintain segregation. Black Virginians, by contrast, boycotted the vouchers, viewing them as an affront. Oliver Hill, one of the NAACP attorneys who filed suit for the student strikers of Prince Edward, stated crisply the principle on which they opposed the grants: "No one in a democratic society has a right to have his private prejudices financed at public expense."[31]

Indeed, even Buchanan's University of Chicago mentor, Frank Knight, expressed some concern about "racists" before a visit to Charlottesville. Buchanan responded that Chicago had far more "race hatred" than any place he had lived in the South. He assured Knight that "the Virginia attitude on the whole mess" stemming from *Brown* had not been based on racism. "The transcendent issue," he instructed his former teacher, was "whether the federal government shall dictate the solutions."[32]

It is true that many observers at the time, and scholars since, have reduced the conflict to one of racial attitudes alone, disposing too easily of the political-economic fears and philosophical commitments that stiffened many whites' will to fight. So a "both/and" construction would be reasonable. Indeed, since the abolitionists had first enlisted the Commerce Clause of the Constitution to try to stop the profitable interstate traffic in human beings, and later when the New Deal had leveraged it to regulate the economy, class and race had been interwoven with property rights and public power in ways that cannot be understood well with a single-factor analysis.[33] To pose the schools conflict as "either/or" in the way Buchanan did, however, was a willful misrepresentation. It waved aside the reality that those who opposed school desegregation had to be coached to invoke the Constitution rather than white supremacy as the reason for their stand. And now he was teaching them to use Mont Pelerin Society economics, too.

Yet why did Buchanan imagine that his proposal for thoroughgoing privatization of public schooling would gain traction with state legislators? Had he not seen the enthusiasm generated by Wensel's campaign and the crowds at the pro–public school rallies? Those crowds were not northerners brought south to stir up trouble, as spokesmen of the right liked to insinuate. Their members were in good part men and women President Eisenhower might have referred to as modern Republicans, the kind of voters he had been trying to attract.[34]

Buchanan had first pitched his program to Colgate Darden as a way to push back against federal overreach in the name of liberty. But the parents' mobilization to save the public schools had revealed harder truths. It wasn't just the northeastern elite that rejected his vision of a free society. It was tens of thousands of white moderate citizens of the state in whose name Byrd was defying federal power. In fact, the legislators who had voted against the school closure law represented more Virginians than those who voted for it, but the state's system of apportioning representation made rural votes count for more than urban and suburban votes (rather like the U.S. Senate and the Electoral College overrepresent rural states with small populations).[35]

Was the problem for those who promoted economic liberty majority rule itself? The economists' next intervention raised that possibility.

In early April of 1959, a little less than two months after Buchanan and Nutter circulated their report, the commission set up to chart the way forward voted 22–16 against recommending a proposed change to the state constitution to enable the privatization of public education, a course so new that the verb "to privatize" had not yet been called into being. Some freedom-of-choice vouchers, yes; changing the constitution to further privatization, no. Infuriated, the massive resistance forces organized to build public pressure for such constitutional change. But where they had dominated the public discussion before the school closures, after the moderates' mobilization, the divide was now closer to a draw. They needed help to have any chance of prevailing in the General Assembly.

Buchanan and Nutter entered the debate again at this moment. The timing of their efforts strongly suggests coordination with Jack Kilpatrick in an eleventh-hour push to persuade the legislators to go further. He editorialized in favor of the changes, which would allow the General Assembly "to authorize any county, on a vote of its [enfranchised] people, to abandon public schools entirely and shift altogether to a scholarship [voucher] approach." This was the plan Prince Edward County was about to put into effect, now that it faced its own court order to cease racial discrimination come fall. White county leaders' answer to the court was that because no one had access to public education, no group was being discriminated against. The state constitutional change would also allow localities to sell off their public school buildings and resources to private operators, as the Buchanan-Nutter report urged. Three days later, the two economists went public with their long report advocating school privatization, as Milton Friedman had earlier urged, publishing it in two full-page installments in the *Richmond Times-Dispatch*.[36]

But when put to a political test, the team failed yet again. The resolution in question—to end the constitutional guarantee of free public schools throughout the state—went down in the House of Delegates by a vote of 53–45. The legislators' reluctance to go that far is not surprising. Not many bought the argument that, as a state legislator from Appomattox, of all places, expressed it, "it's not the education of our children that's so important. It's states' rights." That seemed too radical even for state legislators who had prided themselves on their defiance of the Supreme Court. Most understood that a fire sale of tax-funded public schools to private school operators would be political suicide. They wanted to stop integration, not be ejected from office.[37]

The vote marked the definitive end of the state's official policy of massive resistance to *Brown*. "The Byrd machine," observed one reporter, "misread the feeling of the majority of Virginians."[38] The Organization never recovered its former power.

For his part, Jim Buchanan learned lessons from this experience that informed his thinking for the rest of his life. Faced with majority opinion as expressed in votes, politicians could not be counted on to stand by their stated commitments. Even those who previously had pledged fealty to state sovereignty, individual liberty, and free enterprise would buckle, owing to their self-interest in reelection. Buchanan also learned that his adopted state was more committed to public education than he had realized, having taken his cues from Harry Byrd and Jack Kilpatrick. Of course, he blamed the defeat on "educrats" (as segregationists so often called teachers' associations, principals, PTAs, and school-of-education faculty), whose influence he had underestimated. He learned something else, too: constitutions matter. If a constitution enabled what he would call "socialism" (which, in Virginia's case, meant requiring a system of public schools), it would be nearly impossible to achieve his vision of radical transformation without changing the constitution.

Over the next few years, with the expansion of the southern electorate and the demise of Harry Byrd's approach to governance looming, James Buchanan began developing the innovative approach to political economy for which he was later awarded the Nobel Prize. In these final hours of the massive resistance era, then, can be found the seed of the ideas guiding today's attack on the public sector and robust democracy alike.

Meanwhile, back in the county where Barbara Rose Johns first organized for fair treatment, and where officials continued to insist that they would abandon public education entirely rather than submit to "dictation" by federal courts, the Board of Supervisors voted a few weeks later to close the schools.[39] That September, they padlocked every public school and opened new private schools for the white children while leaving some eighteen hundred black children with no formal education whatsoever. "It's the nation's first county," reported the *Wall Street Journal*, "to go completely out of the public school business." Local black youth remained schoolless from 1959 to 1964, when a federal court intervened to stop the abuse.[40]

Throughout those five years, as James Buchanan developed the Virginia school of political economy, he remained mute about the well-publicized tragedy. He saw no reason to distinguish the liberty white county leaders claimed as self-justification for denying education to a community that had dared to challenge them in federal court from what he was seeking to advance with his new school of thought. Quite the contrary, he aggressively defended his adopted state. As the Prince Edward schools remained padlocked and Virginia used tax revenues to build up an infrastructure of segregated white private schools (in a formally color-blind voucher system that survived court challenge until 1968), while keeping black voters from the polls, another southern-born economist, Broadus Mitchell, reached out to Buchanan. Mitchell, who had resigned from Johns Hopkins University two decades before over its refusal to admit a black student, challenged the Thomas Jefferson Center to leave the realm of fine philosophical abstraction and hold a program on "democracy in education"—and, in the name of "social decency," stand up for the integration of UVA. Buchanan answered curtly that "Virginia, as a state, has, in my opinion, largely resolved her own problems" in education. He then sent the new university president his own rebuke to the "annoying" letter, calling Mitchell "a long-time joiner of all 'soft-headed,' 'liberal' causes," and lied that his critic had made "no notable contributions" as a scholar.[41]

CHAPTER 5

TO PROTECT CAPITALISM FROM GOVERNMENT

Had the contest between states' rights and individual rights abated after *Brown* and its progeny, James Buchanan and the right-wing donors who underwrote his center might have felt less urgency. But that is not what happened. As anticipated, a court that found segregated schooling to be a violation of the Constitution's guarantee of equal protection soon began to heed challenges to other realms of southern life in which state governments were inflicting or safeguarding inequity. Of the many areas of vulnerability, none stood out as more egregious than state actions to suppress citizen participation in the political process, particularly but not only among African Americans, and to misrepresent the will of the majority. So it is not surprising that voting rights cases moved to the forefront of the national agenda. Nor that the results proved transformative all around.

"Between the late 1950s and the early 1970s," writes the historian Alexander Keyssar, "the legal underpinnings of the right to vote were transformed more dramatically than they had been at any earlier point in the nation's history."[1] One after another the changes came, pushed by the surging black freedom movement and its allies in Washington, and joined by others who were denied fair representation. A perplexed Senator Harry Byrd bemoaned that states' rights and property rights arguments, once so effective with northern business interests, could no longer derail racial reform. Some thought the Montgomery bus boycott had tipped the scales.

Watching the news, over thirteen months, of black men and women wearily walking miles to and from work rather than endure the indignity of the Alabama city's bus system shook millions of whites out of their complacency. As did the determination and eloquence of the boycott's leader, the young Reverend Martin Luther King Jr., and the courageous college students who began nonviolent sit-in protests in 1960.[2]

Congress and the courts did their part as well, pushed by citizens to see with fresh eyes. Civil rights organizations, labor unions, and civic groups had long denounced the poll tax, which charged people a fee to vote. In 1964, the Twenty-Fourth Amendment forever outlawed the use of poll taxes as a precondition for voting in *federal* elections. Two years later, in 1966, the Supreme Court heard *Harper v. Virginia Board of Elections*. Wealth or the payment of fees, said Justice William O. Douglas, who had grown up in poverty himself, was "not germane to one's ability to participate intelligently in the political process. . . . The right to vote," he ruled, "is too precious, too fundamental to be so burdened or conditioned."[3] It was the end of the poll tax in state elections.

In 1962, in *Baker v. Carr* and *Reynolds v. Sims,* the Supreme Court ended the practice by which the states simply ignored census data showing population growth in the more moderate urban and suburban areas in order to give rural conservative districts more than their fair share of representation. The officials did so for a reason: so they could continue to vote down attempts by their more moderate and pragmatic fellow citizens to improve tax-funded services—from roads to schools to public health. Now, the high court ruled, state governments must apportion representation on the principle of "one person, one vote."[4] Other cases and laws followed, on matters from access to public accommodations to prohibition of employment discrimination.

For most of us today, the story of this period is one of righting wrongs long overdue for correction. It's about basic fairness and equal treatment under the law. As important, what was happening in the South until that time illustrated the probability of absolute power to corrupt absolutely. When one set of rights—those of propertied whites—rarely, if ever, had to give way to any other rights, even when the inequity they inflicted on others (such as tar-paper-covered schools for black youths) far outweighed the damage they inflicted on those with property (slightly higher taxes), a system that started out with strong protections for property rights became, over time, a system where only property rights were protected. Indeed, only white property rights at that.

But for some at the time and since, the story of this period was one of loss, not advancement. What was happening, in their view, in the civil rights era—and, indeed, the New Deal era before it—was that the majority, without the consent of the elite white minority, was taking something they considered intrinsic to the promise of America—the protection of property rights. Those who had amassed the greatest amount of property often believed that they had made the largest contribution to developing the nation, which deepened their feeling of betrayal. Now, to add insult to injury, others—activists and their allies in government—were casting these same figures as society's villains. Indeed, those whom the propertied considered their social inferiors were refusing to submit to their rule on their terms any longer and instead offering their own ideas about fairer ways of doing things. In this expansion of freedom to others, those being challenged saw, rightly, curbs on their accustomed liberties and power.[5] And some set out to take the shine off those who had achieved these victories—to deglorify the social movements that had won them, to recast the motivations of the government officials who rewrote the laws, and to question the value of the changes in society that these victories would produce.

It was in that spirit that the William Volker Fund, the primary funder of James Buchanan's center at the University of Virginia, sent him a postdoctoral fellow in September 1958, with the small wrinkle that the individual in question had no doctorate in economics or a plan to earn one. But he had something more important to their shared milieu: the backing of Ludwig von Mises, the grandfather of the cause, for a critical analysis of government bureaucracy on which he was working. His name was Gordon Tullock. A square-jawed original, he had been raised, he would later say, in a "solidly Midwestern conservative" household that "hated Roosevelt." Tullock was not afraid to speak his mind. For example, he acknowledged that he had "neither taken nor taught an elementary economics course."

But precisely because of that, he believed himself to be "in a completely unbiased position" to determine "that they are taught wrong."[6]

Buchanan and Tullock should not have gotten along well with each other. Buchanan was a preternaturally productive scholar: awake at dawn, at his desk soon after, and rarely home again until twelve hours after his departure—"always working," in the observation of one student turned colleague. By contrast, Tullock, a voluble gadfly who did nothing in a conventional way, "never seem[ed] to be working." Where Buchanan's desk was "piled high" with papers "like an avalanche waiting to happen," Tullock's was as bare as his trademark smirk. Not to be bothered with writing or typing, the "flighty soul," as one student depicted the lifelong bachelor, preferred to dictate his publications. He attracted almost no graduate students, for, said one only partly in jest, "there is nothing in his conduct that provides instruction for others." But the sixty-hour weeks of the one man and the intellectual long jumps of the other strangely made for synergy. Over time, Buchanan and Tullock became each other's most valued critic. More important, they became inseparable in their shared mission: to expose the foibles of government as the best way to protect the market (and property) from popular interference (the majority).[7]

"I intend to attack the leviathan state from the inside," Tullock had earlier told the Volker Fund; he wanted to prove that the very nature of public bureaucracy would prevent government officials from achieving what they claimed they would. Other Americans at the time, from various points on the political spectrum, were also beginning to look askance at the growing bureaucracies of their society, from the critique of stifling corporate culture in the 1955 novel and film *The Man in the Gray Flannel Suit* to the call for participatory democracy in the 1962 Port Huron Statement of Students for a Democratic Society. What distinguished the Virginia team was its determination to expose government problems alone. Never one for self-doubt, Tullock vowed, "I am certain that I can prove that our present bureaucracies do not perform the tasks that they purport to do." No wonder the leading libertarian foundation was excited; if he pulled it off, it would be much more devastating than the Chicago case for free markets.[8]

The book the two men worked on together over the next few years, *The Calculus of Consent,* was a leap from economics as then practiced. As its subtitle, *Logical Foundations of Constitutional Democracy,* signaled, it was a work of political theory that barely discussed standard economic questions. Instead, it focused on the political process, arguing that politicians must be understood as rational human beings who served their own self-interests (reelection) above all else. The authors recast notions such as "the common good" and "the general welfare" as smoke screens that blocked from view the way in which individual public officials and those who sought to influence these officials pursued their own gain through government. Study the constitution of any society, Buchanan and Tullock suggested, and you can identify both the incentives and the constraints that shape the behavior of so-called public servants and their supposedly in-the-public-interest policy outcomes.[9]

To prove their assertions, they laid out what they considered to be the key question and then went on to answer it the only way it could be answered rationally within their assumptions. Why, they asked, did government spending fail to decline in periods of prosperity, when pump priming was no longer needed?

The only explanation, they argued, was that allocating resources by majority decision-making invited voters to group together as "special interests"—or "pressure groups"—in collective pursuit of "profits" (later called "rent-seeking") from government programs. In turn, candidates for office felt obligated to appeal to these special interests to achieve their own goal of winning elections, so they promised gains to multiple constituencies.[10]

Translation: Because the money would not come from the politicians' own pockets, politicians would continue to distribute the money of third-party taxpayers for self-gain as long as it remained in their interests to do so.

To make matters worse, the system encouraged equally profligate "log-rolling." In order to get the backing of colleagues, elected officials engaged in exchange: saying, in effect, *I'll support your proposals (and grant the money) if you support mine.* Because much of this money had to be overseen by bureaucracies, the bureaucrat, too, had an incentive to keep this money flowing, because the more money there was going out, the more important their jobs and the greater the likelihood of their own fiefdoms expanding.[11]

Here, you might say, is the germ of today's billionaires' bid to shackle democracy. *The Calculus of Consent* claimed to show that simple majority voting thus "tend[ed] to result in overinvestment in the public sector." The public sector battened, Buchanan and Tullock argued, because powerful coalitions of voters, politicians, and bureaucrats could foist most of the cost onto a minority whom they subjected to "discriminatory taxation"—or onto the next generation, which inherited the deficits. The syndrome not only wronged minority interests, the authors averred, but also held down private capital accumulation and investment and therefore overall economic growth. Their case yielded a sobering conclusion. "There are no effective limits" in the current rules to the resources that might be steered to public coffers, even when those monies would be "more productive if left in the private sector of the economy."[12]

Interestingly, these conclusions issued from purely abstract thought experiments, not from any research on political practice. Indeed, even a sympathetic economist soon cited as "the major deficiency" of the Virginia school "the failure to search for empirical tests of the new theories."[13] The lack of proof, however, did not stop Buchanan and Tullock from offering what they considered the only right solution: to stanch the flow of money, change the incentives. Majority rule ought not to be treated as a sacred cow. It was merely one decision-making rule among many possibilities, and rarely ideal. It tended to violate the liberty of the minority, because it yoked some citizens unwillingly to others' goals. Any collective with the power to enlist the state for its members' benefit, Buchanan and Tullock insisted, was illegitimate in "a society of free men." The only truly fair decision-making model to "confine the [political] exploitation of man by man within acceptable limits" was unanimity: give each individual the capacity to veto the schemes of others so that the many could not impose on the few. Only if a measure gained unanimous consent, they argued, could it honestly be depicted as "in the public interest."[14]

They gave their new approach a shorter name, "public choice," to signify that, unlike most economic analysis, theirs focused on nonmarket decision-making—above all, in government. While some could and did use the tools for other ends, for the coauthors, the analysis had a distinct political purpose (even as they originally denied that). It provided the moral vocabulary for a political economy like that which had prevailed in the United States in the late nineteenth century, when property rights were nearly sacrosanct.

The authors made it clear that they preferred the constitutional rules of 1900 rather than 1960—a kind of dog whistle to those who would catch the reference. It was that of the unique period referred to by legal scholars as the era of *Lochner* and *Plessy,* two pivotal Supreme Court decisions that ensured extreme economic liberty for corporations and extreme disempowerment for citizens on matters from limits on working hours to civil rights. "The facts of history" showed that once the floodgates opened to a more inclusive democracy, it always led to "a notable expansion in the range and extent of collective activity" in pursuit of what the authors deemed "differential or discriminatory legislation." By this they meant graduated income taxes that asked more of the wealthy and corporations; protective tariffs for, or investments in, manufacturing; and laws that allowed workers to organize unions. Once those groups were given the ability through the vote to elect officials who would be responsive to their needs, no effort to put in new officeholders, the authors concluded, would make a significant difference. Because the problem was systemic, the only thing that could produce different results was putting "checkreins" on the actors: reviving constitutional constraints. And only the effective curtailment of majority rule would make it possible for such checkreins to be put in place.[15]

As one-sided as the political decisions of their own era seemed to Buchanan and Tullock, they never acknowledged that the system of rules they favored, the one that struck down labor and market regulations along with civil rights and voting rights protections, was just as one-sided. The power of the most propertied to constrain representative government through the courts not only allowed states to legislate racial segregation while keeping wage-earning Americans from effectively advancing their interests, but also hobbled the growing number of middle-class reformers who hoped to steer between what they often viewed as greed on one side and grabbiness on the other in an era marked by veritable rolling wars between corporations and workers.[16]

"We more or less explicitly considered our exercise an implicit defense of the Madisonian structure embodied in the United States Constitution," Buchanan later said.[17] But if he believed that, it was not on the basis of close study of Madison. It was true that Madison was eager to protect property rights, but he also aimed to enable lasting majority self-government, with protection for minority interests—but not domination by them. When John C. Calhoun made his case for minority veto power like that which Buchanan and Tullock were advocating, Madison made clear in unequivocal language that he rejected it, saying that to give "such a power, to such a minority, over such a majority, would overturn the first principle of free government, and in practice necessarily overturn the government itself." Yet Buchanan understood that by claiming the imprimatur of Madison, and Jefferson, too, for his research agenda, he would be better able to fight off critics of the radical vision he was advancing.[18]

A later retrospective in the Cato Institute's journal more accurately credited the book for offering guidance on "protecting capitalism from government."[19] It might more aptly be depicted as protecting capitalism from democracy.

In a famous speech to the Commonwealth Club, President Franklin Roosevelt had used the new phrase "economic constitutional order" to explain back to Americans what so many of them had been seeking in their organizing efforts. Pointing to the chaos of the Great Depression as the climax of structural changes that were leading to "economic oligarchy," he argued that in the age of the large corporation, capitalism had shown that it would demolish itself and society unless constitutional reform precluded such "a state of anarchy" by ensuring economic security.[20] Buchanan, in stark contrast, argued that representative government had shown that it would destroy capitalism by fleecing the propertied class—unless constitutional reform ensured economic liberty, no matter what most voters wanted.

He had a front-row seat to ideas about how that might be done, ideas he translated into the terms of Mont Pelerin Society thought. With the schools crisis heading toward its climax in 1958, the Virginia General Assembly had created a new body, the Virginia Commission on Constitutional

Government (VCCG), to defend its policies. Unlike similar commissions in Mississippi and elsewhere, the Virginia body had a broader mission than the protection of white supremacy: its main target was the New Deal, viewed as the enabler of all subsequent unrest. More specifically, it aimed to combat "the misinterpretation" of the Constitution "during the administration of Franklin Roosevelt." In short, the VCCG was taking aim at the entire structure of constitutional understanding on which federal regulation, organized labor's power, and civil rights protections alike depended.[21]

The commission spread its message far and wide: that the federal government had been acting illegitimately since at least the 1930s—a school of thought that would later be called "the Constitution in Exile" and associated with Justice Clarence Thomas and others on the arch right. As the VCCG's chairman of publications, Jack Kilpatrick ensured that the group's publications reached every state legislator and governor, every member of the U.S. Congress, federal judges, bar associations, business leaders, chambers of commerce, town and law school libraries beyond number, and daily newspapers and national magazines—with, ultimately, two million pamphlets and books that tutored readers in a restrictive understanding of the Constitution.[22]

Regularly in the news, the VCCG also had support from the state's flagship campus. Colgate Darden accepted appointment to it, for example. As Buchanan and Tullock began their work on constitutional matters, Darden and Jack Kilpatrick were planning an extended UVA seminar on constitutional law that would feature federalism as a restraining device on Washington's power. They gave up on the plan only because the law school dean insisted, to their surprise, on having "both viewpoints fully represented."[23] This was, after all, an institution of higher learning. But the interest of powerful Virginians in advancing a more sophisticated Dixie interpretation of the Constitution was hard to miss for anyone with ambition and like inclinations. Buchanan paid attention.

Core VCCG ideas, in fact, became part of the approach of the Virginia school of political economy. Chief among them was, in the words of its chair, a well-regarded corporate lawyer, "that [we] carefully distinguish between the growth of federal power due to the amazing changes in the world since 1787 as contrasted with the needless increase in bureaucracy by those seeking to puff up their jobs or who think that they can best run all the people's affairs."[24] Buchanan and Tullock added more academic vocabulary as they elaborated the idea of self-seeking as the motor of illegitimate government expansion. But the driving analysis was less original in its basic convictions than later reviewers imagined. It was midcentury Virginia wine with a Mont Pelerin label.

With so many of its own allies supporting the VCCG, the Thomas Jefferson Center helped out as it could. Richmond businessman Eugene B. Sydnor Jr. and Darden must have appreciated the economics department's hire of yet another University of Chicago Ph.D., the British economist Ronald Coase, then working out a case for how more strictly defined property rights could obviate the need for government regulation—one that later won him a Nobel Prize. But Buchanan's operation also provided more direct assistance in the form of contracted research for the VCCG, such as a multiyear study of Virginia's tuition grant system. It was outsourced to the man Buchanan dubbed the "father" of the freedom-of-choice approach, Leon Dure, who had personally helped destroy the South's most promising interracial union before going on to promote private schooling. The study reported the private school subsidies to be a great success and, indeed, a model for evading government control. With Buchanan as intermediary, the Virginia Plan method would make its way across the Atlantic and eventually into the think tank advice with which Prime Minister Margaret Thatcher revolutionized British policy to achieve kindred ends.[25]

Buchanan's project was intellectual—creating a new field of scholarship—but in the end, it was not simply ivory tower acclaim that he was after. It was real-world impact. He understood that cultivating thinkers who could alter the public conversation was essential to the quest to transform political economy in a lasting way. And that is no doubt why, as S. M. Amadae notes in her groundbreaking study of Buchanan's work in those years, "he consistently made a point to expressly locate the candidate's place within the political spectrum," a highly unusual and disturbing practice.[26] The Mont Pelerin Society taught that ideas could trickle down, as it were, to the man in the street, or at least be sold to him by what Professor Hayek called "second-hand traders in ideas." It may have been at society meetings that

Buchanan first thought about how a carefully crafted intellectual system could advance the cause's prospects—what he called, privately, among comrades, "the grand strategy."

The Volker Fund had also made clear that it wasn't just supporting intellectual work but seeking real change—indeed, radical change. While it believed that such change required a new cohort of thinkers, it also believed that their ideas must then be put to work. "We can learn a great deal from Lenin and the Leninists," suggested Murray Rothbard, the Manhattan-based talent scout for the Volker Fund, in 1961. He did not mean to suggest violent revolution, he clarified, but that the leaders of the Bolshevik revolution had an unrivaled grasp of strategy and tactics. A Leninist approach for the current cause, Rothbard argued, called for the "advancement of the 'hard core' of libertarian thought and libertarian thinkers," from which all else would in time flow. He was pleased with the Volker Fund's recent investments, which showed recognition of "the overriding importance of the intellectuals and scholars in forming a libertarian cadre." Economists, the most reliable advocates of unlimited liberty, could lead in building that hard core for the future.[27]

Virginia was the most promising outpost for the cause to connect ideas with action. "Let's hope that you soak up a little more states' rights spirit down there," Rothbard had said to Gordon Tullock on his original assignment there, in 1958, as the massive resistance school closures flouted the *Brown* ruling.[28] Buchanan ensured that an investment would yield good dividends. With Volker Fund monies, he brought leading lights of the libertarian cause to Virginia, who in turn helped him to spread the influence of Virginia school thought in Europe. After coming to Charlottesville, Peter Bauer "almost single-handedly" arranged for Buchanan's yearlong visit to Cambridge University in 1961–62, while Bruno Leoni, after his Virginia visit, got his host to "Pavia, Stresa, and elsewhere" in Italy.[29] So, too, Buchanan, Nutter, and Coase made it to the approved list of speakers for Volker-funded lectures at other U.S. colleges.[30]

The Volker Fund also sent representatives to learn from "the private school movement in the Charlottesville area."[31] Milton Friedman visited Charlottesville in 1960, invited by Buchanan and Nutter to give a public lecture on the economics of education, at which the faculty who spoke up in defense of public education "were openly ridiculed" by the economists who commanded the floor.[32] Friedman went home sounding like Lincoln Steffens after his trip to the USSR: "I've seen the future, and it works."[33] After an extended return visit as a guest of the Jefferson Center to give Volker-funded lectures in 1961, F. A. Hayek, too, endorsed Virginia's tuition grants.[34] If Ludwig von Mises had not been eighty years old and homebound in New York, he probably would have come south to see the future, too.

Yet without Buchanan's academic success, the Leninist long march might have come to naught. The reception of *The Calculus of Consent* proved a boon to the cause, with academic reviews—many, but not all, by like-minded thinkers—praising the book as "brilliant," "original," "ambitious," "eloquent," and "important." They highlighted its new theory to explain how governments made decisions about how to allocate resources and how different constitutional rules might change those outcomes. "The public sector is the most understudied part of the economy," noted Anthony Downs of the RAND Corporation, "in spite of the fact that it is very large and is the fastest growing sector" worldwide.[35] Even those who faulted the logic of the book on key points and disputed the "implicit ideological emphasis" praised it as intellectually stimulating.[36]

The University of Virginia promoted Buchanan to a chaired professorship that very year, and the Southern Economic Association elected him president in 1963. The Mont Pelerin Society, for its part, invited Gordon Tullock to become a member, too.[37]

It seemed the perfect time to launch a formal group to develop the new school of thought that could serve as a magnet for drawing together and grooming like-minded intellectuals, building a cadre to advance the cause. In 1963, Buchanan and Tullock organized the first conference of what came to be called the Public Choice Society. The range of scholars who came to Charlottesville for the meeting pleased Buchanan, who noted in his journal that it "takes the right-wing onus off us to an extent, and it establishes our claim to scholarship, so to speak."[38] The field of public choice economics indeed created useful tools for analyzing the incentive structures of public life. Liberals, too, could use the resulting insights.[39] Yet, for the inner circle, the ultimate purpose was never in doubt.

Buchanan's "grand strategy" was humming along brilliantly. He and his colleagues had not only created a new field of inquiry, in an academy that regards nothing so highly as innovation that spurs new research; they also were using that field to advance the cause of economic liberty in ways none could have imagined prior to the era of massive resistance. "Underneath its abstract analysis," Buchanan allowed in hindsight, "the Virginia research program has always embodied a moral passion."[40]

Indeed, as they convened their conference, a political mobilization was under way that brought many threads together. Men of the right all across Dixie were then working with like-minded organizers up north, among them those who had backed Virginia's T. Coleman Andrews in his run for president in 1956, to make Arizona senator Barry Goldwater the next Republican presidential nominee. Jack Kilpatrick captured their thinking. "The South is Goldwater country," he announced in 1963; Virginia "is fairly panting with suppressed Republican desire."[41] Indeed, Professor Warren Nutter would become the candidate's only full-time economic adviser, and Buchanan would teach five weeks of Nutter's class so he could travel with the campaign.[42]

Off to his first faculty position at the University of South Carolina, Tullock readied groundwork for Goldwater's run by cultivating a cohort of young Republicans. "The student body," Tullock told the Volker Fund, had "particularly good targets." Most were very conservative, "but a minority are converted to the *Nation–New Republic* type of 'liberalism.'" Even as the majority lacked "an articulate and rational social philosophy," they instinctually spurned the liberal students and the social sciences faculty, finding them "useless." This tension, Tullock reported, "provides an opportunity to have an effect considerably greater than would be found in most institutions." He was confident that he could "exploit" it for the cause.[43]

With that in mind, he met William F. Buckley for dinner in 1960 to discuss the launching of a campus Young Americans for Freedom (YAF) chapter. Its members were no doubt thrilled when the national organization gave their own senator, the veteran Dixiecrat Strom Thurmond, its Freedom Award in 1962. With help from the YAF chapter, Tullock sent news of "the beginning of a healthy Republican Party in South Carolina." He predicted that "it should at the very least shift the southern branch of the Democratic Party further to the right"—a move few informed contemporaries would have believed possible.[44]

Before long, he was also boasting to Buckley about the new school of political economy. "Virginia is a sort of center," Tullock informed the *National Review* editor, of "a very small but growing movement of scholars" doing an exciting new kind of research, a "science of politics" with "practical implications." It would soon be time, he said, "to move out of our ivory towers and offer worthwhile assistance in the mundane activity of getting votes."[45]

It was a long-term strategy, granted, but Tullock expected public choice thought to yield notable "improvements in propaganda strategy." And their Virginia location and contacts put the team in a position to "make the results we obtain available to people who can use them."[46] Always the more dedicated scholar, Buchanan concentrated, for his part, on building up a libertarian intellectual hard core. His more sensitive hearing registered, even if he did not heed, the mumbling of critics. "Of course, we continue to be called 'eccentric right-wingers,'" Buchanan informed Hayek in 1963, "but this does not especially bother us."[47] Academic critics could carp, but the enterprise was moving forward with the backing of the most powerful men in the state. "In twenty years," Tullock exulted to an audience of kindred spirits, "we may be able to carry out a small revolution." One problem ahead, though, he confessed, was "persuading people to make the requisite changes" that their new field of study deemed necessary.[48]

That problem of unpopularity never went away. For when the revolution came, it turned out to be not the one they anticipated—and its impact made the challenge of majority persuasion all the more intractable.

CHAPTER 6

A COUNTERREVOLUTION TAKES TIME

Democracy, especially as it became more inclusive, kept causing trouble for the men who wanted economic liberty—trouble that illuminates for us why they later adopted the strategy they did. "Prepare the lifeboats for possible emergency," Gordon Tullock advised William F. Buckley in late October 1964. By then it was clear that Barry Goldwater, the candidate whom right-wing activists had worked so hard to make the Republican Party's presidential nominee, was sinking fast in the polls and threatening to take the movement's "morale" down with him.[1] The ever shrewd Buckley was already one step ahead.

In September, the *National Review* editor had warned a convention of young conservatives, still giddy from having secured the nomination for their preferred candidate, to prepare for *"the impending defeat of Barry Goldwater."* Some wept. But Buckley went on to deliver the hard truth they needed to hear. Thanks to their Herculean efforts, a historic opportunity had come—but far before its time. For a candidate such as Goldwater to be elected would presuppose "a great sea change in American public opinion." That had not been achieved; the effort had barely begun. Buckley urged his listeners to see "the necessity of guarding against the utter disarray that sometimes follows a great defeat." The young activists had to accept that "a counter-revolution" takes years of careful preparation.[2]

That work had barely begun, especially outside the South. Goldwater was campaigning on a vision of economic liberty that sounded much like that of Virginia's 1956 States' Rights presidential candidate, T. Coleman

Andrews.[3] And Andrews had garnered the largest share of the vote in only one community in the United States, Prince Edward County, not exactly the kind of place from which most Americans would want to take cues, especially with that county's public schools still closed and black children going without education as the campaign season of 1964 approached. How in the world could Goldwater articulate their shared view of the just society and still get elected?

The man given "major staff responsibility for every one of the campaign's important speeches," as well as an equally important say in "every statement that left the [Republican] National Committee" in the campaign, "including political principles," was Warren Nutter.[4] Nutter would boast that he had personally written most of the candidate's "speech to the platform committee (including [its section on] 'civil rights')," a section that rightly outraged veteran African American Republicans, because it replaced the party's long-standing support for civil rights with a call for states' rights. It also shocked moderate white northern Republicans, veteran GOP voters who were not eager to enforce full citizenship for blacks but also did not like stepping in line with the refractory white South. "For those of us who revere the memory of Abraham Lincoln," a New Jersey woman on the Republican National Committee complained, "this is a difficult pill to swallow."[5]

Part of the problem in reaching moderates lay with the candidate. Enamored of economic liberty and priding himself on calling things as he saw them, Goldwater was determined to make his run a referendum on the cause's ideas. And so, even before his candidacy was official, he went to Tennessee to ask why Washington, D.C., was producing hydroelectric power in Appalachia. "I think we ought to sell the TVA [Tennessee Valley Authority]," the senator said. But that did not play well in Tennessee. "I have contributed to your campaign and helped organize the Goldwater club here, but since you have . . . come out . . . for the sale of the TVA, I am taking off my Goldwater stickers," wrote a Chattanooga resident, one of thousands to recoil in alarm. "Why in the hell did you say that about the TVA?" an Atlanta fan demanded. "The Southeast will never vote for anyone who advocates turning over the TVA to the . . . monopolists."[6]

Goldwater next took on the most popular New Deal program—Social Security—and in a state with one of the nation's largest ratios of retired voters.

On the hustings in New Hampshire, he called for the program to be made "voluntary," knowing that this would cripple—and in time end—the system, because, like Obamacare in the new century, Social Security relies upon a vast pool of contributors to spread risk and ensure adequate provisioning. In an attempt to deal with the backlash, his advisers insisted that he explain that he meant only to see Social Security "strengthened" and made "sound," but most voters knew he had said what he meant originally. For many, the proposed alternative—investing their money in the stock market—raised painful memories of the crash of '29, when families lost their life savings. For others, investing elsewhere was not an option, because they had never earned enough money to save for old age. Without Social Security, they could not get by.[7]

Goldwater was not done educating the American people on the principles of freedom. Medicare, he then argued, was nothing but "socialized medicine." Alas, "the idea of medical insurance for the aged" was a federal initiative that even "most South Carolinians *liked*," one history of the campaign notes.[8]

Still, the chance to argue their ideas to the American people was so intoxicating that none of the libertarians could resist doing so. The Chicago school's Milton Friedman, who served as Goldwater's scholarly surrogate, explained to the press that the goal of the campaign was "to stop the drift toward centralization and collectivism." That drift had helped "to undermine individual responsibility and to weaken the moral fiber of the people."[9] On a visit to Harvard, Friedman devoted most of his speech to criticizing the Civil Rights Act, complaining that it used "coercive" means to make all "conform to the values of the majority," in violation of the liberty of the white minority that opposed reform. Friedman urged reliance instead on "free market principles": prejudice would cause lower wages for black workers, which in turn would reduce production costs for those who employed them, so more employers would hire African Americans, he said—and, presto, "virtue triumph[s]."[10]

Goldwater went even further in his anti-*Brown* position, citing the Virginia Plan's argument: "Freedom of association is a double-edged freedom or it is nothing at all." Liberty entailed "the freedom not to associate," a justification for another innovation in the GOP platform: support for state subsidies for private schools.[11]

Today Goldwater is best remembered for one line in his acceptance speech, the most uncompromising in major-party history, until recently. Critics of "our cause," he suggested, could leave the GOP and take their "fuzzy" Republicanism with them. "I would remind you," the nominee announced in his climax, "that extremism in the defense of liberty is no vice!" Contemporaries and historians interpreted the line in light of the candidate's opposition to the Civil Rights Act that had just been enacted and his suggestion that nuclear weapons could win the war in Vietnam. Those were reasonable inferences, given the candidate's avid backing from segregationists and his many followers in the John Birch Society, known for its bellicose anti-Communism and fierce opposition to the Warren Court and civil rights.[12]

But for Goldwater himself and the team who crafted the passage, Nutter among them, "extremism in the defense of liberty" referred to his stand for "a free society" in the Mont Pelerin Society sense. The speech was a proud rebuff of what they perceived as a "smear," to use Ayn Rand's word. She argued, with some justification, that liberals deployed the label "extremism" to evade head-on engagement with Goldwater's uncompromising "advocacy of capitalism." By implying an association with fascism, Rand said, the critics dodged what libertarians considered "the basic and crucial political issue of our age . . . *capitalism versus socialism*, or freedom versus statism."[13] Nearly a half century later, Milton Friedman still called the speech "splendid. I recall particularly relishing the sentence that came back to haunt Goldwater: 'Extremism in the defense of liberty is no vice.'"[14]

When Election Day came, the cause's standard-bearer suffered the worst defeat of any major-party presidential candidate in a century and a half. Goldwater won the Electoral College votes of only six states: his home state and five states of the Deep South that practiced acute voter suppression, among them Mississippi, where he garnered 87 percent of the almost entirely white vote.[15] By contrast, Goldwater lost the Rim South—Florida, Tennessee, Texas, and Virginia—where a new economy was arising. The Arizona senator repelled voters in the growing southern suburbs, gaining less support there than Eisenhower and Nixon had before him.[16]

The regional concentration of his vote pointed to a larger truth about the Mont Pelerin Society worldview. As bright as some of the libertarian economists were, their ideas made the headway they did in the South because, in their essence, their stands were so familiar. Goldwater did best in the part of Virginia—like that of the nation as a whole—most resistant to civil rights reform: the old plantation counties that were most eager to, as officials of Prince Edward County had put it, get "out of the business of public education."[17] White southerners who opposed racial equality and economic justice knew from their own region's history that the only way they could protect their desired way of life was to keep federal power at bay, so that majoritarian democracy could not reach into the region. That is why Harry Byrd was Barry Goldwater's "philosophical soul mate," in the words of Byrd's biographer.[18]

As the Republican establishment scrambled to cope with the near wreckage of their party, the election affected the leaders of the Chicago school of economics and the Virginia school of political economy in starkly different ways. For Milton Friedman, the exposure he gained as a Goldwater spokesman was a career booster. *Newsweek* magazine invited him to write a regular column, an arrangement that lasted nearly two decades and yielded hundreds of pieces on matters from the minimum wage to financial deregulation. "By the end of the 1960s," a biographer notes, "Friedman was the most prominent conservative public intellectual at least in the United States and probably in the world."[19] As he made the case for libertarian economics, he assumed that the cause would eventually triumph by conversion—voter by voter, as long as it took.

Buchanan, characteristically, drew less sunny conclusions than Friedman. The fate of his institution was now, as it had been from the beginning, tied to the grip of the Byrd machine on Virginia. As citizen organizing, the Supreme Court, and Congress pried that grip open, Buchanan's institutional base became less secure. It did not help his mood that Goldwater pulled down so many other GOP candidates that Lyndon Johnson, one of the most skilled political tacticians ever to sit in the Oval Office, was able to gloat that the incoming Congress "could be better, but not [on] this side of heaven."[20] This Congress would pass everything from work-study programs to help students work their way through college to Medicare and Medicaid, a War on Poverty, and laws to ensure clean air and water. Its crowning achievement was the Voting Rights Act of 1965, designed to allow every American citizen, at last, to participate in the political process.[21]

The once omnipotent Harry Byrd, who had refused to endorse Johnson, decided to retire in 1965. Howard Smith, Byrd's long-serving and similarly archconservative counterpart in the House, was not so savvy; staying in the running, he was swept out of the 1966 Democratic primary by a combination of black voters and white urban and suburban voters. "Many whites and blacks in the new district," his biographer summarizes, "wanted the federal programs and civil rights guarantees that Smith had long fought." Able, finally, to wield power in proportion to their numbers, they delivered "one of the most stunning defeats ever sustained by a Byrd Organization candidate."[22]

With such stalwarts of economic liberty out of power and an era of grand expectations opening, the Virginia General Assembly, in a nod to the new growth-minded business class and residents of the growing cities and suburbs, repealed the "pay as you go" requirements in the state constitution, which had put the Virginia of their day fiftieth in the nation in capital spending for health and welfare. Borrowing money to invest in public schooling and infrastructure in a way that would have been unimaginable with Byrd still in power, they turned Northern Virginia, especially, into a cornucopia of economic growth.[23]

As the state and the nation changed, it would not be long before the University of Virginia did as well. In the early 1960s, President Darden acknowledged that academic excellence at UVA would require more federal research grants, a more distinguished faculty, and a larger and higher-achieving student body recruited from broader sources than the white, country-club South.[24] What he had not foreseen is what it would take to open the campus to such improvement.

Nothing did more to bring the new world to campus than the sit-ins that began in March 1961. "The segregated restaurants, barber shops, and movie theater" in the midst of the campus, reported one former student, had become "an embarrassment to fair-minded white students and faculty and a source of despair and frustration for black students," tiny as their numbers were. Patient efforts to persuade the business owners to stop turning away African Americans proved unavailing. So a hardy band of four black students and two dozen white students and faculty, stirred by the larger sit-in movement then sweeping the South, began a petition-and-picket campaign to open local public accommodations to all. Campus conservatives railed against them, insisting on the business owners' right, as property owners, to discriminate as they wished.[25]

The clash polarized the campus: as the advocates of the Golden Rule founded an interracial group, the defenders of the right to discriminate built a chapter of Young Americans for Freedom (YAF), with encouragement from Gordon Tullock.[26] Things grew tenser still when opponents of racism persuaded the Student Council to declare "all segregated businesses off-limits to University organizations and threaten [campus] violators with censure." This prohibition would include the Farmington Country Club, used by many university programs, among them the Thomas Jefferson Center, to host visitors. Hundreds of critics signed a petition, started by Leon Dure, against "any rule that would dictate to groups or persons where they may or may not go," on the grounds that "individual liberty is a higher good than racial equality."[27]

The new university president, Edgar F. Shannon Jr., relished controversy over desegregation no more than his predecessor had. But Shannon also knew that nondiscriminatory admission, coming quietly if possible, was both right and necessary for academic excellence. In 1965, responding to changing constituents and mindful of running afoul of the new federal ban on discrimination, President Shannon informed university administrators that no further evasions of the antisegregation policy would be allowed.[28]

When the city of Charlottesville that same year abandoned the segregation-enabling "freedom of choice" for a public school policy that would allow more integration, Buchanan grumbled to Tullock that now "the leftists will be attracted" to the University of Virginia.[29] His crankiness hid justified fear. That year, Tullock was denied promotion by the upper administration, something that would never have happened under the old regime. Tullock told Milton Friedman he sensed that "the University administration feels much the same about Nutter [and] Buchanan . . . as it does about me." Buchanan, too, felt a chill wind rising. "If we are forced out," he said darkly, the "knaves and fools" at the helm of the university should know that "we shall not go without stirring up a few people"—

presumably his own elite backers.[30] But the threat was idle: his backers no longer held sway as they once had.

With generous funding from anonymous Virginia business donors, university administrators had just authorized a new institute to study the state's economy, so as to guide them in developing "the kind of Virginia we want in 1980." The creation of the new institute, with its vision of using public policy and tax dollars to enhance economic development, signaled a direct rejection of the approach of Buchanan's center by the state elite represented on the university's Board of Visitors.[31] For the first time, business pragmatists not beholden to the Byrd Organization were in the saddle. Among them were such civic leaders as the corporate lawyer (and future U.S. Supreme Court Justice) Lewis F. Powell Jr. and the banker J. Harvie Wilkinson Jr., both of whom had opposed the 1958 school shutdowns and believed it legally and morally wrong to defy the federal courts as Byrd's men had. Wilkinson called himself a "constructive conservative." He wanted to lure outside investment to build the state's economy, and he knew that they would want good public schools at every level and other public investments to make it happen. "With good business practices, you've got to invest," President Shannon explained. "You've got to borrow some money that you know is going to pay off."[32]

The cofounders of the Thomas Jefferson Center had known from the outset that their secret political mission carried intellectual risk. "The obvious danger," Nutter had once confided to Milton Friedman, with a plan to create a political "rallying point" for the like-minded, "is that of slipping from scholarship to propaganda."[33] He and Buchanan also knew that they must eventually attract "reputable" scholarly grants—not just the right-wing corporate funding they had to date, but what Nutter called "'clean' and respectable" money.[34]

What they had not realized until it was too late was that those around them were also beginning to notice a troubling contradiction. Buchanan and his fellows trumpeted "the free society," yet they brooked no dissent from their assumptions. University leaders had first become troubled about the ideological intensity of the enterprise in 1960, when the program came up empty-handed in a major application to the Ford Foundation, and a follow-up visit only confirmed Ford's fears of dogmatism.[35] Ensuing episodes worsened the worries back home in Charlottesville.[36]

In June 1963, the dean of the faculty alerted the president to "a condition in the Department of Economics that has worried me for quite a while. Doctrinalism tends to breed authoritarianism," he warned. "And absolute doctrinalism breeds absolute authoritarianism absolutely."[37] The zeal of the Thomas Jefferson Center's faculty was scaring others. Colleagues not in the inner circle complained of "the department as being too far to the right." The university opened a secret study, a highly unusual practice. The inquiry found that the center and the economics department were indeed "rigidly committed to a single point of view": the "'Virginia School,' an outlook described by its friends as 'Neo-Liberalism' and its critics as 'Nineteenth-Century Ultra-Conservatism.'" Interviews with untenured faculty exposed a "disquieting" atmosphere: one way of thinking so controlled the department "as to make it difficult or impossible for other views to find expression, whether in instruction or research." The climate was such that two mainstream conservatives had left for other institutions.[38]

In addition, the exclusively private funding of the autonomous center suggested external influence on the scholars' mission, a reference to right-wing corporate donors funding an academic program to advance their political agenda. Hiring some faculty outside the mold, and soon, the study concluded, was vital for introducing "an element of pluralism into an otherwise closed society."[39]

It was a sad circumstance for an enterprise founded "to preserve liberty" to be tarred with the "closed society" label then used for totalitarian states. And it would not be the last time it happened.

Oblivious to the growing uneasiness among administrators answerable to a more inclusive electorate, Buchanan still pushed his approach aggressively at every opportunity. Like his maternal relatives, he became a preacher. Elected president of the Southern Economic Association in 1964, he used his bully pulpit to prescribe "what economists should do." They should cease focusing on problems of resource distribution—what the field called "allocation problems"—because the very idea that inequality was a bad thing led to looking for remedies, which in turn led the discipline toward an applied "mathematics of social engineering." Instead, they should adopt his radical methodological individualism in all that they studied, and assume that individuals always sought personal gain, whether in the economy or in politics. But, he opined, markets were good, whereas politics was bad. In the economy, individuals engaged in voluntary exchange; politics, by contrast, was a "whole system of coercive or potentially coercive relationships," because it relied on government force. Buchanan insisted that his hyper-individualistic method was ideologically "neutral."[40]

But it was not. It took effort to deny that "the market" was not a real thing but rather an intellectual abstraction. In the real world, throughout history, people had created markets, and governments had shaped those markets in various ways, always benefiting some groups more than others. History and the daily news alike showed how hard it was for people with vastly unequal wealth to come to a mutually satisfying solution. One had only to read Charles Dickens to grasp the reality of unregulated capitalism; the unchecked economic power of some enabled the domination of others.

What Buchanan was doing was leveraging the prestige of economic "science" to reject what several generations of scholarship in the social sciences, humanities, and law had exposed: that the late-nineteenth-century notion of a pure market was a fiction. That fiction helped emerging corporate elites to shape law and governance to their advantage while devastating the societies over which they held sway by virtue of their wealth and the control over others it could purchase. Founders of the discipline of modern economics, among them Richard T. Ely and John R. Commons, had demonstrated that social power shaped markets, and they debunked the thinkers such as Herbert Spencer who pretended otherwise. Ely, who had led in the 1885 founding of the American Economic Association, was blunt about the laissez-faire economics his generation aimed to supplant. "This younger political economy," Ely said, "no longer permits the science to be used as a tool in the hands of the greedy and the avaricious for keeping down and oppressing the laboring classes." No one who claimed the mantle of science should advocate "doing nothing while people starve."[41]

It was views like these that Buchanan aimed to defeat with his new school of thought. Take, for example, one of the central concepts of public choice analysis: "rent-seeking." Mainstream economists enlisted the concept of "rents" to describe the additional profits a firm might secure without creating additional value for the economy by productive activity—say, by lobbying to extend the patent on an existing product. Buchanan's team, though, gave the concept a new and distinctive meaning, one in wide use on the right today. They depicted as "rent-seeking" any collective efforts by citizens or public servants to prompt government action that involved tax revenues. And, in their assumption that individuals always acted to advance their personal economic self-interest rather than collective goals or the common good, Buchanan's school went further, projecting unseemly motives onto strangers about whom they knew nothing. Similarly, Virginia school economists deployed the existing term "special interests" to refer primarily to organized citizens seeking government action and occasionally to corporations seeking legislative favor. Their usage of the phrase implied that these people were scheming, trying to extract money from the economic producers through vote gathering and lobbying rather than earning it from personal labor. The scholars were conducting, in effect, thought experiments, or hypothetical scenarios with no true research—no facts—to support them, while the very terms of their analysis denied such motives as compassion, fairness, solidarity, generosity, justice, and sustainability.[42]

A case in point: Tullock argued that Lyndon Johnson had undertaken the War on Poverty because "he probably foresaw a fairly direct exchange of political favors for votes."[43] The allegation was the more absurd because the president had known his policies would cost his party its former hold on the white South from the time he signed the Civil Rights Act. Tullock simply presented his own biases about how the world works to discredit those he opposed. It was an old saw on the American right that the people were so dull and inert that any call for government action could come only from self-interested third parties, outside agitators—whether abolitionists, "labor bosses," Communists, or politicians—seeking to make personal hay.[44]

This school of thought certainly did satisfy corporate donors, but it was sharply at odds with the independent ideas the Virginia school was competing with in this era, when so many other scholars, moved by the hard questions raised by the civil rights movement, reached nearly opposite conclusions. Researchers in history and sociology, for example, including some emerging leaders in UVA's own history department, such as the southern historian Paul M. Gaston, were reaching conclusions that, in effect, echoed the teachings of Martin Luther King and civil rights activists: that radical restructuring would be required to include all Americans in the promise of opportunity, and that for this, federal intervention was essential. It was needed for a simple reason, they showed: because only the federal government had the power to end the long train of damaging injustices shielded by undemocratic state governments.[45]

Not surprisingly, then, even at an institution as relatively culturally conservative as the University of Virginia, more people were looking askance at the project of the Thomas Jefferson Center. A member of the top administration murmured that, in effect, "there was nobody in the Department [of Economics] to the left of the John Birch Society."[46]

In 1967, unnerved by their loss of stature and sensing that they were "being liquidated," the founders of the center shifted its funds to a foundation beyond the university's control. Then, for the third time in as many years, the senior economics faculty, led by Buchanan, again recommended that Gordon Tullock be promoted to full professor. That, too, could be read as brinkmanship. Tullock had never earned a Ph.D. and by his own admission had never completed an economics course. Brilliant though Buchanan and his allies might have believed the law school alumnus to be, he lacked training in the field in which he taught, and his publication record—apart from the book he had coauthored with Buchanan—was undistinguished. He was also an awful teacher. It did not help that Tullock struck many outside the center as an egomaniac—or just a twit. (Once, for example, as a new colleague was unpacking his books, Tullock appeared at the door. "Oh, Mr. Johnson, I'm glad you finally arrived," he said. "I need the opinion of someone obviously inferior to me.")[47] Tullock would not be promoted. Buchanan was furious.

Trying to leverage his standing to avenge his own honor and his colleague's name, Buchanan threatened to leave unless the president reversed himself and made Tullock a full professor. The president held firm. "I have deep and abiding loyalties to the South, Virginia, and the University," Buchanan said upon resigning, but he could tolerate neither the "gross injustice" to Gordon Tullock nor "the long-smoldering internal campaign of slander, malicious gossip and vilification" directed at his program and his own running of it.[48]

So Buchanan left. He accepted a regular faculty position at the University of California at Los Angeles, "a fine" department and among the closest in spirit to Virginia's and Chicago's. Indeed, in subsidizing the free-market training of men from other countries, the libertarian Earhart Foundation treated the Chicago, Virginia, and UCLA economics departments as interchangeable options.[49] It did not feel that way to Buchanan, though. On a visit to Los Angeles he revealed that he disliked the city and found the school "impersonal." He went despondently, knowing that he would no longer be the big fish able to make an outsize splash in a small pond. He also seemed uncomfortable about the number of African Americans living in the city and attending UCLA, commenting to Tullock after a visit to San Diego State about how there were "very few blacks in evidence" and the students seemed "more orderly" than UCLA's.[50] Equally dispirited, Warren Nutter left UVA to serve as President Nixon's assistant secretary of defense for international security affairs.[51] The program, the loyal alumnus James C. Miller III protested, had suffered "emasculation."[52]

Over the ensuing decades, Buchanan and his colleagues would tell the tale of their center's implosion as one of liberal perfidy—the politically motivated backstabbing of innocents. "Things at Virginia have fallen apart," Jim Buchanan informed his former adviser, "due to [a] rotten and wholly dishonest administration."[53]

Buchanan's telling distorted the reality in at least two ways. The administration was not, in fact, liberal, let alone hostile to right-wing ideas. Its members were pragmatic conservatives; Buchanan's men were zealous libertarians. And the administrators had realized that the difference mattered. They were practical men who wanted more investment by the state government in Virginia's future. Shannon and his board understood that "to really serve the needs of the state"—a democratizing state, at that—the university could no longer operate as it had in the Byrd era, certainly not if it wanted to become a nationally reputable research institution. Among other things, it needed to attract not just African American men but women of all groups as well, a change Shannon urged in 1967 and saw to fruition in 1970.[54]

Buchanan also bore more than a little personal blame for his program's fate. He had misgauged his market, one could say, from the time he jumped into the public debate in 1959 to urge wholesale privatization of the state's schools. Colgate Darden had authorized their center to push back on the New Deal, yes, but not to side with the reactionaries who threatened the destruction of public education to save segregation. Public schools were a staple of civilized society, in his view, a view shared by the state's top business leaders. The split only widened under Shannon as Buchanan's conduct as a colleague hurt his cause. Just as he could see no exploitation in the market, so he saw as unremarkable his own taking advantage of his status to get what he wanted, regardless of the opinions of other colleagues who rightly assumed decisions should be made democratically. By his own reports, Buchanan ran his department as though he were the CEO of a private firm, answerable to no one. Where other departments made hires through collective deliberation, he chose those "who fit my requirements," unconcerned that others might not be comfortable with his nonnegotiable choices.[55]

He never acknowledged any fault on his or his fellows' part for their fall from grace. In his telling of his life story, the campus donnybrook took its place alongside the alleged discrimination he had suffered in the Navy, where he had felt the sting of Ivy League northerners' snobbery about Middle Tennessee State Teachers College. He was the victim of mistreatment; he was sure of it. He ascribed the demise of his program to "crude attempts at thought control" by "establishment intellectuals," men who bore "envy-engendered hatred" toward those who rejected their "romance with the state."[56] As Buchanan fled Charlottesville for Los Angeles, he found further grounds for his fury—and more reasons to constrict democracy.

CHAPTER 7

A WORLD GONE MAD

"I felt that I had landed in a lunatic asylum," trapped in "a world gone mad," James Buchanan would say of his time at UCLA. It was 1968–69, the most tumultuous school year in modern history, as the student revolt went global. That January, at the start of the second semester, two young Black Panther Party activists were assassinated by a member of a rival radical group only yards from the economics department, which itself had been the target, a few months earlier, of an anonymous failed bombing for its failure to hire any black faculty. The shooter's group was enraged at having lost a vote over which tendency would have more influence on the Community Advisory Board of UCLA's new Center for Afro-American Studies. The murders horrified student activists across the country and stupefied the campus.[1]

But in Jim Buchanan's mind, the violence just reinforced why money obtained from taxpayers to fund public resources was leading society in a destructive direction. He drew a similar message from the reaction of UCLA students and faculty to the firing of Angela Davis.

To her advocates, Davis was a brilliant intellectual who was bringing fresh thinking to campus. The Alabama-born, Sorbonne-trained assistant professor of philosophy taught "the most widely attended [classes] in the history of the school." To Buchanan and others on the right, she was simply a Black Panther Party supporter and a self-avowed Communist. Pushed by Governor Ronald Reagan to fire Davis for violating the university's policy prohibiting Communist Party membership among the faculty, the administration did so, only to have faculty in every department but economics protest the firing as a violation of her First Amendment rights and the principle of academic freedom. Huge rallies demanded that she be rehired. The courts would eventually agree.[2]

Not Buchanan. He believed that, in the short term, repression was the only appropriate immediate answer to the spreading student unrest. Despite "my long-held libertarian principles," he said, looking back, "I came down squarely on the 'law-and-order' side" of things. He heaped praise upon one administrator who showed the "simple courage" to smash the student rebellion on his campus with violent police action.[3]

But Buchanan's experiences at UCLA left a far deeper legacy, one that ultimately explains why, in our time, governors and state legislators under the influence of the capitalist radical right have been moving aggressively to transform public higher education in states where they are in control. After 2010, as the Koch-funded project moved forward in the states, its representatives sought to slash their states' public university budgets while simultaneously raising tuition, ending need-based scholarships, limiting or curtailing tenure protections, reducing faculty governance, and undermining support for the liberal arts curriculum (particularly those parts of it most known for dissent). In each case, Republican-appointed members of the university governing boards acted with unprecedented speed while at the same time limiting deliberations. At the University of Virginia, they fired a popular president for being an "incrementalist." In Texas, they called themselves "the kick-ass regents." In North Carolina, Louisiana, Mississippi, Iowa, and Wisconsin, they shoved out chancellors who would not do their bidding.[4]

It was in the crucible of the campus upheaval of the 1960s that Buchanan produced the analysis and prescription behind this determination to transform public universities into corporate-style entities. Setting to work on a new book with coauthor Nicos Devletoglou, a young UCLA visiting scholar who had witnessed the era's upheaval at the London School of Economics, Buchanan contended that the leaders of higher education institutions were enabling "a handful of revolutionary terrorists to undo the heritage of centuries."[5]

What made the authors' case distinctive was not that anger—widespread on the broad right and among many older liberal faculty, too—but the totally original public choice argument for why the solution was not to deal with the young radicals on an ad hoc, one-case-at-a-time basis, but to rethink these institutions and their incentive structures. Government and the public, Buchanan and his coauthor would argue, had to stop considering colleges and universities as public resources. They constituted an industry, albeit "a unique industry," in which individuals sought to maximize their personal advantage and minimize their costs.[6]

From that starting point it was easy to explain why state governments should no longer support low-tuition public universities. They provided yet another example of how too much money going from the taxpayers' pockets—where it could actually do good—to government spending on questionable activities in the "public interest" wrought perverse results. Its ill-conceived inducements and lack of proper penalties for misconduct, they said, all but invited protests.

The problem with the university, according to Buchanan and Devletoglou, began with its distinctive structural features: "(1) those who consume its product [students] do not purchase it [at full-cost price]; (2) those who produce it [faculty] do not sell it; and (3) those who finance it [taxpayers] do not control it."

Having obtained the university's services for "free," or close to it, the customer had little reason to value them—or the faculty, administrators, and facilities at his disposal. "Is it to be wondered that he treats the whole university setting with disrespect or even contempt?" asked the coauthors. Indeed, having little of his own money at stake, the student was in an ideal position to disrupt the university whenever he or she chose to do so, even to demand that changes be made to it, without paying any personal price. So, too, the faculty "producers" bore no personal cost for the disruption and damage: tenure insulated them. It was "one of the root causes of the chaos," in fact, for job security meant that faculty members had no driving motivation to stand up to the radical students. They had more reason to be coconspirators, or at least passive observers of the upheaval.[7]

Finally, owing to a management structure that divorced investment and ownership from control, university administrators misunderstood who their true bosses were. They tended to be "prisoners of their faculty," allowing faculty rather than shareholders to set policy (a situation as perverse to the authors as workers' control in industry would be). Equally peculiar in the authors' minds was that "taxpayers and alumni," by which they presumably meant donating alumni, "unlike investing stockholders," paid scant attention to "the results obtained by management," even though their money sustained the institutions.[8]

The cure flowed from the diagnosis. Students should pay full-cost prices, and universities should compete for them as customers. Taxpayers and donors should organize "as other stockholders do" to monitor their investments. "Weak control" by governing boards must end. As agents of the taxpayers (in the case of California, those who had elected Governor Reagan), the boards should enforce order in the enterprise—for example, by adopting "a policy stating that all students arrested in campus demonstrations should be summarily expelled."[9]

Only measures modeled on corporate understandings of responsibility and order would work. Indeed, in the end, the problem was public ownership itself, which left no one clearly in charge and no one with the kind of direct personal incentives for maintenance that came from strictly defined property rights. "Think how much differently," the coauthors nudged, faculty and administrators would react to student occupations of their offices if those offices were more like their own homes: if "they should be required to rent, lease, or purchase office facilities from the universities." Then they might find their spines and stop paying "ransom."[10]

It is hard to read this manifesto and not see the blueprint for the right's current fight to radically transform public higher education: to turn state universities into dissent-free suppliers of trained labor, run with firm managerial hands and with little or no input from faculty, and at the lowest possible cost to taxpayers. In essence, Buchanan and Devletoglou were arguing that if you stop making college free and charge a hefty tuition, ideally enough to cover the entire cost of each education, you ensure that students will have a strong economic incentive to focus on their studies and nothing else—certainly not on trying to alter the university or the wider society. But the authors were also arguing for something else: educating far fewer Americans, particularly lower-income Americans who could not afford full-cost tuition. And they were telling the businesspeople who tended to dominate governing boards that it was time to get tough with their wards, faculty and students alike.

Within a few months the economists had a book manuscript completed. In Buchanan's telling, its content proved "utter poison to a certain type of academic liberal." Whatever the reasons, publishing house after publishing house turned them down. That is, until they met Irving Kristol, an editor at Basic Books who was then attracting attention as a spokesman for neoconservatism, an emerging tendency that backed core New Deal programs but called for a crackdown on campus radicalism, an end to race-based affirmative action, and a more hard-line anti-Communist foreign policy. Basic Books pledged to get the book out within the year.[11]

Academia in Anarchy was dedicated to "The Taxpayer." To those familiar with the Virginia school voucher fight, however, the book's racial undertones came through despite its ostensibly race-neutral economic arguments. Indeed, when talking about campus unrest caused by black students, which they depicted as the core of "the chaos," the authors implied that the unrest was being orchestrated by external revolutionaries, presumably white Communists, who engaged in "usage of black students" for their own ends—as though African American students had no cause to protest and no ability to lead their own fight. "The revolutionary adopts the black students as his most attractive allies," wrote the economists; inciting them to achieve his own radical ends, he exploits white Americans' "guilt complex." The authors maintained that the "reaction would have been total, swift, and severe" if the protesters had been "supporters of George Wallace instead of the Black Student Union or the Students for a Democratic Society." (It would have come as quite a surprise to young African Americans to hear that police showed special leniency toward them.)[12]

In his review of the book in *National Review,* Buchanan's former colleague William Breit seconded the call for a "system of full tuition charges supplemented by loans which students must pay out of their future income."[13] The point was not merely parsimony to save taxpayer money. Privately, Gordon Tullock and Jim Buchanan discussed the social control function of denying a liberal arts education to young people from lower-income families who had not saved to pay for it. "We may be producing a positively dangerous class situation," Tullock said, by educating so many working-class youth who would probably not make it into management but might make trouble, having had their sights raised.[14]

It bears noting, given the current implementation of recommendations first made in *Academia in Anarchy*, that the book's analysis was wrong. The crisis on campus did not come from perverse incentives and outside agitators' exploitation of them. At stake were real issues, about which millions of students felt deeply: racial inequality, a war in Vietnam so misguided that the Army had all but collapsed from soldier dissent, and the students' own lack of voice in colleges, universities, and national politics. While hundreds of thousands were being drafted to kill and perhaps die in a war they opposed, they also could not vote. Not until 1971, with the Twenty-Sixth Amendment to the Constitution, proposed and ratified as a result of this tumult, could those between eighteen and twenty-one vote in national elections.[15] What calmed the campuses was not the violent suppression and top-down transformation *Academia in Anarchy* urged, but the end of the draft and campus reform that treated students as stakeholders with ideas that might improve the quality of education.

It also bears noting that, for a thinker who professed devotion to liberty, Buchanan showed a marked enthusiasm for the armed suppression of rebellion, both at home and abroad. Indeed, he never questioned the rightness of American military policy in Vietnam—except to say that it should be more aggressive.[16] His reductionist analysis turned young Americans with a passion to live up to their nation's stated ideals into menaces who misrepresented their purposes for personal gain and the pure pleasure of disruption. Viewing the protesters, white and black, as spoiled work shirkers who lived off illegitimate extractions from taxpayers, he found it easy to call for the use of clubs to subdue them.

With campus upheavals attracting attention worldwide, this book garnered wider notice than Buchanan's previous publications. Not only the conservative press but also a few newspapers with national readerships alerted readers to it, among them the *New York Times*, the *Los Angeles Times*, and the London-based *Guardian*. British, French, German, and Australian academic journals, across disciplines, reviewed it, often commenting on the creative application of economic analysis, even if they faulted its lack of empirical support and palpable political agenda.[17]

But critics could say what they would. For Buchanan, the upshot of all the commentary was that his audience was broadening. He was changing the conversation—not with the general public or the enemy, granted, but with the like-minded, who would always be the audience that really mattered to him.

It was only a matter of time before the lifelong southerner fled UCLA for the region where he felt at home. It would fall to his former student Charles Goetz to entice his mentor to an institution that, back in his haughty Charlottesville days, Buchanan had scorned as the "state's 'cow college.'" Situated in the small town of Blacksburg, nearly an hour from the closest city, Roanoke, Virginia Polytechnic Institute was unquestionably a second-tier state school. But that also made its administration ecstatic to recruit a scholar of Buchanan's stature and willing to give free rein to his proposed Center for Study of Public Choice. The school had only recently made the transition to a research university. His grateful employers granted his center "a mansion, formerly the university president's residence, on a hill overlooking the campus." Buchanan found there the unchecked liberty and lavish institutional regard he craved. Reassembling a team of like-minded men, attended to by "Mama Betty" and able to sport their Adam Smith ties in peace, and with generous support from right-wing foundations, he and his colleagues set to work. Sharing the same assumptions, they practiced "no-holds-barred combat" in developing their variant of political economy—while, again, keeping out those who questioned their premises.[18]

The orderly, "cloistered" community became, said an Australian who joined the group, "the Mecca for aspiring young public choice and public economics scholars from across the world."[19] Buchanan and his team remained at Virginia Tech, as it is now known, for more than a decade. There, these libertarian radicals of the right deepened their ties to right-wing businessmen and foundations who were looking for ideas to counter the expansion of government from the New Deal and the Great Society, and whose own numbers expanded in these years. It was while Buchanan was at Blacksburg that he first got to know Charles Koch, opening a relationship of mutually beneficial exchange, as the economist might say, that reached fruition a quarter century later.

It helped that the president of Virginia Tech, T. Marshall Hahn Jr., was a kindred spirit to Buchanan and a corporate man himself. (Indeed, he would soon become a director of the largest paper corporation in the world, Georgia-Pacific, later purchased, ironically—and apparently coincidentally—by Koch Industries.) Also helpful was that Virginia's brief flirtation with liberal Republicanism was ending. The state's corporate elite was regrouping, with firm dominance now in both parties and the state General Assembly.[20]

Backed by such partners as the Virginia Bankers Association, Buchanan and his team held periodic briefings to bring "businessmen, scholars, and policy-makers" together for discussion of "crucial economic problems facing the people of Virginia." The new center thus resumed the base building with the state's corporate world that Buchanan's earlier operation at UVA had practiced. It even created a new subdivision called the Center for Economic Education, a prototype for future outreach efforts funded by Charles Koch and aimed at Washington, D.C., policymakers. Each wing would carry the authority of association with scholarly research in a public university, yet operate free of control by or accountability to that university as its operatives joined with corporate partners to promote their shared ideas to policymakers.[21]

In May of Buchanan's first year at Virginia Tech, G. Warren Nutter, his old colleague and now a member of the defense department, came to speak just after four students had been killed by National Guardsmen at Kent State University while protesting the U.S. bombardment of Cambodia and Laos. As Nutter delivered the Nixon administration line on the war, eight students, each with one letter on his or her shirt, stood collectively "to spell out a vulgar word," in the description of the shamed college president, one that began with BULL. The action staggered Buchanan, and put him into a rage.[22]

The following year, after some students broke windows and set fire to a building, Buchanan advised President Hahn not to pay much attention to the university's lawyers but instead to engage in "strategic countermoves." Hahn should punish the protest leaders and their supporters; they might not have personally violated any rules, but they had "stirred up" the campus and should pay for that. Angry taxpayers and their representatives in the General Assembly, upon whom Hahn relied for funding, would likely back him—especially if "the federal courts" sided with the dismissed students. Buchanan himself had long disdained the federal judiciary, he made clear, and he imagined the backers whose support Hahn needed did, too.[23]

The self-styled libertarian went further in outlining "a counterstrategy," one he honed and shared with powerful donors, think tank staff, and like-minded public officials over the ensuing decades, for it had application far beyond the campus. The president should play "a simple tit-for-tat game" with the "undesirables." The students who caused trouble should "be subjected to explicit harassment by the administration," a kind of hounding "always within rules but explicitly designed to keep them busy and off balance." There should also be a new "reward-punishment structure for faculty." Sociology, literature, history, and all such disciplines that encouraged critical thinking: Let them reap what they sowed, he was suggesting. Let them feel some pain. It was time to alter the incentive structures. "This is rough business, and it violates sacrosanct precepts for 'academic freedom.' But," Buchanan intoned, "this is a rough world."[24]

Hahn, wisely, did not follow Buchanan's advice. But in his vocal stand against the campus turmoil, Buchanan made contacts with others who shared his indignation and appreciated his recommendations. They included men with substantial wealth to invest. Those applauding Buchanan's call for harsh measures and the clamping shut of tax coffers to troublesome institutions included the vice president of the Federal Reserve Bank of Richmond (a past student from the 1950s), a top corporate philanthropy official at T. Mellon & Sons, and the president of the Scaife Family Charitable Trusts, with its vast endowment from the oil-and-banking heir Richard Mellon Scaife. These men of means shared his fury over the students' conduct—and over administrators and courts they viewed as enabling protest by insufficient repression.[25]

Buchanan so impressed Richard Larry, the economics specialist at the Scaife Family Charitable Trusts, then emerging as a major funder on the right, that Larry awarded a $240,000 multiyear grant (about $1.5 million in 2016 dollars) to support public choice scholarship and outreach at the economist's new Virginia Tech center. "Our research changes the way people think about the way governments work," Buchanan explained in applying for funds.[26]

The favorable recognition that the Virginia school received in a 1971 journal article by two public choice scholars, Mancur Olson and Christopher K. Clague, helped in fund-raising. The article, which Buchanan shared with prospective funders, highlighted the irony that radical right and radical left economists now seemed to share a "skepticism about bureaucracy, government, and majority rule" that might prove transformative.[27]

Delighted to find allies with deep pockets, Buchanan also reached out to the "libertarian-conservative" Cornell Alumni Committee for Balanced Education. Its members were fighting perceived liberal dominance among arts and sciences faculty by marshaling pressure to hire faculty of a Mont Pelerin Society bent. From the outraged ranks of the Ithaca institution's alumni came one especially consequential contact: John M. Olin. After seeing Cornell administrators cower, in his view, before armed black activists, Olin decided to donate a goodly share of his vast fortune to subsidizing the hiring of pro-capitalist faculty on U.S. campuses.[28]

In the meantime, assigned to speak about education at the Munich meeting of the Mont Pelerin Society, Buchanan minced no words. Modern society, with its widespread affluence, was showing itself "willing to allow for the existence of parasites," freeloaders who took from it without adding value. "This is essentially what the student class has already become," he told the scholars, businessmen, and funders. "If we do not like what we see," the "simple solution" was clear: "close off the parasitic option."[29] Before the decade was out, he would be recommending that for nearly all who looked to government for assistance with one thing or another.

PART II

IDEAS IN ACTION

CHAPTER 8

LARGE THINGS CAN START FROM SMALL BEGINNINGS

On a warm Friday evening in Richmond, Virginia, in late September 1973, James Buchanan took the podium to deliver the opening banquet address. He was speaking to the founders of the International Atlantic Economic Society, at its inaugural meeting. It was to be a scholarly society, but one that welcomed economists from business and government, too, and took interest in how economic thought could be applied to public challenges, ranging from the problems of inner cities to tax reform and energy and ecology. Styling himself as "a social philosopher" and not simply an economist, Buchanan used the opportunity to outline a vision and a plan he had been forming in his head and setting to work on with a small circle of like-minded and trusted men and funding from the Scaife Foundation. This would be the first time he discussed it in public.[1]

Earlier that year, he had privately reached an important conclusion. "The Watergate mess" had set the political right back badly. President Nixon had promised "budget restriction" but was too wounded now to deliver. And those who believed in true economic liberty remained a tiny, embattled minority in the academy and scarcely audible beyond it. The cause was in trouble. Even tax anger was backfiring. Lower- and middle-income taxpayers had begun to bridle at how much they were paying, true, but instead of pointing fingers at a federal government that kept spending, they were calling for the wealthy and corporations to pay more, to relieve the "pocketbook squeeze" on those with less income. The demand for "tax justice," as this campaign became known, proved popular, scoring successes at the local and state levels and inducing alarm on the right.[2]

The time was right for a more ambitious approach, Buchanan believed. Scattered thinkers, even if they were grouped in friendly institutions like Virginia Tech, the University of Chicago, and UCLA, were not going to stimulate a counterrevolution. The more he thought about what the new approach should be, the more he felt that the answer lay in organization, in connecting like thinkers and linking them to funders who could help them create enough surrogates to spread the message across the country from varied locations, yet as with one voice. The reality had to be faced—and might even prove useful: most citizens knew little about government. Gordon Tullock called it "rational ignorance": the individual voter had scant effect on outcomes, so why bother to follow politics closely? Busy with other matters, "they devote relatively little time and effort in acquiring information about social policy alternatives"; rather, "they accept what they are told" by news sources they trust. And so it was incumbent on the cause to change what they were hearing and from whom. His vision was to start by converting people of power in domains that mattered: politics, business, the media, and the courts.[3]

This was why Buchanan had invited a group of close associates to his cabin in the country that March to test out his new plan. "If a history of the Third Century movement is ever written, it can talk about origins in a log cabin deep in the Virginia mountains," he forecast with glee in convening the gathering. "A roaring fire will add a bit of conspiratorial flavor" to the conclave of a small circle with a big plan for the future. It included his longtime ally Tullock; his *Academia in Anarchy* coauthor, Nicos Devletoglou; his fellow Mont Pelerin Society economist J. Clayburn La Force Jr., former department chair at UCLA; and the department chair at Virginia Tech who had brought in Buchanan's team, Wilson E. Schmidt, now President Nixon's deputy assistant secretary of the U.S. Treasury. Schmidt had been seeking the help of like-minded economists to prevent higher taxes from becoming the answer to the emerging "fiscal crisis."[4]

What the cause needed, Buchanan told the men he brought together, was to "create, support, and activate an effective counterintelligentsia" to begin to transform "the way people think about government." A kind of bottleneck existed in which liberal intellectuals influenced the media, which in turn influenced the "elected political leaders," thwarting the men's shared cause. The center-left all but owned the university, and its "intellectual establishment" effectively indoctrinated political actors in both parties. Because of this, any attempt at fundamental change would be "frustrated and subverted." It was essential, therefore, to pull together the like-minded and seed a new crop of surrogates who could be "indoctrinated" with intellectually compelling arguments and then "mobilized, organized, and directed" to spread them in a strategic manner. If the job was done right, ultimately, in time, this new "vast network of political power will *be* the Establishment."[5]

It sounded like the plan he had first proposed to President Darden all those years ago—but on a far grander scale. This was a multitiered vision no longer focused on developing an academic school of thought. He had created that, after all. The new stage was "Practical Strategy." Buchanan made one more important point to his invited guests. The key thing moving forward, he stressed, was that "conspiratorial secrecy is at all times essential."[6]

Now, tonight, in his Richmond banquet address, he would make the dream public (but not the stealth organizing to realize it). "The issue that the Third Century faces," he announced, was how to put manacles on what he referred to as Leviathan. He spelled out what he saw as the world-historic peril of government growth. The Civil War had ended the possibility that states might use the threat of exit to check federal action. The concept of states' rights had also lost its power. As a result, "since the Great Depression, we have witnessed a continuing and accelerating growth in the American Leviathan," evident in the enlarged public sector. "The monster" was "on a rampage."[7]

To give his listeners hope, the economist scanned the news hungrily for signs of popular malaise among taxpayers "against the oppression" of being forced, by the government, to "support unproductive and essentially parasitic members of society."[8] He enlisted the racially coded stereotypes commonly used at the time to decry allegedly freeloading black welfare recipients to tarnish a much broader swath of society that would include, say, laid-off steelworkers granted unemployment compensation, students provided low-cost tuition at state colleges and universities, and retirees who received more from Social Security and Medicare than they had paid in.[9]

Jim Buchanan continued to think of himself as a populist in a fight against the eastern establishment, but his way of seeing the world upended that of the movement whose voters had elected his grandfather in 1890. The original Populists had extolled the ordinary men and women who produced needed goods by the sweat of their brows and reviled as "parasites" the mortgage bankers, furnishing merchants, and robber barons who lived in luxury by exploiting them. The People's Party called on the federal government to intervene, as the only conceivable counterweight to the vast corporate power altering their society. Because that government was representative of the people (or could be made so, through organizing), they saw it as wholly legitimate to endow Congress with new powers that the people believed it needed to ensure justice in a land changed by concentrated corporate power.[10]

By contrast, the twentieth-century libertarian directed hostility toward college students, public employees, recipients of any kind of government assistance, and liberal intellectuals. His intellectual lineage went back to such bitter establishment opponents of Populism as the social Darwinists Herbert Spencer and William Graham Sumner. The battle between "the oppressed and their oppressors," as one People's Party publication had termed it in 1892, was redefined in his milieu: "the working masses who produce" became businessmen, and "the favored parasites who prey and fatten on the toil of others" became those who gained anything from government without paying proportional income taxes. "The mighty struggle" became one to hamstring the people who refused to stop making claims on government.[11]

Still, he told his Richmond audience hopefully, many Americans seemed to be turning against "bureaucratic, governmental solutions"—from George Wallace voters on the right to the "counterculture" on the left. But older means of resolving political grievances would no longer work, he warned. Public choice analysis showed that "a flaw in our basic constitutional structure" made controlling public spending an almost insuperable challenge. Elected officials responded to voters, and most voters were now, in one way or another, dependent on "the federal gravy train." Yet—and here was a good sign—"two broad-based coalitions" seemed to be congealing. One was regionally concentrated in the South, the Midwest, and the West, yet it also included "ethnic [that is, white] blue collar workers in the Northeast." The other consisted of those who benefited most directly from federal spending programs, including the employees of government with a stake "in continued exploitation of the taxpayer" and their allies among the "Eastern Establishment, the media and the intellectuals." The collective enemy he was constructing included nearly everyone in education, it would seem, except academic economists.[12]

His listeners in Richmond could be part of the solution. "Carefully and constructively, a counter-intelligentsia can be mobilized," he assured them. "Large things can start from small beginnings."[13]

Indeed, they can. And in this case, they would. For by decade's end his plan would help guide a major corporate push to transform the nation's courts.

The idea of convening a tight cluster of kindred economists began taking shape first in Buchanan's conversations with Richard Larry of the Scaife Family Charitable Trusts, in early 1972. "Such an effort might have a handsome payoff if carefully planned," the two agreed. Larry had already arranged for Buchanan's new center at Virginia Tech to have a big multiyear grant from the Scaife Trust that included funds for "outreach," after Buchanan pointed out that "many [on the right] have noted the need to have a 'counter-Brookings' [Institution]" to negate the authority of the "alleged economists" who worked for liberal think tanks that backed political intervention in the economy.[14]

In a series of confidential documents, Buchanan spelled out to Larry what he envisioned doing with this money to shape "the way people think about government" with "a 'sound' perspective." Some of it would be used for the "training of teachers for the community colleges" throughout the South. That was a clever way to reach much larger numbers than attended universities—and influence ambitious students of modest means, uncontaminated by the hated eastern establishment, who would likely go on to work for regional corporations or even become entrepreneurs themselves.[15]

As for the national project, Buchanan planned it with meticulous care.

To be effective, he projected, his counterforce could "only be staffed by members of the intelligentsia in the highest standing." Such people existed in decent numbers but often lacked authority in their own institutions. His program would identify these individuals and give them the resources they needed to push back credibly on the other side's ideas.[16]

Also key to his plan was the creation of a small Founders Group of about ten; these men would generate what he called the Blue Book to reach another two hundred people through their own personal contacts. The centerpiece of the operation would be a Society of Fellows that would include political leaders and possible donors, along with scholars. (His notes to himself read: "use quasi-academic jargon with formalities, but not academic criteria for selection.") As a student of incentive structures, Buchanan looked to create a big monetary prize—one to rival the Nobel Prize in Economic Sciences, then just a few years old and without any Mont Pelerin Society winners—to enhance the allure of working for "individual freedom." ("Get Nixon commitment here," read his notes. Remaining were such strategic questions as "How is respectability to be established and maintained? How much hypocrisy is necessary? How much internal criticism is to be allowed?")[17] The key thing moving forward was to maintain secrecy, with outsiders kept in the dark.[18]

Soon after the Richmond address, Buchanan and his trusted team organized a larger gathering in Los Angeles that included members of Governor Reagan's inside circle, hoping to build relationships that would carry forward the grand strategy over the next forty years and more. The gathering included, alongside Buchanan's scholarly allies and Richard Larry of Scaife, four members of Reagan's team, among them his most trusted adviser and chief of staff, Edwin Meese III. "We are living on borrowed time," the Virginia economist informed the assembled men, because America was "changing rapidly." Strenuous behind-the-scenes organizing was the only hope.[19]

In designing strategy to build the needed counterintelligentsia, Buchanan advised, "money talks." Creating a "gravy train" would help "bring men into the fold" and get them "committed to a set of values" so they would do the work that needed doing. (Remember, to him, venal self-interest was at the core of human motivation; the trick was to establish new providers.) Buchanan doubted that business leaders could be approached directly to fund the cause, because few were likely to see value in a long-term intellectual project. The best way to reach them was "through political leaders" who saw the need and could persuade them. The "Reagan connections" to corporate donors illustrated the potential—and Ed Meese's presence at the event augured well for the future.[20]

Did Buchanan's Third Century project succeed? Some parts did, some didn't. Those that worked set the model for others. Some early achievements came from an organization Buchanan set up with Meese in the first of many collaborations between them; another had enormous long-term impact on the courts.

The California-based Institute for Contemporary Studies (ICS) connected scholars with right-wing political actors in the state and businessmen recruited by them. Relying for start-up funding on the Scaife Family Charitable Trusts, its staff stayed in regular contact with the governor's office. Among those recruited were the future Supreme Court Justice Anthony M. Kennedy, then a Sacramento attorney, as vice president, and a board of directors that mingled "sound" economists with agents of corporate interests such as the California Farm Bureau Federation and Shell Oil. ICS set out to remedy "misunderstanding" about how "our free institutions" ought to work by targeting "opinion-making institutions, especially the mass media." One project drafted PBS to let Governor Reagan speak directly to youth in the state's eleven hundred school districts. Another aimed to learn what was being taught in precollegiate economics education and propose new curricula.[21]

The Institute for Contemporary Studies also planned various ways to get its version of economics into the public debate. Its staff trained businessmen, for example, to offer "a persuasive libertarian analysis of social problems" to "the mass media." They also hired journalists and other professionals for "rewriting technical research material [by the economists] into a form usable by the media." As an ICS fund-raising brochure noted, "Economics is an underlying concern if not the primary element of practically every social issue." It was time to teach opinion-makers and decision-makers to understand the field as the ICS economists did.[22] Corporate donors concurred. By 1980, their ranks included Exxon, Mobil, Shell, Texaco, Ford, IBM, Chase Manhattan Bank, U.S. Steel, and General Motors, backed by the Olin, Scaife, and Smith Richardson Foundations.[23]

Another highly influential initiative came about partly as a result of Buchanan's concern, expressed to one of his funders in 1970, that "we are witnessing genuine subversion in our law schools." He was likely referring to the role public interest attorneys had been playing in the War on Poverty and in suing government bodies to make them more accountable to minority citizens and other impoverished Americans, and to the new reliance on class action lawsuits by social justice litigators. Law school faculty fostered both developments. Meese, an attorney by training, shared Buchanan's concern, and ICS devised an effort to train antitrust lawyers and "selected newspaper journalists" in its brand of economics.[24] ICS worked on this effort with the Law and Economics Center at the University of Miami.[25]

That center was run by Professor Henry G. Manne, a leader in the emerging field of "law and economics," a field dedicated to shaping the understanding and practice of law in a manner that CEOs and CFOs could—and did—appreciate. Bringing a corporate-oriented cost-benefit analysis to regulation and legal liberalism more generally, the field sought to do to midcentury legal thought what public choice was doing to social science thought about government: in the words of one history of the effort, to "undermine the intellectual foundations on which its arguments, and its claim to represent the public interest, were based." Manne's own work of the 1960s had argued, for example, that insider trading was good for the economy and that hostile takeovers offered an ideal way for investors to control managers.[26]

Manne had been among the handful of scholars Buchanan first thought of for his Third Century project in 1973—and no wonder, for he, too, saw the need for an organizing strategy and had the talent to convene the right players. "I think we are not too far away from a period when there will be conservative counterparts to the ACLU," Manne consoled Buchanan during the campus upheaval, and when "there will be 'public interest' lawsuits brought on behalf of property owners."[27] Lawsuits waged on behalf of property owners: it was that sense of possibility that had led Henry Manne to launch an annual Summer Economics Institute for Law Professors, in which some of Buchanan's colleagues served as lecturers.[28]

Manne, too, was playing a long game. He looked to transform the legal profession "wholesale" rather than "retail." Instead of turning out individual mentees, Manne planned to alter the way the law was understood and taught by luring existing leaders in the legal academy, from institutions including Harvard and Columbia—eventually more than six hundred of them—to his two-week summer institutes. As the guests went back to their institutions (and he always made sure to take a minimum of two from any given law school so they could back each other and not give in), they would push their skeptical colleagues to be more open to hiring faculty in the field of law and economics, particularly when the new colleagues came at little or no cost because the funds for them were provided by the Olin Foundation or its imitators. Some entire law schools became bastions of Manne's approach to the law. The University of Virginia became the first big "adopter," enticed by Olin money and encouraged by the economics faculty Buchanan had put in place. As his Thomas Jefferson Center had, so Manne's Law and Economics Center now also created a new set of lures to build a counterintelligentsia. As one young legal scholar so drawn, who went on to an Olin position at Yale Law School, recalled of what came to be called Henry Manne camp, "getting a thousand-dollar honorarium to write a paper then was a lot. I drooled over it."[29]

Like Buchanan, and with his guidance early on, Manne transformed a weakness into a strategic asset. Unable to secure a post in a top law school in his early years, he instead persuaded the aspiring presidents of a string of lesser schools to let him re-create their programs in his image. It was easy to transform new or low-ranked law schools: with their shallow institutional roots, they had no encrusted traditions or committed alumni to block the way, and any improved ranking would appear exponential to administrators itching to ascend the ladder. Because the law schools depended entirely on tuition, without cushioning endowments, they were also especially susceptible to outside funders. Moreover, graduates of his kind of program were sure to appeal to corporate personnel departments and donors in a way that ordinary law school alumni would not.[30]

Indeed, also like the economist, the law professor was a canny solicitor of corporate contributors. When he tapped companies for support, Manne avoided their public relations departments, the usual source of gifts, which were often stocked by employees interested in social responsibility, and instead approached their general counsels, defenders of the core enterprise, who tended to be ensconced in the top executive suites and more likely to see the world as he did. General counsels were only too aware of how corporations were faring in court battles with public interest plaintiffs. As Manne recounted in one interview, "a law school especially designed to serve the needs with which these men are familiar could strike a responsive chord that many other law schools do not." His own approach, he said, was "really like sales work, calling on people face to face, offering your product and seeing if you could interest them."[31]

Manne's training programs needed cash flow—and he got it from big business. At the opening of the new decade, for example, he wanted $100,000 for his program, so he asked eleven major corporations for $10,000 each, emphasizing the fight his program would wage against antitrust law. "I said it was a way to get these ideas across to a large number of law professors who create the lawyers and the government officials," he told his contacts. "Within a few weeks I had $10,000 from ten of them," he recalled. U.S. Steel, the eleventh, came in late and begged to have its funds included, even as Manne told the company he had all he needed. "We were not asking for charity," he made clear. "Corporations had a long-range interest in what went on in universities, and if they didn't begin tending to it, it was going to jump up and bite them."[32]

Henry Manne was not averse to gross exaggeration to scare corporate officers into opening their safes. In *The Attack on Corporate America,* he claimed that since the 1960s there had been "an outpouring of corporate and business criticism as venomous as anything seen since Nazi 'scholars' placed responsibility for the ills of an earlier epoch on the Jewish community." Manne warned that if it was allowed to continue, the "free enterprise" system was "in the greatest danger ever of being destroyed." Law and economics scholarship, however, "would be on their side," he pledged to his corporate contacts privately. "We were doing something that they ought to buy." Swayed, they wrote checks. To use an analogy from another law-and-economics figure, such fund-raising was "like knocking over Coke bottles with a baseball bat."[33] Easy exercise, once you got the swing of it.

As Jim Buchanan was assembling his Third Century organizing team in late 1972, Henry Manne outlined his overarching vision for the law profession to Pierre Goodrich, the Indiana entrepreneur who had created and generously endowed the Liberty Fund in 1960. A Mont Pelerin Society member who revered the Austrian economist Ludwig von Mises, Goodrich had determined to use his wealth to promote the cause by investing in scholars he trusted. Even "one law school dedicated" to a libertarian approach, Manne wrote Goodrich, "would do more to discipline all the other law schools (and conceivably other segments of the university) than anything I can think of." Within one generation, his plan "could turn the American legal system back into a productive and desirable channel," the kind that had contained it before the Great Depression.[34] This pitch, too, worked. Like Georges Danton, the French revolutionary famous for his motto *"De l'audace, encore de l'audace, toujours de l'audace!"* ("audacity, more audacity, always audacity!"), Henry Manne set in motion the transformation he promised his donors he could deliver.

One year earlier, Eugene B. Sydnor Jr., the Richmond businessman who, back in the late 1950s, had the vision for the Virginia Commission on Constitutional Government (VCCG) to fight "the ever-quickening pace of Federal intrusion," solicited the so-called Powell Memorandum in his new role as education director of the U.S. Chamber of Commerce. Today it is widely cited as the beginning of the corporate mobilization to transform American law and politics. Lewis F. Powell Jr., its author, was his Richmond neighbor and friend, a leading corporate attorney who went on to serve as president of the American Bar Foundation. Powell's memorandum, said Sydnor, offered "an excellent presentation of the vitally important case for American Business to go on the offensive." Powell warned that "the American economic system is under broad attack," pointing to signs as disparate as the campus revolt, environmentalism, and the rise of pro-consumer litigation, led by Ralph Nader. "Strength lies in organization" and "consistency of action over an indefinite period of years," Powell advised. He urged corporate investment in scholars who "believe in the system," "constant surveillance" of the nation's television networks for "criticism of the enterprise system," the buildup of corporate political power to "be used aggressively," and a new focus on the courts, perhaps "the most important instrument for social, economic and political change." Powell found appreciative ears.[35]

Over the ensuing decade, many American corporations heeded Powell's call to alter the courts. (His authority grew when President Nixon appointed him to the Supreme Court the following year.) "In no other area," observes one scholar, "was the process of strategic investment [by right-wing funders] as prolonged, ambitious, complicated and successful as the law."[36]

The "campaign for the courts," as a critical organization dubbed it, sought "to mold a new jurisprudence" that would radically change "the way justice is dispensed in our society." In particular, those waging the campaign sought "to make the protection and enhancement of corporate profits and private wealth the cornerstones of our legal system." Toward that end, the investors helped fund law-and-economics programs like Henry Manne's and property rights "public interest" law firms such as the Pacific Legal Foundation, which had a close relationship with both the Chamber of Commerce and the Institute for Contemporary Studies.[37] Knowing both the new corporate urgency and Manne's aptitude, as Buchanan did, it was logical for ICS to enlist him to train journalists in an approach to law that was sympathetic to corporations that found themselves in court.[38]

Among the investors in Henry Manne's vision, alongside the blue-chip corporations and the Earhart Foundation, a long-standing libertarian funder, was a relative novice: Charles G. Koch.[39]

CHAPTER 9

NEVER COMPROMISE

Charles Koch did not just become a convert to the ultra-capitalist radical right. He is the sole reason why this movement may yet alter the trajectory of the United States in ways that would be profoundly disturbing even to the somewhat undemocratic James Madison, I believe—and would unquestionably take the "demos" out of American democratic governance. How Koch came to know libertarianism is easy to answer: at his father's dinner table. Less obvious is why he continued to pour untold millions of dollars into this cause, even as he later acknowledged that for some three decades it produced few results. He made clear he was looking for something, but what that something was, beyond a "technology" of revolution, remained unclear.[1] When and where he found it is not: in the ideas of James Buchanan. In the eventual merger of Koch's money and managerial talent and the Buchanan team's decades of work monomaniacally identifying how the populace became more powerful than the propertied, a fifth column movement would come into being, the likes of which no nation has ever seen.

At first it seems hard to imagine why a man who had so much would become consumed with a need to take down those who just wanted "some more" for themselves (in the immortal words of *Oliver Twist*). The answer, to the extent that one can be found in the mysteries of individual human personality, lies in a childhood in which fighting was a leitmotif and government was always the enemy.

Charles G. (de Ganahl) Koch was the second of four sons of Fred Chase Koch, a man who made his millions running an oil-refining business. Through much of his youth, Charles and his brothers watched their father fight round after round of what no doubt seemed to the family, despite its wealth, a David-and-Goliath-style legal battle. It lasted twenty-three years. On one side was a behemoth known as Universal Oil Products, which was owned by a group of major corporations, including what remained of John D. Rockefeller's Standard Oil, and which had monopolistic tendencies. On the other was Fred Koch.[2]

As the plaintiff, Universal Oil claimed that the innovative technical process that had already made Fred Koch a wealthy man violated its patent rights. Koch was up against an adversary that had unlimited funds and therefore access to the best lawyers. They won virtually every lawsuit they filed for patent violations against new competitors. But Koch did not buckle. His attorney argued that his accusers kept control of the industry through a kind of government-backed blackmail, such that "a small refiner . . . is told that if he does not take a license [from the patent-owning company] he will suffer the penalty." At trial, Koch lost. His appeals failed as well. But later he learned, as the investigative reporter Daniel Schulman has put it, that "the ruling that had sealed his company's fate had been bought and paid for" by the company that sued him. It took two decades and the exposure of that corruption, but Koch ultimately prevailed.[3]

Universal Oil Products engaged in what Buchanan's coauthor Gordon Tullock would later define as (and an adult Charles Koch would revile as) "rent-seeking behavior." It referred to all attempts to extract benefits (financial or otherwise) through manipulation of the political or legal system that exceeded what those seeking these advantages would have been able to earn through their own productive activity.[4] Of course, what happened to Fred Koch wasn't rent-seeking behavior; it was criminal behavior. If Universal's lawyers felt confident that the courts would have sustained their claims, then Universal would not have resorted to bribery. One can only wonder if the course of both Fred's and Charles's lives might have been somehow different had the judge in the case refused the bribe and heard the case on its merits.[5]

Then again, there is no gainsaying the fact that Fred Koch did not need a lawsuit to lead him to the right. When asked to describe his father, Charles called him "a John Wayne–type figure, charismatic and forceful," someone who taught his boys to love liberty, venerate hard work, and passionately hate collectivism. "He was constantly speaking to us children about what was wrong with government," recalled David Koch, one of Charles's two younger brothers. But he was even more derogatory about those who turned to government for help, expressing his utter contempt for those who had a "dependence on government" or were even temporarily "feeding at the public trough."[6]

Making and enjoying money was never enough for Fred Koch, as it would not be enough for the son he groomed to be his successor. He had to have things his way. In 1958, after his victory against Universal Oil, Fred co-led a referendum drive to alter the state constitution in order to make it harder for unions to take root in Kansas. Fred was a passionate advocate of so-called right-to-work laws. But what he is most remembered for is his cofounding of the John Birch Society earlier the same year, declaring that he was "thoroughly disgusted with the Eisenhower variety of Republicanism."[7]

Charles was in graduate school at MIT at the time his father helped launch the society, and was keeping his distance from the stern hand of the family patriarch. By all accounts, Charles continued to be more interested in things—above all, how they worked and how to make them work more efficiently—than in philosophy; he earned three engineering degrees before departing from MIT. He liked living in Cambridge and chose to remain in the Boston area in a consulting job after graduation, beyond the reach of the man who had been so bent on hardening him that he had sent Charles, against his will, to a string of boarding schools as a preadolescent and then to an Indiana military academy far from home for high school.[8]

But Charles was raised to respect his parents. So when Fred Koch, ailing, called upon him to help with the family business—or see it sold off—the prodigal son returned to Wichita.

The company he gradually took over had, at the time he returned, annual revenues of $70 million. In 1967, after two heart attacks felled Fred Koch, Charles, then still only thirty-two, succeeded his father. Through the aggressive pursuit of any promising technological breakthrough, and the determined application of it no matter how long it took to yield results, combined with shrewd market and managerial strategy, he would turn Koch Industries into the second-largest privately held company in

America—with yearly revenues of more than $115 billion (well over a thousandfold increase from what it was when he took over) and some sixty-seven thousand employees in almost sixty nations.[9] Indeed, within a decade of his assuming leadership, and at a time when America had only five billionaire families (four of whose fortunes went back to the Gilded Age), the Kochs had already reached the top twenty in wealth through Charles's deft navigation of the family's original industry, crude oil marketing, and smart expansion into other domains.[10] Keeping the company private, he also maintained control.

Koch's competitors learned never to underestimate his determination, his skill at seeing many moves beyond them, and his virtually infinite patience. Playing the long game is his forte, something other Americans are just beginning to understand.

As smart as Charles Koch was as an engineer and entrepreneur, socially he was not very adept; he would not marry until he was forty-one years old. With the business booming and nothing much else to take up his time other than what he called a "compulsion" to learn how the world worked, he devoted more and more of his time to reading books and articles that would enhance his "understanding [of] the principles that lead to prosperity and societal progress." He restricted his study in only one way: to thinkers who believed as he did that the foundation upon which prosperity and social progress had to be built was unhampered capitalism. One work particularly influenced him: F. A. Harper's *Why Wages Rise*, a free-market primer published in 1957.[11]

"Baldy" Harper is one of the least known names in the pantheon of radical right thinkers. But he was a founding member of the all-important Mont Pelerin Society and was Charles's cherished mentor. An agricultural economist by training, Harper was especially concerned with how collective organization among workers affected wages and the "cost of being governed." For the worse, he concluded. Harper compared the impact of unions to that of "a bank robber." They enabled, he sought to show, "a few persons, through power and special privilege" to "gain some short-term advantages at the expense of others who work." In a true, undistorted market society, wages should rise only with increases in productivity. Harper also declaimed against the "little corporate welfare states" created by union contracts that included such fringe benefits as health insurance, pensions, and others. "A small welfare state is perhaps better than a large one, of course," he said, but "it is still an evil," as it is "the essence of communism-socialism." For another thing, such benefits "tend to freeze a worker in his job," thereby "compris[ing] a serious threat to our progress" by inhibiting movement from one job to another. The right way to do things was to put individuals back in charge of negotiating and spending their earnings, and let them purchase what services they needed as individuals in the market, not look to the political system to supply them.[12]

Baldy Harper also hated the idea of "government schools." He fulminated against "financial need" as a criterion for college scholarships as a "Marxian concept," warning, "'Need' grows without bounds whenever it is severed from a responsibility for acquiring satisfaction through one's own endeavors."[13] Harper also worried about moral deterioration in modern society. He claimed to have evidence in his files showing "that the shorter work week is an important source of crime," and that "compulsory unemployment devices, such as child labor laws," and mandatory schooling "during teen-age years, are important causes of juvenile delinquency." By the same token, he argued that so-called government "help" in times of economic depression, such as the 1930s, was "dangerous." The economy would quickly recover, Harper assured, if each individual were "free to continue to work at the best price a free market will offer him." However low that wage might be, allowing the market to right itself would lead to restored prosperity; the key was never to allow wages to stick at too high a level, as with minimum wage laws or union contracts. Such true freedom, with relations between individual employees and employers undistorted by group power or government action, Harper rhapsodized, "would be as near a utopia as can be hoped for in economic affairs this side of heaven."[14]

Harper's thought moved Charles Koch deeply. It echoed his father's core teaching, yet was free of the embarrassing baggage of the John Birch Society, such as the founders' suggestion that President Dwight Eisenhower might be part of the Communist conspiracy. Harper also conveyed ethical urgency about acting on libertarian values, among them emancipation from taxation. "Government in the United States is now taking from persons' incomes an amount equivalent to the complete enslavement of 42 million persons," Harper wrote in another work. "Compare that figure, and the concern about it, with the figure of 4 million privately-owned slaves in the United States at the outbreak of the War Between the States!" Why did so few see the outrage of it? "The power to tax is the power to destroy," he wrote, borrowing words from Daniel Webster and Justice John Marshall in *McCullough v. Madison*, and taking them to ends such early Americans could scarcely imagine. Democratic government was, Harper argued, increasing "the power of certain persons to destroy other persons." It was time to fight such "special privilege," stop "slavery," and "restore liberty."[15]

Harper described the world as Koch understood it, a world in which entrepreneurs were drastically underappreciated and overcontrolled. And he drew a vision of what a society might become if the entrepreneurs were freed from both interference and government-granted favors: a paradise of individual freedom, world peace, and social progress. "Goodness in man can only grow in a climate of liberty" was the message Charles Koch took from his "beloved" teacher: only if one were totally free of coercion and fully self-responsible could one make truly ethical choices. Not surprisingly, Koch credited Harper with the "life-changing" teaching that made the quest for economic liberty the passionate mission of his life.[16]

From Baldy Harper, Koch found his way to Robert LeFevre, a fiercely libertarian onetime businessman who had founded what he named the Freedom School in rural Colorado in the late 1950s to teach an antigovernment, property-supremacist vision of liberty. LeFevre was one of the northerners excited by Virginia's turn to private schools, and was certain that the South's angry whites could be won over to the libertarian cause. He promised Jack Kilpatrick to help by spreading the case that "our government schools have failed us." Americans, he would teach, needed "private and independent schools, completely free from government domination." LeFevre's broader "Platform for a Free America" blamed the Wagner Act for having "enslaved millions" to "Labor Bosses," denounced Social Security as "unsound" and "immoral," and called for "constitutional limits . . . both on taxing and spending."[17] LeFevre's vision, notes one inside history of the libertarian movement, "was like catnip to a certain class of businessmen." Charles Koch was among them. He was so keen on the Freedom School that he persuaded his younger, less political brother David to accompany him on a two-week session at the school; Charles went on to join the board of trustees.[18]

Not surprisingly, then, Koch's first major philanthropic cause was the Wichita-based Center for Independent Education, which pushed private schooling and voucher programs nationwide. It grew out of the Wichita Collegiate School, conceived by his father and Robert Love, his father's partner in the local John Birch Society, to provide a liberty-minded alternative to state-run schools in the wake of *Brown v. Board of Education*. The school's motto was *"Proba te Dignum"*—"Prove Yourself Worthy"—that running theme employed by Jack Kilpatrick for why the federal government had no business helping African Americans: because they should "earn" any improved standing.[19]

In 1965, Koch, having become convinced that finding new thinkers and leaders for the fight for economic liberty was the most pressing need, began contributing substantial amounts to Baldy Harper's organization, the Institute for Humane Studies (IHS), to locate and cultivate these much-needed thinkers and leaders. It was the direct successor to the William Volker Fund, which had brought so many American scholars into the Mont Pelerin orbit, Buchanan among them. (In a fit of the kind of imperiousness to which libertarians seemed especially prone, Volker's president "blew the whole damned thing up," according to one longtime staff member. The IHS took over its mission and attracted its former supporters.)[20]

After joining its board the next year, Koch never left. He devoted not only millions of dollars to the IHS but also the scarcest arrow in a CEO's quiver—his time and his focused attention, even serving a term as president after Harper's death. IHS remained the organization closest to his heart, and he its main benefactor. Koch believed that, as the institute expressed it, "ideas" are "the greatest power." The mission of IHS was, through "basic research," to "search for important truths" to guide the pursuit of liberty. It would do that by "the training in depth of highly talented persons" with "the greatest promise of leadership." That would take time, Koch and Harper knew, because "ideas do not bear fruit immediately." One had only to look at Marxism, decades in development before it bore its "bitter fruit."[21]

It was around this time—1970, to be exact—that Koch was admitted to the Mont Pelerin Society. It was not an easy society to join, even for a man with his wealth and views. Its bylaws specified that any candidate must be nominated by two members and approved by four-fifths of the sitting directors of the association. The new prospect must wait a year for admission, during which time there must be "sufficient enquiry, including where possible among his fellow nationals" to confirm his "suitability." (Virtually all the members were men, so the pronoun is apt.) Dues were modest for a pro-enterprise cause: $20 a year in 1976, about $125 in today's dollars. Once Charles Koch joined, the groups he funded made regular use of the society's newsletter to advertise their events, publications, and employment opportunities.[22]

Urging Koch on in his chosen vocation was something else as well: his belief that his own growing financial success as one of the richest men in the world already justified his slowly taking over the libertarian cause and shaping it to his will. For in his own mind his success confirmed the quality of his intelligence and his fitness as a leader. From Ludwig von Mises, Koch had learned that entrepreneurs were the unsung geniuses of human history, deserving of a kind of reverence reminiscent of the old Puritan doctrine that equated earthly success with divine favor.[23]

Perhaps this arch sense of his own achievement also helped explain the lack of charity (or what most would call compassion) for nearly everyone else—not just wage earners but also businessmen who did not see things as he did. He came to disdain those who ran publicly traded corporations. Such people mistakenly imagined that because they possessed elegant high-rise corner offices, they were his equals, especially the moderate managers who then played an important role in the Republican Party. By his lights, they were just hired hands, beholden to shareholders and lacking in appreciation of true liberty. No, the real heroes were men like himself, from the Midwest, the West, and the South, who had built their own businesses, kept them private, and were not inclined to compromise.[24]

He was even more contemptuous of businesses that failed, arguing that this meant the market was working efficiently, clearing out those who had misgauged the buyer—or their own abilities relative to their competitors. Koch believed that what the famed economist Joseph Schumpeter called "creative destruction" was so critical to the health of the capitalist system that empathy was an obstacle to acceptance of the world that must be brought into being. "Envision what could be," Koch urges; act with "urgency" and "discipline" to "drive creative destruction."[25] A businessman who did not have the savvy to serve the customer "should be a janitor or a worker." In Koch's view of the world, that is what a lifelong wage earner was: the less able or the one sentenced to a form of serfdom by his or her own failures.[26]

Indeed, these notions of what made for superior and inferior people became so intrinsic to his character and sense of the world that when he finally married, he insisted that his wife be similarly indoctrinated into these ideas, lest their marriage lack harmony of purpose, until he was satisfied that the "intense training" had succeeded. (It had. Elizabeth "Liz" Koch complains that America has become "a country of non-risk-takers," of people "who just want to be coddled, and taken care of." Most of her fellow citizens, she says, never stop to think "that they might be able to do it themselves and do it better." Government should not interfere with profit making, she says, because "greed is a return on investment, the risk you took.")[27]

That sense of intellectual and even ethical superiority to others may help explain why Charles Koch bypassed Milton Friedman to make common cause with the more uncompromising James Buchanan. Koch referred to Friedman and the rest of the post–Hayek Chicago school of economics he led, as well as to Alan Greenspan, as "sellouts to the system." Why? Because they sought "to make government work more efficiently when the true libertarian should be tearing it out at the root." They actually tried to help government deliver better results, which could only prolong the disease. Koch believed that only in its "radical, pure form," without compromise, would the ideas "appeal to the brightest, most enthusiastic, most capable people."[28] (Is it any wonder, then, that his allies would now rather bring down the government than improve it?)

In the beginning, though, it was difficult to find bright and capable people who believed as he did. When "I started [bankrolling the cause]," Koch marveled, "we'd be lucky if we could get a half dozen professors or scholars."[29] Still, he continued to invest, undaunted by the eccentricities of the human raw material at hand. At one 1975 gathering of Institute for Humane Studies members in Hartford to promote Koch's favored Austrian economics, one participant remembered "a real team-building afternoon" when the group went on a bus tour. As the young female tour guide drew their attention to the many lovely buildings they were passing, "when it was a government building we all booed deeply and when it was private we all cheered," delighting in the fact that the young woman, not grasping the correlation, was "totally unnerved" by the men's yelling. Apparently, only one attendee of several dozen was "shocked and disgusted" by the boorishness. He was not American.[30]

The next such IHS gathering was held at Windsor Castle, inside the walls of the royal palace used on weekends by Queen Elizabeth, but now with fewer than two dozen participants. They were "booster meetings" to bond new talent with "heroes." Charles and Liz Koch brought so many pieces of matching luggage, the organizer recalled, that an additional big car had to be hired to port it all. It was, he reminisced, like the "forming of a clan."[31]

It is hard to imagine such a clan upending the known world within a few decades, but chance won them a wider hearing. It came with the troubling economic events of the mid-1970s, which undercut the credibility of the prevailing approach to political economy. The worst and longest recession since the Great Depression, followed by a mystifying period of stagflation and compounded by new competition from abroad, enabled the wider right to draw more and more corporate leaders into action. They wanted not just to rein in regulation and taxation, but also to dethrone the dominant paradigm of Keynesian economics that was at the core of the midcentury social contract.[32]

Although deeply interested in this very project, Koch remained on the sidelines of the energetic corporate mobilization then under way. He simply did not trust the big blue-chip, publicly traded companies and established business associations that took the lead to stand on principle (which, in fact, they did not, always making exceptions for themselves), so Koch kept his contributions separate. He would not intermix his money with that of the ideologically impure, those who seemed likely to quit or cut a side deal before the long game was won. As they did.[33]

As important, because he had assured himself that his actions were solely motivated by principle, by allegiance to a set of ideas that would create a better society, he remained religious about the need to discipline CEOs as well as social movements and others who looked to government. "How discrediting it is for us to request [corporate] welfare for ourselves," Charles Koch chided his fellow businessmen in 1978, "while attacking it for the poor." No wonder the enemies of free enterprise called company attacks on big government hypocritical. "We must practice what we preach," he intoned, and cease seeking special privileges and subsidies.[34]

Given the interest of James Buchanan's team in what they called rent-seeking and in new legal rules that might prevent it, the man who jokingly referred to himself as an "adopted Austrian," and who privately speculated about the benefits to the Virginia school of his "assuming the role of the American 'Hayek,'" found himself drawing closer to the people representing Koch's political interests. And when Charles Koch set up his own eponymous foundation in 1974, Buchanan was invited to be the featured dinner speaker for "our first formal activity." Held in Charlottesville, where kindred economists and law school faculty were now working so well together at the University of Virginia, it was the first of a series of gatherings that were not merely for the like-minded to get acquainted. They featured intense deliberations on topics ranging from "The New Monetary Theory" to "The Austrian View of Social Cost."[35]

Koch's team knew of James Buchanan not least because the libertarian milieu was still so small. Earlier, they had welcomed the economist's argument against "appeasement" of campus protests, publishing a pamphlet-size version of *Academia in Anarchy* to reach a broader audience than the book had. Indeed, more than anything else, it was Buchanan's and Koch's shared commitment to school privatization at every level that started a collaboration that deepened over the next two decades.[36]

Being an insatiable reader and an exacting thinker, Koch was made to partner with a man like Buchanan. His questions at the early Charles Koch

Foundation seminars were as probing as any of those asked by the invited academics—indeed, with a sharper sense of the ultimate stakes, we can see in hindsight, because he was deadly serious about implementing the views of Austrian thinkers on matters from labor management to monetary policy. Before long, Koch was writing to Buchanan to share his excitement "about developments in the economics profession" and thank the scholar for his leadership "in bringing them about." The two were also drawing closer through joint work to build up the Institute for Humane Studies, which carried forward "the battle of ideas" on campuses by "building a critical mass of freedom-friendly professors."[37]

When William E. Simon, by 1978 president of the Olin Foundation, urged corporate leaders to "rush [funds] by the multimillions to the aid of liberty," Charles Koch needed little convincing—he was already writing checks.[38] And he was writing them not simply from a desire to broaden public debate. He was seeking the alchemy that might help him take what was then a quirky backwater of a movement and turn it into a rushing river powerful enough to smash through the dam of the twentieth-century state.

Which explains his interest in Murray Rothbard, one of the intellectuals Koch first subsidized. It was Rothbard who explained to him how small numbers could effect big changes. Rothbard suggested that Koch study Lenin.[39]

"I grew up in a Communist culture," Rothbard later said of the extended "family, friends, [and] neighbors" in the New York City milieu he rebelled against. Even as he despised their goals, he took from their heated discussions in the 1930s and 1940s, as well as his own wide reading in the original sources, a deep appreciation of the strategic and tactical genius of Vladimir Lenin, who led a revolution in a place where others said it simply could not be done. A champion of "uncompromising libertarianism," Rothbard, like Lenin, believed that government was "our enemy." He admired Lenin's daring leadership, but most of all he saw that some of his techniques could serve a wholly opposite purpose: namely, to establish a kind of capitalism purer and less restrained than the world had ever known.[40]

In 1976, over a weekend of discussion as Koch's guest in Vail, Colorado, Rothbard explained to his host how a Lenin-like libertarian strategy might work. The Russian revolutionary had once said of the ranks of the revolutionary party, "Better fewer, but better." To create a sound, disciplined movement, Rothbard explained, preparing a "cadre" must be the top priority. What his admiring biographer, a foot soldier himself, summed up as "the general flakiness and counterculturalism" of so many libertarians had had its day, Rothbard told Koch. The survivalist-like stocking up on beans and science fiction novels to last years of exile, with backpacks at the ready to rush for the hills if the statists came, the visions of colonizing remote islands or even of other planets: all that had to go. A new seriousness was needed. It was time for the revolutionary cause to orient itself to Middle America.[41]

In a protracted fight to win, it would be crucial to stay on top of "nourishing, maintaining, and extending the libertarian cadre itself," something Koch's bottomless bank accounts would enable.[42] It was not hard to persuade the midwestern multinational capitalist that the many weirdos were not bringing success any closer. Liking what he'd heard, Charles Koch shushed the older advisers he had on retainer and bet on the brash visitor, who seemed so sure of what was to be done.[43] Not long after that, in one of the publications whose creation Rothbard had recommended as organizing tools, Koch wrote that over his own fifteen years of active involvement, "our biggest problem has been the shortage of talent." To become "an effective force for social change," the CEO intoned, "we need a movement." And to create a sound, disciplined movement, preparing a "cadre" must be the top priority.[44]

The new urgency called for a think tank to be created to serve as a training and reinforcement institution for the cadre. To lead it, both men had their eyes on a steely fellow already in the ranks: Edward Crane III.[45] Crane had served as a precinct captain for Barry Goldwater in 1964, but he was disgusted by "how quickly Goldwater ran away from the issue of privatizing Social Security." Blaming Goldwater's retreat on his effort to win over the majority of voters (and recoiling, too, from the senator's military adventurism), Crane went on to join the Libertarian Party, which had been summoned into being in a Denver living room in December 1971. Its founders sought a world in which liberty was preserved by the total absence of government coercion in any form. That entailed the end of public education, Social Security, Medicare, the U.S. Postal Service, minimum wage laws, prohibitions against child labor, foreign aid, the Environmental Protection Agency, prosecution for drug use or voluntary prostitution—and, in time, the end of taxes and government regulations of any kind.[46] And those were just the marquee targets.

Crane was as insistent as Rothbard and Koch about the need for a libertarian revolution against the statist world system of the twentieth century. "The Establishment" had to be overthrown—its conservative wing along with its liberal wing. Both suffered "intellectual bankruptcy," the conservatives for their "militarism" and the liberals for their "false goals of equality." The future belonged to the only "truly radical vision": "repudiating state power" altogether.[47]

Once Crane agreed to lead the training institute, all that was lacking was a name, which Rothbard eventually supplied: it would be called the Cato Institute. The name was a wink to insiders: while seeming to gesture toward the *Cato's Letters* of the American Revolution, thus performing an appealing patriotism, it also alluded to Cato the Elder, the Roman leader famed for his declaration that "Carthage must be destroyed!" For this new Cato's mission was also one of demolition: it sought nothing less than the annihilation of statism in America.[48]

There was no mistaking libertarianism for conservatism at Cato's 1977 founding. Indeed, Rothbard announced in its first publication, that this label should be "despised." "In its contemporary American form," Rothbard explained, conservatism "embodied the death throes of an ineluctably moribund, fundamentalist, rural, small-town white Anglo-Saxon America." The future belonged not to it, but to the secular libertarian movement, "the party of revolution."[49]

Rothbard's "book-length memo" outlining the Cato Institute's goals and plan of action, titled *Toward a Strategy for Libertarian Social Change,* quoted so liberally from Lenin and so avidly scoured previous revolutions and authoritarian regimes for methods that it was deemed too "hot" for release beyond the inner circle. As the Bolshevik leader taught, the "cadre" was to play the vital role: its full-time devotion to the cause, as a militant minority of foot-soldier ideologues, would assure purity and continuity while building the ranks and expanding the cadre's influence on others.[50]

You cannot understand the influence of the stealth movement that is transforming America today without understanding this critical turning point. "We came to realize," Rothbard later reminisced, "that, as the Marxian groups had discovered in the past, a cadre with no organization and with no continuous program of 'internal education' and reinforcement is bound to defect and melt away in the course of working with far stronger allies." Training was crucial so that the cadre's members could "make strong and fruitful alliances" with partners who might at the time of the alliance be stronger than the cadre without fear of the cadre's going over to the temporary ally.[51]

The Republican Party's officialdom after 2008 could stand as Exhibit A of Koch's success with this model. The venerable major party's leaders did not turn the heads of the cadre, despite their apparently greater authority and power; instead, the disciplined cadre turned them.

The mission of the cadre was, quite literally, revolutionary, although a cause with so much money would not need violence. "The ruling class" to be overthrown consisted of the leaders of labor unions, those corporations and business associations that continued to seek special benefits through lobbying, and the intellectuals who supported government action. The task facing the libertarian cadre who would staff the Cato Institute and related efforts would be to drive home to the populace the parasitic nature of all three groups, exposing every practical instance of it to help larger numbers see the evil of statist corruption—and what must be done to vanquish it.[52]

With a permanent staff and a stable of rotating scholar visitors, Cato could generate nonstop propaganda against this ruling class. Buchanan played a crucial role in such propaganda, for Cato's arguments generally followed analyses provided by his team. Koch, meanwhile, provided new resources as the cadre brought in recruits with ideas for new ways to advance the cause. They would then be indoctrinated in the core ideas to assure their radical rigor, all of this held together with the gravy train opportunities Koch's money made available as they pushed their case into the media and public life. The libertarian vanguard, Rothbard taught, could "guide the peoples to the proper path."[53]

With enough gestures to the nation's founding fathers, even Leninist libertarianism could be made to look appealingly all-American, like a restoration rather than the revolution it was. But Cato would be unbending in its advocacy, whether for taking an axe to taxes, revoking government regulation, ending social insurance, or presenting unfettered personal liberty as the answer to all problems. In that early purity, Cato often shocked the nation's conservatives, as when it criticized American military intervention in other countries and called for legalizing drugs, prostitution, and other consensual sex. That unique stance, its first president said, made it "the think tank for yuppies"—those who liked social freedom with their economic liberty, and never caught on to where all this was headed.[54]

Cato had no need to compromise because it was funded by one of the richest men in the world. Indeed, compromise, Koch had made clear, was the kiss of death. And when their patron spoke, the grantees listened. "It could seem almost comic, this sudden injection of enormous wealth into a small movement," recalled one participant, "this bizarre gravitational shifting as Planet Koch adjusted everyone's orbits."[55] Apparently no one confronted the import of the incentive structure at the outset, for libertarians steadfastly refused to acknowledge wealth as a form of power, but the sheer amount of money Charles Koch was giving would affect all the players in time. "Employees of single-donor nonprofits," said a disenchanted one who left, "follow the moods and movements of their benefactor like flowers in the field, their faces turned toward the sun."[56]

In the same year he attended the founding seminar of what became the Cato Institute, James Buchanan published an article called "The Samaritan's Dilemma," a piece that has been used by the right ever since to show, in effect, that the ethics of Jesus as reported in the Gospel of Luke produced perverse results in the modern world. Buchanan summarized this piece of what he termed "prescriptive diagnosis" thus: "We may simply be too compassionate for our own well-being or for that of an orderly and productive free society." He then applied a game-theory thought experiment—never, of course, empirical research, which he spurned—to make the argument. His "hypothesis" was "that modern man has become incapable of making the choices that are required to prevent his exploitation by predators of his own species, whether the predation be conscious or unconscious." *Predators of his own species?* It was a perverse appropriation of the parable of the Good Samaritan, in which a kind resident of Samaria comes to the aid of a Jewish traveler who has been stripped, robbed, beaten, and left to die—a *victim* of predators, in other words—in the story Jesus used to show his followers that one should love his neighbor as himself, even when the suffering neighbor was a member of a despised out-group, as Jews were to Samaritans.[57]

In the view of the libertarian economist, Jesus was mistaken. Conscripting the Good Samaritan story, Buchanan made his case that "modern man [had] 'gone soft'": he lacked the "strategic courage" needed to restore the market to its proper ordering. By this logic, what seemed to be the ethical thing to do—help someone in need—was not, after all, the correct thing to do, because the assistance would encourage the recipient to "exploit" the giver rather than to solve his own problems. Buchanan used as an analogy the spanking of children by parents: it might hurt, but it taught "the fear of punishment that will inhibit future misbehavior."[58]

Similarly, "the potential parasite" needed curbing to prevent efforts to "deliberately exploit" society's "producers." More than any other piece, this article captured the stark morality of libertarianism, offering, as it were, the cause's prescription for how America's third century could reverse the "soft" errors of its second. The trick, though, was to figure out how to bind the foolish Samaritan, *qua* government, from giving out perverse incentives—how to shackle the Samaritan, so to speak. As Buchanan noted in conclusion, "welfare reform" was "only one of many applications, and by no means the most important."[59] It was true: his eyes were set on much bigger game.

While Cato advocated a wide-ranging libertarian policy agenda in the late 1970s, another Koch-supported think tank, the Reason Foundation, concentrated on making the case for selling off public property and outsourcing public services to private corporations. The effort built on the popularity of a countercultural libertarian magazine called *Reason* that was started in 1968 by an Ayn Rand devotee in a dorm room with a ditto machine.[60] It was then taken over by Robert W. Poole Jr., an MIT-trained engineer of a cohort after Koch's who learned of libertarianism in high school. In college, he joined Young Americans for Freedom and went door-to-door for Barry Goldwater in 1964 as he "devoured *Atlas Shrugged*" and converted to radical libertarianism. He moved to Santa Barbara, California, and took a job "with a local 'think tank,'" the phrase being new enough in 1972 to merit quotation marks. For years he published *Reason* out of his home as a hobby.[61]

But as stagflation set in at mid-decade, Poole grew more serious about influencing public policy. He published a practical how-to pamphlet in 1976 called *Cut Local Taxes—Without Reducing Essential Services*. It took dead aim at the growth of public sector employment as a cause of increasing taxes and spending, and called for contracting out to private companies to contain costs.[62] Ron Paul, a Libertarian Party member of Congress, recommended Poole's approach as wiser than the old "ideological purity" that simply called taxation "theft." To make the appeal nonpartisan, Poole also secured a blurb from U.S. senator William Proxmire, who called the piece "must reading" for public officials. The Wisconsin Democrat had just begun giving Golden Fleece Awards each month to embarrass government agencies for foolish spending.[63]

In the wake of the pamphlet's success, Poole began reading about the Fabian Society in Edwardian England, whose public-debate-changing members included H. G. Wells, George Bernard Shaw, and Virginia Woolf. Poole was taken with the Fabian strategy of effecting small changes that would in time lead to socialism, but he gave the idea a Buchanan-like spin to the right. "I figured that if you could gradually build up to socialism, you could probably undo it, dismantling the state step by step," he later told an interviewer. You could hack away at government, that is, "by privatizing one function after the other, selling each move as justified for its own sake rather than waiting until the majority of the population is convinced of the case for a libertarian utopia."[64] "Selling" was perhaps the key word.

Why wait for popular opinion to catch up when you could portray as "reform" what was really slow-motion demolition through privatization? On the tenth anniversary of *Reason*, in 1978, Poole convened a strategy session. Every man in the room looked to Charles Koch when talk turned to funding an infrastructure of "professional libertarians," for who else could? The Wichita CEO was willing to commit the resources needed, he said, but with one condition: "that libertarians must remain uncompromisingly radical." They had to forswear "the temptation" to "compromise" with those currently in positions of power. Any such conciliation, Koch warned, would "destroy the movement."[65]

With Koch's backing, Poole "started working full-time for the cause," enlisting "economic reasoning and evidence."[66] Poole recruited an advisory board of some two dozen libertarian scholars, including F. A. Hayek, and set to work to advance privatization. The advocacy was no-holds-barred, as Koch had demanded: a sample press release was headlined "Abolish—Don't Reform—Regulatory Agencies." The enterprise's biggest splash was a full-length 1980 book by Poole called *Cutting Back City Hall,* which recommended outsourcing to private corporations and imposing new user charges for access to public goods such as parks. The Reason Foundation was emerging as the nation's premier voice for privatization, not only of public education, through voucher plans like Virginia's, but also for every conceivable public service, from sanitation to toll roads.[67]

Meanwhile, as the Cato Institute and the Reason Foundation set to work, Buchanan was hired by yet another Koch-backed organization, the Liberty Fund, to run what became annual summer conferences for the recruitment and training of young talent (defined as under age thirty-five, later upped to forty) in the social sciences. In essence, he was being asked to identify and begin preparing the intellectual cadre that Koch now believed was so critical to the cause's success.[68]

Buchanan relished the role of gatekeeper. The evaluations he submitted for who had promise and who did not were highly detailed. One participant was "a highly articulate speaker, with basic instincts you and I share," he reported, although "a bit 'slick'" for "the country boys." Another, despite a "poor expository style" and annoying "soft-left" reflexes, was still "interesting" and worth watching. The rankings were blunt: the judge divided the prospects into "Very Strong, Medium, [and] Weak." At the best sessions, he could boast new "camaraderie" and "no misfits."[69] Like Koch, Buchanan was not squeamish about throwing flotsam overboard. Anyone unsound in doctrine or lacking in promise was unlikely to be invited back.

He tried to "insure that no bad apples get into the barrel, for such can spoil the whole thing." He required "explicit recommendation by those we trust for potential participants." And he rewarded himself and his recruits in high style. The man who still called himself a country boy and railed against liberal "elitists" did not stint on frills, personally preselecting wines such as a 1966 Château Lafite-Rothschild that today would retail between $300 and $1,000 per bottle.[70]

Even as Charles Koch was assembling scholars and underwriting think tanks on two coasts, he was also testing electoral politics. Neither of the two main parties was demolition-minded enough for his tastes. He seemed to hold the Republican Party in greater contempt, though, because of what he took to be its leaders' dishonesty. Their claim to stand for free markets was manifest fraud: the GOP was the party "of business accommodation and partnership with government," sneered Koch. "If this is our only hope then we are doomed."[71]

And so he backed the nascent Libertarian Party instead. Its numbers were tiny, and it was less a real party than a protest party, one being kept in the ring by a cluster of quirky characters. But it had chugged through the decade in a way that impressed Koch enough that he decided to invest in the 1978 Golden State gubernatorial race of Ed Clark, associate counsel for an oil company and "a long time dedicated libertarian."[72]

The race excited Koch, he said, "because California is the center of libertarian activity, with the potential for explosive growth." He contributed $5,000 and urged friends to do so, too. Ed Clark, Koch advised, was "ideal because he will not compromise our principles but, at the same time, projects a mature, responsible image," and he "comes across as attractive and articulate on TV," by now such a prime platform. Clark had also pledged to Koch that he would highlight "the need for and benefits of private education," so as to capitalize on the spreading "discontent with public schools."[73]

Koch knew the party had no hope of becoming "a political force." Still he explained, "I didn't see any [other] mechanism to get these ideas out in political discussion." Clark drew more than 5 percent of the state's vote, helped along, no doubt, by another measure on California ballots that year, Proposition 13, the first loud shout of revolt against rising taxes, which he vocally backed. Nationwide, Libertarian Party candidates, who got on the ballot in thirty states, attracted 1.2 million votes.[74] The excitement was palpable: was California's election an augury of a new age of liberty in America?

The faithful went all in to back a run by Ed Clark for president in 1980, against California's own Ronald Reagan and Jimmy Carter—at a much greater cost. Since they could do the math on how a party with fewer than five thousand members would fare in a presidential contest, the strategists sought a way to get around campaign finance laws. They found one: because candidates faced no limits on how much they could contribute to their own races, they could run David Koch for vice president on the ticket with Clark. In the end, Koch contributed $2 million to the $3.5 million campaign. The ticket drew more than nine hundred thousand votes, 1 percent of the overall turnout, much better than any libertarian electoral effort had ever achieved.[75]

But even that small success at the polls came at a troubling cost. Clark so compromised libertarian principle to win votes that he split the fledgling party. Murray Rothbard, as usual the most scathing guardian of orthodoxy, condemned the candidate's campaign promises as "treacle." His ceaseless carping so irritated Charles Koch, who was becoming more pragmatic about tactics if not about his endgame, that Rothbard found himself fired from Cato. He fumed at a libertarian institution being run "like a corporation, where orders are given, dissidents are fired, etc." Never having held a normal job in his lifetime of advocating unalloyed capitalism, he seemed gobsmacked by the experience of being treated as just another hired hand who could be let go at the whim of his boss. Rothbard's pleas went unheeded. And, after the Kochs withdrew their backing, the Libertarian Party all but crashed. How could a party grow with neither masses nor money?[76]

While Charles Koch and his younger brother were experimenting politically, James Buchanan wasted no time on a quixotic third party. Sequestering himself in the mountains of southwestern Virginia, he produced *The Limits of Liberty,* the book he would later describe as the single best statement of his intellectual vision. It was his magnum opus for the cause, the summation of his distinctive revolutionary vision for "America's third century."[77] More a work of political philosophy than of economics, it searched for a balance, as the subtitle expressed it, "between anarchy and Leviathan."

Because "both markets and governments fail," the challenge was how to sort out what each arena did best, to find some middle ground in theory between pure laissez-faire (what he called anarchy) and dreaded socialism. Wrestling with the reality that a modern world required some form of state power to apply rules and adjudicate claims, Buchanan sought to limn out a political order in which no state could impinge more than absolutely necessary upon individuals' "freedom from the coercion of others."[78]

He rued that the cause might already be doomed: the "failures in political and institutional structure" that had so eviscerated liberty might be irreversible by conventional means. He blamed the Great Depression for the rise of unacceptable intrusions on liberty; it had ended what he called the "fortuitous circumstances" that had produced a sixty-year reign of economic freedom, between the end of Reconstruction and the Great Depression. At no point did he address the possibility that if economic inequality had not been so extreme in that era and if the stock market had been regulated, the Depression might not have been so devastating. (Such considerations would lead in the dangerous direction of Keynes.) But Buchanan did observe that the developments of the Depression era might have made it virtually impossible to change direction through the electoral process.[79]

One has to wonder if the seeds of the final addition to his program were taking root in his mind at this moment—the search for unconventional means to achieve the desired reversal. Could a way be found to upend the normal order long enough to rewrite the governing rules of democracy, to separate it from the commitment to majority rule?

Indeed, that was exactly where he was going. But he would take his time getting there, and move from intellectual argument to emotional appeal to reach that destination. Initially, he seemed to be shooting for small changes. He told his readers that the challenge ahead was to develop strategies for "keeping collective action within limits"—not, as one might expect from his previous history, for eliminating collective action. He went on to explain that as an economist, he believed the expanding public sector to be unsustainable.[80] Yet he wanted to address the reader at the level of ethics, too, and so he turned to semi-emotional argument.

As a philosopher, he told his readers, he believed that what was required to support an expansive public sector was profoundly unjust: a system of progressive taxation that would ask more of the wealthy. Buchanan's early work was in public finance, and his first book addressed the growth of public debt. But his concern grew as the baby boom generation moved through its life cycle. With school populations growing and retired people organizing, and calls mounting for new government support and action of all kinds in the 1970s, public coffers became strained, with no relief in sight.

To be fair, Buchanan wasn't the only one worried about this problem. One 1973 book, James O'Connor's *The Fiscal Crisis of the State,* noted that the capitalist system, in order to survive, had to tack between the economic need for corporations to profit and reinvest to remain competitive in a changing market and the political need to rein in that accumulation so as to keep the system from losing legitimacy. Leftists like the author saw an emerging legitimation crisis, as some defined it. A case in point: By 1975, New York City had lost its equilibrium. Spending more than it took in through taxes, the city faced the prospect of default—but cutting services to the people set off revolt. Nationally, too, deficits were mounting. All Americans liked at least some government programs, yet few seemed eager to pay the higher taxes needed to keep the growing number of programs in the black.[81] The pattern was hard to ignore. In fact, some members of the liberal establishment founded the Trilateral Commission in 1973, in part from concern that democracies around the world were becoming too demanding and unruly.[82]

But for Buchanan, once again the issue was personal. "Why must the rich be made to suffer?" he asked pointedly.[83] If "simple majority voting" allowed the government to impose higher taxes on a dissenting individual in the minority—"the citizen who finds that he must, on fear of punishment, pay taxes for public goods in excess of the amounts that he might voluntarily contribute"—what distinguished that from "the thug who takes his wallet in Central Park?" Why should the well-off, he was asking, be forced to pay for *those people,* as the popular euphemism put it? "So long as unanimity is violated," was government action, in fact, truly "legitimate," even if the people's representatives were duly elected? Might "the confiscation through taxation of goods" from an unwilling person not be seen as "criminal"?[84]

The problem was not, Buchanan took pains to clarify, one of bad or misguided people in power, but of the normal functioning of institutions without built-in guardrails, whichever party was in charge. It was not even a matter of one ideology versus another. The George Wallace voter who complained about his tax rate refused to give up his own "special benefits" (things like government-funded highways and unemployment benefits when out of work, a more empirically minded reader could add). So, too, Buchanan pointed to "the suburbanite who is most vehement in his opposition to cross-city bussing of his children," yet never thinks about whether it is fair to "levy taxes, coercively, on all families to finance the schooling of children for some families."[85]

The West's current operating rules exacerbated the trouble, Buchanan argued, by failing to establish ironclad rules for "curbing the appetites of majority coalitions." *The Limits of Liberty* never provided actual examples. But like-minded readers could infer these coalitions from the daily news: unionized public school teachers or health care workers, say, joining with school parents or health care recipients to demand better services and higher taxes to fund them. Buchanan often noted that public employees could enlist the political process to their advantage; this really bothered him. In fact, he concluded, "there are relatively few effective limits on the fiscal exploitation of minorities through orderly democratic procedures in the United States."[86]

Yet even as the theorist projected exploitive motives onto others, it was Buchanan's own understanding of his fellow humans and their relations in society that was truly predatory. "Each person seeks mastery over a world of slaves," he intoned, clarifying that in his view every man desired maximum individual personal freedom of action for himself—and controls "on the behavior of others so as to force adherence with his own desires." As the political theorist S. M. Amadae has painstakingly and luminously shown, Buchanan was breaking with the most basic ethical principles of the classical liberalism he claimed to revere, of the market order as a quest for mutual advantage based on mutual respect. Instead, he was mapping a social contract based on "unremitting coercive bargaining" in which individuals treated one another as instruments toward their own ends, not fellow beings of intrinsic value. He was outlining a world in which the chronic domination of the wealthiest and most powerful over all others appeared the ultimate desideratum, a state of affairs to be enabled by his understanding of the ideal constitution.[87]

The remedy flowed from the diagnosis, ominously. "Democracy may become its own Leviathan," Buchanan warned darkly, "unless constitutional limits are imposed and enforced."[88] The hope he had held in his early career, expressed in *The Calculus of Consent,* that deliberations among citizens of good faith could produce rules for a political economy that all would find acceptable, now appeared naive.

There seemed no way to reconcile robust individual property rights with universal voting rights. For how could the cause ever persuade a majority to agree to rules that might radically disadvantage its members in a society fast growing more unequal? Buchanan implored his readers to face facts: "how can the rich man (or the libertarian philosopher) expect the poor man to accept any new constitutional order that severely restricts the scope for fiscal transfers among groups?" What poor man in his right mind would ever consent to rules that would keep him poor?[89]

But if not by willing consent, then how could the cause stop citizens from turning to government? Buchanan wanted to see, somehow, a "generalized rewriting of the social contract." America needed "a new structure of checks and balances," well beyond that provided for in its founding Constitution, itself already a very pro-property-rights rulebook, as he well knew. He advised "changes that are sufficiently dramatic to warrant the label 'revolutionary.'" The time when it seemed as if normal adjustments might be enough had passed. Buchanan closed with "a counsel of despair" that troubled him. "Despotism may be the only organizational alternative to the political structure that we observe."[90]

There was no sense glossing over it anymore: democracy was inimical to economic liberty.

One reviewer, a historian of economic thought, sounded an alarm about where Buchanan was heading. "His analysis strikes at the heart of self-government," said Warren J. Samuels. He granted that Buchanan was an original thinker and that the book contained some dazzling points. But in its overall case, *The Limits of Liberty* constituted an "extreme and anti-democratic" departure from the constitutional thought of James Madison and Alexander Hamilton, who had, after all, built in plenty of safeguards against possible tyranny by the majority. Buchanan's scheme, by contrast, would empower "a private governing elite" of corporate power freed from public accountability. "I shudder at the uses to which his ideas are capable of being put," Samuels concluded, with unknowing prescience.[91]

Some of Buchanan's and Koch's fellow Mont Pelerin Society members agreed with the book's foreboding analysis and reached conclusions that would have shocked their fellow citizens—if they had been shared widely. Henry Manne thought the book's message so important that he invited Buchanan to give seven distinguished lectures at his center, which awarded the book a law-and-economics prize.[92] The society's then president, George Stigler, the venerable University of Chicago economist, pushed the matter into discussion at the 1978 invitation-only Mont Pelerin meeting in Hong Kong. Facing the reality that he and his assembled allies were destined to remain "a permanent minority" whose ideas were "widely . . . rejected," Stigler pushed on to an "uncomfortable" question: "If in fact we seek what many do not wish, will we not be more successful if we take this into account and seek political institutions and policies that allow us to pursue our goals?" He did not equivocate, adding that this might mean "non-democratic" institutions and policies. One "possible route" Stigler suggested for achieving the desired future was "the restriction of the franchise to property owners, educated classes, employed persons, or some such group."[93]

Willy-nilly, faced with the inescapable reality that they could not win by persuasion, these globetrotting scholars were sounding more and more like the southern oligarchy that had authorized Buchanan's first program.

There is a photograph of Jim Buchanan from the late 1970s that he was said to like. It shows him at his mountain farm, Dry Run, in a fenced ring alongside two animals in a peculiar pose: a dog is riding a donkey, looking scared. The founder of the Virginia school of political economy walks alongside them, riding crop in hand, training the animals to perform this utterly unnatural act. Sometimes, as the old saying goes, a picture is worth a thousand words. Where persuasion failed, the lash might work.

CHAPTER 10

A CONSTITUTION WITH LOCKS AND BOLTS

On September 11, 1973, General Augusto Pinochet led a successful coup that overthrew the elected socialist government of President Salvador Allende in Chile. Ruling in the name of economic liberty, the Pinochet junta became one of the most notorious authoritarian regimes in recent history. With mass killings, widespread torture, and systematic intimidation, Pinochet's forces crushed the trade union movement, vanquished the rural farmers seeking land reform, stifled student activism, and imposed radical and unpopular changes in schooling, health care, social security, and more. As Orlando Letelier, the soon-to-be-assassinated Chilean ambassador to the United States, explained in *The Nation*, the economic program and the repression were inseparable: social and political "regression for the majorities and 'economic freedom' for small privileged groups" went together.[1] The military coup obliterated the citizen-led organizing that had made Chile a beacon to the rest of Latin America of what might be achieved by democratic, electoral means.[2]

To grasp the significance of the Chilean story for our own world today, it is important to remember that the reforms did not begin with Allende. His predecessor, the anti-Communist Christian Democrat Eduardo Frei (whose government lasted from 1964 to 1970), proudly oversaw what he called a "Revolution in Liberty," a kind of Chilean New Deal, supported by the U.S. presidents Kennedy and Johnson, that included support for labor rights, expansion of voting rights, and land redistribution in rural communities. Frei's opening up of Chilean democracy helped encourage the popular mobilization that led to the election of Allende. The military officers who led the coup concluded that, once in power, not only did they have to reverse the gains that had been made under elected governments, but they also wanted to find a way to ensure that Chileans never again embraced socialism, no matter how strong the popular cries for reform.[3] The solution they came up with was to rewrite the nation's constitution to forever insulate the interests of the propertied class they represented from the reach of a classic democratic majority.

As the Pinochet regime became a fulcrum of human rights activism in the 1970s and a cautionary tale thereafter, many critics indicted leading thinkers of the Mont Pelerin Society for abetting the despot. Milton Friedman was widely condemned for advice he provided on a visit to Santiago in 1975 about how to bring down the country's soaring inflation. That advice resulted in draconian policies that inflicted mass hardship, to be sure. But Friedman was a monetarist. Whether or not one approved of the painful "shock treatment" he proposed, what Friedman recommended was ultimately reversible policy. The society's aging founder, F. A. Hayek, also visited Pinochet and shared with the dictator his own distaste for "unlimited democracy." Such moral support from scholars helped the junta weather the international storm of condemnation. But while Hayek became an apologist for the regime, there is no evidence that he left a lasting mark on Chile, either.[4]

The same cannot be said of James Buchanan. His impact is still being felt today. For it was Buchanan who guided Pinochet's team in how to arrange things so that even when the country finally returned to representative institutions, its capitalist class would be all but permanently entrenched in power. The first stage was the imposition of radical structural transformation influenced by Buchanan's ideas; the second stage, to lock the transformation in place, was the kind of constitutional revolution Buchanan had come to advocate.[5] Whereas the U.S. Constitution famously enshrined "checks and balances" to prevent majorities from abusing their power over minorities, this one, a Chilean critic later complained, bound democracy with "locks and bolts."[6]

The first phase was a series of structural "reforms" devised by a young devotee of the Virginia school, Minister of Labor José Piñera. Piñera had been working toward his doctorate at Harvard University when the coup occurred; elated, he came home "to help found a new country, dedicated to liberty." His contribution was a series of deep alterations in governance, collectively dubbed "the seven modernizations." Their common threads were privatization, deregulation, and the state-induced fragmentation of group power.[7]

Under the new labor code Piñera promulgated in 1979, for example, industry-wide labor unions were banned. Instead, plant-level unions could compete, making one another weaker while their attention was thus diverted from the federal government ("depoliticizing" economic matters, in Buchanan terms). Individual wage earners were granted "freedom of choice" to make their own deals with employers. It would be more accurate to say that they were forced to act solely as individuals. "One simply cannot finish the job," Piñera later explained to would-be emulators, if workers maintain the capacity to exercise real collective power.[8]

Piñera designed another core prop of the new order: privatization of the social security system. This freed companies of the obligation to make any contributions to their employees' retirement and also greatly limited the government's role in safeguarding citizens' well-being. Ending the principle of social insurance, much as Barry Goldwater had advocated in 1964, the market-based system instead steered workers toward individual accounts with private investment firms. As one scholar notes, it "was essentially self-insurance." Fortunately for the plan, the regime had full control of television. At a time when three of every four households had televisions, Piñera made weekly appearances over six months to sell the new system, playing to fear of old-age insecurity owing to "this sinkhole of a bureaucracy," the nation's social security system. "Wouldn't you rather," he queried viewers, holding up "a handsome, simulated leather passbook," see your individual savings recorded every month in such a book "that you can open at night and say, 'As of today I have invested $50,000 toward my golden years?'" The junta overruled the suggestion that Chileans might decide which system they wanted in a referendum—after all, "who could say where such a precedent might lead?"—and imposed Piñera's plan by military decree. In short order, two private corporations—BHC Group and Cruzat-Larrain, both with strong ties to the regime—acquired two-thirds of the invested retirement funds, the equivalent, within ten years, of one-fifth of the nation's GDP. (José Piñera, for his part, went on to work for Cruzat and then promoted U.S. Social Security privatization for Charles Koch's Cato Institute.)[9]

Other "modernizations" included the privatization of health care, the opening of agriculture to world market forces, the transformation of the judiciary, new limits on the regulatory ability of the central government, and the signature of both the Chicago and Virginia schools of thought: K–12 school vouchers. In higher education, the regime applied the counsel of Buchanan's book on how to combat campus protest. As the nation's premier public universities were forced to become "self-financing," and for-profit corporations were freed to launch competitors with little government supervision, the humanities and liberal arts were edged out in favor of utilitarian fields that produced less questioning. Universities with politically troublesome students stood to lose their remaining funding.[10] Through these combined measures, education, health care, and social insurance, once provided by the state, ceased to be entitlements of citizens.

With the seven modernizations in place, Pinochet's appointees could now focus fully on drafting a constitution to entrench this new order behind what they hoped would be impassable moats. In preparation, the BHC Group's management translated James Buchanan's recent book, *The Limits of Liberty*, into Spanish.[11] So, too, the founders of a pro-regime think tank, the Centro de Estudios Públicos (CEP), translated several works of public choice, including a basic primer by Buchanan.[12]

Buchanan then visited for a week in May 1980, a pivotal moment, to provide in-person guidance. A few months earlier, the regime had begun a mass purge of teachers from the nation's public universities, firing those considered "politically unreliable," reported the *New York Times*.[13] Dozens of other, less prominent citizens were simply found guilty of breaching a prohibition on political activity and banished to faraway villages, with no chance of appeal.[14]

As a result of the assassination of Ambassador Letelier and an American associate in rush-hour traffic on Washington, D.C.'s Embassy Row, Chile faced U.S. sanctions for having carried out a terrorist act. This meant that the economists' visits had to come on the invitation of private actors—in

Buchanan's case, from the Adolfo Ibáñez Foundation's business school. Its dean, Carlos Francisco Cáceres, and Buchanan had had a long conversation at the 1979 Madrid meeting of the Mont Pelerin Society. Cáceres, one of the most vehemently antidemocratic members of the Council of State, a body created in 1976 to advise Pinochet, was eager to bring Buchanan's "opinions" into the regime's discussions of the new constitution. It worked. The Virginian's true host, in fact, was the Chilean minister of finance, Sergio de Castro, the regime's leading thinker and an economist indebted to Pinochet for enabling him and his colleagues to expunge a "half century of errors" when "public opinion was very much against [us]."[15]

Which is why de Castro and others saw a pressing need for a new constitution that would make public dissatisfaction irrelevant—or at least sharply curtail the public's ability to reverse the transformation he and his junta colleagues had imposed by force. When Cáceres set up a meeting for Buchanan with the BHC Group, he told him directly that "our main interest in your visit" was to explore how public choice economics might help inform the "new Constitution which will define our future republican life." They sought input on questions from "the way to elect the political authorities" to "the economic matters which should be included" in the document.[16]

Buchanan responded with detailed advice on how to bind democracy, delivered over the course of five formal lectures to top representatives of a governing elite that melded the military and the corporate world, to say nothing of counsel he conveyed in private, unrecorded conversations. He spoke plainly and in the imperative mode, suggesting the government "must" and "should" do this or that. He defined public choice as a "science" (even though he, of all people, knew that there was no empirical research to back its claims) that "should be adopted" for matters ranging from "the power of a constitution over fiscal policy" to "what the optimum number of lawmakers in a legislative body should be." He said of members of his school of thought, "We are formulating constitutional ways in which we can limit government intervention in the economy and make sure it keeps its hand out of the pockets of productive contributors."[17]

Buchanan understood what his hosts were asking for: a road map. He thus explained that the constitution needed "severe restrictions on the power of government." He instructed that "the first" such restriction "is that the government must not be free to spend without also, at the same time, collecting the necessary taxes to offset expenses"—Harry Byrd's sacred pay-as-you-go principle. "It must have a constitution that requires a balanced budget"—no more Keynesian deficits under any circumstances. Also, "the independence of the Central Bank should be enshrined in the constitution"; the government should be denied the authority to make "monetary policy because doing so would surely lead to inflation." A last restriction he urged was to require supermajorities for any change of substance. "It must be ensured that a system exists in which only a large majority," he said, "2/3 or 5/6 of the legislative body, can approve each new expense."[18] With this formula the scholar overshot the mark even with the junta's members, just as he had in his proposal for a fire sale of public schools to Virginia's legislature in 1959: none had the nerve to float a five-sixths requirement.

So intrinsic was the influence of economic libertarians that Chile's new constitution bore the same name as Hayek's classic *The Constitution of Liberty*.[19] "It promised a democracy," remarked the leading American historian of the Pinochet era, Steve Stern, "protected from too much democracy." The new constitution guaranteed the power of the armed forces over government in the near term, and over the long term curtailed the group influence of nonelite citizens. The document guaranteed the rule of General Pinochet and his aides until a 1988 plebiscite that might extend his term to 1997, when "a new generation," as Stern notes, "would have learned the role of the citizen in a restrictive democracy."[20]

The devil is in the details, goes the old adage, and it is true: the wicked genius of Buchanan's approach to binding popular self-government was that he did it with detailed rules that made most people's eyes glaze over. In the boring fine print, he understood, transformations can be achieved by increments that few will notice, because most people have no patience for minutiae. But the kind of people he was advising can hire others to make sure that the fine print gets them what they want. The net impact of the new constitution's intricate rules changes was to give the president unprecedented powers, hobble the congress, and enable unelected military officials to serve as a power brake on the elected members of the congress. A cunning new electoral system, not in use anywhere else in the world and clearly the fruit of Buchanan's counsel, would permanently overrepresent the right-wing minority party to ensure "a system frozen by elite interests."[21] To seal the elite control, the constitution forbade union leaders from belonging to political parties and from "intervening in activities alien to their specific goals"—defined solely as negotiating wages and hours in their particular workplaces. It also barred advocating "class conflict" or "attack[ing] the family." Anyone deemed "antifamily" or "Marxist" could be sent into exile, without access to an appeal process.[22]

Pinochet personally reviewed the penultimate document, making well over a hundred changes, then announced that citizens would have to vote a simple yes or no on whether to adopt the new constitution, in its entirety, in a plebiscite to be held within a month of its release. The balloting would take place during the prolonged "state of emergency" in which all political parties were outlawed, no voter rolls existed to prevent fraud (because the junta had had them burned), and no scrutiny or counting by foreign observers was to be allowed. When a group of moderate jurists and civic leaders composed a truly democratic alternative document, the regime prohibited its release. The mayors charged with running the plebiscite and counting the votes owed their jobs to the dictatorship.[23]

Election rules forbade electioneering by "no" activists. When some individuals flouted the ban by leafleting and inviting people to a speech by the former Christian Democratic president Eduardo Frei, nearly sixty found themselves arrested; some were tortured. "With my own eyes," reports a political scientist and later ambassador, "I saw people being dragged off a public bus and beaten for shouting, 'Vote "no" on the charter!'" The junta allowed only a single indoor gathering to oppose the document. More than ten thousand citizens filled every seat in the theater for the first legal rally in seven years, while as many as fifty thousand craned to hear from outside. Frei had opposed Allende yet also denounced the proposed constitution as "illegal" in its conception and "a fraud" in its content. A reporter from one of the few media outlets allowed to cover the rally was fired later that night for his refusal to read on the air a prepared report that smeared the speaker and lied about the event. Against such odds, "dissidents could not block the steamroller." Only three in ten Chileans voted no on the transparent paper used for ballots; 67 percent assented.[24]

If Jim Buchanan had qualms about helping to design a constitution for a dictatorship or about the process by which the final product was ratified, matters widely reported in the press, he did not commit them to print. Instead, he wrote Sergio de Castro with thanks for "the fine lunch you held in my honor" and shared how he "enjoyed the whole of my visit to Chile." Mrs. Buchanan, who accompanied him, appreciated "the nice gifts, the beautiful flowers, the Chilean jewelry, [and] the wine."[25]

What's perplexing is how a man whose life's mission was the promotion of what he and his fellow Mont Pelerin Society members called the free society reconciled himself, with such seeming ease, to what a military junta was doing to the people of Chile. The new Chile was free for some, and perhaps that was enough, as they were the same kind of people who counted in Virginia in the era when Buchanan pledged to his new employer that he would work to preserve liberty. It was also, always, a particular type of freedom the libertarians cared most about. One Chilean defined it well in rejoicing to fellow members of the society that the "individual freedom to consume, produce, save and invest has been restored."[26]

But perhaps above all, for Buchanan, the end justified the means: Chile emerged with a set of rules closer to his ideal than any in existence, built to repel future popular pressure for change. It was "a virtually unamendable charter," in that no constitutional amendment could be added without endorsement by supermajorities in two successive sessions of the National Congress, a body radically skewed by the overrepresentation of the wealthy, the military, and the less popular political parties associated with them.[27] Buchanan had long called for binding rules to protect economic liberty and constrain majority power, and Chile's 1980 Constitution of Liberty guaranteed these as never before.[28]

The political economist also gained from this episode the adulation of his allies in the Mont Pelerin Society. The society showcased his thought by inviting him to present the main paper at its annual meeting that September at the Hoover Institution, in Palo Alto.[29] Exhilarated by what had been achieved, the society's leaders chose for the site of its November 1981 regional meeting the coastal Chilean city of Viña del Mar, where military leaders had hatched the coup and President Allende's remains lay in an unmarked grave. Buchanan and two pro-junta Chilean colleagues together organized the program. The sessions they designed sounded like rationales—indeed, justifications—for the dictatorship's choices. Among the panels were "Social Security: A Road to Socialism?"; "Education: Government or Personal Responsibility?"; and finally Buchanan's own contribution, "Democracy: Limited or Unlimited?"[30] For the society's members, Chile was a beacon. The constitution, in the summary of one scholar, removed "major social questions—such as macroeconomic policy—from democratic influence."[31]

Interestingly, Buchanan never spoke of the Chilean consultation in his later publications. He did include his multiple speaking commitments there in his center's annual report to the Virginia Tech administration and to donors in 1980, likely as evidence of his increasing international stature.[32] But he never mentioned the Chilean case in print as an example of the application of his thought. For someone who devoted the remainder of his scholarly career to constitutional analysis and prescription, it was a telling omission. Perhaps his conscience troubled him or he feared condemnation. After all, even a conservative newspaper condemned Jesse Helms for how he "doggedly ignored the country's atrocious human rights record." After the North Carolina senator visited with Pinochet in 1986 and came home defending the junta from critics, the *Raleigh Times* mockingly urged a public collection to buy him better glasses and a hearing aid, because the senator was "deaf, blind, and dumb to official policies of corruption and torture."[33] Whatever the reason, Buchanan's enduring silence spoke loudly.

Looking back, though, one can only wonder what would have happened if someone had suggested to Buchanan that he apply his public choice analysis to the decision-making calculus of General Pinochet and his colleagues when they sought his counsel. Would he have been able to step back a minute and examine the military officers and their corporate allies as self-interested actors? As they set about devising binding rules to limit what other political agents could do, would he have seen that they might be using the rule-writing process to keep themselves in power? Buchanan would title one of his later books *Politics by Principle, Not Interest.*[34] But there is no evidence that he ever recognized what was happening in Chile as naked interest-driven action, bereft of any classical liberal principle. Or that he acknowledged that his own counsel had encouraged it.

If he had treated his school of thought as the neutral analytical framework he proclaimed it to be, Buchanan should also have anticipated how General Pinochet—having done away with independent media, freedom of speech, political parties, and so many regulations—could easily purloin public monies to enrich himself and his family, as he did. In the wake of the 9/11 attacks on the United States, Congress began investigating foreign money-laundering and discovered that the very year after the Constitution of Liberty was ratified, Pinochet had established, under false names and with the collaboration of leading banks, 125 separate accounts in seven countries to stash what became an illicit fortune of at least $15 million—this for a man who had sworn that he had only $120,000 in savings when he took power. Even Pinochet's Chilean loyalists were appalled. The disgraced general was indicted in his home country for tax evasion and tax fraud; theft was harder to prove. Yet two years later, after these exposures, James Buchanan ended his memoirs with the words "Literally, I have no regrets."[35]

Nor did Buchanan ever publicly criticize the final constitution as promulgated by the junta. On the contrary, he continued to promote constitutional revolution, thereafter more single-mindedly, and to seek out support from wealthy funders who might help effect it. From this we can only conclude that he was well aware of the Pandora's box he had helped open in Chile for the genuine, not merely metaphorical, corruption of politics, but he valued economic liberty so much more than political freedom that he simply did not care about the invitation to abuse inherent in giving nearly unchecked power to an alliance of capital and the armed forces.

His silence, it must be said, safeguarded his reputation. Buchanan had surely noticed that Milton Friedman never lived down having advised the junta on how to combat inflation: protesters disrupted the 1976 award ceremony in Stockholm at which he received the Nobel Prize and hounded his speaking engagements thereafter.[36] Whereas Friedman's name became permanently and embarrassingly paired with Pinochet's, Buchanan, the stealth visitor, largely escaped notice for the guidance he provided. But, then, unlike Friedman, Buchanan never craved the spotlight. He was content to work in the shadows.

Meanwhile, predictable trouble loomed for the political-economic model imposed on Chile. The year after the Mont Pelerin Society celebrated in the resort city of Viña del Mar, Chile's economy went into a tailspin, contracting by more than 14 percent. The devastation was so bad that, despite the dangers, a broad-based opposition emerged among workers, students, and homemakers that shook the regime as nothing else had to date. The causes of the crisis were not only internal; the world economy also stumbled that year. But the economic model urged by the society's thinkers and implemented by their local colleagues made it especially disastrous. Chile's now unregulated banks engaged in reckless lending that threatened to sink the entire economy when the reckoning arrived.[37]

The only thing that averted a total collapse was Pinochet's firing of the Mont Pelerin Society zealots, in particular Sergio de Castro, Buchanan's leading host, whose proposed solution to the free fall included cutting the minimum wage and other deflationary measures that seemed too risky even to a dictatorship. Pinochet replaced the ideologues with individuals who were willing to enlist government to right the ship. That November, the state took control of four banks and four finance companies to prevent "the collapse of the entire banking system." The outcome will sound familiar to Americans who lived through a virtual replay in 2008: "During the boom, Chile's economic gains had been privatized; now, in the crunch, the country's losses were socialized." Among those hardest hit were those who had invested their life savings in the new individual retirement accounts in corporate mutual funds that failed.[38]

Meanwhile, the opposition's attention turned to the new constitution. Buoyed by the public outcry, they used its provision for a 1988 plebiscite to achieve surprising success—only to discover how its "tricky" mechanisms, in the words of one Chilean legal scholar, would block "channels for the majority to express itself or for just laws to be passed." Voters were given only one choice: to vote yes or no on whether General Pinochet could rule for another eight years. Visiting to report on the worsening human rights situation, which now included aggressive attacks on the Catholic Church, the political scientist Alfred Stepan explained to American readers what was "really at stake." The call for a yes vote was "an effort to institutionalize a new type of authoritarian regime that has not been seen in a Western country like Chile since the 1930s."[39]

The whole process was so absurdly rigged in the dictatorship's favor that at first, virtually all its opponents urged a boycott. But this was the only chance people had to register rejection of Pinochet at the polls, so most reconsidered. Joining together to form the center-left Concertación de Partidos por la Democracia (Coalition of Parties for Democracy), they urged a no vote, and worked so intently to register voters that 92 percent of Chileans regained the right to vote. On October 5, lines formed early and stayed late, until the stunning result was announced: despite a manifestly stacked deck, voters refused General Pinochet the additional term he sought by a margin of 55 percent to 43 percent. Ten of the nation's twelve regions voted no, leaving the erstwhile potentate "humiliated." As the new constitution stipulated, Pinochet held on to power for another year, until, in July 1989, after tireless work from activists, Chileans elected a president and a congress for the first time in nearly twenty years.[40]

The new Concertación government inherited a society of surging inequality and economic insecurity—and a constitution that made it all but impossible to change course. The document baked in the fundamental rules of Pinochet's economic model, albeit as modified modestly by the pragmatists who took over after 1982. "The free market model as applied under Pinochet had an enormous social cost," explains one political scientist. "Whereas in 1970, only 23 percent of the population was classified as poor or indigent, by 1987 that proportion had reached 45 percent—almost half—of the population," while wealth had become more concentrated among the richest.[41]

The novel labor "flexibility" heralded by the regime's enthusiasts had taken away protections that working people won over generations of organizing and political action. "Precarious and low-income work [became] the staple for over 40 percent of the Chilean labor force," a marginality compounded by the fact that individuals were now forced to save the full cost of their retirement pensions, with no contribution by their employers, and pay for other goods that had previously come with citizenship. Not to mention those who had dutifully put away money only to have it lost in the downturn. One salesman who called himself part of the "white-collar poor" told journalists, "Today there are two Chiles": "one with credit cards and computers, and one that is just trying to survive."[42] Yet "Pinochet's sinister constitution," as the acclaimed refugee author Ariel Dorfman has called it, by design "mak[es] urgently needed reforms especially difficult to carry out."[43]

From the very beginning, then, the pro-democracy forces saw their task as twofold: mitigating the injustices the dictatorship had left and reducing the authoritarian aspects of the constitution. That first elected government proposed and won overwhelming approval of fifty-four amendments, among them one to eliminate the requirement that supermajorities of two successive sessions of the congress must approve any future constitutional amendments. Yet the skewed electoral system still remains in place, with its provision effectively granting the one-third minority of right-wing voters the same representation as the typical two-thirds majority attracted by center-left candidates.[44]

It is deeply troubling, then, that Chile is held up today as an exemplary "economic miracle" by the Cato Institute, the Heritage Foundation, and others on the U.S. right.

After the toppling of Saddam Hussein, *National Review* senior editor Jonah Goldberg went so far as to announce, "Iraq needs a Pinochet." Trumpeted the Heritage Foundation's country-by-country annual global ranking, "Chile's economic freedom score is 78.5, making its economy the 7th freest in the world in the 2015 Index," with no peer in South America. A global "example" of economic liberty, "Chile is second in the world in protecting property rights," surpassed only by Hong Kong. Charles Koch, too, cites Hong Kong and Singapore as model "free societies." Admitting that they lack the "social and political freedom" of other countries, he stresses what matters to him: "the greatest economic freedom" and "thus some of the greatest opportunities." For whom, he does not specify.[45]

Few Chileans take pride in that standing, however; most deplore its effects but are stuck with it regardless of their wishes. A nation that once stood out as a middle-class beacon in Latin America now has the worst economic inequality it has seen since the 1930s—and the worst of the thirty-four member states in the Organization for Economic Cooperation and Development (OECD). Yet even among those who have profited most from the concentration of wealth, a feeling has spread that the chasm between those favored under the new rules and those hurt is "immoral."[46]

The damage done during the Pinochet years by public choice economics goes beyond the legacy of economic inequality it left behind. The imposition of nationwide school "choice" had dire effects as well. Pupil performance diverged sharply, owing to "increased sorting" by income, which naturally took place with the voucher system. Meanwhile, college tuition costs now equal 40 percent of the average household's income, making a higher education in Chile the most expensive on the planet, relative to per capita income. A huge student movement began in 2011–12 that featured marches of up to 200,000 and had the support of 85 percent of Chileans. The young people demanded the end of "profiteering" in schooling and a free education system with quality and opportunity for all. What they were asking for "is that the state take a different role," said one leader, Camila Vallejo. "People are not tolerating the way a small number of economic groups benefit from the system."[47]

In 2015, prosecutors charged leaders of the Penta Group, among the top beneficiaries of pension privatization, with massive tax evasion, bribery, and illegal financing of right-wing politicians. The prosecution found that the company, with some $30 billion in assets, had become "a machine to defraud the state." That case lifted a huge rock, leading to inquiries that are ongoing and involve numerous companies tied to the dictatorship and the political parties to which they give. "The depth of corruption is enormous," observed a law professor at the University of Chile in 2016. "Public interest has been subordinated to private interest, and when there is no clear distinction between them, it opens the door to endless opportunities for corruption."[48]

What makes it so hard for Chile to address these pressing problems is precisely the constitution that still, even after multiple waves of reform, grossly favors wealthy, conservative interests at the expense of others.[49] In the wake of the student struggle, the center-left candidate Michelle Bachelet, running for president in late 2013, promised vast reforms in education, social security, health care, and taxation, as well as additional reform of the 1980 constitution. She won almost two-thirds of the vote, yet she still found it difficult to carry out the platform. "Democratic processes are held back by authoritarian trammels," President Bachelet complained in 2014. "We want a constitution without locks and bolts."[50]

But durable locks and bolts were exactly what James Buchanan had urged and what his Chilean hosts relied on to ensure that their will would still prevail after the dictator stepped down. And today the effectiveness of those locks and bolts is undermining hope among citizens that political participation can make a difference in their quality of life. Frustrated by how the junta's economic model remains so entrenched nearly three decades after Pinochet was voted out, many are disengaging from politics, particularly the young, who have never known any other system. Some legal scholars fear for the legitimacy of representative government in Chile as disgust spreads with a system that is so beholden to corporate power, so impermeable to deep change, and so inimical to majority interests.[51]

For his part, Buchanan came home from his consultation in Chile with a hunger to see radical change in his own country and a new sense of efficacy. He was finished with "the classic American syndromes, incrementalism and pragmatism." It was time for "changes in the whole structure of social and economic institutions."[52] The challenge, he soon learned, would be securing them in a functioning democracy.

CHAPTER 11

DEMOCRACY DEFEATS THE DOCTRINE

Fairfax County, Virginia, just across the Potomac River from Washington, D.C., was little more than a mass of dairy farms on land long ago ruined by tobacco plantations when a group of entrepreneurial developers set to work to make something more of it. To anchor their plan, they convinced the state to open a two-year college that was given the name George Mason. Housed in a shopping mall, it opened in 1957 to an enrollment of seventeen students.[1] But the developers knew it could be more. They envisioned it as a magnet for the kind of high-tech businesses they wanted to attract.[2] Twenty-five years later, George Mason, now a university, recruited its first marquee professor: James McGill Buchanan. Over time, especially with Buchanan's talent for fund-raising with businessmen, the institution found a purpose that it never announced publicly, but which enabled its ambitious administrators to realize their dreams of expansion in a tight-fisted state. The campus—or rather, members of its economics department and law school—created the research and design center of a right-wing political movement determined to undo the modern democratic state.

For all their talk of an overweening federal government intruding on states' rights, Virginia's legislature and the businessmen attempting to make a fortune from Fairfax County property were elated to be the beneficiaries of a new federally funded Capital Beltway that connected Fairfax with the nation's capital. Feeder highways would carry drivers to the Pentagon; the CIA headquarters at Langley, Virginia; and Washington National Airport in just minutes (at least before the traffic came). By the late

1960s, more and more of the employees hired by the federal government, many of them highly educated staff in its dreaded regulatory bureaucracy, brought their families to Fairfax to enjoy large and still relatively inexpensive houses, not to mention the state's low property taxes, the result of its continuing efforts to protect the wealth of its richest residents.

As Fairfax grew, so did George Mason. In 1978, the university hired a new and highly entrepreneurial president, George W. Johnson, who avidly cultivated "relationships with the CEOs" of the area and then helped them convince the federal government to outsource work to local corporate contractors. "Johnson knew," reports a history of Fairfax commissioned by the developers themselves to tell their story in their own way, "that if these [Beltway] 'bandits' could band together, they could help combat the anti-contractor bias that was rampant in many Washington circles." It became a source of great pride to the Fairfax movers and shakers that, as their palace history reports, "these corporate leaders were able to work in ways that would have been impossible without the cover of the university."[3]

Whether or not James Buchanan knew anything of this plan by the president and local CEOs to feast off the government table (an unambiguous example of intentional rent-seeking, in public choice terms) is unclear. Probably not, because while all this was going on, Buchanan was still at Virginia Tech. But by 1981, after a dozen years there, he was ready to leave and eager to do so quickly. Once again, as it was at UVA, his arrogance and obliviousness to the reasonable needs and concerns of others caused his scholarly enterprise to implode.

Convinced that he was meant, like an Ayn Rand hero, to be the dominant force in whatever he did, even going so far as to suggest at one point that his "embodiment of authority" was "genetically determined," he didn't have that many options when disagreement arose.[4] Certain that ultimate control should belong to him, Buchanan was shocked when others wanted to negotiate important matters that affected them, too. His department chair at Virginia Tech, Daniel Orr (himself no liberal), described Buchanan as "the sort of person who has to have his way with everything. He will not compromise."[5]

Orr's disagreements with Buchanan were not ideological but practical. Because Buchanan's program was based on his theories, not on research as academic economists defined the term, Orr was rightly concerned that its graduates would not be marketable for faculty positions because they lacked the mathematical skills and technical training that most economics departments valued. Orr respected Buchanan's work, yet argued on behalf of a balance of approaches when it came to hiring new faculty. But Buchanan refused to allow any dilution of his enterprise.[6]

Worse, when challenged, he became, by Orr's telling, not simply "unrelenting," but "explosive" and "unforgiving." (Even among his comrades, Buchanan's red-faced rages were the stuff of legend.) His insistence on having his way, other colleagues also reported, wrecked the give-and-take on which communal life depended. It set off an internal "war." Of course, as he had in Charlottesville, Buchanan saw his downfall in Blacksburg differently. Why should he share power? His team had built an international reputation, so "we felt our opinions should count for more."[7] To his own shock, his secret behind-the-scenes effort to have Orr fired failed. Once again, even administrators who appreciated Buchanan's contributions lost patience with his bullying.[8]

Denied what he believed was his due, and realizing his welcome had again worn out, he started to look elsewhere. In his own terms, he "exercised the academic exit option" so as to block "those who might have tried to modify the direction" of his program. Through relocation, he was able to protect his minority rights from the majority will in a manner he would soon suggest to corporations for the avoidance of taxation and regulation. Some might call it secession; Buchanan did.[9]

Humbled momentarily, Buchanan depicted himself as underappreciated to allies when he attended the annual meeting of the American Economic Association in December 1981. At a cocktail party, he let one of his mentees in the Liberty Fund conferences know that he and his team were interested in making a move. Karen Vaughn, of the George Mason University economics department, was stunned that Buchanan would even consider the underfunded and, as she later put it, "spectacularly undistinguished" school. Knowing what a difference a hire like this could make to her department and the university administration, Vaughn discussed it with an ally and then "jumped on the chance."[10] She assured Buchanan that with "no entrenched interest groups to oppose the public choice agenda . . . they could pretty much run the place."[11]

At GMU, Buchanan marveled at how everyone "from the lowest janitor to the [university] president moved heaven and earth" to lure his program. His starting nine-month salary of $103,000 was more than most university presidents were paid and more than the state's governor made. So as not to ruffle feathers, Johnson arranged for a large chunk of it to be paid by a local banker. He and Vaughn also arranged for the hire of six other Blacksburg economics professors and, of course, Buchanan's cherished assistant, Betty Tillman. They also secured the "separate quarters" Buchanan always insisted on for his centers. The new hire would never teach undergraduates, in a school where other faculty taught four courses each semester, and so would have more time to hobnob and fund-raise. Before the year was out, Buchanan had brought in $800,000 in corporate contributions for his center's research, graduate student training, and outreach programs (over $2 million in 2016 dollars).[12]

The phrase "corporate university" is often used by critical faculty and students today to evoke the sweeping and troubling changes taking place in higher education, most dramatically in public institutions, as university presidents who want to build up the reputations of their schools yet know they can no longer expect much help from parsimonious legislatures actively court corporate donors. And more and more, those corporate donors, particularly the ideologically driven ones, seek in exchange for their contributions a voice in the content of the academic programs they fund and even in the overall direction of the university. For their part, state legislatures are often pleased to have private donors keep an eye on the university to make sure it serves the interests of the corporations that supply many of the jobs and taxes that sustain the state. (Faculty members are typically less enamored of the expanding external influence.)[13]

An entrepreneurial president can also pole-vault a university up the national rankings that now obsess nearly all university governing boards. "Literally millions of dollars" came to George Mason in the 1980s owing to Buchanan's "presence," the university's then senior vice president later reported. He specifically noted that the incoming economist's "very strong support from corporations and foundations" enabled the school to start producing economics doctorates, among other things.[14]

Charles Koch was among those taking an interest in George Mason's economics program even before Buchanan's arrival. He paid expenses for participants in Karen Vaughn's Austrian Economics Forum, which studied the ideas of his idols Ludwig von Mises and F. A. Hayek, among others. Vaughn also helped arrange the deal that brought a newly minted assistant professor named Richard H. Fink to join the Austrian team GMU already had. "Richie," as he was known, was a *macher*—only the Yiddish word can capture his brash way of getting things done. He had reached out to Koch when still in graduate school in the nation's sole Austrian economics Ph.D. program, at New York University, and talked the CEO into funding a small training program, which he brought to GMU upon joining the faculty.[15]

Fink did his best to get the George Mason graduate students "hyped up," as one fondly put it—more militant, that is, in their advocacy. "We're gonna be like Malcolm X," Fink goaded them. Except where Malcolm X promoted Black Power and pride, the GMU alumni would be "Austrian and proud." He urged that they be "in your face with the Austrian economics." It was the style Koch had longed for when he warned that in order to excite smart young people, the cause must never compromise. Buchanan predicted to the patron, more aptly than he could have imagined, "Richie Fink will make his mark in the years ahead."[16]

But without Buchanan's intellectual leadership, professional stature, and pragmatic vision, success was "inconceivable," said Vaughn. "Our biggest problem has been the shortage of talent," Koch had earlier complained; the GMU team was building a pipeline to remedy that problem. Before long the program attracted more than two hundred graduate students, most of whom would go on to apply what they learned for hire outside academia. Indeed, summer writing workshops trained some students to write journal articles and others to carry out policy studies for think tanks. With Washington, D.C., so near, Buchanan solved the employment problem that had worried his former chair: his program's students might not land teaching jobs, but they could find eager buyers for their counsel in the corporate-funded libertarian milieu. "We had to make our way in policy circles instead" of universities, one of them explained.[17]

Buchanan gave a wink to the growing politicization of his program, pointing out to one of his longtime funders, the Scaife Family Charitable

Trusts, how its new location "will surely make us more accessible to where things happen and will allow us to provide solid academic input to the more applied emphases of our friends in the area." Among those friends in Washington that his team could now better assist in applying public choice ideas were the Cato Institute and the Heritage Foundation. Both hosted receptions to welcome Buchanan.[18] In the meantime, he coached his new colleagues in the economics department: "Of course, we cannot be revolutionaries in the overt sense." But by combating the "ruling orthodoxies," he counseled, they could contribute to the cause.[19]

Indeed, within a few years of Buchanan's arrival, a *Wall Street Journal* writer dubbed George Mason "the Pentagon of conservative academia."[20] The university had "built a stable of economists who have become an important resource for the Reagan administration," another reporter noted, helping with its plans to spur economic recovery by cutting taxes, regulations, and domestic programs, and its promise to return authority to the states.[21] Three doctoral students who were trained in Buchanan's first program—James C. Miller III, Paul Craig Roberts, and Robert D. Tollison—would be tapped to play important roles in the administration, while the new George Mason master's degree students would find jobs with think tanks and work their way up, particularly with the Koch-funded Cato Institute and the Scaife- and Coors-funded Heritage Foundation and the American Enterprise Institute.[22]

Yet despite their high hopes for the Reagan administration, ambitions for radical transformation ran aground far sooner than anyone expected. Except Buchanan. Never a backslapper, James Buchanan had sought to tamp down the euphoria that swept the Mont Pelerin Society after the elections of Ronald Reagan, and Margaret Thatcher in the United Kingdom. In his address at the Viña del Mar meeting in November 1981, Buchanan warned his comrades, "We should not be lulled to sleep by temporary electoral victories of politicians and parties that share our ideological commitments." Success at the polls, while heartening, must not "distract attention away from the more fundamental issue of imposing new rules for limiting government." Much as he admired Reagan—and he did, greatly—Buchanan understood that even such an ideologically driven president could succumb to the pressures of modern majoritarian democracy.[23] That proved a prophetic reading.

Still, most on the right believed that Ronald Reagan would deliver on his word to make tax and spending cuts large enough to undo the mode of government the Mont Pelerin Society had condemned since its founding in 1947. Reagan certainly wanted to, having told the American people in his inaugural address that "in this present crisis, government is not the solution to our problem; government *is* the problem." But the actual work of coming up with a proposal for which programs to cut and which tax cuts to authorize fell to the revolution's field general, budget director David A. Stockman.

Stockman had come to his work in the White House as an avid libertarian. Like Buchanan, he believed that "the politicians were wrecking American capitalism. They were turning democratic government into a lavish giveaway auction" and "saddling" those who created wealth with "punitive taxation and demoralizing and wasteful regulation."[24]

But something went terribly awry in the heady rush of the first year. The budget director, it turned out, had failed to make clear to the president and his political advisers—much less to the American people—that the colossal Kemp-Roth tax cut, as it came to be known, would necessitate tearing up the social contract on a scale never attempted in a democracy. To this day, it is unclear how such a consequential misunderstanding occurred. Was it that the electoral wing of the Republican right had for so long racially coded "special interests" and "government spending" that they genuinely failed to realize that slashing on this scale would hurt not only poor blacks but also the vast majority of white voters, among them many millions of Republican voters?[25] However it happened, it spelled the end of the libertarian dream of lasting change under Reagan.

"A true economic policy revolution" of the size Reagan and the right had requested, David Stockman explained in the wake of its rout, "meant risky and mortal political combat with all the mass constituencies" who looked to Washington for help. They would have to fight "Social Security recipients, veterans, farmers, educators, state and local officials, [and] the housing industry," with its mass market of middle-class buyers who relied on their mortgage tax deductions. The president could rail all he wanted about "welfare queens" and government "waste," but Social Security, veterans' benefits, and Medicare "accounted for over *half* the domestic budget"—and were dear to his followers. "Minimalist government" would "dislocate and traumatize" not a minority but the vast majority of Americans, in a "ruthless"—indeed, "bone-jarring"—way before delivering any of its promised benefits. And that was the summary not of a critic but of the policy's primary salesman.[26]

"By 1982," Stockman reported, "I knew the Reagan Revolution was impossible." It simply could not happen in "the world of democratic fact." Indeed, once the public became aware of just how drastic a plan the president's economic team intended—including immediate changes to Social Security (as Stockman put it, "a frontal assault on the very inner fortress of the American welfare state," a program "on which one seventh of the nation's populace depended for its well-being")—the jig was up. Even a South Carolina House Republican squawked, furious that his phones were "ringing off the hook" with calls from constituents "who think it's the end of the world." As powerful groups rallied to protect the popular program, the mobilization to "Save Our Security" worked. A *Washington Post* headline read, "Senate Unanimously Rebuffs President on Social Security." From then on, it was over, said Stockman. "The democracy had defeated the doctrine."[27]

What was not evident then but is now is that this moment became a turning point in the Republican Party, the prod for a historic, albeit unnoticed, three-way split. Stockman represented one wing, a lonely one. He learned from this experience that the libertarian dream had been a dangerous illusion. Sure, "special interest groups do wield great power, but their influence is deeply rooted in local popular support." Stockman concluded that trying to impose an ideologically driven "exacting blueprint" on the people of "a capitalist democracy" was a mistake of the highest order. As important was what he said next. "It shouldn't have been tried." The correct inference from the episode, Stockman concluded, was that voters must be told the truth. To have all the things they wanted, from clean air and water to retirement security (to say nothing of military power), Americans needed "a moderate social democracy," and to get this, they needed to pay higher taxes. It was that simple: higher taxes could solve the problem, without permanent deficits or economic disaster.[28]

The Republican right's political leadership, however, looked on Stockman as a turncoat. Its members followed the president and his advisers on a second path, one that forsook the fact-based universe. Abandoning any attempt to cut core entitlements significantly, but unwilling to give up on their promised huge tax cuts or on their desire for massive military spending, they went ahead with both, even though, as Stockman pointed out repeatedly, the outcome would be a fiscal train wreck. He was shocked: not one member of the president's political team had studied the budget or had the slightest idea how it worked. When presented with dire news that confounded their hopes, they simply refused to believe the bothersome information. The result? By the time President Reagan left office, the deficit was three times larger than the one he inherited from Jimmy Carter. At $2.7 trillion, it was the worst in U.S. history: the national debt by 1989 accounted for 53 percent of gross domestic product.[29] The path from refusal to face the outcome of their policy to denial of the human role in climate change would be a short one.

The libertarian milieu influenced by Virginia school thinking went a third way. In their view, Reagan hadn't "failed," in Buchanan's summary conclusion; he had "forfeited" his chance "to change the structure of politics." True, the economist said approvingly, Reagan had fed "widespread public skepticism about government's capacities" and about "the purity of the motives of political agents," a crucial contribution to the cause. But the president had proved to be too much of a pragmatist, too deferential to public opinion and those concerned about the health of his party, and so he allowed "the rent-seekers" to continue to practice "exploitation through the political process."[30]

These libertarians seemed to have determined that what was needed to achieve their ends was to stop being honest with the public. Instead of advocating for them frontally, they needed to engage in a kind of crab walk, even if it required advancing misleading claims in order to take terrain bit by bit, in a manner that cumulatively, yet quietly, could begin to radically alter the power relations of American society. The program on which they tested this new strategy was Social Security.[31]

Social Security, as both Buchanan and Stockman had observed, was the linchpin of the American welfare state.[32] The most popular New Deal reform, its very success had made it a far-right target ever since its creation, in 1935. Indeed, one of the radical right's indictments of Dwight Eisenhower and moderate Republicans after him was that they had accepted the legitimacy of Social Security. They did so, quite simply, not only because the overwhelming majority of American voters liked the system and were terrified of facing old age without it, but also because they, too, recognized it as a good program that worked.

Now, no doubt inspired by Chile's conversion to private pensions, Charles Koch's Cato Institute turned to Buchanan to teach its staff how to crab walk. Having relocated from San Francisco to Washington, D.C., in late 1981 to achieve greater influence, Cato made the privatization of Social Security its top priority. Buchanan labeled the existing system a "Ponzi scheme," a framing that, as one critic pointed out, implied that the program was "fundamentally fraudulent"—indeed, "totally and fundamentally wrong."[33]

It was fundamentally wrong in the view of libertarians, but with Buchanan's tutelage, the cause learned that opposing it candidly meant "political suicide," because the majority of voters wanted the system to continue as it was. "There is no widespread support for basic structural reform, among *any* membership group" in the American polity, the professor warned, the italics his own—"among the old or the young, the black, the brown, or the white, the female or the male, the rich or the poor, the Frost Belt or the Sunbelt."[34] The near-universal popularity of Social Security meant that any attempt to fight it on philosophical grounds was doomed.

Buchanan therefore devised and taught a more circuitous and sequential—indeed, devious and deceptive—approach, but one that served the new crab-walking cause well. "Those who seek to undermine the existing structure," he advised, must do two things. First, they must alter beneficiaries' view of Social Security's viability, because that would "make abandonment of the system look more attractive."[35] If you have ever seen a television ad showing older people with worried faces wondering if Social Security will be around when they need it, or heard a politician you think is opposed to the retirement program suddenly fretting about whether it will be there for you and others, listen more carefully the next time for a possible subliminal message. Is the speaker really in favor of preserving the system as we know it? Or is he or she trying to diminish the reputation of the system with the public, so that when the right time comes to make changes to it, even small ones that in fact reduce benefits or change the rules for beneficiaries, those affected will be less likely to feel that something good is being taken away from them?

While step one would soften public support for the system by making it seem unreliable, step two would apply a classic strategy of divide and conquer. Recipients could be split apart in this way.

The first group he defined as those already receiving Social Security benefits and (although Buchanan did not include them, his ideological heirs would) those nearing the age when they could begin to collect. These current recipients and those close to retirement (some said within ten years; more recently politicians on the right have suggested five years) should be reassured that *their* benefits would not be cut. This tactic Buchanan referred to as "paying off" existing claims. The reasoning behind it is vintage public choice analysis: as the citizens most attentive to any change in the system, they were the ones who would fight the hardest to preserve it. Getting them out of the struggle to preserve the system would greatly enfeeble the remaining coalition (to say nothing of the resentment their departure would cause among those who found they were being denied something others had secured for themselves).[36]

The second group, Buchanan coached, consisted of high earners. The plan here would be to suggest that they be taxed at higher rates than others to get their benefits, thus sullying the image of Social Security as an insurance program in the minds of the wealthy by making it look more like now-unpopular means-tested income transfer programs popularly understood as "welfare." Progressives would likely fall for a proposal to make the wealthiest pay more, not realizing the damage that could do to Social Security's support among group two. And if the message was repeated enough, such that the wealthy began to believe that others are not paying their fair share, they in turn would also become less opposed to altering the program.[37]

The third group would consist of younger workers. They needed to be constantly reminded that their payroll deductions were providing "a tremendous welfare subsidy" to the aged.[38]

Finally, those who would just miss the cutoff for the old system should be targeted for short-term changes. As Buchanan put it, "those who seek to undermine the support of the system (over the longer term) would do well to propose increases in the retirement age and increases in payroll taxes," so as to irritate recipients at all income levels, but particularly those who are just on the wrong side of the cutoff and now would have to pay more and work longer.[39]

This "patchwork pattern of 'reforms'" (the quotation marks around "reforms" were added by Buchanan, to make sure the message was clear that reform was not really the endgame) could tear asunder groups that hitherto had been united in their support of Social Security. Better still, Buchanan noted, the member groups of the once unified coalition that protected it might be induced by such changes to fight one another. When that happened, the broad phalanx that had upheld the system for a half-century might finally fracture.[40]

Yet Buchanan's projections left unanswered how to identify those who would benefit from the end of Social Security and turn them into active allies of the cause. To answer that question, two staff members at the Heritage Foundation wrote a follow-up plan. It was titled, notably, "Achieving a 'Leninist' Strategy." As the Russian revolutionary had taught, the coauthors explained, a radical cause must succeed in both "isolating and weakening its opponents" and "creat[ing] a focused political coalition" to work for change.[41] In other words, the revolutionaries must find the people who would gain from the end of Social Security and draw them into the battle alongside the cadre.

In the case of Social Security, the answer was clear: the financial sector. The right was not against people putting away for their retirements. To the contrary, they wanted people to save, early and actively, for their own retirements as part of their philosophy of personal responsibility. They just wanted those savings taken out of the hands of the federal government and put into the hands of capitalists, just as was done in Chile. And to end employer contributions as Chile had.

Once again, an incremental strategy was proposed. First push for legislation to make private retirement saving easier and more remunerative to the industry; then pull into the fight the financial corporations that would profit from the replacement of social insurance with private savings accounts. Individual retirement accounts (IRAs), the report argued, were "a powerful vehicle for introducing a private Social Security system," not least because the tax deductions granted for them had become popular. By thus "strengthen[ing] the coalition for privatizing Social Security," backers of change would be better positioned to take advantage of any crisis in the system.[42]

The Cato team translated Buchanan's ideas into a battle plan. The top priority was to assure current Social Security recipients that they would not lose anything; as "a very powerful and vocal interest group," they required "neutralizing."[43] Phase two would be "guerrilla warfare," albeit of the legislative kind, to break up the coalition that sustained Social Security by "buying out, or winning over" its various elements. Those who could not be bought out or won over should be weakened and defeated. (For example, AFL-CIO unions had helped organize the Save Our Security fight against the Stockman cuts; breaking the spine of the labor movement would hobble any future defense.)[44] Phase three would cultivate new partners in the private sector who would benefit from all that money being shifted to savings accounts and investment.[45]

But the overall message shared among insiders was always this: "If the political dynamics are not altered," no "radical reform of Social Security is possible."[46]

For the libertarian right, Social Security privatization meant a savvy triple win, in which ideological triumph over the most successful and popular federal program was the least of the gains. First, it would break down citizens' lived connection to government, their habit of believing it offered them something of value in navigating their lives. Second, it would weaken the appeal of collective organization by inducing fracture among groups that had looked to government for solutions to their common problems. But third and just as important, by putting a vast pool of money into the hands of capitalists, enriching them, it would both make them eager to lobby for further change and willing to shell out dollars to the advocacy groups leading the charge for change. The stronger these already well-heeled right-wing advocacy groups became, the more powerful partners shared their interests, the quicker they would be able to alter power relations in America in a manner that advanced the libertarian revolution. Charles Koch later used an apt metaphor that captures this process, too. "I often think of what we do," Koch says of his firm, as "stonemasonry. Once a stone has been carefully selected and set, it shapes a new space in which the mason can set yet another well-chosen stone. Each stone is different, but they all fit together to create a framework that is mutually reinforcing."[47]

His dreamed-of revolution no longer seemed so pie in the sky as it had when he set to work. By the second half of the 1980s, the political scientist Jeffrey Henig has noted, privatization "moved from an intellectual fringe to become a centerpiece in contemporary public policy debates." The Virginia school of political economy in particular helped effect "the intellectual de-legitimation of the welfare state," which prepared the way for privatization and, with it, in the words of one enthusiast, "the goal of fundamentally and irreversibly changing" the nature of politics.[48]

Many liberals then and since have tended to miss this strategic use of privatization to enchain democracy, at worst seeing the proposals as coming simply from dogma that preferred the private sector to the public.[49] Those driving the train knew otherwise. Privatization was a key element of the crab walk to the final, albeit gradual, revolution—the ends-justify-the-means approach that allowed for using disingenuous claims to take terrain that would make the ultimate project possible.

The disappointments of Reagan's presidency notwithstanding, the libertarian cause emerged much stronger at the era's end than it had been at the outset. Its cadre had learned invaluable lessons that some veterans would go on to apply in the years to come. Chief among them was Reagan's closest and most trusted adviser, Edwin Meese III, who to this day plays a pivotal role in the Heritage Foundation, above all, but also in a string of less prominent organizations funded by the Koch network and other wealthy donors. Advising influential political players such as Meese would be strategists such as Stuart Butler, a British-born economist who applied Buchanan's thinking in fine-tuning the Leninist strategy to permanently alter the political dynamics of budget growth. Butler became so deft at turning Buchanan's ideas into measures that could be pushed by allies in Congress that the Heritage Foundation promoted him to director of its Center for Policy Innovation.[50]

Because they became so interconnected by the late 1980s, it is nearly impossible to identify a sharp boundary between the insider cadre of strategists and the right-wing Republican officials such as Ed Meese and Congressman Jack Kemp and lower-level staff to whom they brought their proposals.[51] More research than is feasible for this book will be needed to determine who among the latter knew the actual objectives of the plans at any given point. But the cadre's numbers were growing, as evidenced by the expansion of the Heritage Foundation and the Cato Institute and lesser operations, and so was their influence, as evidenced by media attention to the products of these institutions and the representation of their members on bodies such as the President's Commission on Privatization.

The move to George Mason had been a godsend. It was easy to cross the Potomac to speak with political leaders and their staff members or to bring them into Northern Virginia to attend programs. With supportive donors, Buchanan's center made use of its new site to attract and train many more foot soldiers for the cause. Among the most lastingly important of the many trainees was Stephen Moore, an early M.A. alumnus hired by the Heritage Foundation's program on budgetary affairs, where he worked throughout the eighties, in the first of many such movement positions. In 1987, Moore was named research director of President Reagan's Commission on Privatization. In time he would move on to the *Wall Street Journal* editorial board, where he gained a platform from which to promote the cause to its most important audience: power brokers and potential donors who could benefit from its success.[52]

Moore was but one highly visible product of the pipeline being constructed at George Mason. The most promising would be hired upon completion of their training in Koch-funded operations. As they began to hear their own ideas echoed in the statements of politicians, agency political appointees, and such respected publications as the *Wall Street Journal*, confidence grew among the cadre that the very terrain of public life could be altered without their ever having to argue openly for their real goals.

While others focused on advancing the new stealth strategy, Buchanan never lost sight of the fact that such rearguard assaults on the welfare state would take the movement only so far. What was needed was a way to amend the Constitution so that public officials would be legally constrained from offering new social programs to the public or engaging in regulation on their behalf even when vast constituencies were demanding them. Again and again, at every opportunity he had, he told his allies that no "mere changing of the political guard will suffice," that "the problems of our times require attention to the *rules* rather than the *rulers*." And that meant that real change would come "only by Constitutional law." The project must aim toward the practical "removal of the sacrosanct status assigned to majority rule."[53]

In 1985, the ever enterprising university president George W. Johnson, no doubt having heard and understood Buchanan's oft-repeated message, acquired a tiny, floundering law school housed in what had been a department store, and invited Jim Buchanan and Gordon Tullock to advise him on how to use the purchase to "make a splash." The public choice team told Johnson that Henry G. Manne, Buchanan's old friend and a Koch grantee whose career at Emory had just capsized owing to conduct similar to Buchanan's at Virginia Tech, was a "hot property" to serve as dean of the law school. "They had a hidden agenda; they were going to find conservatives for him," Manne recounted.[54]

Johnson was happy to go along, "because he had heavy financial support from Republican interests in Northern Virginia" and he needed to please the right-leaning General Assembly to keep George Mason growing. The "extremely conservative" economics department "creates comfortable relationships," noted the *Washington Post,* "with the legislature and the businesses to which universities look for support." Manne accepted the position on the condition that he would be granted a free hand to operate the school his way. "Act fast," the president warned in regard to how he should deal with the existing faculty who came along with the school, "because by next April they'll be organized." Within two weeks Manne had fired every untenured professor and proposed buyouts to those he could not summarily send packing. "There weren't enough of them left" to resist once they recovered from the shock, he gloated. Like Buchanan,

Manne rejected the idea of open searches for the best talent, in favor of hiring kindred thinkers, all white men who felt "underappreciated" at other schools.[55] "At George Mason," he could soon advertise to prospective right-wing donors, "the entire curriculum is permeated with a distinctive intellectual flavor, emphasized and developed by almost every professor."[56]

For example, Manne's law school would stake out a position on the side of corporations against "consumerism and environmentalism," two causes that had grown in popularity and influence since the 1970s. His faculty would advocate for the superiority of "unregulated corporate capitalism" and assert, as Manne himself argued in print, that companies needed liberation from "the distortions introduced by government intervention."[57] That included full freedom for Wall Street financial firms from government regulation.

Serendipity brought another gift to this quiet base-building project in the Reagan era: in October 1986, James Buchanan was awarded the Nobel Prize in Economic Sciences for his "contributions to the theory of political decision-making and public economics." The Swedish Academy called him "the leading researcher in the field of what has come to be known as 'public choice theory.'" Back when he left Charlottesville in fury and disgrace, the moment would have been unimaginable. His persistence had paid off handsomely.[58]

The prize was "a vindication of the outsider," Buchanan would write, someone "far outside the mainstream"—the first southerner to have won in economic science, and also the first to have "worked almost exclusively at southern universities." No other Nobel in economics, he pronounced, sounding almost presidential, "gave hope and encouragement to more people." He recited his story with glee. "Here was Jim Buchanan, a country boy from Middle Tennessee, educated in rural public schools and a local public teachers college, who is not associated with an establishment university, who has never shared the academically fashionable soft left ideology, who has worked in totally unorthodox subject matter with very old-fashioned tools of analysis, chosen by a distinguished and respected Swedish committee."[59]

The Stockholm judges recognized Buchanan for his foundational public choice work, mentioning particularly *The Calculus of Consent* (and, by neglect of his coauthor, Gordon Tullock, permanently complicating that relationship) and two of his books on public finance, as well as his "visionary approach" in more recent years to constitutional "systems of rules." Traditional economic theory illuminated the decisions of producers and consumers in marketplace settings, the Nobel citation noted, but made no effort to explain the behavior of political actors. Buchanan's attention to political actors' quests for gains through exchange (of votes, benefits, or coalition partners rather than profits, per se) directed new attention to "'the rules of the game,' i.e., the constitution in a broad sense." These rules, far more than actors' stated inclinations, "determined" the results of political processes, for different types of constitutions could be predicted to produce different results. What public choice revealed, in the end, was the fallacy of assuming that market failure could be remedied through the political process, for there, too, people "behave[d] selfishly."[60]

"This type of analysis has become universal in recent years," the judges observed, with more aspiration than accuracy. (Indeed, the all-important judge Assar Lindbeck, a professor at Stockholm University, was himself a devotee of Buchanan's diagnosis of what Lindbeck had called "Vote Purchasing Democracy" a few years earlier. Under his leadership, reports a study of the economic prize's history, the committee "veered to the right in its awards.") Its members also commended Buchanan's related philosophical case for "the principle of unanimity" in constitutional rules choice and reform to make it so that "the political process" ceases to be "a means for redistributing resources." Buchanan's "foremost achievement," said the judges, "is that he has consistently and tenaciously emphasized the significance of fundamental rules."[61]

In a final, fitting coincidence, the day he received the Nobel Prize, the federal government temporarily shut down, "having spent all its money," in the gleeful words of one Virginia editor.[62]

Back home in the United States, Buchanan's ideas were producing "a quiet revolution in politico-economic thinking," observed the *New York Times*—"quiet" because their "public recognition quotient is near zero."[63] Still, signs of that unobtrusive intellectual revolution abounded for those who knew how to read them. As the think tanks with which Buchanan worked were attracting more media attention, some converts in the

Reagan administration were setting out to change the incentives of public life over the long term.

The cause would be helped along, too, by the fact that popular trust in government was dropping precipitously. The fall was due above all to the conduct of elected officials, from Lyndon Johnson's lying about the war in Vietnam to Richard Nixon's Watergate crimes. Buchanan believed his school's work had contributed, too.[64] It had long urged seeing political actors as self-aggrandizing individuals rather than the civic-minded altruists they portrayed themselves as. "What we did was take the bar-room approach to politics, and bring it out in the open," as Tullock later put it with his usual bluntness, by presuming that politicians were "crooks," voters were "selfish," and "bureaucrats" were "incompetent." With these portrayals, the libertarian mavericks had aimed to show that government action would cause worse trouble than the problems it was called on to cure.[65]

Buchanan's Nobel advanced the cause as nothing else had to that point, invigorating his allies and quickening their ambitions. Since founding the Thomas Jefferson Center in 1956, Buchanan had worked with nearly every libertarian think tank, publication, and training endeavor, among them the Cato Institute, the Independent Institute, the Center for Libertarian Studies, and the Earhart Foundation—as well as their counterparts abroad, including the Institute of Economic Affairs and the Adam Smith Institute in England, the Fraser Institute in Canada, and the Centro de Estudios Públicos in Chile. For all the money flowing in, the libertarian "movement" was small enough that those there from the beginning—mainly academics and idea-oriented businessmen—were well acquainted. "I think I know personally each and every member of the board that is listed in your letter," Buchanan thus told the Center for the Defense of Free Enterprise in 1980. He spoke at conferences, served on advisory boards, and helped select fellows for career investment from libertarian funders.[66] Two leading libertarian think tanks organized large national black-tie dinners to honor him. "All my friends," Buchanan joked, seemed to be tripping over themselves in competition to host such events.[67]

Was it the high energy he saw coming out of Buchanan's team that led Charles Koch to move the institution nearest to his heart, the Institute for

Humane Studies, from California to George Mason at mid-decade? Did his earlier decision to give up on the Libertarian Party as a hopeless cause make him more receptive to other routes forward? We don't know.

We do know that the university administration invited the move and promised the institute's staff carte blanche. And that the institute's president, Leonard P. Liggio, a loyal member of the cadre himself, was thrilled to be relocating to a community with "nearly twenty faculty members closely associated with our work," Buchanan the towering eminence among them. "The imprimatur of George Mason University," he exulted, "alone will aid our program." And, he happily reported to Buchanan, a "crucial point" in the negotiations was that "we will retain *complete program and financial autonomy,*" while "our post doctoral programs will have full and equal standing" with other GMU programs. He foresaw "crop after crop" of advocates.[68]

Charles Koch, Liggio's boss, became a more regular campus visitor after the IHS moved to George Mason. And more and more he looked to Buchanan and his team to teach and inspire the participants in the institute's annual summer training programs for "intellectuals and scholars." Within a decade, a listing of IHS alumni with faculty positions ran to ten pages; its growing staff would offer generous grants to graduate students to bring them into the fold.[69]

The wider circles of the right were eager to get closer to Buchanan as well. *National Review* marveled at the "sea change" Buchanan's work had produced in economists' thinking about government, making reliance on it "seem not nearly so credible as in the Fifties or Sixties." The Virginia school's was "a more fundamental critique than the usual free-market economist's," it informed novice readers. "By casting doubt on whether [government] can" do what citizens look to it for, "Buchanan challenges the idea that it ought to try."[70] President Reagan commended the Virginia school's founder on his "wide influence inside and outside of government" on behalf of "economic freedom."[71]

So it was not surprising that before long, the head of the Institute for Humane Studies was writing to invite Buchanan to speak on "Constitutional Economics" for the national conference of a recently launched organization that over the next few decades would do more than any other to transform the nation's judiciary and law schools. Liggio reported that "IHS has been working with the Federalist Society for several years"—that is, since roughly its creation with inspiration from Ed Meese.[72]

No wonder some insiders began to speak of the "Kochtopus": there were so many arms that when they all got to waving at once, it was hard to notice the human body behind them, the man whose checks kept everything moving. For his part, Charles Koch came to see, perhaps in the light of all the Nobel attention and talk of a new economic constitution for America, that Buchanan possessed the key he had been searching for over so many years. Public choice thought could guide the strategy he needed to get what he wanted. It was time to go from theory to practice in a way that even Koch-supported operatives had never been asked to do before.

CHAPTER 12

THE KIND OF FORCE THAT PROPELLED COLUMBUS

By the mid-1990s, a colleague reported, Charles Koch had grown increasingly frustrated with the lack of progress being made in furtherance of the cause.[1] Among trusted allies, he revealed his weariness with the sometimes cultlike libertarian movement, "ossified by purity tests" and plagued as it was by "personality cults."[2] Nor was he all that impressed with the elected officials to whom he was more and more looking for help. The cause's most recent near miss—the "Contract with America," with its marquee pledge to amend the U.S. Constitution to require a balanced budget—might have caused someone with a less steely determination to give up. But Koch just kept on looking, firm in the belief that somewhere out there was the set of ideas that could break through the impasse.[3] That search would lead him back to James Buchanan's front door, which the scholar opened wide, not knowing that after doing so he would find himself exiting out of the back.

The Contract with America was not a public choice document, per se, although the man most responsible for its creation, Richard "Dick" Armey, could not have been a more loyal, dedicated, or hardworking convert to the cause. A believer in public choice theory, he had earlier been chair of the economics department at North Texas State (now the University of North Texas). "The market's rational, the government's dumb" was "Armey's Axiom No. 1," which he repeated constantly, as if that settled the matter. When the university grew too "liberal and politically correct" for his comfort, a right-wing oilman on the board of regents persuaded him to run for Congress on the Republican ticket in 1984. Armey brought a zealot's determination to the fight for "drastic reforms," including abolishing the minimum wage and ending Social Security. Once elected to the House of Representatives, he turned to the Cato Institute for help in staffing his congressional office. His first decade had gone well.[4]

With his trademark cowboy boots and Texas swagger, and a readiness to roll up his sleeves when needed to do the hard work of shepherding stray Republicans back into line, he quickly became something of a hero among his fellow GOP congressmen. When they learned that Armey was the true intellectual and strategic force behind one of the most daring forays in modern U.S. politics, every one of the 367 Republican candidates for the House and nearly all the incumbents got on board. On a late September afternoon, nearly two hundred staged a signing of the contract before news cameras at the Capitol, one by one publicly affirming their commitment to the agenda.[5]

The signing occurred six weeks before the 1994 elections, midway through President Bill Clinton's first term in office. The signers promised that if the American people voted Republican, giving them the majority of seats, their new majority would bring up every item of the contract for a vote within the first one hundred days of the 104th Congress. They would radically "transform the way Congress works." The candidates pledged, above all, to back ten legislative bills that together would answer the American people's deep-seated desire for change.[6]

Six weeks later, on Election Night, Republicans swept both houses of Congress in what one political historian called "the most impressive off-year comeback in modern times." Talk filled the press and the airwaves of an impending "Republican Revolution" to complete what Ronald Reagan had begun. White southerners—and those who identified with the South's traditions, even if born elsewhere—now so dominated the GOP delegation that one of the first acts of the new leadership was to hang a portrait of Virginia's old warhorse Howard W. Smith in chamber where the Rules Committee met. Smith had been Harry Byrd's alter ego in the U.S. House of Representatives. He had led the fight against the Wagner Act, "bottled up" the Fair Labor Standards Act, helped defeat President Harry Truman's push for national health care, and tried to sink the Civil Rights Act. As chairman of the Rules Committee, Smith became a legendary tactician of the manipulation of legislative rules to prevent the majority from achieving its will. Not just Democrats, the new leadership was saying, but their own party's "moderates got too much deference."[7]

In the weeks and months that followed, the media flocked to Georgia's Newt Gingrich, who was coauthor of the contract and now, as a result of its success, Speaker of the House. But although he became the visible voice and limelight seeker of the cause, the real work of getting the agenda passed, in particular the balanced budget amendment so important to the libertarians, was being done by Armey.[8]

Armey was in some ways like Koch, in that he was very systematic in pursuit of his goals as the cause's "legislative tactician," in the words of one seasoned observer, not simply its chief ideologue. Armey studied the fine print of the House's complex rules in order to determine with precision how best to move the items in the contract through the knotty legislative process. To shore up doubters, he walked the corridors daily, answering questions and, where necessary, using his new power as House majority leader to enforce discipline. Anything less than unity would have doomed the plan, for, as team member John Kasich of Ohio noted, their budget proposals would mean cuts in Medicare "unlike any this town has ever seen before." Another team member boasted that his subcommittee was so tight, "we could kill motherhood tomorrow if it was necessary."[9]

Because every vote counted, Armey urged that a school prayer amendment be added to the contract to keep the Christian Coalition on board. He lost on that and some other tactical suggestions, in a pattern that ultimately contributed to the defeat of the most ambitious goals of the promised revolution—including the balanced budget amendment. Worse, loss turned to failed brinkmanship when the House Republicans voted for two protracted government shutdowns in order to, in effect, force the government to stop spending by refusing to raise the debt ceiling. Turning public opinion against "the extremists," the shutdowns also, according to one study, made them seem both "heartless and reckless."[10]

In the end, as their representatives in Washington should have known all along, even those voters who revered Ronald Reagan, and cheered on the contract-signing candidates in principle, were not ready when they learned that freed markets would leave them with sole responsibility for their own fates, to give up their Social Security and Medicare, their public schools, and their government-backed air, water, and earth protections. As important, Bill Clinton's legendary ability to "triangulate"—taking on as his own some of the goals they proposed while drawing the line against such extreme measures as a balanced budget amendment—took the steam out of the House GOP's sails. To be repeatedly outwitted by Clinton, a president the radical right had spent much effort and untold treasure trying to undermine, made the sting of defeat all the more sharp.[11]

Buchanan dismissively explained the disappointing outcome by concluding, once again, that most people desired to remain, as he put it, in "dependency status."[12] What Charles Koch concluded is not recorded in the available documentation, but what we do know is this: rather than throw up his hands in despair, he decided to double down and "speed up the whole process" of radical transformation. He let go of his earlier demand for ideological consistency, a demand that was nonnegotiable for him in the 1970s; now what mattered was practical "results."[13] But how to achieve them?

Koch had been giving to Buchanan's center as well as Henry Manne's Law and Economics Center at George Mason University since the mid-1980s—along with other radical right efforts. He knew Buchanan's signature ideas, having invited him to more than one discussion. But it was only now, when his mind was laser-focused on producing results, that he circled back to the Nobel laureate and ultimately decided that the missing piece he was looking for was close at hand. There was one thinker in the movement who did more than just elaborate on the vision of a just society laid out by his intellectual heroes, von Mises and Hayek, both now deceased. Only James Buchanan had also developed an operational strategy for how to get to that radically new society, one that took as axiomatic what both Buchanan and Koch understood viscerally: that the enduring impediment to the enactment of their political vision was the ability of the American people, through the power of their numbers, to reject the program. What was holding the movement back now became clear: the lack of a strategy to break that power, or at least to debilitate it, the very approach Buchanan had spent a lifetime thinking about and designing.

Operationally, as Buchanan had repeatedly explained, such a program must ultimately change the rules, not simply *who* rules. In the near term, it had to have two components. First, it had to create a pathway from here to there that could be executed in small, piecemeal steps that on their own polled well enough with the American people that they could win passage without raising the public's ire. But each step had to connect back to the previous step and forward to the next one so that when the entire path was laid, all the pieces would reinforce the route to the ultimate destination. By then it would be too late for the American public to cry foul.

Second, and as important, because some of those piecemeal steps, no matter how prettified, could not be fully disguised, where necessary they had to be presented to the American public as the opposite of what they really were—as attempts to shore up rather than ultimately destroy—what the majority of Americans wanted, such as sound Medicare and Social Security programs. For such programs, the framing should be one of the right's concern to "reform" the programs, to protect them, because without such change they would go bankrupt—even though the real goal was to destroy them. For both men, the ends justified whatever means seemed necessary, although those means should remain technically within the law.

While many details are lodged in private records beyond the reach of researchers, it is clear that Koch had so convinced himself of the goodness of his self-appointed mission and of the "prosperity and social well-being" it would bring that he had no moral doubts about the duplicity of the plan he was about to throw his weight behind.[14] He trusted his superior intellect. Buchanan also had something of a God complex that seemed to free him, too, of moral uneasiness, as his aid to Chile's junta showed. What remained to be seen was how these two men would get along once they had to work together to achieve their vision. "Hawks," the novelist Ernest Hemingway once memorably observed, "do not share."[15]

The message Koch delivered in January 1997, along with the $10 million gift he pledged to support a new and enlarged James Buchanan Center, made clear that he believed he had found the missing tool he had been searching for, the one that would produce "real world" results. James Buchanan's theory and implementation strategies were the right "technology," to use Koch's favored phrase. But the professor's team had not employed the tools forcefully enough to "create winning strategies." Koch chastised gently at first: "Since we are greatly outnumbered, the failure to use our superior technology ensures failure."[16]

In essence, he was saying to Buchanan's cadre: *You have a novel analysis of how government grew over the twentieth century to become the Leviathan we detest. I believe your analysis is so valuable to the cause that I am investing $10 million in your work over the next few years, with more to come if I like what I see. Now, use your understanding to take down the beast. Don't go for small gestures. Go for the big win.* "Our skepticism," he said pointedly to any who might hesitate, "needs to be directed toward rationalizations for not applying the framework rather than toward the framework itself." Indeed, Koch concluded his challenge to them by equating the project to the Protestant Reformation, waged by Martin Luther against the corrupt hegemon of an earlier century.[17]

The Mont Pelerin Society's golden anniversary provided an opportunity for Buchanan and his colleague Henry Manne, the newly retired dean of the George Mason School of Law, to define the content of the push to come. Manne had by then more than proved his value to Koch. His summer legal programs had provided intensive training in applying free market economic analyses to legal decision-making for law professors and for federal judges, luring them with luminaries and luxury accommodations. To name just one index of how successful Manne had been: by 1990, *more than two of every five* sitting federal judges had participated in his program—a stunning 40 percent of the U.S. federal judiciary had been treated to a Koch-backed curriculum.[18]

Not surprisingly, early discussion between Manne and Buchanan identified several barriers to economic freedom to be overcome. Excessive "government regulation of business" was an overarching theme, with the biggest threat, the two men now determined, coming from the environmental movement. Because environmentalists were, in the eyes of Manne and Buchanan, on a "quest for control over industry," they had to be not merely defeated, but defamed, with their personal "hidden agenda" exposed.[19]

Another impediment to the society's vision of liberty was government-backed "health and welfare," which impaired "the normal workings of labor markets." Social Security, Medicare and Medicaid, employer-provided pensions and insurance: all those needed to be phased out—or, rather, over time, converted to individual savings accounts.[20]

"Any modern democracy's tax policy" was likewise trouble, because the voters' "inevitable egalitarian instincts" would lead them, if unobstructed, to "redistribution."[21] To solve this problem, they had to bring about the end of the graduated income tax adopted after 1913 with passage of the Sixteenth Amendment, in favor of a single-rate flat tax.[22]

Another absolutely critical target for the new century, they agreed, should be education. As "the most socialized industry in the world," the GMU team complained, public schools, from kindergarten through university, nurtured "community values, many of which are inimical to a free society." Its continuing dominance was an affront to the cause that, since Milton Friedman's 1955 manifesto, had sought to end the "government monopoly" of schooling.[23]

Finally, the golden anniversary discussions should also figure out how to deal with feminism, which the men found to be "heavily socialistic for no apparent reason."[24] A kind of cultural war was therefore in order against this movement that relied so heavily on government action.[25]

The two men, it should be noted, acknowledged the surprising resilience of the enemy. But whom they defined as the "enemy" may surprise you. It was not, as most of us would assume, liberalism. It was socialism.

Soon after the collapse of the Soviet Union, Buchanan had observed that "'socialism in the small' [was] on the ascendency."[26] What he was referring to was not what you and I were taught in school as the definition. Socialism, as the Mont Pelerin Society members defined the term, was synonymous with any effort by citizens to get their government to act in ways that either cost money to support anything other than police and military functions or encroached on private property rights. By that definition, socialism was indeed alive and well in the 1990s.

What concerned them even more was that it was not just liberals who exhibited these socialistic tendencies. By 1990, with the fall of the Soviet Union, even conservative heads of state such as George H. W. Bush and Margaret Thatcher no longer saw the need to devote vast sums to an arms race and a Cold War against the USSR. But rather than return that money to the people from whom they took it—the wealth makers—they were speaking of a "peace dividend," of shifting vast sums of money from the military to home-front concerns.[27]

Abetting that socialist tendency, Buchanan and Manne believed, was passage of the National Voter Registration Act of 1993, a measure pushed for by organizers of low-income Americans who wanted to bring their voices into the political process. As Alex Keyssar writes in his history of voting in America, the National Voter Registration Act "was the final act of the drama that had begun in the 1960s; it completed a lurching yet immensely important forty-year process of nationalizing the voting laws and removing obstacles to the ballot box" that had been put in place from the 1850s to World War I to deter nonelite voters. It instructed states to facilitate participation in elections by allowing citizens to register by mail, when visiting public agencies for assistance, or when obtaining or renewing licenses at motor vehicle facilities (hence its nickname, the Motor Voter Act). By 1997, nine million net new voters had joined the electorate.[28] To believers in voting rights, it was a huge achievement. To those who scorned the idea of a broad and inclusive electorate, it was cause for mourning. "We are increasingly enfranchising the illiterate," grumbled Jim Buchanan, "moving rapidly toward electoral reform that will not expect voters to be able to read or follow instructions."[29] It could have been Harry Byrd speaking.

But for Koch, now there was finally a way to stop all this. The answer he had spent his entire adult life looking for was at hand. There was no time to waste. Three million of the $10 million grant, Koch announced, would be given out in the first installment, with a reorganization to suit the plan. Buchanan's Center for Study of Public Choice and the fast-growing Center for the Study of Market Processes, which had been brought to GMU by Richie Fink in 1980, would now both become divisions of the new James Buchanan Center for Political Economy at George Mason University. Fink was overseeing the merger while also serving as director of the Charles Koch Foundation, executive vice president of Koch Industries, and Koch's master political strategist, even though not long before he had been Buchanan's junior colleague at George Mason. Notably, the ten-year agreement, lasting until 2008, made Buchanan and Koch, rather than Buchanan and Fink, the cochairs of the governing board of the combined center. According to its charter document, the center's nonprofit, tax-deductible mission was "conducting world-class research, education and outreach on political economy and related topics."[30]

Yet if Buchanan was reassured that Fink had not been named his co-equal, he soon discovered that he had let down his guard unwisely. Koch was known for wanting to maintain control over enterprises in which he invested; large contributions to nonprofits were no different, in his mind, from commercial investments. It was his money. Where George Mason was concerned, he and his team were shrewd enough to know they did not need to take over the whole university, which might attract attention and protest (and cost more), but just the corner they needed in order to accomplish what they wanted to in the wider world. And now, with Buchanan to be counted in that corner, as a veritable acquisition among others, Richie Fink bragged to him, "We *have* you, some talented faculty, the B[oar]d of Visitors [which now included such top libertarian cadre members as Dick Armey, Ed Feulner of the Heritage Foundation, *Weekly Standard* editor William Kristol, James C. Miller III, and, of course, Fink himself], the Administration [namely, the president, Alan Merten, and the provost, David Potter], a capable staff, the Governor, former Governor (maybe the next governor), many state legislators, a plethora of funders, the law school dean [Mark F. Grady] and some law school faculty all in support of the concept we discussed." The unspoken message was that the Koch operation had learned a lot from what had happened to Mont Pelerin outposts at other institutions, including Chicago, UCLA, and Buchanan's own previous Virginia bases.[31] Before long, Buchanan was to learn what the Koch people took from those lessons. It was not what he was expecting.

While some of those brought in by the Koch team to staff the outreach project were trained academics, most were not. They were operatives, pure and simple, doing the take-no-prisoners work that operatives everywhere are paid to do, and they were legion. Apparently Buchanan never gave a thought to the possibility that these operatives would not be constrained by the fact that, although they were working for Koch, who had made clear that he expected big and bold steps, they were now operating under the cover of an academic institution and therefore must take those big steps in a quiet manner.

But they were blissfully unaware of any need for restraint. While

Buchanan's various centers had done extensive "outreach" throughout their existence, Koch's team was redefining "outreach" as whatever was necessary to win the war. And apparently, no one took the time to sit down with the Nobel laureate, the star on their masthead, and explain all this to him, or alert him that, although he and Koch were ostensibly codirectors of the new Buchanan Center, it was Koch who was really in charge. The CEO's right-hand man, Fink, would continue to offer unctuous reassurances whenever Buchanan might question something, and make sure to shower him with flattery and prestigious-sounding titles. But defer to him on operations? No way.

Still, Buchanan understood better than Koch that the ball of fire they were putting in play might come back to burn them. And initially he was right. The new combined operation almost crashed before it really got started, as a result of the crude tactics the operatives employed, inadvertently giving the rest of us a taste of what was to come as the twentieth century gave way to the twenty-first.

As one of her first acts as a member of the new Buchanan Center board appointed by the Koch team, Wendy Lee Gramm blasted out a nine-page fund-raising letter in May 1998 to appeal to potential donors who, like Koch, were "frustrated our freedoms haven't advanced more." She offered them "one of America's best-kept secrets," the James Buchanan Center, as a novel vehicle for advancing "personal liberty and economic freedom." She explained that "coming from a university, the Buchanan Center's ideas pack power and credibility."[32]

Then, laying claim to the authority of Buchanan's Nobel Prize, she boasted of the unique "outreach" work the center was doing to promote deregulation and market-based politics. She was outlining, in print, the vision for how this base camp at a public university would seek to influence government. "Through specialized seminars," the center "reaches out to key, influential policymakers—U.S. Senators, Congressmen and state legislators, legislative staff and regulators"—to tutor them in how to "apply free market principles to public policy work." "Over half of congressional offices, from both sides of the political aisle, send staff to Buchanan Center events," her fund-raising letter bragged. If that was not enough, "more than one-third of the federal judiciary have participated" in GMU programs that taught them to apply free-market economics in judging legal cases.[33]

If any potential donor still had doubts, Gramm made clear that, unlike other universities, George Mason was no ivory tower. "With its close proximity to Washington, D.C., the Buchanan Center is uniquely positioned to advance freedom . . . to the very people who'll make a difference." As a case in point, she highlighted the efforts of House Majority Leader Dick Armey, who was then promoting radical cuts in personal, corporate, and capital gains taxes. (She might have added her husband and fellow economist, Phil Gramm, a sitting U.S. senator who was Armey's counterpart in the upper chamber of Congress, where he was pushing for deregulation of the financial sector.)[34]

This fund-raising appeal was not just a deviation from academic norms and from the more scholarly fund-raising efforts Buchanan had spearheaded his entire academic career; it may have broken the law. The center had been chartered as a nonprofit entity, a 501(c)(3), which made it a tax-deductible charity for IRS purposes—a status that requires abstention from partisan activity. And someone, who chose not to reveal his or her identity, took the time to send Buchanan, as well as the chair of the economics department at GMU and the dean of the college, copies of the letter Gramm had sent out, pointing out that her solicitation "involves clear violations" of tax law. Surely, he or she said, something had to be done about "the blatant political activities of the JBC."[35]

The dean of the college, who had not been consulted about the fund-raising letter or its contents, as well as a few faculty members in the economics department who were not involved with the Buchanan Center, bristled at the naked power play by the cadre. They expressed alarm to the president and the provost that "the JBC tie with Koch may 'politicize'" its members' scholarship. Once the scheme was exposed, others began protesting more vocally. Robert Tollison, a Buchanan student from the University of Virginia era who was now on the economics faculty at GMU and the chief faculty overseer of the project, reported to Koch that some colleagues had stopped speaking to him. Even those "folks who allegedly share our interests in entrepreneurship and market-based teaching and research" proved themselves to be "pseudo-libertarians," Tollison complained. They were "defiantly critical" of Charles Koch, Richie Fink, and "Koch funding in general."[36]

What no one likely expected was Buchanan's reaction. "Quite frankly, I am 'pissed off,'" he told Fink. What was being done under his name "verges on fraud and surely, at a minimum amounts to exploitation of me, of you, of JBC, of the university."[37]

But why the moral outrage? Buchanan knew exactly who Richie Fink was. Years earlier he had recommended him personally to Koch, knowing him to be an operator who made things happen without worrying much about standard norms of conduct. It's not as if it were a secret to anyone how sleazy an operation Richie Fink had built with James C. Miller III, Buchanan's former student, after his hire by Koch. Even the *Wall Street Journal* had run stories about how that joint project, Citizens for a Sound Economy, was operating in a "secretive" manner and claiming as members organizations that never consented to joining—using as "pawns" even the Boy Scouts and the Girl Scouts.[38] CSE was run right under Buchanan's nose, moreover, with both men on the payroll of George Mason as they politicked in Washington, Fink as research associate professor at George Mason, mysteriously released from teaching, and Miller running for a U.S. Senate seat while a John M. Olin fellow at Buchanan's center.[39] And the whole new George Mason scheme had been worked out in its broad contours in "lengthy discussions" at the Cato Institute and over "days at the Mont Pelerin Society meetings."[40]

Buchanan had been played like a fine fiddle. Richie Fink had grandly predicted to him that with Koch's support, the new Buchanan Center at GMU would have "the scholarly impact of the University of Chicago and the outreach credibility and impact of the Kennedy School of Government," knowing that Buchanan had repeatedly expressed his irritation at always finding himself in Milton Friedman's shadow and hated the Kennedy family. Did Buchanan ask himself now if anyone, even Koch's operatives, would have had the nerve to use Friedman's name as they had used his, without his knowledge or permission?

Although far more politically engaged throughout his entire academic career than he ever publicly admitted, he chose to tell himself that this debacle was all the fault of others. "Embarrassed personally," incensed "by the usurpation of authority" that had exposed him to shame, and fearing that no matter what attempts were made to ameliorate the situation, the integrity of the research program he had spent four decades developing had been seriously, perhaps permanently, damaged, he refused to have anything further to do with the operatives in Fink's orbit.[41]

Alas, the colleague to whom Buchanan looked for support was Tyler Cowen, just appointed general director of the Buchanan Center, the "front-man role," in the words of one academic insider. The son of a Goldwater Republican who had served as president of the local chamber of commerce and "became an increasingly radical libertarian," Cowen had been introduced by his father to key leaders and organizations of the cause as an adolescent. The young Cowen met Richie Fink at the age of fifteen at Austrian economics seminars in New York, came up through Koch's Institute for Humane Studies, and followed Fink to George Mason in 1980 as an undergraduate, before heading off to Harvard to earn his Ph.D. "I learned more from Rich than is possible to say," he later gushed, not only about economics "but also about institution building, strategy, personalities and many other matters." Fink was a "role model" for him. But Cowen knew something of strategy himself, having been a chess lover from the age of ten. He was already a key player in the project to create an academic base camp for the libertarian revolution. As both a true believer and a so far undistinguished researcher whose career was taking off thanks to Koch largesse, he was not about to alter the ship's course. By self-description autistic and an "upper-middle-class white male who all his life felt like he belonged to the dominant group," Cowen was not inclined to sentimentality or solidarity.[42]

To maintain nominal academic integrity, Buchanan insisted on the divorce of his enterprise from the "outreach programs" of the Center for the Study of Market Processes. The Koch people agreed and moved all their various programs to the Arlington campus of GMU, where the School of Law was already situated, bringing them even closer to Washington, D.C. The incoming team also agreed to strip the self-aggrandizing titles from power-grabbing nonacademic operatives, even as these operatives moved up the organizational hierarchy, and to take down the Web site boasting of the "Programs for Policymakers," so as not to invite prosecution. It would not do to show on the staff listing that an academic center had a director of congressional programs, Lawson Bader, who had no plausible connection with academic economics—or to let the world know that all four "fellows" of the Buchanan Center were acting as political hands, including Wendy Lee Gramm, James Miller, and another GMU alumnus, Dr. Jerry Ellig, who worked with Miller on Citizens for a Sound Economy. The new staff had shown terrible judgment in advertising the "Chief of Staff Weekend Retreats" at which figures such as sitting U.S. Supreme Court Justice Antonin Scalia and "experts" from such think tanks as Cato and Reason addressed "senior congressional staff" on "a variety of important policy issues, while maintaining relevance to the legislative calendar." And ordinary Web surfers, to say nothing of IRS employees, did not need to know that the Buchanan Center had been tutoring top legislative staff in such areas as strategies for privatizing Social Security and Medicare, "downsizing government," and promoting unlimited campaign spending as a form of free speech.[43]

But when Buchanan went one step further and tried to bring the GMU administration over to his way of thinking by warning the top leaders of the university that Fink's center was out of control—quite literally, "since there is no one with academic standing involved at all"—he got nowhere. GMU had never been offered a larger gift, reported the *Washington Post*.[44]

"We are determined to pursue this initiative," Provost David Potter informed Buchanan; indeed, he and the president made clear that they wanted to better "align the Department of Economics with the Buchanan Center."[45] In other words, they wanted to do still more to please Koch, even subordinating an academic department to the political project. As long as there was money on the table, they were not about to forgo it.

When the waters calmed, Ed Meese, now the rector of GMU's Board of Visitors, charged with university oversight, awarded Charles Koch and James Buchanan each a George Mason Medal, the institution's highest honor, for contributions to "our nation and the world."[46] But the Nobel Laureate was too savvy not to know that this and the minor changes made at his request were face-saving gestures to soothe his wounded pride. He was no longer in charge, not even of the center that bore his name. Rather than face such a future, Jim Buchanan effectively retired to the log cabin where he had first convened his Third Century project. When he died in 2013, neither Koch nor Fink, nor Cowen nor Meese, bothered to attend his memorial service.[47] Why should they? His days of his usefulness to them had passed.

With a respectable base camp secured, minutes from the capital, Koch would turn to assembling the kind of force that had propelled Columbus—this time, to put democracy in chains.

PART III

THE FALLOUT

CONCLUSION

GET READY

"What happens if individuals do not value liberty sufficiently highly?" James Buchanan's colleague and friend Charles K. Rowley asked after the failure of the Reagan revolution. "Should they be forced to be free?"[1]

Rowley was not an outside critic. He was a dedicated libertarian who had been part of the Virginia school of political economy since joining the George Mason economics department in 1984. At the time of his death, in 2013, he was working on a biography of James Buchanan, whom he still deeply admired. Indeed, with words perhaps prescient, he depicted Buchanan as "perhaps the most hated and feared enemy of left-leaning economists throughout the world."[2]

As for his question about those who did not share the cause's zeal, we do not know whether anyone answered it explicitly or whether those answers satisfied his concerns. What we do know is that by the opening of the new century, he seems to have become more uneasy about the movement's direction. As the Mont Pelerin Society was making plans to celebrate its golden anniversary in Washington, D.C., Rowley refused invitations from Edwin J. Feulner, head of the Heritage Foundation, to serve on the host committee. He told him frankly that he did not like what big money was doing to an organization that had once focused on ideas. The "large subsidies from corporations" and "wealthy individuals" led to "extravagant junketing" that disturbed him. "This was not the original intent of Friedrich von Hayek" in creating the society, Rowley protested. "Too many meetings are now dominated by wealthy individuals, foundation executives and the like."[3]

Rowley did not detail the corruption of purpose that unsettled him, at least not in the documents I've been able to find, but it's not difficult to read between the lines in order to understand his confusion. The core claim of this movement—certainly Buchanan's core claim going all the way back to *Brown*—was that government did not have the right to "coerce" the individual, beyond the basic level of the rule of law and public order. If liberty, as Buchanan and others in the movement would use that term, had any hard and fast meaning, it lay in the conviction that every person, up to the very wealthiest among us, had the same right to control the earnings of his own labor as he saw fit, even when the majority thought that this money might be put to better use serving the public interest. In the movement's view, government was the realm of coercion, and the market was the realm of freedom, of freely chosen, mutually valued exchange.

But what Rowley saw—up close—was two equally troubling patterns that did not square with that way of thinking. First, the sheer scale of the riches the "wealthy individuals" brought to bear turned out to have subtle, even seductive, power. And second, under the influence of one wealthy individual in particular, the movement was turning to an equally troubling form of coercion: achieving its ends essentially through trickery, through deceiving trusting people about its real intentions in order to take them to a place where, on their own, given complete information, they probably would not go. This was not classical liberalism, no matter how often cadre members claimed that mantle. When you combine the emerging deceitful and therefore coercive strategy—one that owed much to James Buchanan—with the fact that those attending the Mont Pelerin Society golden anniversary meeting, intellectuals and operatives alike, were ever more beholden for their sustenance to a single man, Rowley's discomfort is easy to explain. It is a contradiction in terms to remain a self-governing intellectual and be part of a messianic movement. Messiahs don't entertain doubts. I suspect Rowley felt the change under way; if it didn't bother others about themselves, it bothered him about himself.[4]

For we also know that once the Koch people settled in—and then took over—at George Mason University, concern turned into contempt, then disgust, until Rowley came to viscerally despise the team of operatives and their academic enablers who were now, as far as Rowley was concerned, occupying his campus. He called Richie Fink, Charles Koch's top strategist, "a third-rate political hack" and "a man who is very appropriately named."[5]

Rowley said what others never dared to admit: "Far too many libertarians have been seduced by Koch money into providing intellectual ammunition for an autocratic businessman." It had reached the point, he came to believe by 2012, that there was no hope that any of those who participated in the "free market think tanks" would "speak out." He was blunt about the reason why: "Too many of them benefit financially from the pocket money doled out by Charles and David Koch."[6]

Did Rowley include Buchanan, as well, in this suggestion of so many having been bought? While Buchanan no longer came to campus after 1998 to teach strategy to a new generation of operatives with the alacrity he once showed, nor did he play any other ongoing direct role that I have been able to trace in what had now become Koch's movement, he continued to accept the honors and emoluments that Koch's people made sure to send his way. In his memoirs, published ten years later, he went out of his way to say that, looking back over his lifetime's work, "I have no regrets."[7]

Perhaps. But Buchanan was far too smart not to remember the young man who had once promised UVA president Colgate Darden that he would seek to defeat Keynesian economics and liberal politics by winning the war of ideas against the other side—not by writing training manuals for subversion by stealth. Had he withdrawn after the Wendy Gramm episode so that he would not have to personally witness what his decades of work had wrought? Again, we don't know.

Rowley clearly continued to respect Buchanan, but perhaps not so blindly, for he predicted, as the 2012 election approached, that the libertarian cause they shared "may well suffer," at least in principle, "serious harm" for having become the instrument of a tyrant. Watching how Koch commandeered the Cato Institute for his "crude" plan to speed up the libertarian conquest of America by using the very governmental apparatus that libertarians had long criticized made him angry. He saw, too, that Koch had "no scruples concerning the manipulation of scholarship"; he wanted Cato's output to aid his cause, period. When a few veteran libertarian board members and staff raised questions, he replaced them with his own people, who now included the kind of "social conservatives" and political party figures who were once anathema to libertarians. In the end, though, Rowley's loyalty was to the cause, not to his adopted country. (He was born and educated in England.) He was concerned about Cato, not America, and certainly not the fate of majority rule. Neither he nor any other insider ever went public with their concerns. Nor did anyone else sound the alarm for the rest of us about what Koch's "proxy army," as one Rowley reader called it, was doing to the country.[8]

Intrepid investigative journalists had by then reported on many of the maneuvers of that proxy army. They revealed how it was operating on more fronts through more ostensibly separate organizations than ordinary mortals could easily follow. It was occupying the Republican Party, using the threat of well-funded primary challenges to force its elected officials to do the cause's bidding or lose their seats. It was pushing out radical right laws ready to bring to the floor in every state through the American Legislative Exchange Council (ALEC). It was selling those laws through the seemingly independent but centrally funded and operationally linked groups of the State Policy Network. It was leveraging the anger of local Tea Party groups to move the legislative agenda of Americans for Prosperity and FreedomWorks. Its state affiliates were energizing voter turnout with deceitful direct mail campaigns. Its elected allies were shutting down the federal government; in effect, using its employees and the millions who rely on it as hostages to get what they otherwise could not—and much, much more.[9]

In the shock-and-awe-style coordinated push to implement radical change in record time, without customary transparency or deliberative process, is it any wonder that no one noticed how many of the leading operatives in this vast project had been trained in economics at Virginia institutions, especially at Buchanan's last home, George Mason University? No. Nor is it any wonder that in the scramble to keep up with all the action, no one inquired about the source of the ideas that made these efforts cohere or identified their endgame. Surely, this was just partisan hardball played with astonishing new viciousness.

The acclaimed jurist Louis Brandeis, who over the course of his lifetime amassed considerable wealth, once warned the American people that as a nation, "we must make our choice. We may have democracy, or we may have wealth concentrated in the hands of a few, but we can't have both." I suspect, however, that even Brandeis (who also spoke of the need for unions, and for social justice and wise regulation in an earlier age when capital ran amok) never imagined that enough wealth could be concentrated in the hands of a few to launch such an audacious stealth attack on the foundational notion of government being of, by, and for the people.[10]

But Brandeis also bequeathed us the maxim "Sunlight is said to be the best of disinfectants." In that spirit of bringing secrets from the shadows out into the open light of day, where they can be examined by all those they affect, I will use this conclusion to convey what is in store if we do not take this assault on our governance and our way of life seriously and respond effectively to it. For all its horror, this portrait can be painted in good part with the words of the people who seek to create it.

"If you tell a great lie and repeat it often enough, the people will eventually come to believe it," Joseph Goebbels, a particularly ruthless, yet shrewd, propagandist, is said to have remarked. Today the big lie of the Koch-sponsored radical right is that society can be split between makers and takers, justifying on the part of the makers a Manichaean struggle to disarm and defeat those who would take from them. Attend a Tea Party gathering and you will hear endless cries about the "moocher class."[11] Read the output of the libertarian writers subsidized by wealthy donors and you will encounter endless variations. David Boaz of the Cato Institute, to choose just one, speaks of the "parasite economy" that divides us into "the predators and the prey."[12] Addressing an audience of $50,000-per-plate donors, Mitt Romney famously remarked that "47 percent" of voters were, in effect, leeches on "productive" Americans.[13]

Is there any evidence to suggest that close to half of American society is intent on exploiting the rich through the tax system? That they contribute nothing, while using government to gang up on a defenseless minority that somehow, all on its own, generates wealth? Is it true that the wealthiest among us are being unfairly fleeced by government? If so, how do we square that with what is now common knowledge: that the secretary to a billionaire will often pay a higher tax rate than her boss?

Might such motivated arguments belie a deeper purpose, a compulsion to control others, to limit their freedoms, in the name of ensuring one's own liberty? Surprisingly, the cause—so secretive in so many other respects—has given us the answer.

Charles Koch has always argued that his vision of a good society will bring prosperity to all. But his trusted cadre, the people he relies upon to justify and advance his messianic vision, apparently believe otherwise. They have sketched out the society that will emerge if their cause succeeds (while wiping their own fingerprints from the story of its emergence). What does that society look like? And what will they have to do to our people and our democracy to secure it?

Koch learned as a young adult, from his mentor Baldy Harper, that "the great social problem of our age is that of designing the preventive medicine that will stop the eroding of liberty in the body politic." Harper warned that "once the disease has advanced, a bitter curative medicine is required to gain already-lost liberty."[14] James Buchanan revealed just how bitter the medicine would be. People who failed to foresee and save money for their future needs, Buchanan wrote in 2005, "are to be treated as subordinate members of the species, akin to . . . animals who are dependent."[15]

Tyler Cowen, the man who succeeded Buchanan and now directs the cause's base camp at George Mason, the Mercatus Center, has explained that with the "rewriting of the social contract" under way, people will be "expected to fend for themselves much more than they do now." While some will flourish, he says, "others will fall by the wayside." And because "worthy individuals" will manage to climb their way out of poverty, "that will make it easier to ignore those who are left behind." Cowen foresees that "we will cut Medicaid for the poor." Also, "the fiscal shortfall will come out of real wages as various cost burdens are shifted to workers" from employers and a government that does less. To "compensate," the chaired professor in the nation's second-wealthiest county recommends, "people who have had their government benefits cut or pared back" should pack up and move to lower-cost states like Texas. Granted, he says, "Texas is skimpy on welfare benefits and Medicaid coverage," and nearly three in ten of its residents have no health insurance, but the state does have jobs and "very cheap housing" to offset its "subpar public services."[16]

Indeed, Cowen forecasts, "the United States as a whole will end up looking more like Texas." His tone is matter-of-fact, as though he is simply reporting the inevitable. And he enjoys great authority, as his blog, *The Marginal Revolution*, is the most visited intellectual blog in professional economics, known for criticizing Republicans as well as Democrats, and also respected for Cowen's signature incorporation of economic concepts to analyze cultural phenomena from food to travel. He presents himself as a pragmatic libertarian (indeed, the blog's motto is "small steps toward a much better world"). Yet when one reads his flip remarks on the fate now facing his fellow citizens with the knowledge that he has been the leader of a team working in earnest with Charles Koch for two decades to bring about the society he is describing, the words assume a different weight. They sound like a premeditation. For example, the economist prophesies lower-income parts of America "recreating a Mexico-like or Brazil-like environment" complete with favelas like those in Rio de Janeiro. The "quality of water" might not be what U.S. citizens are used to, but "partial shantytowns" would satisfy the need for cheaper housing as "wage polarization" grows and government shrinks. "Some version of Texas—and then some—is the future for a lot of us," the economist advises. "Get ready."[17]

Those who subscribe to the libertarian philosophy believe that the only legitimate role of government is to ensure the rule of law, guarantee social order, and provide for the national defense. That is why they have long been fervent opponents of Medicare, Medicaid for the poor, and, most recently, Obamacare. The House budget chairman, Paul Ryan, has explained that such public provision for popular needs not only violates the liberty of the taxpayers whose earnings are transferred to others, but also violates the recipients' spiritual need to earn their own sustenance. He told one audience that the nation's school lunch program left poor children with "a full stomach—and an empty soul."[18]

Less well known is that these zealots do not believe that the government should be involved in trying to promote public health, period. We are not talking about subsidized hip replacements and birth control. We are talking about things like basic sanitation, something governments have committed to since the Progressive Era as the single most important measure to stop waterborne epidemics such as cholera and typhoid.

The Republican majority in Congress has "systematically cut public health budgets that address Zika, Ebola and other ailments," notes the columnist Nicholas Kristof.[19] The insiders' thinking helps explain why. Thom Tillis, a North Carolina state senator elevated to the U.S. Senate in 2014 with backing from the Koch apparatus, has said that restaurants should be able "to opt out of" laws requiring employees to wash their hands after using the toilet, "as long as they post a sign that says, 'We don't require our employees to wash their hands after leaving the restroom.' The market will take care of that."[20]

Even before Obamacare was enacted, a public choice economist funded by the Liberty Fund, Gary M. Anderson, produced a study alleging that the field of public health was, from its beginning in the early twentieth century, nothing more than "a major device used by organized interest groups to redistribute wealth to themselves."[21] Amity Shlaes, a libertarian journalist on the *Wall Street Journal* editorial board and author of a best-selling book based on Buchanan's ideology, *The Forgotten Man*, came to a similar conclusion as the fight over Obamacare began. She "found that public choice theory explained everything," including that "health officials' interest in testing small children's blood for lead made sense when one considered that finding poisoned children validated their jobs."[22]

The largely African American population of Flint, Michigan, knows firsthand what will happen to "people who fall by the wayside" in the new political economy run by people who think this way. The Flint scandal broke because of a mother who would not give in. When she appealed to the appointed city manager and Republican governor in late 2014 because her daughter's hair was falling out, her older son was suffering abdominal pain, and her twins were developing untreatable rashes, they brushed aside her concerns. It was not until she found scientific experts from another state who were willing to help that most Americans learned of the worst public health disaster in state history. "For 18 months, 100,000 residents were exposed to toxic water," explained one Ph.D. student. No amount of lead in water is safe, especially for children, whose developing brains and bodies are so vulnerable; exposure can cause irreversible mental impairment.[23]

What happened in Flint was not a natural disaster. Nor a case of governmental incompetence. What happened there was directly attributable to the prodding of the Mackinac Center, one of the first Koch-funded—and in this case, Koch-staffed—state-level "think and do" tanks that now exist in all fifty states and are affiliated with the State Policy Network (SPN), also Koch-concocted, to coordinate efforts to prevent state governments from responding to the demands of the "takers."[24]

"When the Mackinac Center speaks, we listen," said Michigan governor John Engler in 1994. Indeed, so did his successors. In 2011, the center pushed hard for legislation that would allow the governor to take over all aspects of local government in any community facing a "financial emergency" and hand control over to an emergency manager. The powers of these unelected managers to impose austerity measures would be vast, including the authority to unilaterally abrogate collective bargaining agreements, outsource services, sell off local resources to private companies, and change suppliers at will. By 2009, more than half of the deindustrializing and economically troubled state's black voters were being governed by such appointed emergency managers, among them the residents of Detroit, Benton Harbor, and Flint. "It's dictatorship, plain and simple," one city commissioner said of the new system. To save money, Flint's appointed city manager switched the source of the city water supply to the polluted Flint River. The Mackinac Center lobbyists, by the way, made sure that the law incorporated provisions to protect the appointed managers from lawsuits. Given the scale of the damage they had every reason to know they would inflict, that was a wise protection of potential future foot soldiers for the cause.[25]

Is it any surprise, then, that those who would put public sanitation and clean water at risk are now the leading proponents of climate change denial? Or that before embarking on this mission, Buchanan's students and colleagues were producing economic analyses funded by the tobacco industry to discredit the "paternalists" who would deny cigarette companies, smokers, and those in their immediate surroundings their "voluntary choice" in a misguided "majoritarian" quest, pushed by "rent-seeking interest groups" whose "appeal to the 'public's health' is essentially just political rhetoric designed to camouflage the coercion"? Or that these economists would insinuate that government-funded researchers would never find a cure for cancer because that "would put many cancer bureaucrats out of work"?[26]

Just as the property rights supremacists would rather let people die than receive health care assistance or antismoking counsel from government, so they would rather invite global ecological and social catastrophe than allow regulatory restrictions on economic liberty. The Koch cadre identified the public's embrace of environmentalism as a problem early on. Back in 1997, for example, the same year that Charles Koch made his first big contribution to George Mason, yet another Koch operation, Citizens for a Sound Economy, warned its corporate allies that 76 percent of Americans thought of themselves as environmentalists. "Worse, 65 percent" told industry pollsters that they "do not trust business" to take action against pollution, and "79 percent of voters think current regulations are about right or 'not strict enough.'"[27] The lesson the cadre took from this was that it could not win majorities to its true goals. So what was to be done? "It might be hard to admit," said the chair of the economics department at George Mason, Donald J. Boudreaux, but because public choice showed that a government cure would be worse (from their perspective, of course) than the disease, global warming "is best left alone."[28]

That advice was rejected by serious scientists and concerned citizens, so the Cato Institute and the Independent Institute joined a circle of less-known Koch-funded libertarian think tanks driving what two science scholars describe as systematic environmental "misinformation campaigns." They spread junk pseudoscience to make the public believe that there is still doubt about the peril of climate change, a tactic they learned from the tobacco companies that for years sowed doubt about science to keep the public from connecting smoking and illness.[29] Even more galling are the personal attacks on scientists that suggest, as one Koch-subsidized organization has done, that climate scientists are seeking personal monetary rewards. "All Aboard the Climate Gravy Train" reads a typical headline (a smear more scandalous when you consider that it was coming from operatives on retainer to a billionaire).[30]

The Koch team by then could count on its Club for Growth to fund primary challenges to ensure that the party line on environmentalism would be maintained by Republican members of Congress. That explains why Senator John McCain is but the best-known—and once most principled—Republican to flip his position after being faced with a Tea

Party primary challenge. By 2014, only 8 of 278 Republicans in Congress were willing to acknowledge that man-made climate change is real.[31] "We're looking at a party," the economist and columnist Paul Krugman rightly points out, "that has turned its back on science at a time when doing so puts the very future of civilization at risk."[32]

Backing up that chokehold on federal action is what one reporter called a "secretive alliance" between red-state attorneys general and fossil fuel corporations to litigate in federal courts with "unprecedented" coordination to obstruct environmental and other regulatory efforts.[33] The use of state government power to undercut national reforms follows a strategy of "competitive federalism" advocated by Buchanan and inspired by John C. Calhoun's constitutional theory and Jack Kilpatrick's application of it to fight the implementation of *Brown v. Board of Education*. You could call it the "race to the bottom" by intentional design, now led by the American Legislative Exchange Council and advocated by the entire Koch-funded State Policy Network, which provides scholarly legitimacy for the state legislators' actions.[34] Advised by the Wisconsin affiliate on his agenda since taking office as governor, Scott Walker's administration imposed a gag order in 2015 to prohibit employees charged with oversight of state-owned land from even discussing climate change on the job.[35]

To put all this another way: if the Koch-network-funded academics and institutions were not in the conversation, the public would have little doubt that the evidence of science is overwhelming and government action to prevent further global warming is urgent.[36] Sadly, however, their campaigns are working. The number of Americans who believed that "the continued burning of fossil fuels would alter the climate" dropped from 71 percent in 2007 to 44 percent in 2011.[37]

A different kind of catastrophe is under way in the nation's public school system, a target of the Mont Pelerin Society cause since the 1950s—well before the rise of powerful teachers' unions, it bears noting. Rather than admit their ideological commitment to ending public education, they have convinced a sizable segment of the American population that the problems in schools today are the result of those teachers' unions having too much power. In the states where they have won control, like my own state of North Carolina, the cadre's allied elected officials, pushed by affiliates of the State Policy Network, have rushed to pass laws to debilitate teachers' unions, one bill being hurried through passage after midnight. The Republican-dominated North Carolina General Assembly then also cut seven thousand teacher assistants, allotted $100 million less than the state budget office said was needed merely to maintain the schools, and budgeted $500 million less to public schools than it had in 2008. Even the school supplies budget was cut by more than half; students can no longer take home textbooks in some poor communities, for fear they may be lost.[38]

Where is this money going? Into corporate America, to a new "education industry" of private schools, many of which are held to no standards or even disclosure requirements. One shocked superior court judge found that the North Carolina General Assembly had violated the state constitution in sending children with tax subsidies to "private schools that have no legal obligation to teach them anything." (His verdict was overruled by the state supreme court, which the Koch cadre had spent handsomely to control for just such eventualities.) The new for-profit virtual charter schools, whose CEO personally earned $4 million in 2014, were found, by one Stanford University research study, to have left their enrolled students falling far behind their public school counterparts, equivalent to missing "72 days of learning in reading and 180 days of learning in math" in a 180-day school year. In other words, the online schools in this study taught nothing in math, and little in reading.[39] As a result of all this, North Carolina, which during the twentieth century, through wise investments in public education, had climbed from the poorest of southern states to one of the best-off, now ranks beneath Mississippi in per-pupil spending.[40]

Just as the radical right seeks, ultimately, to turn public education over to corporations, so it pushes for corporate prisons. The mission seems important enough that Alexander Tabarrok, a GMU economist then moonlighting as research director for the Koch-funded Independent Institute, issued a whole book on the subject in 2003, with the coy title *Changing the Guard*. "We now know that private prisons can be built more quickly, operated at lower cost, and maintained at a quality level at least as high as government-run prisons," Tabarrok announced. While warning of "special-interest groups, in particular the correctional agencies and the prison guard unions" that push for more prison spending, he neglected to note how the profit motive could lead private prison corporations to push for tougher sentencing to drive up prison populations and to cut costly items such as job training and substance abuse counseling.[41]

After all, it was by then a common operating principle among insiders that, as the cause's Stephen Moore had argued two decades earlier, turning public functions over to corporations was a "potent strategy" to "create new pro-privatization coalitions," because the corporations that profit from the spun-off government functions would push for further change.[42] And sure enough, the Corrections Corporation of America (CCA) has become a powerful lobbying force for further privatization—as well as a donor to Koch's Reason Foundation, which pushes it.[43] "Cashing In on Cons" was the apt title of an undercover report on a sector with annual revenue of more than $50 billion, CCA being among the most profitable players—and a very generous one with the Republican legislators who received 92 percent of its political contributions.[44]

In one emblem of the perverse incentives for-profit prisons have created, a Pennsylvania judge was convicted in a "'cash for kids' scheme" in which private detention centers paid judges $2.8 million in kickbacks for sentencing thousands of children to their facilities.[45] With no rights or collective voice and few allies, detained immigrants have proven to be even more ideal commodities for a reliable cash stream to such corporations, so lucrative that one recent report on the facilities that house them bore the title "Banking on Detention."[46]

If the nation's health, schools, and prisons, and the world's climate, are at a watershed moment, so, too, is the U.S. labor force. A large body of research by economists and political scientists over the past two decades has demonstrated that the surging inequality on display in America today is not an inevitable result of impersonal developments such as globalization and new technology, even as these have contributed. Rather, the extremity of our current situation is in good part due to the outsized power of corporations and wealthy donors over our politics and public policy. A case in point: According to the International Monetary Fund, an organization known for decades of draconian fiscal prescriptions, "the decline in unionization is strongly associated with the rise of income shares at the top." The

IMF concluded that the rights of workers to bargain collectively must be restored to slow the growth of inequality and enable economic growth.[47]

Yet the cause is pushing hard in the opposite direction: willful destruction of workers' ability to organize into unions and negotiate for better wages and conditions. At midcentury, the former slave states of the South led the nation in passing antiunion right-to-work laws, with only a smattering of imitators elsewhere, mostly in places of sparse population. Yet between 2012 and 2016, guided by Buchanan's ideas and pushed by the Koch-funded organizations ALEC, the SPN, and Americans for Prosperity, four former free states passed such laws: Indiana, Michigan, Wisconsin, and West Virginia.[48]

The new antiunion rules unfurled first by Governor Scott Walker in Wisconsin in 2011 are more devilishly lethal in their cumulative impact than anything the cause had theretofore produced. Their elaborate precision evoked the analogous changes in Chilean labor law instituted in the Pinochet era with Buchanan's input. In the new Wisconsin, public employees would no longer be allowed to negotiate working conditions and benefits, only wages (with those held to the rate of inflation). Each contract would be only a year in duration, thus draining staff time and energy away from addressing the concerns of existing members and from organizing new members in order to prepare for now back-to-back annual negotiations. Unions would lose the right to have dues deducted from members' paychecks and instead have to chase down individuals who did not pay. And, in a final slap, with the unions no longer able to do anything of substance for their members, they would face recertification elections *each year*.[49] No wonder Walker boasted that "we dropped the bomb."[50] His approach cut in half, over just five years, the share of public employees who belong to unions.[51]

The combination of hobbling unions and privatizing public services has taken a particular toll on African Americans, who were able to move into the middle class in significant numbers specifically because of measures preventing discrimination in government jobs. "Public employment," explained the authors of a large interdisciplinary research study on U.S. inequality, "has been the principal source of black mobility, especially for women, and one of the most important mechanisms reducing black poverty." One recent headline captures the impact succinctly: "Public Sector Jobs Vanish, Hitting Blacks Hard." The austerity measures induced by the Great Recession have contributed, but public sector employment's failure to rebound also results from deliberate choices to cut taxes and services and outsource or privatize what remains.[52]

The historian of women Ruth Rosen looks at the impact of the spreading attack on government from yet another perspective. "Who will care for America's children and the elderly," she asks, now that two-thirds of mothers with children under six are in the workforce, yet "market fundamentalism—the irrational belief that markets solve all problems—has succeeded in dismantling so many federal regulations, services and protections?"[53] But the cause would argue that it has answered that question over and over again: *You will.* And if you can't, you should have thought of that before you had kids or before you grew old without adequate savings. The solution to every problem—from young people loaded down with student loan debt to the care of infants and toddlers and the sick and the elderly—is for each individual to think, from the time they are sentient, about their possible future needs and prepare for them with their own earnings, or pay the consequences. Indeed, George Mason's Tyler Cowen and a Mercatus colleague told young Americans a few years ago that they "should not be occupying Wall Street, they should be occupying AARP" (to keep retirees from taking from them).[54]

But the elderly, too, and those now aging will have plenty of problems of their own. Social Security offers another tragic illustration of the destructive import of privatization and "personal responsibility," with Chile's experience again hinting at America's future. Our nation's retirement system is "the soft underbelly of the welfare state," leading cadre member Stephen Moore has said. "Jab your spear through that" and you can kill the whole thing.[55] The Koch team, led by Cato, continues to push the Pinochet model of individual investment accounts, a model for which they have won the support of many Republican elected officials. But in reality, that model proved so disastrous that after the dictatorship ended, a nearly universal consensus emerged on bringing back key elements of social insurance. The system of individual accounts proved a huge boon to the financial corporations that received the automatic deductions from workers' paychecks. The companies exploited that access mercilessly, achieving an average annual profit rate of more than 50 percent over a five-year period, thanks, not least, to their taking between a quarter and a third of workers' contributions as fees. (One senator decried them as "thieves in jackets and ties" who "rob people of their pensions.") Even Sebastián Piñera, a conservative billionaire elected president of Chile in 2010 and the brother of the Pinochet labor minister who imposed the system, said it needed "deep reforms, because half of Chileans have no pension coverage, and of those who do, 40 percent are going to find it hard to reach the minimum level" needed for retirement.[56]

Meanwhile, the United States, distracted by the false fearmongering of the libertarians from the true challenge ahead, faces a retirement shortfall on a scale of more than $6 trillion as wage earners, in particular, have been thrown back on their own resources. Pushed by market pressures and encouraged by Mont Pelerin Society thought, U.S. corporations have nearly all discontinued the defined benefit pensions that a generation ago covered half the labor force. And with wages essentially stagnant for the majority since the 1970s, very few Americans have 401(k) accounts or other savings equivalent to what has been lost. Two authorities offer this stark summary: "The harsh reality is that the majority of today's workforce—probably the large majority—are heading toward increasingly difficult and, in some cases, financially disastrous retirements." The researchers also show, however, that this bleak future does not need to be. Social Security "remains the most widespread, effective, secure, and significant source of retirement income" for the vast majority of Americans. To stave off the crisis, the need is precisely the opposite of what the libertarian cadre argues: the nation's social insurance system should be expanded to compensate for the spread of low-wage work and the shortfall from other sources.[57]

The ultimate target of the well-heeled right's stealth plan, though, as Buchanan for so long urged, is the nation's most important rule book: the U.S. Constitution itself. To understand where that endgame fits with all that has already unfolded, it may help to take a step backward and review the planning of the whole project that has unfurled since 2008, when the combined impact of the financial crisis that set off the Great Recession and the election of the nation's first African American president, Barack Obama, gave the cause the opening for which Charles Koch had patiently waited after setting up shop at George Mason in 1997.[58]

That very year, Tyler Cowen was commissioned to lay the conceptual groundwork for the planned push to transform America with a paper titled "Why Does Freedom Wax and Wane?"[59] The paper was a review of research that could guide the Mercatus Center in its quest to eradicate the "restrictions on liberty" characteristic of twentieth-century democracies.[60]

What did Cowen discover? One key finding was that by the 1920s, in both Europe and the United States, "the expansion of the voter franchise" beyond "wealthy male landowners" had produced the unfortunate result of enlarged public sectors. Alas, "the elimination of poll taxes and literacy tests leads to higher turnout and higher welfare spending."[61]

"The freest countries have not generally been democratic," Cowen noted, with Chile being "the most successful" in securing freedom (defined not as most of us would, as personal freedom, but as supplying the greatest economic liberty). Cowen pointed to Hong Kong and Singapore as other lasting examples, as well as to two other cases: Peru under Alberto Fujimori and New Zealand from the mid-1980s to the early 1990s, which deregulated financial markets, privatized extensively, slashed taxes on the wealthy to create "a (nearly) flat tax," and undermined labor unions' bargaining power.[62]

The professor identified another commonality in the success stories: "In no case were reforms brought on by popular demand for market-oriented ideas." The pro-liberty cause faced the same problem it always had: it wanted a radical transformation that "find[s] little or no support" among the people. Cowen delivered the action implication of its minority following without mincing words: "If American political institutions render market-oriented reforms too difficult to achieve, then perhaps those institutions should be changed."[63]

The economist was creating, it seems fair to say, a handbook for how to conduct a fifth-column assault on democracy.

"The weakening of the checks and balances" in the American system, Cowen suggested, "would increase the chance of a very good outcome." Alas, given the pervasive reverence for the U.S. Constitution, a direct bid to manipulate the system could prove "disastrous." Cowen's best advice, informed by the Chilean experience, was sudden percussive policy bombing, akin in nature, one could say, to the military doctrine of shock and awe, which uses colossal displays of force and calculated interlinked maneuvers to shock the enemy into submission. When the right opportunity arose, the economist advised, "big-bang style clustered bursts" could dispense with multiple democratic constraints on economic liberty in the same surge (rather like, one could infer, the radical policy changes imposed on multiple fronts in the same sessions in newly Republican-dominated states like mine after 2011, among them education, employment, environment, taxation, and voting rights).[64]

In the meantime, shaping public opinion was crucial. Efforts should probably focus on men, because they "are more likely to think like economists," whereas women tend to anticipate the downside of economic liberty and so support government intervention. Research being done at George Mason also suggested a good deal of irrationality in the electorate, which could be turned to advantage. "It might be possible for 'irrationally held' views to in fact support good policies," particularly if the cause were to enlist insights from "cognitive science and perhaps evolutionary biology." Knowledge of just how vulnerable humans are to hardwired drives that resist reasoned evidence, it seemed, might prove helpful in getting voters to unwittingly enable an "unpopular" agenda.[65]

Changes under way in the media offered still more promise for the cause. Television's new fixation on private peccadilloes, as seen in the Clinton era, could leave citizens jaded and suspicious, thus sowing helpful mistrust of government (although some caution was in order, as the "cynicism may undercut some of the values needed to sustain a free society"). The emerging Internet, for its part, "appears especially well suited for rumor, gossip, and talk of conspiracy."[66]

Before we turn to how American "political institutions could be changed" to enable "weakening of the checks and balances" as recommended by Cowen, ultimately through altered interpretation among sitting judges followed by constitutional amendment, a little orientation may be helpful, because, in truth, the U.S. Constitution already restrains what we the people can do to a degree not seen in any other democratic nation. Fittingly for a cause whose lineage traces back to John C. Calhoun, the

Koch-funded cadre works to exaggerate the most troubling features of what one legal scholar fairly called "slavery's constitution."[67]

Let me explain.

Americans are taught from an early age to revere the checks and balances built into our political system by that document, features designed to act as imposing speed bumps, if not complete roadblocks, to radical change from hotheaded majorities, particularly those who may encroach upon the property rights of the minority. The most obvious among these binding features is our grossly malapportioned Senate, designed to put brakes on the House of Representatives, which was to represent the people directly. A state with comparatively few residents, such as Wyoming, has the same Senate representation as the most populous state, California. That means the vote of a Wyoming resident carries nearly seventy times more weight than the vote of a Californian in Senate elections and deliberations.[68] How fair is that? It's not. It is precisely the kind of malapportionment that the Supreme Court, in the early 1960s, ruled unconstitutional in internal affairs of the states, whose officials were purposely overrepresenting rural residents over urban and suburban residents—indeed, a much more egregious departure from the "one person, one vote" standard. But because the apportionment of Senate seats is written into the Constitution, in the one section that cannot be amended, the remedy cannot be applied nationally.

On the one hand, this constitutional system has helped make the United States the most stable republic in the modern world. On the other hand, it has also made ours by far the least responsive of all the leading democracies to what the people want and need. It takes upheaval of truly historic proportions to achieve significant change in America, even when it is supported by the vast majority—as evidenced by the civil war required to end slavery, the tens of thousands of strikes and other struggles needed to achieve reform during the Great Depression, and the mass disruption and political crisis that civil rights activists had to bring about in order to win for African Americans the same constitutional rights enjoyed by other citizens.[69] The existing checks and balances, in short, create an all but insuperable barrier to those seeking to right even gross social injustice.

The problem is systemic. Built into our Constitution, the change-blocking mechanisms prevent us as a polity from addressing our most profound challenges until there is supermajority support for doing so. We can see the toll of these constraints by looking at the problem of economic inequality. As it has swelled in the United States to a degree not seen in any comparable nation, intergenerational mobility—the ability of young people to move up the economic ladder to achieve a social and financial status better than that of their parents, which was once the source of America's greatest promise and pride—has plummeted below that of all peer nations, with the possible exception of the United Kingdom. Many thinkers seek to explain this divergence by citing a uniquely individualistic culture. We have all heard those claims, perhaps even floated them ourselves.

But two of the country's most distinguished comparative political scientists, Alfred Stepan and Juan J. Linz, recently approached the puzzle of U.S. singularity in another way: they compared the number of stumbling blocks that advanced industrial democracies put in the way of their citizens' ability to achieve their collective will through the legislative process. Calling these inbuilt "majority constraining" obstacles "veto players," the two scholars found a striking correlation: the nations with the fewest veto players have the least inequality, and those with the most veto players have the greatest inequality. Only the United States has four such veto players. All four were specified in the slavery-defending founders' Constitution: absolute veto power for the Senate, for the House, and for the president (if not outvoted by a two-thirds majority), and a Constitution that cannot be altered without the agreement of two-thirds of the states after Congress. Other features of the U.S. system further obstruct majority rule, including a winner-take-all Electoral College that encourages a two-party system; the Tenth Amendment, which steers power toward the states; and a system of representation in the unusually potent Senate that violates the principle of "one person, one vote" to a degree not seen anywhere else. Owing to such mechanisms, Stepan and Linz note, even in the late 1960s, "the heyday of income *equality* in the United States, no other country in the set [of long-standing democracies] was as unequal as America, and most were substantially more equal." As arresting, even the most equal U.S. state is less equal than any comparable country. What makes the U.S. system "exceptional," sadly, is the number of built-in vetoes to constrain the majority.[70]

To this already singularly restrictive system the cadre seeks to add still more veto points. In the dream vision of the apparatus Charles Koch has funded to carry out Buchanan's call for constitutional revolution, it would be all but impossible for government to respond to the will of the majority unless the very wealthiest Americans agree fully with every measure.[71] The project has multiple prongs.

One is a vast legal shift, also anchored at GMU; it illuminates how quietly executed changes in legal rules can bind citizens as never before. In 2015, the *New York Times* headlined an investigative report, "Arbitration Everywhere, Stacking the Deck of Justice." The journalists' intensive research revealed "a far-reaching power play by American corporations" to include in the extensive fine print of applications for, say, employment, credit cards, cell phone service, medical practices, or long-term care, language to which exhausted and unwitting consumers routinely agree without reading. That language prevents the signers from participating in class action lawsuits over corporate malpractice and compels them to accept mandatory arbitration in a system in which the corporations in question write the rules and choose the decision-makers. That is: the contracts take away citizens' constitutional right to sue in court, proclaiming their signatures as consent.[72]

"This is among the most profound shifts in our legal history," warns a Reagan-appointed federal judge. His words bear slow reading: "Ominously, business has a good chance of opting out of the legal system altogether and misbehaving without reproach." A subsequent headline noted that it amounts to a "Privatization of the Justice System."[73]

In their bid for constitutional revolution by combined increments, the operatives of the apparatus tell themselves and those in their listening audience that they are restoring the founders' vision. Some even call themselves "Madisonians."[74]

That, too, is misinformation. Rather, the cadre is promoting a view of the Constitution that comes from a unique era of U.S. history: the period after the defeat of Reconstruction and leading up to the Great Depression. Buchanan acknowledged as much in the book that built his career, when he and coauthor Gordon Tullock said that the nation's decision-making rules were closer to "the 'ideal' in 1900 than in 1960."[75] The year 1900 was the age of both *Lochner v. New York* and *Plessy v. Ferguson*—decisions remembered today because they blocked majority desire for meaningful employment reform, in the one case, and allowed state-legislated racial oppression, in the other. Both decisions twisted the Fourteenth Amendment to serve the already privileged rather than the embattled citizens whose rights the amendment was designed to protect.

In short, Buchanan's desired constitutional order enabled an era of unmatched corporate dominance, in which elites North and South reunited in a shared disdain for the political participation of the great mass of the citizenry. His view of the Constitution allowed mass disenfranchisement in the South, suppression of working-class voting in the North and the West, treatment of workers that was odious enough to set off veritable rolling civil wars between capital and labor, ruin of the environment in community after community, and more. The heyday of what millions of contemporaries dubbed a "plutocracy," it was a time that saw, in the words of the legal scholar Barry Friedman, "a colossal loss of faith in the efficacy of law" as citizens concluded that judges always and unfailingly took the bosses' side. Not coincidentally, it was also a time that, the journalist Ida M. Tarbell wrote, "dripped with blood."[76]

Had Buchanan's ideal system of 1900 endured at the national level in the Great Depression, the United States might well have experienced a revolution from the right or the left, instead of pulling off the achievement of being the sole liberal democracy to survive the global catastrophe. That feat was made possible by an emergent understanding of the Constitution that put some constraints on property rights in the name of freedom for all and collective self-government in the age of the large corporation.[77]

There is another, biting irony to note: the goal of this cause is not, in the end, to shrink big government, as its rhetoric implies. Quite the contrary: the interpretation of the Constitution the cadre seeks to impose would give federal courts vast new powers to strike down measures desired by voters and passed by their duly elected representatives at all levels—and would require greatly expanded police powers to control the resultant popular anger. An omen: after years of criticizing "judicial activism" by the Supreme Court for greater equity, Koch grantees are now making, as one

Cato publication puts it, *the Case for an Activist Judiciary* to secure economic liberty.[78]

To advance their constitutional revolution, the donor network has pumped hitherto unheard-of sums into state judicial races. While media attention has focused on the impact of *Citizens United* on the presidential and congressional races, the opening of the spigots in state judicial races may prove more consequential over the decades ahead as corporate donors invest in those they believe will interpret the Constitution and the laws in their favor. The Republican majorities that are rushing through "radical reform" know that citizens of their states are likely to turn to the only branch of government left that might blunt the blows. That is why the large donors have invested so heavily in judicial races: to elect judges who will allow the revolution to go forward. One North Carolina insider summarized the danger bluntly: "Lose the courts, lose the war."[79]

At this writing, though, the flagship success of the constitutional wing of the cause was Chief Justice John Roberts's decision in the Affordable Care Act case, *National Federation of Independent Business v. Sebelius*. While some on the right excoriated Roberts for having upheld the ACA, smart court watchers noted not the verdict but what Roberts said about the Commerce Clause.

Some context: In 1937, when the Supreme Court upheld a minimum wage law for the first time and then the Wagner Act, too, signaling its acceptance of the New Deal, it did so by agreeing with government attorneys that the Commerce Clause of Article I of the Constitution gives Congress the ability to regulate interstate trade. Under the rubric of regulating interstate trade, the federal government then dramatically increased its oversight of what used to be considered strictly private or state matters. But in the Affordable Care Act case, Roberts, who in his first year on the bench did more to limit the reach of *Brown v. Board of Education* than any previous justice, commented that "the Commerce Clause is not a general license to regulate an individual from cradle to grave" (a proposition no one has suggested). Justice Ruth Bader Ginsburg, in her opinion, rightly picked up on that surprising assertion, calling the chief justice's claim "stunningly retrogressive." But as court watcher Jeffrey Toobin notes, "Roberts' narrow conception of the Commerce Clause is now the law of the land"—and an invitation to legal challenges to other federal legislation and programs.[80]

A Stanford law professor dubbed Roberts's ruling "a loaded gun."[81] Faculty at the George Mason School of Law, now aptly named after Antonin Scalia, are urging the court to fire it by going back to its pre-1937 jurisprudence, when the justices routinely struck down government action to advance popular economic security or social justice goals.[82]

As the push for aggressive judicial activism on behalf of economic liberty illustrates, for all the small-government rhetoric, the cadre actually wants a very strong government—but a government that acts only in a way they deem appropriate. It wants our democracy to be curbed as Chile's was, with locks and bolts on what the majority can do. Three additional battlefronts illuminate this truth, highlighting the stark restructuring of power under way.

One is a power grab by affiliated state legislators reaching down to deny municipal governments the right to make their own policies on matters hitherto within their purview, not least local election rules. Pushed by State Policy Network affiliates and guided by ALEC-affiliated legislators, GOP-controlled states have been passing what are called preemption laws that deny localities the right to adopt policies that depart from the model being imposed by the network-dominated state legislatures.[83]

Typically, the GOP state governments are preventing city and suburban governments from enacting measures to raise local minimum wages, protect the environment, or enact antidiscrimination measures that would protect LGBTQ citizens. In Texas, for example, the City of Dallas lost the autonomy to discourage local retailers from using plastic bags, because, its people were told, it ran counter to "the Texas model" of "low taxes, limited government and free markets."[84]

But the pattern now emerging is not a paradox after all: the cause understands that, as in the 1950s, corporate and conservative interests can make their will felt most easily in state governments—and are more likely to be challenged successfully by the citizenry at the federal and local levels—partly because state affairs are less well monitored by the people and the press.[85] Tractability was thus state officials' prime qualification for the cadre's plans. Virtually every state government, according to a recent study by the nonpartisan Center for Public Integrity, kowtows to business and the wealthy, underrepresents citizens of lesser means, lacks transparency, and does a poor job of enforcing ethics laws. The promotion of states' rights is not an atavistic racial reflex for the insiders, that is to say, but a cold-eyed way to secure minority rule.[86]

If the cadre has its way, in fact, and its allied legislators continue to comply, a nation that stands at 138th of 172 democracies in the world in voter turnout will have even fewer people participating in the political process.[87] After America elected its first black president, operatives throughout the apparatus and their allied officeholders systematically kindled the irrational conviction that Barack Obama had won through massive voter "fraud," and that, unless a battery of new laws prevented it, such fraud would be used to "steal" more elections. This was the cadre at its most cynical. But so avidly has this big lie been spread that nearly half of registered voters, and even federal judges and Supreme Court justices, came to believe that fraud was a big problem—and cases have been decided on those fallacious assumptions.[88]

With fewer people voting, everything will be so much easier to achieve. In the two years after Republican candidates swept the 2010 midterm elections, ALEC-backed legislators in forty-one states introduced more than 180 bills to restrict who could vote and how. The measures would most reduce the political influence of low-income voters and young people, who had been inclining leftward. America had not witnessed such a burst of limits on voting rights since the calculated mass disenfranchisement instituted by southern states a century ago.[89] But now the effort was national, not only regional, and before long it was affecting outcomes.[90]

A related strategy further distorts political representation to advance the property rights supremacist project. One part of this initiative was the most audacious gerrymander in U.S. history, with the purpose of ensuring systematic underrepresentation of Americans viewed as troublesome by the cause and overrepresentation of the more manageable—while lining up the supermajority of reliably controlled states needed to hold a constitutional convention. Journalists—in particular, Jane Mayer and David Daley—have done an excellent job of exposing the evil genius of the 2010 midterm elections campaign plan called the Redistricting Majority Project, or REDMAP. It was a cunning project to amass state-level power to transform the nation by using the decennial redistricting process to sharply boost the power of Republicans, even where majorities backed Democrats, and to pull the Republican Party to the right of its own voters in the process.[91]

Understandably, many saw the power grab in purely partisan terms, but it was much more. The breathtaking import is conveyed well by *Salon* editor in chief David Daley: "Without the protection of a fairly drawn district, the citizen is a pawn of billionaires who use the map of the country" to get what they want. And the game was a long one, all but invisible to those it was locking out. Daley points out that the GOP is an election away "from achieving an unimaginable goal in a country that sees itself as a beacon of democracy: a veto-proof supermajority operating without majority support."[92] The ever strategic Koch grantee Grover Norquist equates the cause's expanding chokehold over the states with a Roman *pilum*—a spear powerful enough to penetrate any shield, and barbed, so it "could not be pulled out."[93]

A final example of the new bullying we can expect from the plan to enchain democracy also harks back to the midcentury South, with its inquisition-minded state and private bodies to investigate and intimidate dissenters. In 2015, the journalist Kenneth Vogel revealed that the Koch network had "quietly built a secretive operation that conducts political surveillance and intelligence gathering on its liberal opponents, viewing it as a key strategic tool in its efforts to reshape American public life."[94] A case in point: when Jane Mayer began to expose the operations of the Koch brothers and their network, they dispatched private investigators in a fruitless quest to find dirt with which to discredit her and tried to convince her employer to fire her. Anyone who tries to expose what this cause is up to thus must ask herself: Will I become the target of a similar scurrilous attack? Wouldn't it be wiser to keep quiet? The cadre even has an economics euphemism for harassment designed to intimidate—they call it "upping the transaction costs for the other side."[95]

"Democracy," the towering African American historian John Hope Franklin observed in the midst of World War II, "is essentially an act of faith."[96] When that faith is willfully exterminated, we should not be surprised that we reap the whirlwind. The public choice way of thinking, one sage critic warned at the time James Buchanan was awarded the Nobel Prize in Economic Sciences, is not simply "descriptively inaccurate"—indeed, "a terrible caricature" of how the political process works. It also constitutes an insidious attack on the very "norm of public spiritedness" so crucial to shaping good government policy and ethical conduct in civic life. That is to say, public choice theory was wrong in its explanations, and would be toxic if believed by the public or its representatives. We have seen the truth of that prediction.[97]

The United States is now at one of those historic forks in the road whose outcome will prove as fateful as those of the 1860s, the 1930s, and the 1960s. To value liberty for the wealthy minority above all else and enshrine it in the nation's governing rules, as Calhoun and Buchanan both called for and the Koch network is achieving, play by play, is to consent to an oligarchy in all but the outer husk of representative form.[98]

The question this stealth plan presents Americans with is, at one level, quite simple: Do we want to live in a cosmetically updated version of midcentury Virginia, in a country that so elevates property rights as to paralyze the use of government for democratically determined goals and needs? That extinguishes "the political we"?

For what is the substance of James Buchanan's and Charles Koch's idea of liberty but Harry Byrd's Virginia, the state subjected to the "most thorough control by an oligarchy," with tools now to be grafted upon the nation as a whole? Byrd's state-mandated racial oppression would go; the cause would not publicly advocate for that. But nearly all else about the political economy of midcentury Virginia enacts their dream: the uncontested sway of the wealthiest citizens; the use of right-to-work laws and other ploys to keep working people powerless; the ability to fire dissenting public employees at will, targeting educators in particular; the use of voting-rights restrictions to keep those unlikely to agree with the elite from the polls; the deployment of states' rights to deter the federal government from promoting equal treatment; the hostility to public education; the regressive tax system; the opposition to Social Security and Medicare; and the parsimonious response to public needs of all kinds—not just the decent schools sought by aspiring teenagers like Barbara Rose Johns and John Stokes but also the care and shelter of the elderly poor, the mentally ill, and others in whose names

Dr. Louise Wensel ran her 1959 Senate campaign against Old Harry. Her core criticism, after all, was that he worshipped "the golden calf": that he prized the accumulation of private wealth over the Golden Rule and democracy, "no matter what the cost."

The libertarian cause, from the time it first attracted wider support during the southern schools crisis, was never really about freedom as most people would define it. It was about the promotion of crippling division among the people so as to end any interference with what those who held vast power over others believed should be their prerogatives. Its leaders had no scruples about enlisting white supremacy to achieve capital supremacy. And today, knowing that the majority does not share their goals and would stop them if they understood the endgame, the team of paid operatives seeks to win by stealth. Now, as then, the leaders seek Calhoun-style liberty for the few—the liberty to concentrate vast wealth, so as to deny elementary fairness and freedom to the many.

Is this the country we want to live in and bequeath to our children and future generations? That is the real public choice. If we delay much longer, those who are imposing their stark utopia will choose for us. One of them has announced flatly: "America will soon make a decision about its future. It will be a permanent decision. There will be no going back." As we consider the future of our democracy in light of all that has happened already, we may take heed of a Koch maxim: "Playing it safe is slow suicide."[99]

ACKNOWLEDGMENTS

They say that a liberal arts education prepares one for lifelong learning, which is true. But less often acknowledged is how your earlier teachers prime you for both. I wish all children could experience the quality of education I enjoyed in some of America's great suburban public schools. I am deeply grateful for the mentors I found there, foremost among them Franklin J. Wiener. After giving up a lucrative career in advertising to pursue his true vocation of teaching high school English, Mr. Wiener earned the love of generations of grateful students. In the belief that no starting teacher should have to work two jobs to pay the bills, he also supported his colleagues through his union activism. For years, I had over my desk a mounted newspaper photo of him walking a picket line with his signature pipe and a sign that read TEACHERS PAY TAXES, TOO. I lost the photo in a move, but his devotion to young people and belief in us changed my life.

I also had some amazing lucky breaks in the informal teachers to whom this research led me, and it is to them, above all, that the book is dedicated. When I first became interested in the Prince Edward County story, several people familiar with it said I must talk with Ed Peeples. An e-mail inquiry proved the start of a lasting friendship. As Ed welcomed me into his Richmond attic archive and he and his kind wife, Karen, put me up in their home, he taught me about life in Harry Byrd's Virginia.

Ed's friend James H. Hershman Jr. had never met me when I first contacted him after learning of James Buchanan from a footnote in his work. Yet Jim instantly understood the stakes of the research I was pursuing and took me under his wing, becoming my personal guide through the thickets of Virginia history, as well as a dear friend. His knowledge of the state's past is encyclopedic, his analyses unfailingly illuminating, and his generosity as a scholar absolutely without peer. I have whole files of material from him, including scores of primary sources I would not otherwise have found, along with his own astute capsule histories on various matters. In short, I could never have written this book in this way had I not had the good fortune to be included on the ever lengthening list of researchers whom Jim has assisted over the years. I like to think he had special enthusiasm for this project because it tracked the stages of his own life in Virginia so closely, but either way, I am grateful beyond words that he also read the entire manuscript, saving me from errors while providing superb advice on interpretive matters large and small. If I still managed to get anything wrong, it is owing to my effort to simplify matters of byzantine legal and political complexity for a general readership, not to any want of careful guidance on his part.

Another teacher I wish to thank is S. M. Amadae, whose groundbreaking first book, *Rationalizing Capitalist Democracy,* alerted me to the existence of the Buchanan House Archives. When I called her to ask how she gained access, not only did she generously share her experience with research in this unusual setting, but she also allayed my fear that I might somehow be imagining things, because no one else had discovered the plan I was seeing take shape in the sources—and on the floor of the North Carolina General Assembly after 2010. There was a long pause on the other end of the line; then she said, "You have to realize that most of the critics of neoliberalism never read the theory." That observation was a turning point; it made me determined to keep following the trail I was on to its end, wherever it led. The conversation also proved the start of another enlightening and sustaining friendship. No one I have read or met understands Buchanan's philosophy of political economy as astutely as Amadae does; in her most recent book, *Prisoners of Reason,* she demonstrates the predatory will to power at the level of theory that I have shown in its practical application.

My deepest gratitude, though, is to my agent, Susan Rabiner, the most exacting teacher I have ever had and the dream coach for this project. From our very first conversation, Susan understood like no one else the stakes of this story, and she worked far beyond the call of duty to help realize its potential. She was, I thought more than once, the Anne Sullivan to my Helen Keller, patiently yet firmly teaching me how to speak to be understood outside my academic world. She has been the most brilliant interlocutor, supportive coach, and talented advocate a writer could dream of—and she has made the work fun. My editor, Wendy Wolf, showed tremendous faith in this project from the outset, and her reading of the manuscript taught me much about storytelling for a general readership. Will Palmer proved a peerless copy editor; his was the most meticulous and helpful review my work has ever enjoyed. I also thank Georgia Bodnar and Megan Gerrity at Viking for their expert work. Pamela Haag improved the book immensely with her incisive freelance editing. Her hard queries and helpful suggestions brought it to a new level.

I could never have persuaded Rabiner and Wolf to take me on had it not been for teachers closer to home: the members of my writing group. Laura Edwards, Jacquelyn Dowd Hall, and Lisa Levenstein are a dream team of relevant historical expertise, as well as some of the smartest critics and most loyal friends a writer could hope for. For generously taking time from their own summers to read the entire penultimate manuscript and send me comments and suggestions that vastly improved it, I am also deeply grateful to another dream team of scholars: Alice Kessler-Harris, who believed in and supported this project and its author from the very beginning; Jason Brent, whose grasp of the varied traditions of economic thought saved me from missteps and sharpened the overall analysis; Joseph A. McCartin, whose knowledge of public sector workers and their history is unrivaled; and Sonya Amadae, whose critical command of the relevant body of theory is unrivaled and who took time from her research appointment in Finland to help me get it right. I also want to thank two leading Latin Americanists, John French and Jeffrey Rubin, for reading the chapter on Chile and offering keen insights. Thanks, too, to my colleagues in the Labor and Working-Class History Association, from whom I have learned much about the substance and stakes of the history recounted in this book.

Lisa Levenstein deserves a paragraph all her own for additional brilliant editing at the eleventh hour. I will never forget her generosity over the Christmas and New Year's break, carrying out heroic and inspired surgery to shorten and sharpen each chapter, sometimes more than once. Possessed of an amazing editorial mind, she is a singular friend I am incredibly lucky to have.

I am profoundly grateful to the other distinguished historians who believed in this work enough to write letters in support of my applications for fellowship support: Linda Gordon, Linda Kerber, Alice Kessler-Harris, Charles Payne, Michael Sherry, and Daniel T. Rodgers. And thank you to these institutions for heeding those letters and underwriting the research and writing: the American Council of Learned Societies, the National Endowment for the Humanities, the National Humanities Center, and the Northwestern University Institute for Policy Research.

I would also like to thank some people I have never met but have learned from immensely: the dedicated journalists who have been covering the impact of big money on American politics. Many are named in the notes but all merit collective recognition here because I could never have pieced together the last two decades of this book's story without their intrepid investigations.

One of the many joys of teaching is the two-way flow of information and insight. My graduate students have enriched my understanding of many topics touched on in this book; I thank them for sustaining me with the inspiration of their own research and fellowship. So, too, do I appreciate the many undergraduate students whom I have had the pleasure of learning from in the course of writing this book. I also want to thank the outstanding research assistants who helped at various stages of this project, first at Northwestern and later at Duke: Anthony Abata, Eladio Bobadilla, Jon Free, Alexander Gourse, Natalie Jean Marine-Street, Parvathi Santhosh-Kumar, Hunter Thompson, Brad Wood, and Martin Zacharia.

Many other colleagues and friends shared sources, ideas, and encouragement on various parts of this work, among them Ed Balleisen, Martha Biondi, Jack Boger, Christopher Bonastia, Eileen Boris, Andy Burstein, Margot Canady, Eduardo Caneda, Patrick Conway, Saul Cornell, Nancy Cott, Joseph Crespino, Emma Edmunds, Lane Fenrich, Melissa Fisher, Mary Foley, Nancy Fraser, Estelle Freedman, Paul Gaston, Jonathon Glassman, Thavolia Glymph, Sally Greene, Brian Grogan, Roger Horowitz, Nancy Isenberg, Jennifer Klein, Bob Korstad, Kevin Kruse, Matt Lassiter,

Jules Law, Kelley Lawton, Brian Lee, Ariane Leendertz, Andrew Lewis, Nelson Lichtenstein, Mary Anne McAlonan, Joseph A. McCartin, Laura McEnaney, Alan McGinty, Jennifer Mittelstadt, Julie Mooney, Bethany Moreton, Alice O'Connor, Julia Ott, Joseph J. Persky, Christopher Phelps, Kim Phillips-Fein, Jedediah Purdy, Bernhard Rieger, Kyle Schaefer, Edward H. Sebesta, David Steigerwald, David Stein, Wolfgang Streeck, Shelton Stromquist, Kerry Taylor, Heather Thompson, Eckard Vance Toy (and his daughter Kelly Dittmar, for reaching out to me after his death and sending me valuable materials from his personal research collection on the far right), Kara Turner, Nick Unger, Jean-Christian Vinel, Daniel Williams, Peter H. Wood, Celeste Wroblewski, and Jack Wuest. If I have neglected to mention anyone, please know it is only from exhaustion!

As always, I am indebted to the many archivists and librarians whose knowledge, professionalism, and openhandedness assisted my research (though I will refrain from naming any, lest it cause some of them trouble). So, too, I appreciate the invitations to speak on aspects of this project and the hosts and audiences who helped sharpen the ideas.

Lastly, but most importantly, I am grateful to the many beloved friends (you know who you are, and I know how blessed I am to have you) and the family members who sustained my spirits throughout this work: Mary Anne, Ray, and Ryan McAlonon; David and Jacquie MacLean; Eli, Eve, and Les Orenstein; Celeste Wroblewski; and Ann Golden. Mary Anne arrived like a miracle in the final month, each day of which confirmed my belief that she is the world's best sister. In a category all his own is Bruce Orenstein, my first reader and my soul mate, without whose love, vision, everyday help, sage advice, and sense of humor I could never have done this. Thank you all, so much.

NOTES

EPIGRAPH

1. Pierre Lemieux, "The Public Choice Revolution," *Regulation*, Fall 2004, 29. Lemieux was writing for one Koch-funded organization, the Cato Institute, as a fellow of another, the Independent Institute.

INTRODUCTION: A QUIET DEAL IN DIXIE

1. "Working Papers for Internal Discussion Only" (December 1956), record group 2/1/2.634, box 9, Office of the President, Papers of the President of the University of Virginia, Office Administrative Files, Manuscripts Division, Alderman Library, University of Virginia. The best introduction to Darden's thought is Guy Friddell, *Colgate Darden: Conversations with Guy Friddell* (Charlottesville: University Press of Virginia, 1978). See chapters 2 and 3 for the full story of the center's founding.
2. "Working Papers for Internal Discussion Only."
3. Trip Gabriel, "Teachers Wonder, Why the Heapings of Scorn?" *New York Times*, March 3, 2011, A1, 18.
4. See, for example, Andrew Burstein and Nancy Isenberg, "GOP's Anti-School Insanity: How Scott Walker and Bobby Jindal Declared War on Education," *Salon*, February 9, 2015; Richard Fausset, "Ideology Seen as Factor in Closings at University," *New York Times*, February 20, 2015; and the superb documentary *Starving the Beast*, directed by Steve Mims, www.starvingthebeast.net.
5. Ari Berman, *Give Us the Ballot: The Modern Struggle for Voting Rights in America* (New York: Farrar, Straus and Giroux, 2015), 260, 263.
6. Elizabeth Koh, "Justice Clarence Thomas: 'We Are Destroying Our Institutions,'" *News & Observer*, October 27, 2016, 1.
7. William Cronon, "Who's Really Behind Recent Republican Legislation in Wisconsin and Elsewhere? (Hint: It Didn't Start Here)," *Scholar as Citizen* (blog), March 15, 2011, http://scholarcitizen.williamcronon.net/tag/wpri. The Wisconsin Republican Party became so nervous that it demanded his e-mails: David Walsh, "GOP Files FOIA Request for UW Madison Professor William Cronon's Emails," History News Network, March 25, 2011, http://historynewsnetwork.org/article/137911.
8. Jane Mayer, "Covert Operations: The Billionaire Brothers Who Are Waging a War Against Obama," *The New Yorker*, August 30, 2010; and, more recently, Jane Mayer, *Dark Money: The Hidden History of the Billionaires Behind the Rise of the Radical Right* (New York: Doubleday, 2016). See also Lee Fang, *The Machine: A Field Guide to the Resurgent Right* (New York: New Press, 2013); Kenneth P. Vogel, *Big Money: 2.5 Billion Dollars, One Suspicious Vehicle, and a Pimp—On the Trail of the Ultra-Rich Hijacking American Politics* (New York: Public Affairs, 2014), and Daniel Schulman, *Sons of Wichita: How the Koch Brothers*

Became America's Most Powerful and Private Dynasty (New York: Grand Central Publishing, 2014).

9. Numerous journalists pointed to Rand and/or Friedman. Among scholarly accounts that focus on Hayek and Friedman, see, for example, the astute work of Philip Mirowski, *Never Let a Serious Crisis Go to Waste: How Neoliberalism Survived the Financial Meltdown* (New York: Verso, 2013). A brilliant historian of neoliberal thought, Mirowski is in plentiful company in paying only passing attention to Buchanan, though he says more than most. The one notable exception is S. M. Amadae, *Prisoners of Reason: Game Theory and Neoliberal Political Economy* (New York: Cambridge University Press, 2016). Her luminous explication of Buchanan's thought reveals the falsity of his claim of being a classical liberal and the chilling will to power driving his intellectual program.
10. James H. Hershman Jr., "Massive Resistance Meets Its Match: The Emergence of a Pro-Public School Majority," in *The Moderates' Dilemma: Massive Resistance to School Desegregation in Virginia*, ed. Matthew D. Lassiter and Andrew B. Lewis (Charlottesville: University of Virginia Press, 1998), 222n49; Alfred Stepan, "State Power and the Strength of Civil Society in the Southern Cone of Latin America," in *Bringing the State Back In*, ed. Peter B. Evans, et al. (Cambridge, UK: Cambridge University Press, 1985), 341n13.
11. I learned of the archive from the pathbreaking work of S. M. Amadae, *Rationalizing Capitalist Democracy: The Cold War Origins of Rational Choice Liberalism* (Chicago: University of Chicago Press, 2003), whose emphasis here was on his early involvement with the RAND Corporation. Her work has been a beacon to me.
12. George Zornick, "Vice President Mike Pence Would Be a Dream for the Koch Brothers," *The Nation*, July 14, 2016. To take but one index of his reliability, Pence was one of only four governors awarded a grade of A by the Cato Institute; *Fiscal Policy Report Card on America's Governors* (Washington, DC: Cato Institute, 2014), 2–3, https://object.cato.org/sites/cato.org/files/pubs/pdf/fprc-on-americas-governors_1.pdf.
13. Charles G. Koch, *Creating a Science of Liberty* (Fairfax, VA: Institute for Humane Studies, 1997). The occasion was a speech to a Fellows Research Colloquium addressed also by James Buchanan in January 1997 at GMU.
14. Richard Austin Smith, "The Fifty-Million-Dollar Man," *Fortune*, November 1957, 177.
15. Thomas Frank identified the spread of this novel understanding of corruption on the right in *The Wrecking Crew: How Conservatives Ruined Government, Enriched Themselves, and Beggared the Nation* (New York: Metropolitan Books, 2008), and brilliantly conveyed the scale of the damage prior to 2008, without quite pinpointing the ideas driving it. He discovered a second-generation public choice scholar, Fred S. McChesney, but missed the long lineage that produced him, which began with Buchanan (245–49).
16. "Working Papers for Internal Discussion Only."
17. For the premier treatment of that campaign and its import, see Rick Perlstein, *Before the Storm: Barry Goldwater and the Unmaking of the American Consensus* (New York: Hill & Wang, 2001).
18. Koch, *Creating a Science of Liberty.*
19. For his first invocation of constitutional revolution in print, see James M. Buchanan, "America's Third Century," *Atlantic Economic Journal* 1 (November 1973): 9–12. Scholars and journalists in many nations are now grappling with how numerous democracies have been, in effect, losing sovereignty and responsiveness to voters, and hence popularity. Yet most write in the passive voice, focusing on impact more than sources, and attributing the action to abstract nouns rather than human agents. See, for example, the powerful indictment of "democracy's conceptual unmooring and substantive disembowelment" by political theorist Wendy Brown, *Undoing the Demos: Neoliberalism's Stealth Revolution* (New York: Zone Books, 2015); and the bracing exploration of the fiscal crisis that is undermining the legitimacy of Western democracies by Wolfgang Streeck, *Buying Time: The Delayed Crisis of Democratic Government* (London: Verso, 2014). What no one has

identified with adequate clarity is the individuals and institutions that are intentionally insulating the economy from intervention, in what has become a bipartisan and transnational project. It is beyond the scope of this book, but I anticipate that when others become familiar with Buchanan's ideas and their transnational transmission in the wake of his Nobel Prize, they will gain a better knowledge of where many of the troubling practices came from. See also Stephen Gill and A. Claire Cutler, eds., *New Constitutionalism and World Order* (Cambridge, UK: Cambridge University Press, 2015); also, Jeffrey Rubin and Vivienne Bennett, *Enduring Reform: Progressive Activism and Private Sector Responses in Latin America's Democracies* (Pittsburgh: University of Pittsburgh Press). The Koch-funded Atlas Network now has 457 partner organization members operating in 95 nations, https://www.atlasnetwork.org. For more on the global libertarian network, see Steven Teles and Daniel A. Kenney, "Spreading the Word: The Diffusion of American Conservatism in Europe and Beyond," in *Growing Apart? America and Europe in the Twenty-First Century*, ed. Jeffrey Kopstein and Sven Steinmo (Cambridge, UK: Cambridge University Press, 2008), 136–69.

20. James M. Buchanan, "Constitutions, Politics, and Markets," draft prepared for presentation, Porto Allegre, Brazil, April 1993, Buchanan House Archives.
21. For a sense of how the addition worked, see Grover G. Norquist, *Leave Us Alone: Getting the Government's Hands Off Our Money, Our Guns, and Our Lives* (New York: HarperCollins, 2008).
22. Already in the late 1980s, the Cato Institute was showing nervousness about the potential impact on alliance building of the long history of libertarian "denunciations of religion, specifically targeting Christianity as deleterious to individual liberty," and so hired a fellow who could make the case in terms evangelicals could accept; Ben Hart, "When Government Replaces God," *Wall Street Journal*, December 30, 1988, A5. Because the religious right has been the subject of its own extensive literature and because it had virtually no connection to Buchanan's project until the organizations funded by Charles Koch began looking for partners that could help them gather the numbers they needed to prevail, I say little about this vast part of the modern American right. But for the canny ideological affinity of white evangelical Protestant political entrepreneurs and libertarian economics, see, for example, Michael Lienesch, *Redeeming America: Piety and Politics in the New Christian Right* (Chapel Hill: University of North Carolina Press, 1993), 94–138; Linda Kintz, *Between Jesus and the Market: The Emotions That Matter in Right-Wing America* (Durham, NC: Duke University Press, 1997); Bethany E. Moreton, *To Serve God and Wal-Mart: The Making of Christian Free Enterprise* (Cambridge, MA: Harvard University Press, 2009). Feminist scholars such as Moreton have long pointed out that when government sheds functions, women lose twice: as public sector workers who lose good jobs and as unpaid workers in the home, on whose shoulders the additional burdens tend to fall.
23. For an early alert, see Jacob M. Schlesinger, "As Opponents of 'Corporate Welfare' Mobilize on Left and Right, Business Has Reason to Worry," *Wall Street Journal*, December 18, 1996, A22.
24. Arlen Specter, *Life Among the Cannibals: A Political Career, a Tea Party Uprising, and the End of Governing as We Know It* (New York: Thomas Dunne, 2012); Howard Berkes, "GOP-on-GOP Attacks Leave Orrin Hatch Fighting Mad," National Public Radio, April 12, 2012, www.npr.org/sections/itsallpolitics/2012/04/12/150506733/tea-party-again-targets-a-utah-gop-senator-and-orrin-hatch-is-fighting-mad; Alan Rappeport and Matt Flegenheimer, "John Boehner Describes Ted Cruz as 'Lucifer in the Flesh,'" *First Draft* (blog), *New York Times*, April 28, 2016.
25. See, for example, the illuminating work of Thomas E. Mann and Norman Ornstein, *It's Even Worse than It Looks: How the American Constitutional System Collided with the New Politics of Extremism* (New York: Basic Books, 2012); Geoffrey Kabaservice, *Rule and Ruin: The Downfall of Moderation and the Destruction of the Republican Party, from Eisenhower to the Tea Party* (New York: Oxford University Press, 2012); David Daley, *Ratf**ked: The True Story Behind the Secret Plan to Steal America's Democracy* (New York: Liveright,

2016); and E. J. Dionne Jr., *Why the Right Went Wrong: Conservatism—From Goldwater to Trump* (New York: Simon & Schuster, 2016).

26. For a very readable early sounding of the alarm about privatization, without the Buchanan angle but with a good sense of the effects, see Si Kahn and Elizabeth Minnich, *The Fox in the Henhouse: How Privatization Threatens Democracy* (San Francisco: Berrett-Koehler, 2005).
27. Mark Holden, the head of Koch Industries' government and public affairs operation, told an invitation-only audience of billionaire and multimillionaire donors that those who are worried about what is happening to American politics are "afraid of us," but ineffectual in stopping the assembled donors and operatives. "We're close to winning. I don't know how close, but we should be," he told them, because "they [the critics] don't have the real path"; Kenneth P. Vogel, "The Koch Intelligence Agency," *Politico*, November 18, 2015, www.politico.com/story/2015/11/the-koch-brothers-intelligence-agency-215943#ixzz47cZ8Bqci.
28. Jeb Bush and Clint Bolick, *Immigration Wars: Forging an American Solution* (New York: Threshold Editions, 2013). Bolick, a libertarian attorney who cofounded the Koch-funded Institute for Justice to litigate for the restoration of the pre–New Deal Constitution, helped the Cato Institute's Roger Pilon get Clarence Thomas nominated to and approved for the U.S. Supreme Court, and derailed the nomination of law professor Lani Guinier to head the Civil Rights Division of the Department of Justice. See Jane Mayer and Jill Abramson, *Strange Justice: The Selling of Clarence Thomas* (New York: Houghton Mifflin, 1994), quotes on 179–80, 186, 198; Nina J. Easton, *Gang of Five: Leaders at the Center of the Conservative Crusade* (New York: Simon & Schuster, 2000), 89–110, 260–65; Clint Bolick, "Clinton's Quota Queens," *Wall Street Journal*, April 30, 1993, A1.
29. For a masterful exposition of this, see Ira Katznelson, *Fear Itself: The New Deal and the Origins of Our Time* (New York: Liveright, 2013). For stark contrast, see the Buchanan-influenced revisionist quest by a popular libertarian financial reporter to prove that FDR was acting in his personal self-interest, a skewed case that neglects not only the global context but also the mass popular demand for a new political economy; Amity Shlaes, *The Forgotten Man: A New History of the Great Depression* (New York: Harper, 2007). For the signal achievements of active government, see Jacob S. Hacker and Paul Pierson, *American Amnesia: How the War on Government Led Us to Forget What Made America Prosper* (New York: Simon & Schuster, 2016). For a superb accounting of the bipartisan move away from Keynesianism in the 1970s, see Judith Stein, *Pivotal Decade: How the United States Traded Factories for Finance in the Seventies* (New Haven, CT: Yale University Press, 2010).
30. The historical literature on Friedman and Hayek is vast, yet it typically pays far less, if any, attention to Buchanan. The works I have learned most from include Philip Mirowski and Dieter Plehwe, eds., *The Road from Mont Pelerin: The Making of the Neoliberal Thought Collective* (Cambridge, MA: Harvard University Press, 2009); Angus Burgin, *The Great Persuasion: Reinventing Free Markets Since the Depression* (Cambridge, MA: Harvard University Press, 2012); Daniel Stedman Jones, *Masters of the Universe: Hayek, Friedman, and the Birth of Neoliberal Economics* (Princeton, NJ: Princeton University Press, 2012); and Daniel T. Rodgers, *Age of Fracture* (Cambridge, MA: Harvard University Press, 2011).
31. For an early incisive critique of how Buchanan's ideas "threaten to become self-fulfilling," in that, by discrediting the aspirational behavioral norm of public spirit, "our society would look bleaker and our lives as individuals would be more impoverished," see Steven Kelman, "'Public Choice' and Public Spirit," *The Public Interest* 87 (March 1987): 80–94. In the light of the 2016 election, Kelman's analysis reads like prophecy.
32. William P. Carney, "Madrid Rounds Up Suspected Rebels," *New York Times*, October 16, 1936, 2.
33. On the "Brown Scare," see Leo Ribuffo, *The Old Christian Right: The Protestant Far Right from the Depression to the Cold War* (Philadelphia, PA: Temple University Press), 178–224. The literature on the Red Scare is voluminous.
34. Matt Kibbe, *Hostile Takeover: Resisting Centralized Government's Stranglehold on America* (New York: HarperCollins, 2012), 342.

35. Theda Skocpol and Alexander Hertel-Fernandez, "The Koch Effect: The Impact of a Cadre-Led Network on American Politics" (paper presented at the Inequality Mini-Conference, Southern Political Science Association, San Juan, Puerto Rico, January 8, 2016), www.scholarsstrategy network.org/sites/default/files/the_koch_effect_for_spsa_w_apps_skocpol_and_hertel -fernandez-corrected_1-4-16_1.pdf, quote on 8. I am grateful to Nancy Cott for alerting me to this paper. "Not a single grassroots Tea Party supporter we encountered argued for privatization of Social Security or Medicare along the lines being pushed by ultra-free-market politicians like Representative Paul Ryan (R-WI) and advocacy groups like FreedomWorks and Americans for Prosperity," Skocpol and coauthor Vanessa Williamson reported in an earlier work, *The Tea Party and the Remaking of Republican Conservatism* (New York: Oxford University Press, 2012), 61.
36. James M. Buchanan, "Saving the Soul of Classical Liberalism," reprinted in *Cato Policy Report*, March/April 2013, after his death, www.scribd.com/document/197800481 /Saving-the-Soul-of-Classical-Liberalism-Cato-Institute-pdf. The same operative who spoke of ginning up hostility in Washington similarly portrays the cause's goals in appealing language to attract the numbers needed to move the unstated antidemocratic agenda; Matt Kibbe, *Don't Hurt People and Don't Take Their Stuff: A Libertarian Manifesto* (New York: William Morrow, 2014).
37. For a recent claim to the Madisonian mantle by a cause insider in the course of encouraging thoroughly un-Madisonian mass right-wing civil disobedience, backed by donor-funded legal defense funds, "to open a new front" in the "war" on the federal government in order to obtain what ordinary democratic politics has blocked, see Charles Murray, *By the People: Rebuilding Liberty Without Permission* (New York: Crown Forum, 2015), quote on 8.

PROLOGUE: THE MARX OF THE MASTER CLASS

1. Richard Hofstadter, *The American Political Tradition and the Men Who Made It* (New York: Random House, 1948), 68.
2. Alexander Tabarrok and Tyler Cowen, "The Public Choice Theory of John C. Calhoun," *Journal of Institutional and Theoretical Economics* 148 (1992): 655, 661, 665.
3. Ibid., 661, 665. For more appreciation from the public choice fold, see Peter H. Aranson, "Calhoun's Constitutional Economics," *Constitutional Political Economy* 2 (1991): 31–52. Cowen and Tabarrok are chaired professors of economics and leaders of George Mason University's Mercatus Center, which has been heavily funded by Charles Koch since at least 1997. Cowen has served as general director of the center since then and was originally a codirector with Koch, who remains on the governing board. "The strategy of Mercatus is to integrate theory and practice," supplying what in today's parlance are called "deliverables" to policy-makers, think tanks, foundations, and media; Tyler Cowen, "Why Does Freedom Wax and Wane: Some Research Questions in Social Change and Big Government," Mercatus Center, GMU, 2000. The piece was reprinted online in 2015.
4. Cowen, "Why Does Freedom Wax and Wane."
5. A venerable publishing house on the right recently republished both in H. Lee Cheek Jr., ed., *John C. Calhoun: Selected Writings and Speeches* (Washington, DC: Regnery, 2003). For a case that "the southern states' rights theory has become the constitutional orthodoxy of the conservative movement," see Michael Lind, *Up from Conservatism: Why the Right Is Wrong for America* (New York: Free Press, 1996), 208–34.
6. Murray N. Rothbard, *Power & Market: Government and the Economy* (Menlo Park, CA: Institute for Humane Studies, 1970), 12–13. Rothbard credits the "devoted interest" of Charles Koch in the acknowledgments, saying that his "dedication to inquiry into the field of liberty is all too rare in the present day." Calhoun's analysis also appeared in the successive Libertarian Party platforms that divide the citizenry into "an entrenched privileged class" that benefits from tax funds and "an exploited class—those who are the net

taxpayers"; Joseph M. Hazlett II, *The Libertarian Party and Other Minor Parties in the United States* (Jefferson, NC: McFarland & Co., 1992), 86.

7. Walter Johnson, *River of Dark Dreams: Slavery and Empire in the Cotton Kingdom* (Cambridge, MA: Belknap Press of Harvard University Press, 2013), 5.
8. Louis Hartz, *The Liberal Tradition in America* (New York: Harcourt, Brace, 1955), 158–59, 163.
9. Hofstadter, *American Political Tradition*, 69–70, 72–76. On Calhoun's resolute antiliberalism, see Minisha Sinha, *The Counter-Revolution of Slavery: Politics and Ideology in Antebellum South Carolina* (Chapel Hill: University of North Carolina Press, 2000).
10. See Jacob S. Hacker and Paul Pierson, *American Amnesia: How the War on Government Led Us to Forget What Made America Prosper* (New York: Simon & Schuster, 2016).
11. David L. Lightner, *Slavery and the Commerce Power: How the Struggle Against the Interstate Slave Trade Led to the Civil War* (New Haven, CT: Yale University Press, 2006), 99–100. On the extensive protections Calhoun considered inadequate, see David Waldstreicher, *Slavery's Constitution, from Revolution to Ratification* (New York: Hill & Wang, 2009), and Paul Finkelman, "The Proslavery Origins of the Electoral College," *Cardozo Law Review* 23 (2002): 1500–1519. Both authors, and many others, have published extensively on these themes.
12. Sinha, *Counter-Revolution of Slavery*, 64, 74, 77.
13. John C. Calhoun to Alexandre Dumas, August 1, 1847, reprinted in *The Friend: A Religious and Literary Journal*, February 26, 1848, and cited in Hofstadter, *American Political Tradition*, 77.
14. Laura F. Edwards, *The People and Their Peace: Legal Culture and the Transformation of Inequality in the Post-Revolutionary South* (Chapel Hill: University of North Carolina Press, 2009), 9, 12, 259, 278; William W. Freehling, *Secessionists at Bay, 1776–1854*, vol. 1 of *The Road to Disunion* (New York: Oxford University Press, 1991), 37.
15. For recognition by seasoned commentators of a kinship between the antebellum southerner and the obstructionism pushed by the post-2010 radicals in Congress, see Sam Tanenhaus, "Original Sin: Why the GOP Is and Will Continue to Be the Party of White People," *New Republic*, February 10, 2013; Bruce Schulman, "Boehner Resurrects the Antebellum South," *Great Debate* (blog), Reuters, January 17, 2013, http://blogs.reuters.com/great-debate/tag/john-c-calhoun; and Stephen Mihm, "Tea Party Tactics Lead Back to Secession," *Bloomberg View*, October 8, 2013, www.bloomberg.com/news/articles/2013-10-08/tea-party-tactics-lead-straight-back-to-secession.
16. Hofstadter, *American Political Tradition*, 68–92. See also the astute analysis on which Hofstadter built his argument, Richard N. Current, "John C. Calhoun, Philosopher of Reaction," *Antioch Review* 3 (1943), especially 225, 227 for quotes.
17. Hofstadter, *American Political Tradition*, 71, 78, 84.
18. Robin L. Einhorn, *American Slavery, American Taxation* (Chicago: University of Chicago Press, 2006), 3, 5, 7–8.
19. Ibid., 7. For the related case that the tradition the right now upholds is that of the Anti-Federalist opponents of the Constitution, not of its authors, see Garry Wills, *A Necessary Evil: A History of American Distrust of Government* (New York: Doubleday, 2000). For how that original alchemy continues to do its work in our own time, relying on assumptions of racial difference to justify inequality of all kinds and refusal of public policy solutions to address it, see Karen E. Fields and Barbara J. Fields, *Racecraft: The Soul of Inequality in American Life* (New York: Verso, 2014). For deeper roots in the tradition of political theory from which James Buchanan drew, see Charles W. Mills, *The Racial Contract* (Ithaca, NY: Cornell University Press, 1997).
20. Waldstreicher, *Slavery's Constitution*. Madison believed that the more slavery existed in a state, the more "aristocratic in fact" it would become, "however democratic in name." "The power lies in a part instead of the whole" in such states, he explained, "in the hands of property, not of numbers"; Lacy Ford Jr., "Inventing the Concurrent Majority: Madison, Calhoun, and the Problem of Majoritarianism in American Political Thought," *Journal of Southern History* 60 (February 1994): 41–42.

21. Current, "John C. Calhoun," 230. Recent important works on slavery and capitalism include Sven Beckert, *Empire of Cotton: A Global History* (New York: Alfred A. Knopf, 2014); Edward E. Baptist, *The Half Has Never Been Told: Slavery and the Making of American Capitalism* (New York: Basic Books, 2014); and Johnson, *River of Dark Dreams*.
22. Hofstadter, *American Political Tradition*, 78–80.
23. Ibid., 80.
24. Calhoun to Dumas, August 1, 1847, 21, 23.
25. Eric Foner, *Free Soil, Free Labor, Free Men: The Ideology of the Republican Party Before the Civil War* (New York: Oxford University Press, 1970).
26. Hofstadter, *American Political Tradition*, 77.
27. William J. Novak, *The People's Welfare: Law and Regulation in Nineteenth-Century America* (Chapel Hill: University of North Carolina Press, 1996); Brian Balogh, *A Government Out of Sight: The Mystery of National Authority in Nineteenth-Century America* (Cambridge, UK: Cambridge University Press, 2009).
28. Ford, "Inventing the Concurrent Majority," 49.
29. For a similar point on mobilizations in the century since the income tax took effect, see Isaac William Martin, *Rich People's Movements: Grassroots Campaigns to Untax the One Percent* (New York: Oxford University Press, 2013).
30. On the long shadow of the South's "regime of racial capitalism," see James L. Leloudis and Robert Korstad, *To Right These Wrongs: The North Carolina Fund and the Battle to End Poverty and Inequality in 1960s America* (Chapel Hill: University of North Carolina Press, 2010).
31. J. Morgan Kousser, *The Shaping of Southern Politics: Suffrage Restriction and the Establishment of the One-Party South* (New Haven, CT: Yale University Press, 1974). The scholarly work on the role of race in American political development and on the fusion of race and class motives and appeals in politics since the nineteenth century is so extensive as to defy individual citation, but for concise discussion of the narrower point made here, see Rogers M. Smith, *Civic Ideals: Conflicting Visions of Citizenship in U.S. History* (New Haven: Yale University Press, 1997).

CHAPTER 1: THERE WAS NO STOPPING US

1. For the most memorable treatment of the Reverend Vernon Johns as a liberation theologian, "forerunner" to Dr. King, and mentor to his niece, see Taylor Branch, *Parting the Waters: America in the King Years, 1954–1963* (New York: Simon & Schuster, 1988), 7–26.
2. Kathryn Orth, "Going Public: Teacher Says She Encouraged 1951 Student Strike," *Richmond Times-Dispatch*, May 30, 1999, C1; Inez Davenport Jones, "Students Went on Strike to Challenge Jim Crow," *Virginian-Pilot*, August 20, 2007, A15; Robert C. Smith, *They Closed Our Schools: Prince Edward County, Virginia 1951–1964* (Chapel Hill: University of North Carolina Press, 1965), 34. The strike and all that followed have been the subject of three recent and rich explorations, by a historian, a historical sociologist, and a white journalist who grew up in Prince Edward County: Jill Ogline Titus, *Brown's Battleground: Students, Segregationists, and the Struggle for Justice in Prince Edward County* (Chapel Hill: University of North Carolina Press, 2011); Christopher Bonastia, *Southern Stalemate: Five Years Without Public Education in Prince Edward County, Virginia* (Chicago: University of Chicago Press, 2011); and Kristen Green, *Something Must Be Done About Prince Edward County: A Family, a Virginia Town, a Civil Rights Battle* (New York: HarperCollins, 2015).
3. On the equalization campaign, see Doxey A. Wilkerson, "The Negro School Movement in Virginia: From 'Equalization' to 'Integration,'" *Journal of Negro Education* 29 (Winter 1960): 17–29; and J. Douglas Smith, *Managing White Supremacy: Race, Politics, and Citizenship in Jim Crow Virginia* (Chapel Hill: University of North Carolina Press, 2002). I thank James H. Hershman Jr. for alerting me to the import of this campaign.

4. For the best short treatment of Virginia's poll tax, see Brent Tarter, "Poll Tax," *Encyclopedia Virginia*, www.encyclopediavirginia.org/poll_tax#start_entry; see also the classic V. O. Key Jr., *Southern Politics in State and Nation* (New York: Alfred A. Knopf, 1949), especially 580, 594.
5. Smith, *They Closed Our Schools*, 42, 61–62.
6. Smith, *They Closed Our Schools*, 15–17, 19, 24.
7. Inez Davenport Jones, speech in Farmville, VA, 1999, in *Above the Storm*, ed. Charles Gray and John Arthur Stokes (n.p.: Four-G Publishing, 2004), 91–93. She did not confess her role to her future husband until two days into the strike (Orth, "Going Public," C1). For uncovering of her role and resolution of questions about it, see Kara Miles Turner, "'It Is Not at Present a Very Successful School': Prince Edward County and the Black Educational Struggle, 1865–1995" (PhD diss., Duke University, 2001), 197n159. Textile workers were just then gearing up for a general strike, with Virginia's Dan River Mills as the epicenter; see Timothy J. Minchin, *What Do We Need a Union For? The TWUA in the South, 1945–1955* (Chapel Hill: University of North Carolina Press, 2000).
8. Kara Miles Turner, "'Liberating Lifescripts': Prince Edward County, Virginia, and the Roots of *Brown v. Board of Education*," in *From the Grassroots to the Supreme Court: Prince Edward County, Virginia, and the Roots of Brown v. Board of Education*, ed. Peter F. Lau (Durham, NC: Duke University Press, 2004), 95; John Stokes with Lois Wolfe and Herman J. Viola, *Students on Strike: Jim Crow, Civil Rights,* Brown, *and Me: A Memoir* (Washington, DC: National Geographic, 2008), 54–62; Smith, *They Closed Our Schools*, 32–33.
9. Barbara Rose Johns Powell, handwritten account held by the Robert Russa Moton Museum, Farmville, VA; Stokes, *Students on Strike*, 71.
10. Stokes, *Students on Strike*, 54–62; Smith, *They Closed Our Schools*, 32–33.
11. Stokes, *Students on Strike*, 63–68; Davenport Jones, speech in *Above the Storm*, 90.
12. Stokes, *Students on Strike*, 63–68, 75, 78; Richard Wormser, *The Rise and Fall of Jim Crow* (New York: St. Martin's, 2003), 180; Smith, *They Closed Our Schools*, 40–42.
13. "The Lonely Hero of Virginia School Fight," *Jet*, May 18, 1961, 20–24; "The Shame and the Glory," *Christian Century*, August 15, 1962, 977; Smith, *They Closed Our Schools*, 7, 11–13.
14. Smith, *They Closed Our Schools*, 43, 45–46; Richard Kluger, *Simple Justice: The History of* Brown v. Board of Education *and Black America's Struggle for Equality* (New York: Random House, 1975), 473; and, more generally, Genna Rae McNeil, *Groundwork: Charles Hamilton Houston and the Struggle for Civil Rights* (Philadelphia: University of Pennsylvania Press, 1983); and Kenneth Mack, "Law and Mass Politics in the Making of the Civil Rights Lawyer, 1931–1941," *Journal of American History* 93, no. 1 (June 2006): 60.
15. Smith, *They Closed Our Schools*, 47–48.
16. Ibid., 51–54.
17. Smith, *They Closed Our Schools*, 9, 58–59; Branch, *Parting the Waters*, 470–79.
18. Stokes, *Students on Strike*, 106.
19. Orth, "Going Public," C1; Smith, *They Closed Our Schools*, 75–76; Stokes, *Students on Strike*, 102–3, 107.
20. Smith, *Managing White Supremacy*.
21. James H. Hershman Jr., "A Rumbling in the Museum: The Opponents of Virginia's Massive Resistance" (PhD diss., University of Virginia, 1978), 28.
22. Mark Whitman, *Brown v. Board of Education: A Documentary History* (Princeton, NJ: Markus Wiener, 2004), 80–81; Kluger, *Simple Justice*, 482–84. Kenneth Clark thought Garrett "a model of mediocrity" as a professor (Kluger, 502).
23. Numan V. Bartley, *The Rise of Massive Resistance: Race and Politics During the 1950s* (1969; repr., Baton Rouge: Louisiana State University Press, 1997), 114–15.
24. The literature here is voluminous, from older classics such as James T. Ely Jr., *The Crisis of Conservative Virginia: The Byrd Organization and the Politics of Massive Resistance* (Knoxville: University of Tennessee Press, 1996), to newer works such as Smith, *Managing White Supremacy.* To my reading, Hershman's "A Rumbling in the Museum" best captures the contingency of

the moment and the dynamics of the moderate challenge that was assembling by the 1950s. See also Matthew D. Lassiter and Andrew B. Lewis, eds., *The Moderates' Dilemma: Massive Resistance to School Desegregation in Virginia* (Charlottesville: University Press of Virginia, 1998).

25. Philip J. Hilts, "The Saga of James J. Kilpatrick," *Potomac Magazine (Washington Post)*, September 16, 1973, 15, 69; Robert Gaines Corley, "James Jackson Kilpatrick: The Evolution of a Southern Conservative, 1955–1965" (unpublished MA thesis, University of Virginia, 1970), 7; William P. Hustwit, *James J. Kilpatrick: Salesman for Segregation* (Chapel Hill: University of North Carolina Press, 2013), 29–31, 39–40; donkey quote from Hollinger F. Barnard, ed., *Outside the Magic Circle: The Autobiography of Virginia Foster Durr* (Tuscaloosa: University of Alabama Press, 1985), 314.
26. Editorial, *Richmond News Leader*, May 7, 1951.
27. Gene Roberts and Hank Klibanoff, *The Race Beat: The Press, the Civil Rights Struggle, and the Awakening of a Nation* (New York: Alfred A. Knopf, 2006), 70–72.
28. Bartley, *Rise of Massive Resistance*, 128–29. For the original arguments, see H. Lee Cheek Jr., ed., *John C. Calhoun: Selected Writings and Speeches* (Washington, DC: Regnery, 2003); for a classic explication that holds up well, see Richard N. Current, "John C. Calhoun, Philosopher of Reaction," *Antioch Review* 3 (1943).
29. Joseph J. Thorndike, "'The Sometimes Sordid Level of Race and Segregation': James J. Kilpatrick and the Virginia Campaign Against *Brown*," in *The Moderates' Dilemma*, 51–71.
30. James J. Kilpatrick, *The Southern Case for School Segregation* (New York: Crowell-Collier Press, 1962), 8; Hilts, "Saga of James J. Kilpatrick," 69; Garrett Epps, "The Littlest Rebel: James J. Kilpatrick and the Second Civil War," *Constitutional Commentary* 10 (1993): 19.
31. James J. Kilpatrick, "Nine Men, or 36 States?" in *Interposition: Editorials and Editorial Page Presentations, 1955–1956* (Richmond, VA: Richmond News Leader, 1956); Hilts, "Saga of James J. Kilpatrick," 72.
32. Thorndike, "'The Sometimes Sordid Level,'" 51–59; Hustwit, *James J. Kilpatrick*, 45–49.
33. Hershman, "A Rumbling in the Museum," 46–47, 88–89, 115–17.
34. "Virginia's Senator Harry Byrd," *Time*, August 17, 1962, 11–15; *Edward P. Morgan and the News*, transcript, American Broadcasting Network, October 9, 1958, Louise O. Wensel Papers, Special Collections Department, Manuscript Division, University of Virginia Library, Charlottesville; see also October 27, 1958, transcript.
35. *Edward P. Morgan and the News*, transcript, October 9, 1958; "Virginia's Senator Harry Byrd." For the stark exploitation allowed by such programs, see the pathbreaking study by Cindy Hahamovitch, *No Man's Land: Jamaican Guestworkers in America and the Global History of Deportable Labor* (Princeton, NJ: Princeton University Press, 2013).
36. For a recent, hard-hitting summary of "the Byrdocracy," see chapter 11 of Brent Tarter, *The Grandees of Government: The Origins and Persistence of Undemocratic Politics in Virginia* (Charlottesville: University of Virginia Press, 2013), 281–304; James H. Hershman Jr., private communication to author, August 2, 2013.
37. Nick Kotz, *Judgment Days: Lyndon Baines Johnson, Martin Luther King Jr., and the Laws That Changed America* (New York: Houghton Mifflin, 2003), 36; Robert Caro, *The Passage of Power* (New York: Alfred A. Knopf, 2012), 466, 468–69.
38. Steven F. Lawson, *Black Ballots: Voting Rights in the South, 1944–1969* (1976; repr., Lanham, MD: Lexington Books, 1999), 14–15; C. Vann Woodward, *Origins of the New South, 1877–1913* (Baton Rouge: Louisiana State University Press, 1951), 345; James H. Hershman Jr., "Massive Resistance Meets Its Match: The Emergence of a Pro-Public Education Majority," in *The Moderates' Dilemma*, 104–5, 109; J. Douglas Smith, *On Democracy's Doorstep: The Inside Story of How the Supreme Court Brought "One Person, One Vote" to the United States* (New York: Hill & Wang, 2014), 19.
39. Frank B. Atkinson, *The Dynamic Dominion: Realignment and the Rise of Virginia's Republican Party Since 1945* (Fairfax, VA: George Mason University Press, 1992), 4; Key, *Southern Politics in State and Nation*, 19–20.

40. See Smith, *Managing White Supremacy.*
41. Tarter, *Grandees of Government.*
42. "Virginia Outlaws Closed-Shop Pacts," *New York Times,* January 19, 1947, 4. Thanks to James H. Hershman Jr. for sending me this story.
43. This practice is captured well in Edward H. Peeples, *Scalawag: A White Southerner's Journey Through Segregation to Human Rights Activism* (Charlottesville: University of Virginia Press, 2014).
44. Harry F. Byrd to James Kilpatrick, November 8, 1957, box 245, Harry Flood Byrd Sr. Papers; Byrd to Kilpatrick, July 26, 1957, box 413, ibid.; Byrd to Kilpatrick, December 23, 1955, box 7, series B, James J. Kilpatrick Papers, Special Collections Department, University of Virginia Library (hereafter cited as JJKP).
45. James Kilpatrick to Harry Flood Byrd, December 26, 1955, box 7, series B, JJKP; Roberts and Klibanoff, *The Race Beat,* 109, 111, 116–19; Joseph Crespino, *Strom Thurmond's America* (New York: Hill & Wang, 2012), 105–7.
46. Hershman, "A Rumbling in the Museum," 188, 189–90, 208–9, 214, 263; American Jewish Congress, *Assault upon Freedom of Association: A Study of the Southern Attack on the National Association for the Advancement of Colored People* (New York: American Jewish Congress, 1957), 27–29. For fuller discussion, see the classic treatment by Benjamin Muse, *Virginia's Massive Resistance* (Bloomington: Indiana University Press, 1961).
47. Among other sources, see the reports in James R. Sweeney, ed., *Race, Reason, and Massive Resistance: The Diary of David J. Mays, 1954–1959* (Athens: University of Georgia Press, 2008), 167, 168, 178, 190.
48. Smith, *Managing White Supremacy,* 278, 285–88, 294–95; record group 2/1/2, Board of Visitors Files for 1956, 1957, and 1958, box 9, Office of the President, Papers of the President of the University of Virginia, Office Administrative Files, Manuscripts Division, Alderman Library, University of Virginia; *Colgate Darden: Conversations with Guy Friddell* (Charlottesville: University of Virginia Press, 1978), 103–5, also 175.

CHAPTER 2: A COUNTRY BOY GOES TO THE WINDY CITY

1. James M. Buchanan, *Better than Plowing and Other Personal Essays* (Chicago: University of Chicago Press, 1992), 1, 19, 25. My depiction of Middle Tennessee comes from a gem of national heritage enabled by the New Deal: the Federal Writers' Project collection of state studies. I used *The WPA Guide to Tennessee* (1939; repr., Knoxville: University of Tennessee Press, 1986).
2. Buchanan, *Better than Plowing,* 1; Wilma Dykeman, *Tennessee: A Bicentennial History* (New York: W. W. Norton, 1975), 167–68; Carlton C. Sims, *A History of Rutherford County* (Murfreesboro, TN: privately published), 210; Manuscript Census, 1920, 1940 (accessed online), and additional information courtesy of the Rutherford County Archives and Kelley Lawton of Duke Libraries. For a very different view of an African American journalist who grew up just down the road in Middle Tennessee, see the tellingly titled work by Carl Rowan, *South of Freedom* (New York: Alfred A. Knopf, 1952).
3. Buchanan, *Better than Plowing,* 2; Sims, *History of Rutherford County,* 210; Manuscript Census, 1920, 1940 (accessed online), and additional information courtesy of the Rutherford County Archives and Kelley Lawton.
4. Buchanan, *Better than Plowing,* 1; Karin A. Shapiro, *A New South Rebellion: The Battle Against Convict Labor in the Tennessee Coalfields, 1871–1896* (Chapel Hill: University of North Carolina Press, 1998), 8, 108, 246.
5. Buchanan, *Better than Plowing,* 1, 5, 26–27.
6. Shapiro, *New South Rebellion,* 2, 47, 109, 139, 235, 242, 243.
7. Buchanan, *Better than Plowing,* 21, 30.
8. Shapiro, *New South Rebellion,* 8–9, 11, 90, 93, 133, 186, 196.
9. Dykeman, *Tennessee,* 133–34, 148; Buchanan, *Better than Plowing,* 1, 2, 5, 19, 21, 37.

10. Buchanan, *Better than Plowing*, 1–3, 75, 126; Robert D. Hershey Jr., "An Austere Scholar: James McGill Buchanan," *New York Times*, October 17, 1986; Hartmut Kliemt remarks at James M. Buchanan Memorial Conference, George Mason University, September 28, 2013 (author's notes).
11. Twelve Southerners, *I'll Take My Stand: The South and the Agrarian Tradition* (1930; repr., Baton Rouge: Louisiana State University Press, 1977); R. Blakeslee Gilpin, *John Brown Still Lives! America's Long Reckoning with Violence, Equality, & Change* (Chapel Hill: University of North Carolina Press, 2011), 120; Dykeman, *Tennessee*, 177. For the rich and varied internal dissent, see Glenda Elizabeth Gilmore, *Defying Dixie: The Radical Roots of Civil Rights, 1919–1950* (New York: W. W. Norton, 2009).
12. Gilpin, *John Brown Still Lives!*, quotes on 123, 124, 127, 141, 143; Buchanan, *Better than Plowing*, 126. See also Paul V. Murphy, *The Rebuke of History: The Southern Agrarians and American Conservative Thought* (Chapel Hill: University of North Carolina Press, 2001).
13. Donald Davidson, *The Attack on Leviathan: Regionalism and Nationalism in the United States* (1938; repr., Gloucester, MA: Peter Smith, 1962), 5, 10, 12, 26. For illuminating discussion, see Murphy, *Rebuke of History*, 92–113.
14. Buchanan, *Better than Plowing*, 25, 171; Jane Seaberry, "GMU Teacher Wins Nobel in Economics," *Washington Post*, October 17, 1986.
15. Davidson, *Attack on Leviathan*, 163, 168.
16. Buchanan, *Better than Plowing*, 49.
17. Ibid., 4, 49–50. For contrast with a white working-class southerner whose experience of prejudice in the North led him to identify with the black freedom struggle, see Edward H. Peeples with Nancy MacLean, *Scalawag: A White Southerner's Journey Through Segregation to Human Rights Activism* (Charlottesville: University of Virginia Press, 2014).
18. James M. Buchanan, "Afraid to Be Free: Dependency as Desideratum," first draft, Buchanan House Archives, Center for Study of Public Choice, George Mason University, Fairfax, VA (hereafter cited as BHA), 9, later published in *Public Choice* 120, no. 3 (September 2004). For contrast, see W. E. B. Du Bois, *Black Reconstruction in America: An Essay toward a History of the Part which Black Folk Played in the Attempt to Reconstruct Democracy in America, 1860–1880* (New York: Oxford University Press, 1935), quote on 726—and just about any reputable work on Reconstruction published since the 1960s.
19. Rob van Horn and Philip Mirowski, "The Rise of the Chicago School of Economics and the Birth of Neoliberalism," in *The Road from Mont Pelerin: The Making of the Neoliberal Thought Collective*, ed. Philip Mirowski and Dieter Plehwe (Cambridge, MA: Harvard University Press, 2009), 169n5.
20. Buchanan, *Better than Plowing*, 1–4, 66.
21. Ibid., 68.
22. Ibid., 24, 77, 79; George J. Stigler, typescript tribute to Frank Knight, May 24, 1972, BHA.
23. Buchanan, *Better than Plowing*, 5, 70, 72. On Chicago social history in these years, see Meg Jacobs, *Pocketbook Politics: Economic Citizenship in Twentieth-Century America* (Princeton, NJ: Princeton University Press, 2005); Laura McEnaney, *World War II's "Postwar": A Social and Policy History of Peace, 1944–1953* (Philadelphia: University of Pennsylvania Press, forthcoming, 2017).
24. Jacobs, *Pocketbook Politics*, 221–37; Patricia Sullivan, *Days of Hope: Race and Democracy in the New Deal Era* (Chapel Hill: University of North Carolina Press, 1996).
25. Milton Friedman and Rose D. Friedman, *Two Lucky People: Memoirs* (Chicago: University of Chicago Press, 1998), 158–61; Richard Cockett, *Thinking the Unthinkable: Think-Tanks and the Economic Counter-Revolution, 1931–1983* (London: HarperCollins, 1995), 110; additional description from www.du-parc.ch/en/heritage.
26. Daniel Stedman Jones, *Masters of the Universe: Hayek, Friedman, and the Birth of Neoliberal Politics* (Princeton, NJ: Princeton University Press, 2012), 57.

27. Cockett, *Thinking the Unthinkable,* 4, 28, 31, 97; Alan Ebenstein, *Friedrich Hayek: A Biography* (New York: Palgrave Macmillan, 2001), 231.
28. Quotes from Kim Phillips-Fein, *Invisible Hands: The Making of the Conservative Movement from the New Deal to Reagan* (New York: W. W. Norton, 2009), 41; George H. Nash, *The Conservative Intellectual Movement in America, Since 1945* (1976; repr., Wilmington, DE: Intercollegiate Studies Institute, 1996), 5; Cockett, *Thinking the Unthinkable,* 100–101; Angus Burgin, *The Great Persuasion: Reinventing Free Markets Since the Depression* (Cambridge, MA: Harvard University Press, 2012), 89. See also van Horn and Mirowski, "The Rise of the Chicago School," 147, 150–51.
29. Friedrich A. Hayek, *The Road to Serfdom* (Chicago: University of Chicago, 1944); Cockett, *Thinking the Unthinkable,* 5.
30. Hayek, *Road to Serfdom,* 4–6.
31. Ibid., 7, 35.
32. Ibid., 13, 16, 17, 19.
33. Phillips-Fein, *Invisible Hands,* 5, 322.
34. Ibid., 41–42; van Horn and Mirowski, "The Rise of the Chicago School," 139–68; Alan O. Ebenstein, *Milton Friedman: A Biography* (New York: Palgrave Macmillan, 2007), 139. For the ironic evolution of the fund, see Michael J. McVicar, "Aggressive Philanthropy: Progressivism, Conservatism, and the William Volker Charities Fund," *Missouri Historical Review* 105 (2011): 191–212.
35. Hayek, *Road to Serfdom,* 262; Cockett, *Thinking the Unthinkable,* 89; Burgin, *Great Persuasion,* 103, 107–8; for Keynes's full comment, see Stedman Jones, *Masters of the Universe,* 67. Burgin's book deftly charts the society's change over time to more full-throated, unequivocal advocacy.
36. Friedman and Friedman, *Two Lucky People,* 158–61; Dieter Plehwe, introduction to *Road from Mont Pelerin,* 3–25.
37. R. M. Hartwell, *History of the Mont Pelerin Society* (Indianapolis: Liberty Fund, 1995), xii; Friedman and Friedman, *Two Lucky People,* 161.
38. Buchanan, *Better than Plowing,* 75; Stigler, tribute to Knight. For an excellent overview, see the collection edited by Robert van Horn, Philip Mirowski, and Thomas A. Stapleford, *Building Chicago Economics: New Perspectives on the History of America's Most Powerful Economics Program* (New York: Cambridge University Press, 2011).
39. Buchanan, *Better than Plowing,* 16, 94–95. On Nutter, see John H. Moore, "Gilbert Warren Nutter," *American National Biography Online,* February 2000; William Breit, "Creating the 'Virginia School': Charlottesville as an Academic Environment in the 1960s," *Economic Inquiry* 25 (October 1987): 648–49.
40. Buchanan, *Better than Plowing,* 5, 70, 72.
41. James M. Buchanan, *Economics from the Outside In: "Better than Plowing" and Beyond* (College Station: Texas A&M Press, 2007), 195.
42. For the relationship today, see Marc J. Hetherington, *Why Trust Matters: Declining Political Trust and the Demise of American Liberalism* (Princeton, NJ: Princeton University Press, 2005).
43. Quoted and discussed in James M. Buchanan, "The Constitution of Economic Policy," Nobel Prize lecture, December 8, 1986, www.nobelprize.org/nobel_prizes/economic-sciences/laureates/1986/buchanan-lecture.html.
44. Buchanan, "Constitution of Economic Policy."
45. Buchanan, *Better than Plowing,* 6. For illuminating analysis of Buchanan's departure from Wicksell, essentially turning the Swede's purpose on its head, see Amadae, *Prisoners of Reason,* 193–200.
46. Buchanan, *Better Than Plowing,* 8–9, 83–88; James M. Buchanan, *Public Principles of Public Debt: A Defense and Restatement* (Homewood, IL: Richard D. Irwin, 1958), vi, vii.

CHAPTER 3: THE REAL PURPOSE OF THE PROGRAM

1. James M. Buchanan, *Better than Plowing and Other Personal Essays* (Chicago: University of Chicago Press, 1992), 16, 94–95.
2. "Working Papers for Internal Discussion Only" (December 1956), record group 2/1/2.634, box 9, Office of the President, Papers of the President of the University of Virginia, Office Administrative Files, Manuscripts Division, Alderman Library, University of Virginia.
3. Warren Nutter, typescript reminiscences, 1975, box 80, William J. Baroody Papers, Manuscript Division, Library of Congress, Washington, DC.
4. Buchanan, *Better than Plowing*, 6–7, 8–9, 97, 100; James M. Buchanan, ed., *Political Economy, 1957–1982: The G. Warren Nutter Lectures in Political Economy* (Washington, DC: American Enterprise Institute for Public Policy Research, 1982), 4, 7, 11; John Kenneth Galbraith, *American Capitalism: The Theory of Countervailing Power* (Boston: Houghton Mifflin, 1952).
5. Kim Phillips-Fein, *Invisible Hands: The Making of the Conservative Movement from the New Deal to Reagan* (New York: W. W. Norton, 2009), 3–12, quote on 13; Guy Friddell, *Colgate Darden: Conversations with Guy Friddell* (Charlottesville: University Press of Virginia, 1978), 129–30.
6. Friddell, *Colgate Darden*, 57.
7. Ibid., 129. On right-wing businessmen more generally in these years, see Elizabeth Fones-Wolf, *Selling Free Enterprise: The Business Assault on Labor and Liberalism, 1945–1960* (Urbana: University of Illinois Press, 1994).
8. For the classic history of legal realism, see Morton J. Horwitz, *The Transformation of American Law, 1870–1960: The Crisis of Legal Orthodoxy* (New York: Oxford University Press, 1992), quote on 197; see also, for the legal context of *Brown*, Horwitz's *The Warren Court and the Pursuit of Justice* (New York: Hill & Wang, 1998).
9. For a small sample of a deep and rich literature, see Morton White, *Social Thought in America: The Revolt Against Formalism* (Boston: Beacon Press, 1947); Ellen Fitzpatrick, *Endless Crusade: Women Social Scientists and Progressive Reform* (New York: Oxford University Press, 1990); Daniel T. Rodgers, *Atlantic Crossings: Social Politics in a Progressive Era* (Cambridge, MA: Belknap Press of Harvard University Press, 1998); Genna Rae McNeil, *Groundwork: Charles Hamilton Houston and the Struggle for Civil Rights* (Philadelphia: University of Pennsylvania Press, 1983); Jonathan Scott Holloway, *Confronting the Veil: Abram Harris, Jr., E. Franklin Frazier, and Ralph Bunche, 1919–1941* (Chapel Hill: University of North Carolina Press, 2002).
10. "Working Papers for Internal Discussion Only"; see also James M. Buchanan, "The Thomas Jefferson Center for Studies in Political Economy," *University of Virginia News Letter* 35, no. 2 (October 15, 1958): 1, 6. The last three words in the center's name ("and Social Philosophy") were later dropped for brevity's sake.
11. Buchanan, "Thomas Jefferson Center," 7; Buchanan, *Better than Plowing*, 95.
12. Brian Doherty, *Radicals for Capitalism: A Freewheeling History of the Modern Libertarian Movement* (Philadelphia, PA: PublicAffairs, 2007), 182–83; Phillips-Fein, *Invisible Hands*, 42, 51; H. W. Luhnow to Colgate Darden [1957], record group 2/1/2.635, series 1, box 11, Office of the President, Papers of the President of the University of Virginia, Office Administrative Files, Manuscripts Division, Alderman Library, University of Virginia. On Volker's earlier interest in UVA, T. Coleman Andrews to President Colgate W. Darden, February 4, 1952, box 3, T. Coleman Andrews Papers, Division of Special Collections, University of Oregon Libraries (hereafter cited as TCAP); also, Andrews to Darden, June 8, 1950, TCAP. The Volker Fund invested well: six of its early grantees went on to win the Nobel Prize in economics: F. A. Hayek, James Buchanan, Milton Friedman, Ronald Coase, Gary Becker, and George Stigler (Doherty, *Radicals*, 183).
13. Record group 2/1/2, Board of Visitors files for 1956, 1957, and 1958, Office of the President, Papers of the President of the University of Virginia, Office Administrative Files. On Smith, see Don Oberdorfer, "'Judge' Smith Rules with Deliberate Drag," *New York Times Magazine*,

January 12, 1964; and Bruce J. Dierenfield, *Keeper of the Rules: Congressman Howard W. Smith of Virginia* (Charlottesville: University of Virginia Press, 1987).

14. Record group 2/1/2, Board of Visitors files for 1956 and 1957, Office of the President, Papers of the President of the University of Virginia, Office Administrative Files.
15. On Garrett's appointment, see J. Kenneth Morland, *The Tragedy of Public Schools: Prince Edward County, Virginia,* report for the Virginia Advisory Committee to the United States Commission on Civil Rights (Lynchburg, VA: unpublished report, 1964), 22. For Garrett's testimony as the "backbone" of the state's case, see Taylor Branch, *Parting the Waters: America in the King Years, 1954–1963* (New York: Simon & Schuster, 1988), 484; and "Henry E. Garrett, Psychologist, Dies," *New York Times,* June 28, 1973.
16. William R. Duren Jr. to Edgar F. Shannon Jr., June 29, 1962, box 9, Office of the President, Papers of the President of the University of Virginia.
17. Ronald L. Heinemann, *Harry Byrd of Virginia* (Charlottesville: University Press of Virginia, 1996), 246, 290, 454n63. I am grateful to James Hershman for alerting me to Byrd's interest in Hayek. "Old Harry," as some in Washington called him, also fought passage of every law that violated his conception of liberty, among them the progressive income tax; the Wagner Act, which empowered workers to join unions; the Tennessee Valley Authority, which supplied electricity to so much of the rural South; the Social Security Act, which provided old-age pensions; the Fair Labor Standards Act, which regulated working conditions; and the Fair Employment Practices Committee, which barred discrimination in wartime industries. Robert Caro, *The Passage of Power* (New York: Alfred A. Knopf, 2012), 466, 468–69.
18. "The idea has interesting possibilities altogether separate from segregation," Chodorov suggested, and could bring welcome new "competition" to schooling; "All Men Are Created Equal" (editorial), *The Freeman,* June 14, 1954, 655–66. Kilpatrick had recommended Chodorov for editor, so it is possible that they discussed his ideas for private schooling; James Kilpatrick to Florence Norton, June 17, 1954, box 18, series B, JJKP. On Chodorov's foundational role, see George H. Nash, *The Conservative Intellectual Movement in America Since 1945* (1976; repr., Wilmington, DE: Intercollegiate Studies Institute, 1998), 22–25.
19. Robert LeFevre to Jack Kilpatrick, July 1, 1954, series B, box 31, JJKP; LeFevre to Kilpatrick, July 6, 1954, with attachment, series B, box 31, JJKP. LeFevre proved to be too extreme even for Kilpatrick, as their correspondence shows, but he became something of a guru among libertarians, not least among them Charles Koch.
20. Doherty, *Radicals for Capitalism,* 200, 203, 205; F. A. Hayek, "Postscript: Why I Am Not a Conservative," *The Constitution of Liberty* (1960; repr., Chicago: Regnery, 1972); James M. Buchanan, *Why I, Too, Am Not a Conservative: The Normative Vision of Classical Liberalism* (Northampton, MA: Edward Elgar, 2005); Ralph Harris, *Radical Reaction: Essays in Competition and Affluence* (London: Institute of Economic Affairs, 1961).
21. Nash, *Conservative Intellectual Movement,* 15; "Regnery Publishing," in *American Conservatism: An Encyclopedia,* ed. Bruce Frohnen, et al. (Wilmington, DE: ISI Books, 206), 722–23.
22. Henry Regnery to Kilpatrick, May 19, 1955, box 39, Henry Regnery Papers, Hoover Institution Archives, Stanford University.
23. Hilts, "Saga of James J. Kilpatrick," 72; Henry Regnery to Kilpatrick, March 14, 1956, box 66, series B, JJKP; James Jackson Kilpatrick, *The Sovereign States: Notes of a Citizen of Virginia* (Chicago: Henry Regnery, 1957), 234–51. "When we published it," Regnery gushed to Kilpatrick years later, "I was so convinced by the lucidity and persuasiveness of your argument that I fully expected to see the 14th Amendment repealed momentarily and the Doctrine of Interposition recognized by the Supreme Court. The fact that these things didn't happen is merely an indication of how deeply we have allowed ourselves to be taken in by the lure of centralized power"; Regnery to Kilpatrick, April 17, 1972, box 39, Regnery Papers.
24. Kilpatrick called those comments "the greatest single boost the book has had"; Kilpatrick to Donald Davidson, April 29, 1957, box 8, Donald Grady Davidson Papers, Special Collections, Jean and Alexander Heard Library, Vanderbilt University, Nashville, TN. See also John

Chamberlain, "The Duty to Interpose," *The Freeman*, July 1957, 55. Henry Regnery solicited corporate subsidies to put Kilpatrick's book in the "hands of every Governor, every U.S. Senator and every member of Congress"; Henry Regnery to Kilpatrick, January 10, 1957, box 39, Regnery Papers; Regnery to Roger Milliken, January 23, 1957, box 51, Regnery Papers.

25. Ivan R. Bierly to Jack Kilpatrick, July 8, 1959, box 26, series B, JJKP; Bierly to Kilpatrick, October 2, 1959, box 26, series B, JJKP; David Greenberg, "The Idea of 'the Liberal Media' and Its Roots in the Civil Rights Movement," *The Sixties* 2, no. 1 (Winter 2008–2009). On the plan by segregationist editors to fight what today would be called "the liberal media," see Gene Roberts and Hank Klibanoff, *The Race Beat: The Press, the Civil Rights Struggle, and the Awakening of a Nation* (New York: Alfred A. Knopf, 2006), 214–20. For interest from the Volker Fund in helping, see Bierly to Kilpatrick, October 2, 1959, box 4, series B, JJKP.
26. For an overview, see Robert Griffith, "Dwight D. Eisenhower and the Corporate Commonwealth," *American Historical Review* 87 (February 1982): 87–122, quote on 102. For the wider right's anger at Eisenhower, see Nash, *Conservative Intellectual Movement;* and Rick Perlstein, *Before the Storm: Barry Goldwater and the Unmaking of the American Consensus* (New York: Hill & Wang, 2001).
27. Francis Crafts Williams to Kilpatrick, [nd. but 1956], box 55, series B JJKP.
28. T. Coleman Andrews to Leonard E. Reed, January 30, 1956, box 4, TCAP; Andrews to Harry F. Byrd, December 5, 1947, box 2, TCAP; Andrews to Byrd, October 10, 1950, box 18, TCAP; Andrews to Byrd, May 16, 1952, TCAP; Andrews to Byrd, July 17, 1952, TCAP; Andrews to Byrd, July 27, 1952, TCAP.
29. "Andrews Files for President," *Washington Post*, September 18, 1956, 24; "Andrews Says Fight Is Against Socialism," *Washington Post*, October 28, 1958, B5.
30. "Tax Rebellion Leader: Thomas Coleman Andrews," *New York Times*, October 16, 1956, 26; "Why the Income Tax Is Bad: Exclusive Interview with T. Coleman Andrews," *U.S. News & World Report*, May 25, 1956. Andrews's revolt against the Democratic Party had begun with anger over FDR's support of labor and corporate regulation and his involvement in Europe's "troubles"; Harry F. Byrd to T. Coleman Andrews, July 2, 1935, box 2, TCAP; Andrews to Byrd, October 13, 1939, TCAP.
31. J. Addison Hagan to Harry F. Byrd, October 18, 1956, box 2, TCAP; Numan V. Bartley, *The Rise of Massive Resistance: Race and Politics During the 1950s* (1969; repr., Baton Rouge: Louisiana State University Press, 1997), 161–65; Joseph Crespino, *In Search of Another Country: Mississippi and the Conservative Counterrevolution* (Princeton, NJ: Princeton University Press, 2007).
32. Jonathan M. Schoenwald, *A Time for Choosing: The Rise of Modern American Conservatism* (New York: Oxford University Press, 2002), 65, 68; Claire Conner, *Wrapped in the Flag: A Personal History of America's Radical Right* (Boston: Beacon Press, 2013), 26–27. For others' backing, see Doherty, *Radicals*, 179, 258; T. Coleman Andrews to Leonard E. Reed, November 23, 1956, box 4, TCAP; Perlstein, *Before the Storm*, 10–12; Bartley, *Rise of Massive Resistance*, 149, 163.
33. For his opposition to "every extension of socialistic philosophy" as Richmond chamber president, see text of his testimony in box 5, TCAP. Statewide, he got 6 percent of the vote, doing better in Virginia than anywhere else in the nation.
34. Roberts and Klibanoff, *The Race Beat*, 159–65; editorial, *Richmond News Leader*, September 12, 1957, 12.
35. Roberts and Klibanoff, *The Race Beat*, 151, 158, 171.
36. Ibid., 172, 175–80; Bartley, *Rise of Massive Resistance*, 266.
37. James Jackson Kilpatrick, "Right and Power in Arkansas," *National Review*, September 28, 1957, 273–75.
38. "The Lie to Mr. Eisenhower" (editorial), *National Review*, October 5, 1957, 292–93; "The Court Views Its Handiwork" (editorial), *National Review*, September 21, 1957, 244. Government "weeps over the civil rights of certain minorities," concurred industrialist E. F. Hutton in the leading libertarian journal, "but punishes no one when labor union monopolies" cause disruptions; E. F. Hutton, "Contempt for Law," *The Freeman*, April 1957, 20. For Faubus's action

as issuing from Kilpatrick's theory, see Garrett Epps, "The Littlest Rebel: James J. Kilpatrick and the Second Civil War," *Constitutional Commentary* 10 (1993): 26–27; and Benjamin Muse, *Virginia's Massive Resistance* (Bloomington: Indiana University Press, 1961), 172.

39. "Bayonets and the Law" (editorial), *National Review,* October 12, 1957, 316–17.
40. James M. Buchanan to Frank H. Knight, October 24, 1957, box 3, Frank Hyneman Knight Papers, Special Collections Research Center, University of Chicago Library.
41. Breit, "Creating the 'Virginia School,'" 645–47, 652; Richard E. Wagner, speech at memorial program for James Buchanan, September 29, 2013, George Mason University, Fairfax, VA. For one of the many references to the "boys," see Buchanan to Gordon Tullock, July 19, 1965, BHA.
42. Buchanan, *Better than Plowing,* 97.
43. Breit, "Creating the 'Virginia School,'" 645–47, 652; James M. Buchanan to David Tennant Bryan, May 18, 1970, BHA.
44. Breit, "Creating the 'Virginia School'"; Carl Noller to James Buchanan, March 16, 1971, BHA.
45. "Everyday Hero," *Mason Gazette,* June 16, 2005; Fabio Padavano, remarks at Buchanan memorial conference; Betty Tillman to Gordon Tullock, July 12, 1965, box 95, Gordon Tullock Papers, Hoover Institution Archives, Stanford University.
46. Alexander S. Leidholdt, "Showdown on Mr. Jefferson's Lawn: Contesting Jim Crow During the University of Virginia's Protodesegregation," *Virginia Magazine of History and Biography* 122 (2014): 236, 237.
47. Ibid., 241, 256.
48. Friedrich A. Hayek to James Buchanan, November 15, 1957, and March 8, 1958, box 72, Friedrich A. von Hayek Papers, 1906–1992, Hoover Institution Archives; H. W. Luhnow to Hayek, December 7, 1956, box 58, ibid.
49. William J. Baroody Jr., foreword to James M. Buchanan, ed., *Political Economy, 1957–1982: The G. Warren Nutter Lectures in Political Economy* (Washington, DC: American Enterprise Institute for Public Policy Research, 1982).
50. Indeed, the National Right to Work Committee, founded in 1954, suffered immediate embarrassment in the mainstream national press for being run by a southern CEO who was, in the words of one legal historian, "fresh from a bitter but successful fight against unionization"; Sophia Z. Lee, *The Workplace Constitution, from the New Deal to the New Right* (New York: Cambridge University Press, 2014), 123.
51. Philip D. Bradley, ed., *The Public Stake in Union Power* (Charlottesville: University of Virginia Press, 1959), quote on 168; Friedrich A. Hayek to James Buchanan, November 15, 1957, and March 8, 1958, box 72, Hayek Papers; H. W. Luhnow to Hayek, December 7, 1956, box 58, ibid. The Austrian summarized Hutt's case as showing that when federal legislation and union power managed to "win for some groups of workers higher compensation than they would have collected on an unhampered market, they victimize other groups." The right way to reduce unemployment and lift wages was "the progressive accumulation of capital"; Ludwig von Mises, preface to *The Theory of Collective Bargaining,* by W. H. Hutt (Glencoe, IL: Free Press, 1954), 9–10; Lawrence Fertig to James M. Buchanan, August [1961], BHA. On Relm Foundation and Lilly Endowment subsidies, see H. W. Hutt to Henry Regnery, January 3, 1962, box 33, Regnery Papers; Regnery to Hutt, December 26, 1962, Regnery Papers; and Warren Nutter to James Buchanan, May 6, 1965, BHA.
52. James M. Buchanan, lecture notes, Introductory Economics, Spring 1959, BHA. The notion of union monopoly was another of the Mont Pelerin Society's departures from classical liberalism. Some of its thinkers averred that early free-market economists such as Adam Smith were wrong to worry so much about corporate monopoly; that came about only when government meddled. For workers to join together in collective organizations enabled by law, they said, was the real danger. See Yves Steiner, "The Neoliberals Confront the Trade Unions," in *The Road from Mont Pelerin: The Making of the Neoliberal Thought Collective,* eds. Philip Mirowski and Dieter Plehwe (Cambridge, MA: Harvard University Press, 2009), 181–203.

53. James Buchanan to Gordon Tullock, June 13, 1965, BHA; Roger Koppl, ed., *Money and Markets: Essays in Honor of Leland B. Yeager* (New York: Routledge, 2006), 38. There is extensive correspondence with donors in the Buchanan House Archives, George Mason University.

CHAPTER 4: LETTING THE CHIPS FALL WHERE THEY MAY

1. For the premier published account of the moderates' mobilization to save the schools, see Hershman Jr., "Massive Resistance Meets Its Match," in *The Moderates' Dilemma*. For a fuller account, with notable resonance for today, see, also by Hershman Jr., "A Rumbling in the Museum." On the pivotal role of southern white moderates more broadly, see David L. Chappell, *Inside Agitators: White Southerners in the Civil Rights Movement* (Baltimore: Johns Hopkins University Press, 1994).
2. For a first-person account of how effective that culture was at indoctrination from someone who managed to get free eventually, see Edward H. Peeples, *Scalawag: A White Southerner's Journey Through Segregation to Human Rights Activism* (Charlottesville: University of Virginia Press, 2014). His archived records contain abundant riches on Virginia social and political history in this era and beyond; see Edward H. Peeples Jr. Collection, James Branch Cabell Library, Special Collections and Archives, Virginia Commonwealth University, Richmond, VA.
3. For more detail and illuminating analysis, see the excellent essays in *The Moderates' Dilemma*.
4. Dr. Louise Wensel, press release, July 25, 1958, Louise O. Wensel Papers, Special Collections Department, Manuscript Division, University of Virginia Library, Charlottesville (hereafter cited as LOWP); George Lewis, "'Any Old Joe Named Zilch'? The Senatorial Campaign of Dr. Louise Oftedal Wensel," *Virginia Magazine of History and Biography* 107 (Summer 1999). The *New York Times Magazine* featured Wensel in a 1958 article six months before her run. Margaret and William Meacham, "The Country Doctor Is Now a Lady," *New York Times Magazine*, January 19, 1958, unpaginated offprint in LOWP.
5. Peter Montague, "Senatorial Candidate Wensel Blasts Byrd Organization, School Closures," *Cavalier Daily*, November 4, 1958; Louise O. Wensel, typescript editorial for *Northern Virginia Sun*, November 1958, LOWP. Full—and very moving—documentation of this extraordinary and largely unrecognized campaign can be found in Wensel's papers, including her own narrative, Louise Oftedal Wensel, "Running for the United States Senate in 1958," typescript, LOWP.
6. Wensel, press release, July 25, 1958.
7. The state AFL-CIO leader had long condemned Byrd's practice of barring would-be voters from the polls to maintain elite control. In fact, at the same time the Virginia General Assembly was passing the massive resistance package, it also authorized ordinances to require labor organizers to register with county clerks—pure and simple intimidation. "Union Organizer Freed in Virginia," *Washington Post*, August 25, 1956. Thanks to James H. Hershman Jr. for this; also, "Dr. Wensel Is Backed by Virginia AFL-CIO," unidentified clipping, September 7, 1958, LOWP.
8. See, for example, Mark Newman, "The Baptist General Association of Virginia and Desegregation," *Virginia Magazine of History and Biography* 105 (Summer 1997): 268. Hershman notes that "the few white voices speaking publicly in favor of the *Brown* decision" after its issue "came almost entirely from religious organizations" (34–35, 49, 51, 56, 64–67, 133, 280).
9. Matthew D. Lassiter, "A 'Fighting Moderate': Benjamin Muse's Search for the Submerged South," in *The Moderates' Dilemma: Massive Resistance to School Desegregation in Virginia*, ed. Matthew D. Lassiter and Andrew B. Lewis (Charlottesville: University Press of Virginia, 1998), 182.

10. "The Changing Scene" (editorial), University of Virginia *Cavalier Daily,* September 19, 1958; Andrew B. Lewis, "Emergency Mothers: Basement Schools and the Preservation of Public Education in Charlottesville," in *The Moderates' Dilemma,* ed. Lassiter and Lewis, 72–102.
11. "Rally of Citizens Calls for Schools," *Virginian-Pilot,* October 14, 1958.
12. Gene Roberts and Hank Klibanoff, *The Race Beat: The Press, the Civil Rights Struggle, and the Awakening of a Nation* (New York: Random House, 2006), 210; Lewis, "Emergency Mothers," 80–81, 85–86, 216n37.
13. Editorial, "Political Lethargy Dispelled as David Faces Goliath," Waynesboro *News-Virginian,* July 28, 1958.
14. Robert E. Baker, "Protest Vote Is Heavy, but Byrd Wins Easily," *Washington Post,* November 5, 1958.
15. Kristin Norling, "Joel's in by a Nose," *Staunton Daily News,* November 5, 1958, 5; "The Election" (editorial), Norfolk *Journal and Guide,* November 8, 1958; Lewis, "'Any Old Joe,'" 316; "Dr. Wensel Says Byrd Win Is No Indication School Closings Have Full Favor," unidentified clipping, November 5, 1958, LOWP.
16. James H. Hershman Jr., "Massive Resistance Meets Its Match: The Emergence of a Pro-Public Education Majority," in *The Moderates' Dilemma,* ed. Lassiter and Lewis, 104–5, 109.
17. Lewis, "Emergency Mothers," 92, 217n59.
18. Stuart Saunders, Memo on Virginia Industrialization Group, 6, in section 1.2, box 1, Lewis F. Powell Jr. Papers, Washington and Lee University School of Law, Lexington, VA; Charles H. Ford and Jeffrey L. Littlejohn, "Reconstructing the Old Dominion: Lewis F. Powell, Stuart T. Saunders, and the Virginia Industrialization Group, 1958–1965," *Virginia Magazine of History and Biography* 121 (2013): 146–72.
19. Lewis, "Emergency Mothers," 96.
20. James M. Buchanan and G. Warren Nutter, "The Economics of Universal Education," Report of the Thomas Jefferson Center for Studies in Political Economy, February 10, 1959, C. Harrison Mann Papers, Special Collections and Archives, George Mason University (also in BHA); James M. Buchanan and G. Warren Nutter to Leon Dure, April 1, 1959, box 1, Leon Dure Papers, Manuscripts Division, Alderman Library, University of Virginia. They could see the consequences of letting the chips fall where they may right in Charlottesville. See Lewis, "Emergency Mothers" in *The Moderates' Dilemma,* 72, 102.
21. Buchanan and Nutter, "Economics of Universal Education."
22. Ibid. Their recklessness went deeper, in that they never recognized that to sell off school facilities, as they proposed, someone would have to come up with "money from somewhere to pay off $200 million of bonded indebtedness." Benjamin Muse, "It Is Also a Matter of Principal," *Washington Post,* February 22, 1959, E2. Thanks to James H. Hershman Jr. for this.
23. See Lorin A. Thompson, "Some Economic Aspects of Virginia's Current Educational Crisis," typescript report, September 1958, original in Special Collections Department, University of Virginia Library; "Virginia's Economic Advancement Will Come to an End If Public School System Is Completely Abandoned," *Cavalier Daily,* January 8, 1959; "Abandonment of Public Schools Seen as Threat to Virginia's Economic Growth," Charlottesville *Daily Progress,* January 7, 1959.
24. Buchanan and Nutter, "Economics of Universal Education"; Ford and Littlejohn, "Reconstructing the Old Dominion."
25. "Faculty Statement Supports Schools," *Daily Progress,* January 31, 1959. Faculty from ten other campuses across the state followed a few days later. "College Instructors Urge Open Schools," *Daily Progress,* February 6, 1959. Buchanan and Nutter were also, implicitly, seeking to refute the influential report of a UVA business school faculty member: Lorin A. Thompson, "Some Economic Aspects of Virginia's Current Educational Crisis," typescript report, September 1958, original in Special Collections Department, University of Virginia Library; "Virginia's Economic Advancement Will Come to an End If Public School System

Is Completely Abandoned," *Cavalier Daily,* January 8, 1959; "Abandonment of Public Schools Seen as Threat to Virginia's Economic Growth," Charlottesville *Daily Progress,* January 7, 1959.

26. Milton Friedman, "The Role of Government in Education," in *Economics and the Public Interest*, ed. Robert A. Solo (New Brunswick, NJ: Rutgers University Press, 1955), 123–44. Friedman's manifesto had proved helpful to some massive resisters in the trenches in the fall run-up to the January 1956 tuition grant referendum, particularly in the expanding suburbs of Northern Virginia, where they had to contend with the moderate "save the public schools" movement. One organization in Fairfax County repeated his arguments almost to the letter and held a public forum featuring a local Chicago-trained economist to urge that the state subsidize private schools to enable true school "choice." Harley M. Williams, "Virginia School Proposal," *Washington Post and Times Herald*, October 16, 1955, E4; Mollie Ray Carroll to JJK, March 21, 1956, Series 6626-B, JJKP. I thank James H. Hershman Jr. for this material.
27. Friedman, "The Role of Government in Education," 123–44. While telling the legislators that their brief was pure science, Nutter told Friedman it was "a mixture of persuasion and analysis"; Nutter to Friedman, February 18, 1959, and attached reply, box 31, Friedman Papers.
28. Roger A. Freeman, *Federal Aid to Education—Boon or Bane?* (Washington, DC: American Enterprise Association, 1955). For their joint work, see membership roster, National Tax Association's Committee on Financing of Public Education, December 11, 1958, box 346, Roger Freeman Papers, Hoover Institution Archives, Stanford University, Palo Alto, CA. "Several corporation" members, along with Freeman, complained that the tax group was "swinging left" and abetting "brainwashing" by "the 'liberal' side" on the need for higher taxes. Roger A. Freeman to Alvin Burger, November 21, 1958, and December 30, 1958, box 346, Roger Freeman Papers.
29. Freeman to Burger, November 21, 1958, and December 30, 1958, box 346, Roger Freeman Papers; Freeman, *Federal Aid to Education.*
30. Roger A. Freeman, "Unmet Needs in Education," typescript report for the Volker Fund, July 15, 1959, 2, 16, 25, 28, in box 311, Roger Freeman Papers. On the efficacy of contemporary women's groups on such matters, see, for example, Susan Lynn, *Progressive Women in Conservative Times: Racial Justice, Peace, and Feminism, 1945 to the 1960s* (New Brunswick, NJ: Rutgers University Press).
31. Hill quoted in Hershman, "Massive Resistance Meets Its Match," 129.
32. James M. Buchanan to Frank Hyneman Knight, October 24, 1957, box 3, Frank Hyneman Knight Papers, Special Collections Research Center, University of Chicago Library. His was the kind of rebuttal Jack Kilpatrick regularly made to northern critics of southern segregation. On Kilpatrick's rhetorical strategy, shared by other segregationist editors, see Roberts and Klibanoff, *The Race Beat*, 216–220.
33. For lucid introductions to the relevant legal history, see David L. Lightner, *Slavery and the Commerce Power: How the Struggle Against the Interstate Slave Trade Led to the Civil War* (New Haven, CT: Yale University Press, 2006); Laura F. Edwards, *A Legal History of the Civil War and Reconstruction: A Nation of Rights* (New York: Cambridge University Press, 2015); and "AHR Forum: The Debate over the Constitutional Revolution of 1937," *American Historical Review* 110, no. 4 (2005): 1046–51.
34. For astute analysis of the politics of Republican moderates in the growing suburbs of the South, see Lassiter, *The Silent Majority.*
35. J. Douglas Smith, *On Democracy's Doorstep: The Inside Story of How the Supreme Court Brought "One Person, One Vote" to the United States* (New York: Hill & Wang, 2014), 19.
36. "Constitutional Roadblocks" (editorial), *Richmond News Leader,* April 9, 1959, 12; G. Warren Nutter and James M. Buchanan, "Different School Systems Are Reviewed," *Richmond Times-Dispatch,* April 12, 1959, D3; G. Warren Nutter and James M. Buchanan, "Many

Fallacies Surround School Problem," *Richmond Times-Dispatch*, April 13, 1959, 7. See also, for explanation of the Hobson's choice facing moderates, Robert D. Baker, "The Perrow Report: Virginia Faces 2nd Dilemma," *Washington Post*, April 5, 1959, B3. My thanks to James H. Hershman Jr. for hunting down this sequel and sending these sources.

37. Benjamin Muse, "Some Sounds and Signs of the Times," *Washington Post*, April 12, 1959; "Segregation Bill Loses in Virginia," *New York Times*, April 21, 1959, 25.
38. Robert D. Baker, "Serious Blow to Byrd Machine," *Washington Post*, April 25, 1959, A1.
39. Jack Kilpatrick egged on the closures in a speech in Prince Edward County, praising its imminent stand for the "old liberties" against the "tyrannous aggrandizement of the central state," while other Americans dozed "under the narcotic illusions of a welfare state." The "battle" against "this monster," he told his white audience, "cannot be won without occasional acts of unyielding resistance," such as "courageous action" to close the schools rather than submit to "federal dictation"; "Farmville High School Commencement Speech," June 4, 1959, box 2, series C, JJKP.
40. Paul Duke, "Dixie Eyes a Virginia County, First to Shut All Its Public Schools," *Wall Street Journal*, December 1, 1959. The chilling story has received extensive coverage. Among the most illuminating recent scholarly works are Bonastia, *Southern Stalemate* and Titus, *Brown's Battleground*. For a more memoir-like treatment, see Green, *Something Must Be Done About Prince Edward County*.
41. Broadus Mitchell to James Buchanan, November 15, 1960, BHA; Buchanan to Mitchell, November 28, 1960, ibid.; Buchanan to Edgar F. Shannon Jr., November 21, 1960, ibid.; Joan Cook, "Broadus Mitchell, 95, Professor, Historian and Hamilton Authority," *New York Times*, April 30, 1988.

CHAPTER 5: TO PROTECT CAPITALISM FROM GOVERNMENT

1. Alexander Keyssar, *The Right to Vote: The Contested History of Democracy in the United States* (New York: Basic Books, 2000), 256.
2. Harry F. Byrd to T. Coleman Andrews, August 7, 1957, box 2, TCAP; on Montgomery, see the classic by Taylor Branch, *Parting the Waters: America in the King Years, 1954–1963* (New York: Simon & Schuster, 1988).
3. Keyssar, *Right to Vote*, 236–37, 262, 269, 271. Virginia charged $1.50 per year, on a cumulative basis (about $12 in 2016 dollars), and required that the taxes be paid in full six months prior to Election Day, thus before campaigns began. On the poll tax as "the cornerstone" of its "electoral controls," see Frank B. Atkinson, *The Dynamic Dominion: Realignment and the Rise of Virginia's Republican Party Since 1945* (Fairfax, VA: George Mason University Press, 1992), 15, also chapter 12, "Suddenly, an Expanded Electorate," on the Byrd machine's demise. Buchanan had earlier argued that "a uniform per-head poll tax would be appropriate as a major revenue source," with the additional value that it would "encourage continued out-migration of unskilled agricultural labor"; undated manuscript [c. early 1960s], "Optimum Fiscal Policy for Southern States," in BHA.
4. See especially J. Douglas Smith, *On Democracy's Doorstep: The Inside Story of How the Supreme Court Brought "One Person, One Vote" to the United States* (New York: Basic Books, 2014). Referring to concerns about property rights and taxation, James Buchanan worried about "dangers . . . [becoming] more urgent since the reapportionment decision"; James M. Buchanan to Colgate Darden Jr., June 24, 1965, BHA.
5. While not writing about the same figures as I am, the political theorist Corey Robin has captured this relational dynamic with keen insight in his book *The Reactionary Mind: From Edmund Burke to Sarah Palin* (New York: Oxford University Press, 2011), 3–28.
6. Gordon Tullock, "How I Didn't Become a Libertarian," August 7, 2003, LewRockwell.com; Gordon Tullock to James Buchanan, February 12, 1962, BHA.
7. J. E. Moes to James Buchanan, January 21, 1962, BHA; Richard E. Wagner, "Public Choice as Academic Enterprise," *American Journal of Economics and Sociology* 63 (January 2004):

64, 66. "Your absence from Charlottesville makes it hard to get good criticism of anything," Gordon Tullock once complained; Tullock to Buchanan, May 21, 1965, BHA.

8. Tullock to Richard C. Cornuelle, July 28, 1956, box 88, Tullock Papers. For Volker's interest in legal theory, training, and practice, see Ivan Bierly to Tullock, March 21, 1958, box 86, Tullock Papers.
9. James M. Buchanan and Gordon Tullock, *The Calculus of Consent: Logical Foundations of Constitutional Democracy* (1962; reprinted as vol. 3 of *The Collected Works of James M. Buchanan* [Indianapolis: Liberty Fund, 1990]), 286. My understanding in this chapter and beyond is indebted to the pathbreaking work of S. M. Amadae, *Rationalizing Capitalist Democracy: The Cold War Origins of Rational Choice Theory* (Chicago: University of Chicago Press, 2003), 133–55. No other scholar outside the public choice fold has studied Buchanan's thought as deeply, or identified as acutely the damage it augers for collective action and democracy.
10. Buchanan and Tullock, *Calculus of Consent*, 21, 286.
11. Ibid., 123, 158–61, 234.
12. Ibid., 166–68, 171. As S. M. Amadae notes, the analysis of the work "obliterates the concept of the public" in political theory, a sharp distinction from classical liberalism. See Amadae, *Rationalizing Capitalist Democracy*, 143.
13. George J. Stigler, "Proof of the Pudding?" *National Review*, November 10, 1972, 1258; see also Steven G. Medema, "'Related Disciplines': The Professionalization of Public Choice Analysis," *History of Political Economy Annual Supplement* 32 (2000): 313.
14. Buchanan and Tullock, *Calculus of Consent*, 96, 284.
15. Ibid., 286, 289, 303. On the legal history, Barry Friedman, *The Will of the People: How Public Opinion Has Influenced the Supreme Court and Shaped the Meaning of the Constitution* (New York: Farrar, Straus and Giroux, 2009), 141–94.
16. On the social and political history, Nell Irvin Painter, *Standing at Armageddon: The United States, 1877–1919* (New York: W. W. Norton, 1987).
17. Buchanan, *Better than Plowing*, 9. James M. Buchanan, *Better than Plowing and Other Personal Essays* (Chicago: University of Chicago Press, 1992).
18. James Madison to Edward Everett, August 1830, Constitution Society, www.constitution.org/rf/jm_18300801.htm. For the economist's claim that his program was "indigenous" to Virginia whereas his "antagonists" were "aliens," see Buchanan, *Better than Plowing*, 106.
19. Dwight R. Lee, "*The Calculus of Consent* and the Constitution of Capitalism," *Cato Journal* 7 (Fall 1987): 332.
20. Ira Katznelson, *Fear Itself: The New Deal and the Origins of Our Time* (New York: Liveright, 2013), 249.
21. Eugene B. Sydnor Jr. obituary, Virginia House of Delegates, January 14, 2004, http://lis.virginia.gov/cgi-bin/legp604.exe?041+ful+HJ208; "Sydnor Recalls Birth of Constitution Agency," *Richmond News Leader*, February 5, 1966. My thanks to James Sweeney for this research and to James H. Hershman Jr. for bringing it to my attention. See also George Lewis, "Virginia's Northern Strategy: Southern Segregationists and the Route to National Conservatism," *Journal of Southern History* 72 (February 2006).
22. Lewis, "Virginia's Northern Strategy," 122; Hustwit, *Salesman for Segregation*, 170–72, 181, 184; for a sampling, see the pamphlets R. Carter Glass, *Equality v. Liberty: The Eternal Conflict* (Richmond: Virginia Commission on Constitutional Government, 1960); and Virginia Commission on Constitutional Government, *Did the Court Interpret or Amend?* (Richmond: Virginia Commission on Constitutional Government, 1960).
23. James R. Sweeney, ed., *Race, Reason, and Massive Resistance: The Diary of David J. Mays, 1954–1959* (Athens: University of Georgia Press, 2008), 248, 251, 260–61.
24. Sweeney, *Race, Reason*, 219, 220, also 224, 261, on the strategy of avoiding the southern schools conflict and showcasing constitutional concerns shared by right-leaning northerners.

25. Ralph Harris to James M. Buchanan, October 21, 1965, BHA; Ralph Harris and Arthur Seldon, "Offering a Choice by Voucher," attached undated clipping from the London *Times;* Buchanan to Arthur Seldon, November 4, 1965, BHA; Edwin West to Gordon Tullock, January 14, 1966, box 84, Tullock Papers. The Volker Fund helped subsidize the study; see Arthur D. Little to Leon Dure, September 25, 1961, box 3, Dure Papers. On the IEA's shaping role in Thatcher's agenda, see Richard Crockett, *Thinking the Unthinkable: Think-Tanks and the Economic Counter-Revolution, 1931–1983* (New York: HarperCollins, 1994). On Dure's successful effort to destroy the union, see Robert Rodgers Korstad, *Civil Rights Unionism: Tobacco Works and the Struggle for Democracy in the Mid-Twentieth-Century South* (Chapel Hill: University of North Carolina Press, 2004), 321–27.
26. Amadae, *Rationalizing Capitalist Democracy*, 144.
27. Murray Rothbard to F. A. Harper, "What Is to Be Done," known as "Rothbard's Confidential Memorandum to the Volker Fund," July 1961, https://mises.org/library/rothbard's-confidential-memorandum-volker-fund-what-be-done". On Rothbard's stature in the cause, see Brian Doherty, *Radicals for Capitalism: A Freewheeling History of the Modern Libertarian Movement* (Philadelphia, PA: PublicAffairs, 2007), 247.
28. Rothbard to Gordon Tullock, November 4, 1958, box 88, Tullock Papers.
29. Buchanan, *Better than Plowing*, 89, 95; James Buchanan, "The Sayer of Truth: A Personal Tribute to Peter Bauer," *Public Choice* 112 (September 2002): 233.
30. Volker Fund announcement, 1961, box 58, Hayek Papers.
31. Janet W. Miller to Leon Dure, September 25, 1961, box 3, Dure Papers; Kenneth S. Templeton to Dure, July 7, 1960, ibid. For the foundation's post-1955 project to promote private schooling, see William Volker Fund Records, 1953–1961, boxes 1 and 2, David R. Rubenstein Rare Book and Manuscript Library, Duke University. Anyone who sought Volker funding, one ally quipped, "should make it clear that he does not believe in public schools, highways, police departments, and other evil statist enterprises." Doherty, *Radicals for Capitalism*, 187.
32. See, for example, Milton Friedman to G. Warren Nutter, May 4, 1960, box 31, Friedman Papers; Nutter to Dure, February 24, 1960, box 1, Dure Papers; Dure to Francis P. Miller, May 8, 1960, box 1, Dure Papers; Milton Friedman, *Capitalism and Freedom* (1962; repr., Chicago: University of Chicago Press, 2002), 6, 31, 35–36, 116.
33. Friedman reported that he had "been told" that the vouchers were a success. That was no doubt true, because Nutter and Buchanan arranged for him to have cocktails with their friend Leon Dure, the chief advocate of the freedom-of-choice vouchers (and fund-raiser for two segregation academies). "The appropriate solution of the school segregation problem," Friedman then instructed Chicagoans, in their own fight over school integration, "is to eliminate the public schools and permit parents to send their children to the schools of their choice, as Virginia has done"; Nutter to Dure, February 24, 1960, box 1, Dure Papers; Friedman to Nutter, May 4, 1960, box 31, Friedman Papers; "U.C. Economic Experts Advise Goldwater," *Chicago Tribune*, April 12, 1964, 8.
34. F. A. Hayek to Ivan Bierly, February 2, 1961, box 58, Hayek Papers; Dure to Segar Gravatt, June 4, 1964, box 2, Gravatt Papers.
35. Review of *Calculus of Consent* by Anthony Downs, *Journal of Political Economy* 72 (February 1964): 88; in a similar vein, review of *Calculus of Consent* by J. E. Meade, *Economic Journal* 73 (March 1963): 101. On Buchanan's ties to RAND thinkers and how they reviewed one another's work to build the authority of the enterprise, see Amadae, *Rationalizing Capitalist Democracy.*
36. Review of *Calculus of Consent* by Mancur Olson Jr., *American Economic Review* 52 (December 1962): 1217. Too numerous for individual citation, the other reviews, most positive, can be found in a simple library search.
37. Bruno Leoni to Gordon Tullock, January 25, 1963, box 4, Tullock Papers.

38. Medema, "'Related Disciplines,'" 309. Unfortunately, the journal has since disappeared. On the society, see also Amadae, *Rationalizing Capitalist Democracy,* 145–49.
39. See, for example, the recent book by Obama's regulation adviser, the legal scholar Cass R. Sunstein, *Why Nudge? The Politics of Libertarian Paternalism* (New Haven, CT: Yale University Press, 2014).
40. Buchanan, *Better than Plowing,* 106–7.
41. James J. Kilpatrick, "Goldwater Country," *National Review,* April 9, 1963, 281–82; see also James J. Kilpatrick, "Crossroads in Dixie," *National Review,* November 19, 1963, 433–35.
42. On the class, see Richard E. Wagner at Buchanan memorial conference, 2013 (author's notes). The literature on Goldwater's candidacy and the right turn of the Republican Party is quite large. The works I have found most illuminating for this book's themes are Rick Perlstein, *Before the Storm: Barry Goldwater and the Unmaking of the American Consensus* (New York: Hill & Wang, 2001) and Kim Phillips-Fein, *Invisible Hands: The Making of the Modern Conservative Movement from the New Deal to Reagan* (New York: W. W. Norton, 2009).
43. Gordon Tullock to Kenneth Templeton, May 1, 1959, box 88, Tullock Papers; Tullock to Ivan Bierly, March 27 [1959], box 86, Tullock Papers; Tullock to Bierly, May 6, 1959, box 86, Tullock Papers.
44. Tullock to William F. Buckley Jr., August 8, 1961, series I, box 37, William F. Buckley Jr. Papers, Manuscripts and Archives, Yale University, New Haven, CT; Tullock to Buckley, September 19, 1961, series 1, box 37, Buckley Papers; Tullock to Douglas Cady, January 16, 1963, box 84, Tullock Papers; Joseph Crespino, *Strom Thurmond's America* (New York: Hill & Wang, 2012), 132, 159. For Tullock's later advice on how the Republican Party might exploit racism to promote realignment, see his "The Heredity Southerner and the 1968 Election," *The Exchange* 29 (January 1969), box 111, William A. Rusher Papers, Library of Congress, Washington, D.C.
45. Tullock to Buckley, October 14, 1964, part I, box 33, Buckley Papers; Tullock to Buckley, November 19, 1965, part I, box 37, Buckley Papers; Buckley to Tullock, December 22, 1965, Buckley Papers.
46. Tullock to G. Warren Nutter, September 1964, box 95, Tullock Papers.
47. James Buchanan to F. A. Hayek, January 10, 1963, BHA.
48. "Colloquium on the Welfare State," Occasional Paper 3, December 1965, 25, Thomas Jefferson Center for Studies in Political Economy, University of Virginia, Charlottesville.

CHAPTER 6: A COUNTERREVOLUTION TAKES TIME

1. Gordon Tullock to William F. Buckley Jr., October 14, 1964, part 1, box 33, William F. Buckley Jr. Papers, Manuscripts and Archives, Yale University, New Haven, CT.
2. John A. Andrew III, *The Other Side of the Sixties: Young Americans for Freedom and the Rise of Conservative Politics* (New Brunswick, NJ: Rutgers University Press, 1997), 203–4. Buckley had been a doubter from the outset; see Rick Perlstein, *Before the Storm: Barry Goldwater and the Unmaking of the American Consensus* (New York: Hill & Wang, 2001), 471–73.
3. Goldwater had no qualms, for example, in calling for what today is known as a flat tax, as Andrews had before him. Reporter Stewart Alsop put it to him to confirm: did he really believe "a man with five million a year should pay the same rate as a man with five thousand?" "Yes. Yes, I do," Goldwater replied. He added, as today's advocates of capital formation would, that "the poor man would benefit from the rich man's investments"; Stewart Alsop, "Can Goldwater Win in 64?" *Saturday Evening Post,* August 24, 1963.
4. Reminiscences of William J. Baroody Sr. of the American Enterprise Institute to Barry Goldwater, January 7, 1970, box 11, Baroody Papers; Don Oberdorfer, "Nixon Eyes Ex-CIA Official," *Washington Post,* February 28, 1969, clipping in box 80, Baroody Papers; James Buchanan to Warren Nutter, November 4, 1964, box 80, Baroody Papers; Karl A. Lamb, "Under One Roof: Barry Goldwater's Campaign Staff," in *Republican Politics: The 1964 Campaign and Its Aftermath for the Party,* ed. Bernard Cosman and Robert J. Huckshorn (New York: Praeger, 1968), 31.

5. Hobart Rowen and Peter Landau, "Goldwater's Economists," *Newsweek*, August 31, 1964, 62–64; Warren Nutter to Gordon Tullock, July 10, 1964, box 95, Tullock Papers; Perlstein, *Before the Storm*, 462; Robert D. Novak, *The Agony of the G.O.P., 1964* (New York: MacMillan, 1965), 439–64; Katherine K. Neuberger to Charlton H. Lyons Sr., January 4, 1963, box 155, Rusher Papers.
6. Joseph E. Lowndes, *From the New Deal to the New Right: Race and the Southern Origins of Modern Conservatism* (New Haven, CT: Yale University Press, 2008), 68; Kim Phillips-Fein, *Invisible Hands: The Making of the Conservative Movement from the New Deal to Reagan* (New York: W. W. Norton, 2009), 65–66; Robert Alan Goldberg, *Barry Goldwater* (New Haven, CT: Yale University Press, 1995), 177.
7. Republican National Committee, "Senator Goldwater Speaks Out on the Issues," advertising reprint from *Reader's Digest*, 1964. Goldwater was not the first to make this case; neither libertarian intellectuals nor the business right had ever accepted Social Security as legitimate. See Phillips-Fein, *Invisible Hands*, 12, 21, 114, 147; Perlstein, *Before the Storm*, 260, 500–502; Goldberg, *Barry Goldwater*, 184, 188; David W. Reinhard, *The Republican Right Since 1945* (Lexington: University of Kentucky Press, 1983), 8, 49.
8. Dennis W. Johnson, *The Laws That Shaped America: Fifteen Acts of Congress and Their Lasting Impact* (New York: Routledge, 2009), 347; Perlstein, *Before the Storm*, 169.
9. Milton Friedman, "The Goldwater View of Economics," *New York Times Magazine*, October 11, 1964; see also Alan O. Ebenstein, *Milton Friedman: A Biography* (New York: Palgrave Macmillan, 2007), 367–69.
10. Milton Friedman and Rose D. Friedman, *Two Lucky People: Memoirs* (Chicago: University of Chicago Press, 1998), 367–70; "U.C. Economic Experts Advise Goldwater," *Chicago Tribune*, April 12, 1964, 8; "Right Face," *Newsweek*, January 13, 1964, 73; Robert D. Novak, *The Agony of the G.O.P., 1964*, 334; "Friedman Cautions Against [Civil] Rights Bill," *Harvard Crimson*, May 5, 1964.
11. Perlstein, *Before the Storm*, 462; Lowndes, *From the New Deal*, 105. William Rusher, the publisher of *National Review* and an early Goldwater backer, also argued for "freedom of association" as the best possible conservative frame for opposition to civil rights enforcement; Rusher to William F. Buckley Jr., June 18, 1963, box 40, Buckley Papers.
12. Nicol C. Rae, *The Decline and Fall of the Liberal Republicans: From 1952 to the Present* (New York: Oxford University Press, 1989), 74; on Birch Society influence, see 53, 57. See also Perlstein, *Before the Storm;* Andrew, *Other Side of the Sixties*, 175–76.
13. Ayn Rand, "'Extremism,' or the Art of Smearing," reprinted in Ayn Rand, *Capitalism: The Unknown Ideal* (New York: Signet, 1967), 176, 178.
14. Friedman and Friedman, *Two Lucky People*, 368.
15. Nick Kotz, *Judgment Days: Lyndon Baines Johnson, Martin Luther King Jr. and the Laws That Changed America* (Boston: Houghton Mifflin, 2005), 261.
16. On Virginia, see Frank B. Atkinson, *The Dynamic Dominion: Realignment and the Rise of Virginia's Republican Party Since 1945* (Fairfax, VA: George Mason University Press, 1992), 30–31; Rae, *Decline and Fall*, 76. For astute analysis of the politics of the growing suburbs as anti-Goldwater, see Matthew D. Lassiter, *The Silent Majority: Suburban Politics in the Sunbelt South* (Princeton, NJ: Princeton University Press, 2006).
17. "Days Ahead" (editorial), *Farmville Herald*, November 6, 1964; "Record Vote Goes to Goldwater," *Farmville Herald*, November 6, 1964. For the statewide vote, see Atkinson, *Dynamic Dominion*, 30–31; Rae, *Decline and Fall*, 76. My thanks to Chris Bonastia for sharing the *Farmville Herald* articles from his own research.
18. Ronald L. Heinemann, *Harry Byrd of Virginia* (Charlottesville: University Press of Virginia, 1996), 106, 412. On how the Fourteenth Amendment forever connected civil rights and federal power in law, a connection that enabled *Brown v. Board of Education* and much later legal reform, see Laura F. Edwards, *A Legal History of the Civil War and Reconstruction: A Nation of Rights* (New York: Cambridge University Press, 2015).
19. Ebenstein, *Milton Friedman*, 169–71, 181.

20. Kotz, *Judgment Days*, 261.
21. For an excellent summary of the legislative achievements, see Calvin G. MacKenzie and Robert Weisbrot, *The Liberal Hour: Washington and the Politics of Change in the 1960s* (New York: Penguin Press, 2008).
22. Bruce J. Dierenfield, *Keeper of the Rules: Congressman Howard W. Smith of Virginia* (Charlottesville: University of Virginia Press, 1987), 209, 218. In an omen of the future, however, a very conservative Republican won the general election for Smith's former seat.
23. William K. Klingaman, *J. Harvie Wilkinson Jr.: Banker, Visionary* (Richmond, VA: Crestar Financial, 1994), 120–33. I am grateful to James H. Hershman Jr. for this understanding and source. On southern development efforts, see Bruce J. Schulman, *From Cotton Belt to Sunbelt: Federal Policy, Economic Development, and the Transformation of the South, 1938–1980* (New York: Oxford University Press, 1991).
24. Alexander S. Leidholdt, "Showdown on Mr. Jefferson's Lawn: Contesting Jim Crow During the University of Virginia's Protodesegregation," *Virginia Magazine of History and Biography* 122 (2014): 243, 245, 248.
25. Bryan Kay, "The History of Desegregation at the University of Virginia, 1950–1969" (unpublished MA thesis, August 1979), held by University Archives, University of Virginia, 66–70.
26. Some of his former YAF mentees at the University of South Carolina were, reported one, "picketing the newly de-segregated lunch counters"—for having conceded to violation of their liberty; John Warfield to Gordon Tullock, April 26, 1965, box 84, Tullock Papers.
27. Kay, "History of Desegregation," 107, 117, 120; Paul M. Gaston, *Coming of Age in Utopia: The Odyssey of an Idea* (Montgomery, AL: New South Books, 2010), 271. On center use, see James Buchanan to Frank Knight, October 14, 1957, box 3, Knight Papers.
28. Kay, "History of Desegregation," 107, 117, 120; Gaston, *Coming of Age*, 271.
29. James Buchanan to Gordon Tullock, July 12, 1965, BHA.
30. Buchanan to Warren Nutter, June 2, 1965, BHA; also Gordon Tullock to Milton Friedman, April 21, 1965, box 116, Tullock Papers.
31. "$225,000 Given for New Institute," *Washington Post*, December 9, 1965, A16; "Study Slated on Potential of Virginia," *Washington Post*, April 14, 1967, C6. Thanks to James H. Hershman Jr. for alerting me to the institute and sending the sources.
32. The new vision and its application is captured well in Klingaman, *J. Harvie Wilkinson*, 83, 87, 125, 127–30, 133.
33. Warren Nutter to Milton Friedman, July 15, 1961, box 31, Friedman Papers.
34. Nutter to James Buchanan, October 28, 1960, BHA.
35. Ibid. The revealing documentation, with the Ford program officer raising reasonable concerns and Buchanan defending the dogmatic approach, is in Folder D-234 (University of Virginia, Educational Program of Thomas Jefferson Center for Studies in Political Economy), Ford Foundation Records, Rockefeller Archive Center, Sleepy Hollow, NY.
36. Buchanan to Edgar F. Shannon Jr., January 9, 1961, box 79, Baroody Papers. More extensive documentation can be found in this box.
37. Rowland Egger to Weldon Cooper, administrative assistant to the president, June 17, 1963, box 6, RG-2/1/2.635, series I, Papers of the President of the University of Virginia, Office Administrative Files, Manuscripts Division, Alderman Library, University of Virginia.
38. Gordon Tullock to James Buchanan, February 2, 1962, BHA; [University of Virginia] Department of Economics, "Excerpt from Self-Study Report," 1963, box 80, Baroody Papers; George W. Stocking to Robert J. Harris, November 14, 1964, box 12, RG-2/1/2.635, series I, Papers of the President of the University of Virginia, Office Administrative Files.
39. [University of Virginia] Department of Economics, "Excerpt from Self-Study Report," and Stocking to Harris, November 14, 1964.
40. James M. Buchanan, "What Economists Should Do," *Southern Economic Journal* 30 (January 1964): 215–21; Ely quoted in Richard Hofstadter, *Social Darwinism in American Thought* (Boston: Beacon Press, 1955), 146.

41. For a classic, unsurpassed exposition of the devastation inflicted by the "stark utopia" of the allegedly "self-adjusting market," see Karl Polanyi, *The Great Transformation: The Political and Economic Origins of Our Time* (1944; repr., Boston: Beacon Press, 1957), 3. On the tradition of legal realism, conceived in refutation of the kinds of claims Buchanan was reviving, see Morton J. Horwitz, *The Transformation of American Law, 1870–1960: The Crisis of Legal Orthodoxy* (New York: Oxford University Press, 1992), especially 194–98, for the realist scholars' critique of the notion of a natural market, as opposed to markets socially and historically constructed through the policy choices of actors. They demonstrated that property itself was, per Oliver Wendell Holmes Jr., "a creation of law" (197).
42. For a luminous, and quite chilling, explication, see S. M. Amadae, *Prisoners of Reason: Game Theory and Neoliberal Political Economy* (New York: Cambridge University Press, 2016), especially 175–92, on Buchanan.
43. Gordon Tullock, "Welfare for Whom?" paper for a session on "The Role of Government," Mont Pelerin Society, Aviemore Conference, 1968, BHA.
44. In fact, the U.S. Chamber of Commerce's Virginia-based research director, a veteran of the fight for private school vouchers, approached kindred economists seeking just such analysis in 1960. Emerson P. Schmidt to Milton Friedman, December 7, 1960, box 32, Friedman Papers. Friedman agreed on the "importance" of such analysis and suggested he contact two scholars then at the University of Virginia; Friedman to Schmidt, January 24, 1961, box 32, Friedman Papers.
45. The scholarship is so voluminous as to defy citation, but a review of those elected to the presidency of the Organization of American Historians, beginning in 1968, with the don of southern history C. Vann Woodward, and continuing to the present, reveals the overarching consensus on such matters, www.oah.org/about/past-officers. For the historian Paul Gaston's growing influence on campus at UVA, see his memoir *Coming of Age in Utopia*.
46. G. Warren Nutter to President Edgar F. Shannon Jr., January 29, 1968, box 80, Baroody Papers; Warren Nutter to James Buchanan, May 6, 1965, BHA. There is no evidence that any center faculty belonged to the society or shared its conspiracy theories about Communist infiltration of the U.S. government. Yet the Birch Society's economic thought was largely indistinguishable from theirs. The JBS was a significant presence in the state in 1965, moreover, as William J. Story, a JBS member and the Conservative Party of Virginia candidate for governor, attracted more than 13 percent of the vote in a four-way race; Atkinson, *Dynamic Dominion*, 155–56.
47. William Breit, "Creating the 'Virginia School': Charlottesville as an Academic Environment in the 1960s," *Economic Inquiry* 25 (October 1987): 650; John J. Miller, "The Non-Nobelist," *National Review*, September 25, 2006, 32–33; Gordon Tullock, "The Origins of Public Choice," in *The Makers of Modern Economics*, vol. 3, ed. Arnold Heertje (Cheltenham, UK: Edward Elgar, 1999), 1123; "Chronology of Significant Events," April 1976, box 80, Baroody Papers; Warren Nutter to Edgar F. Shannon Jr., January 29, 1968, box 80, Baroody Papers.
48. James M. Buchanan to President Edgar F. Shannon Jr., April 4, 1968, box 80, Baroody Papers.
49. Richard A. Ware to Milton Friedman, July 22, 1966, box 26, Friedman Papers.
50. James Buchanan to Gordon Tullock, July 8, 1965, BHA; Buchanan to Tullock, April 28, 1968, box 11, Tullock Papers. Buchanan admitted to the Relm Foundation that he "should have been more careful about building internal bridges earlier" to stave off "trouble"; Buchanan to Otto A. Davis, January 19, 1968, BHA; Buchanan to Richard A. Ware, April 23, 1968, BHA.
51. Steven G. Medema, "'Related Disciplines': The Professionalization of Public Choice Analysis," *History of Political Economy Annual Supplement* 32 (2000): 289–323.
52. James C. Miller to the Rector and Board of Visitors, September 23, 1976, box 80, Baroody Papers.
53. Buchanan to Frank Knight, July 7, 1967, box 3, Knight Papers.

54. Virginius Dabney, *Mr. Jefferson's University: A History* (Charlottesville: University of Virginia Press, 1981), 347–48; Jan Gaylord Owen, "Shannon's University: A History of the University of Virginia, 1959 to 1974" (PhD diss., Columbia University, 1993), 18, 25–26, 30, 32.
55. James M. Buchanan, "The Virginia Renaissance in Political Economy: The 1960s Revisited," in *Money and Markets: Essays in Honor of Leland B. Yeager*, ed. Roger Koppl (New York: Routledge, 2006), 35; on Tullock, even Nutter had misgivings (37).
56. James M. Buchanan, *Better than Plowing and Other Personal Essays* (Chicago: University of Chicago Press, 1992), 177.

CHAPTER 7: A WORLD GONE MAD

1. James M. Buchanan, "Public Finance and Academic Freedom," Center Policy Paper No. 226-30-7073, Center for Public Choice, Virginia Polytechnic Institute and State University, Fall 1971, 4; James M. Buchanan, notes for Charlotte talk to VPI alumni, January 19, 1970, BHA; "Potent Unexploded Bomb Found at UCLA," *Los Angeles Times*, November 12, 1968. On the killings, see Curtis J. Austin, *Up Against the Wall: Violence in the Making and Unmaking of the Black Panther Party* (Fayetteville: University of Arkansas Press, 2008), 224–26; Martha Biondi, *The Black Revolution on Campus* (Berkeley: University of California Press, 2012), 68–71; and Elaine Browne, *A Taste of Power: A Black Woman's Story* (New York: Pantheon, 1992), 160–67. On how provocateurs in the FBI's COINTELPRO program had been stirring conflict between the two organizations to undermine the Black Panther Party, see Joshua Bloom and Waldon E. Martin Jr., *Black Against Empire: The History and Politics of the Black Panther Party* (Berkeley: University of California Press, 2013), 218–29.
2. Angela Davis et al., *If They Come in the Morning: Voices of Resistance* (New York: New American Library, 1971), 185–86; J. Clay La Force to James M. Buchanan, May 19, 1970, BHA.
3. James M. Buchanan, *Better than Plowing and Other Personal Essays* (Chicago: University of Chicago Press, 1992), 114. For his praise of President S. I. Hayakawa at San Francisco State University, see James M. Buchanan, notes for Charlottesville talk. The global unrest was significant enough to move the United States and the USSR to détente, according to historian Jeremy Suri, in *Power and Protest: Global Revolution and the Rise of Détente* (Cambridge, MA: Harvard University Press, 2003).
4. See, for example, Andrew Burstein and Nancy Isenberg, "GOP's Anti-School Insanity: How Scott Walker and Bobby Jindal Declared War on Education," *Salon*, February 9, 2015; Richard Fausset, "Ideology Seen as Factor in Closings at University," *New York Times*, February 20, 2015; and the superb 2016 documentary *Starving the Beast*, directed by Steve Mims, www.starvingthebeast.net.
5. James M. Buchanan and Nicos E. Devletoglou, *Academia in Anarchy: An Economic Diagnosis* (New York: Basic Books, 1970), x–xi.
6. Ibid., 8.
7. Ibid., 48–50.
8. Ibid., 76, 78.
9. Ibid., 78–79.
10. Ibid., 80, 86.
11. Buchanan to Glenn Campbell, April 24, 1969, BHA; Buchanan to Bertram H. Davis, May 5, 1969, BHA; Buchanan to Arthur Seldon, [late June] 1969, BHA; Thomas Medvetz, *Think Tanks in America* (Chapel Hill: University of North Carolina Press, 2012), 104. Kristol soon came to Buchanan's center as a visiting lecturer, in a long relationship nurtured also by shared membership in the Mont Pelerin Society (1971 Annual Report). On Kristol and the affirmative action conflict, see Nancy MacLean, *Freedom Is Not Enough: The Opening of the American Workplace* (Cambridge, MA: Harvard University Press, 2006).
12. Buchanan and Devletoglou, *Academia in Anarchy*, x, 128–29. Their analysis echoes that of the John Birch Society leader Fred C. Koch, who alleged Communists' "use [of] the colored people" in *A Business Man Looks at Communism* (Farmville, VA: Farmville Herald, n.d.).

Challenged in South Carolina about the firing of Angela Davis, Buchanan similarly said that "her hiring was part of a conspiracy to get a Communist on the faculty"; Winthrop College *Herald*, clipping, October 7, 1971, BHA.

13. William Breit, "Supply and Demand of Violence," *National Review*, June 30, 1970, 684–85.
14. Gordon Tullock to James Buchanan, January 22, 1969, box 11, Tullock Papers. An appreciative reviewer drew out the implied alternative: "the bifurcation of the university system into professional training schools supported and strictly controlled by the state; and culture-consumption colleges privately supported and publicly scorned"; Harry G. Johnson, review of *Academia in Anarchy* in *Journal of Political Economy* 79 (January–February 1971), 204–5.
15. Predictable opposition came from Virginia's own James J. Kilpatrick, by then a national columnist: "The States Are Being Extorted into Ratifying the Twenty-Sixth Amendment," in *Amendment XXVI: Lowering the Voting Age*, ed. Sylvia Engdahl (New York: Greenhaven Press, 2010), 123–27. On the Army's unraveling, see Scovill Currin, "An Army of the Willing: Fayette'Nam, Soldier Dissent, and the Untold Story of the All-Volunteer Force" (PhD diss., Duke University, 2015). For how the president whom Buchanan loathed saved the day through dialogue and reform, see Jan Gaylord Owen, "Shannon's University: A History of the University of Virginia, 1959 to 1974" (PhD diss., Columbia University, 1993), 140, 212–13, 218–19; and Gaston, *Coming of Age*, 289. For Buchanan's attempt to have Shannon fired, see Buchanan to David Tennant Bryan, May 18, 1970, BHA.
16. A more consistent libertarian of the era was Murray Rothbard. He reviled the public sector and democracy, but he also opposed the Cold War and its offspring, the war in Indochina, as an imperial contest; Murray N. Rothbard, *The Betrayal of the American Right* (Auburn, AL: Ludwig von Mises Institute, 2007), 186, 196.
17. Meghnad Desai concluded, presciently, that the book's "analysis is a search for an easy panacea—*Homo Oeconomicus* on horseback"; Meghnad Desai, "Economics v. Anarchy," *Higher Education Review* 3 (Summer 1971): 78. Too numerous for individual citation, the other reviews can be found in a simple library search.
18. Steven G. Medema, "'Related Disciplines': The Professionalization of Public Choice Analysis," *History of Political Economy Annual Supplement* 32 (2000): 305–23; James M. Buchanan, "Heraclitian Vespers," *American Journal of Economics and Sociology* 63 (January 2004): 266; Center for Study of Public Choice, introductory brochure, Virginia Polytechnic Institute and State University, Blacksburg, VA, c. 1979; Loren Lomasky, "When Hard Heads Collide: A Philosopher Encounters Public Choice," *American Journal of Economics and Sociology* 63 (January 2004): 192. On the Smith ties, see Buchanan to Douglas Mason, September 23, 1971, BHA.
19. Geoffrey Brennan, "Life in the Putty-Knife Factory," *American Journal of Economics and Sociology* 63 (January 2004): 86, 87.
20. Frank B. Atkinson, *Dynamic Dominion: Realignment and the Rise of Virginia's Republican Party Since 1945* (Fairfax, VA: George Mason University Press, 1992), especially 200, 227–28, 231–54; Martin Koepenick, "T. Marshall Hahn Jr. on the New Georgia Pacific," *PIMA Magazine* 72 (May 1990): 35; James H. Hershman Jr., personal communication to author, May 2, 2015; Brennan, "Life in the Putty-Knife Factory," 85, 87.
21. Center for Economic Education, "Economic Issues Facing Virginia," seminar, November 15, 1972, BHA; James Buchanan to Gordon Tullock, "Five-Year Plan," October 9, 1973, BHA.
22. Buchanan to G. Warren Nutter, May 7, 1970, BHA. For his team's call for harsh measures, see Gordon Tullock to T. Marshall Hahn, May 7, 1970, box 47, T. Marshall Hahn Papers, 1962–1974, Special Collections, Virginia Polytechnic Institute and State University, Blacksburg, VA. See also Charles J. Goetz to Hahn, May 6, 1970, box 47, Hahn Papers; Hahn to Goetz, May 11, 1970, box 47, Hahn Papers.
23. Buchanan to Hahn, June 8, 1971, box 57, Hahn Papers.
24. Ibid.

25. William F. Upshaw to Buchanan, May 25, 1970, BHA; Buchanan to Benjamin Woodbridge, May 8, 1970, BHA; T. Marshall Hahn Jr. to Charles J. Goetz, May 11, 1970, Hahn Papers; Buchanan to Roy Smith, May 14, 1970, BHA; Buchanan to Senator Garland Gray, May 15, 1970, BHA; Buchanan to Richard M. Larry, June 3, 1971, BHA.
26. C. E. Ford to Buchanan, March 25, 1971, BHA; Buchanan to Richard M. Larry, January 14, 1972, BHA; Buchanan to Larry, February 22, 1972, and May 8, 1972, BHA; Buchanan, "Notes for discussion with Richard M. Larry on 4/26/73," April 25, 1973, BHA. For Scaife's multimillion-dollar strategic contributions in this formative decade, see John S. Saloma, *Ominous Politics: The New Conservative Labyrinth* (New York: Hill & Wang, 1984), 27–28, 30–31.
27. Mancur Olson and Christopher K. Clague, "Dissent in Economics: The Convergence of Extremes," *Social Research* 38 (Winter 1971): 751, 764, included by Buchanan with correspondence to Richard A. Ware (director of the Earhart Foundation), March 7, 1972, BHA.
28. J. D. Tuller to Buchanan, October 20, 1970, BHA; Tuller to Buchanan, September 25, 1970, with attachment; Buchanan to Donald A. Collins, June 9, 1970, BHA. For an overview of Olin's work, see Jason DeParle, "Goals Reached, Donor on the Right Closes Up Shop," *New York Times*, May 29, 2005, A1, 21.
29. James M. Buchanan, "The 'Social' Efficiency of Education," for 1970 Munich meeting of the Mont Pelerin Society; later version published in *Il Politico* 25 (Fall 1970), BHA. He turned this line of thought into a theoretical intervention he called "The Samaritan's Dilemma": that the help charity might provide someone in getting back on their feet might be overwhelmed by the harm it could do in enabling sloth (essentially, reinventing Gilded Age "scientific charity"); James M. Buchanan, "The Samaritan's Dilemma," in *Altruism, Morality and Economic Theory*, ed. Edmund S. Phelps (New York: Russell Sage Foundation, 1975), 71–85.

CHAPTER 8: LARGE THINGS CAN START FROM SMALL BEGINNINGS

1. John M. Virgo, "A New Forum on the Economic Horizon," *Atlantic Economic Journal* 1 (November 1973): 1–2; James M. Buchanan, "America's Third Century," *Atlantic Economic Journal* 1 (November 1973): 3. I am grateful to Alexander Gourse for bringing this piece to my attention through his fascinating study of the California origins of the conservative legal movement, which shows how Buchanan's approach influenced Governor Ronald Reagan's administration in its fight against Legal Services and the state legislature; see Alexander Gourse, "Restraining the Reagan Revolution: The Lawyers' War on Poverty and the Durable Liberal State, 1964–1989" (PhD diss., Northwestern University, 2015).
2. James Buchanan to Emerson P. Schmidt, May 1, 1973, BHA; Buchanan to Clay La Force, May 9, 1973, BHA. On the push for tax justice, see Joshua M. Mound, "Inflated Hopes, Taxing Times: The Fiscal Crisis, the Pocketbook Squeeze, and the Roots of the Tax Revolt" (PhD diss., University of Michigan, 2015).
3. Buchanan, "America's Third Century," 9. Gordon Tullock, *Toward a Mathematics of Politics* (Ann Arbor: University of Michigan Press, 1967).
4. James M. Buchanan to Nicos Devletoglou, February 27, 1973, BHA; Buchanan, "The Third Century Movement," typescript planning document, [mid-February] 1973; Buchanan, "Plans, Steps, and Projections—Provisional," March 3, 1973, BHA; Wilson Schmidt to Buchanan, May 26, 1972, BHA; Buchanan to Schmidt, May 1, 1973; BHA.
5. Buchanan to Nicos Devletoglou, February 27, 1973, BHA; Buchanan, "Private, Preliminary, and Confidential" document, February 16, 1973, BHA; Buchanan, "Third Century Movement" document. The term "counter-intelligentsia" entered public discussion five years later when William E. Simon published *A Time for Truth*, a book commonly cited as the origin of the push to convene a counterestablishment. That makes some sense, because Simon, secretary of the Treasury under Nixon, went on to do yeoman labor for the cause as head of the John M. Olin Foundation, exposing and stopping "the injustices to businessmen" at the hands of "a redistributionist state" that obstructed capital accumulation. But in point of

fact, Buchanan used the term first, shared it with Simon's undersecretary at Treasury, and had his own distinctive ideas about how to coax the desired entity into action, which are reflected in Simon's text; William E. Simon, *A Time for Truth* (New York: McGraw-Hill, 1978), 191, 210. Simon's diagnosis and prescription also built, in part, on public choice economics (216, 219, 221) and Buchanan's Third Century project (222–31).

6. Buchanan, "Third Century Movement" document.
7. Buchanan, "America's Third Century," 4, 6–7.
8. Ibid., 7–8.
9. For acute analysis of the ingrained, and lately inflamed, stereotypes in play, see Lisa Levenstein, *A Movement Without Marches: African American Women and the Politics of Poverty in Postwar Philadelphia* (Chapel Hill: University of North Carolina Press, 2009); and Marisa Chappell, *The War on Welfare: Family, Poverty, and Politics in Modern America* (Philadelphia: University of Pennsylvania Press, 2009).
10. The literature on the original Populism is vast, but for the best recent overview and interpretation, see Charles Postel, *The Populist Vision* (New York: Oxford University Press, 2007); for organized farmers' leadership in an alliance of "producers versus plutocrats" that shaped the early American regulatory state, see Elizabeth Sanders, *Roots of Reform: Farmers, Workers, and the American Regulatory State, 1877–1917* (Chicago: University of Chicago Press, 1999).
11. Bruce Palmer, *"Man over Money": The Southern Populist Critique of American Capitalism* (Chapel Hill: University of North Carolina Press, 1980), 170. On Buchanan's desk when I visited GMU was a copy of *Social Darwinism: Selected Essays of William Graham Sumner*, ed. Stow Persons (Englewood Cliffs, NJ: Prentice-Hall, 1963); Spencer was in the bookcase.
12. Buchanan, "America's Third Century," 9–12. Whether or not he had read it, his delineation echoed that of the Nixon strategist Kevin Phillips's 1969 *Emerging Republican Majority*.
13. Buchanan, "America's Third Century," 11–12. It is not clear from the sources whether anyone at the Richmond conference became involved, but Buchanan used his published speech as an organizing tool. Buchanan to Clay La Force, May 9, 1973, BHA.
14. Buchanan to Richard M. Larry, January 14, 1972, February 22, 1972, and May 8, 1972, BHA; Buchanan, "Notes for discussion with Richard M. Larry on 4/26/73," April 25, 1973, BHA; C. E. Ford to Buchanan, March 25, 1971, BHA. For Scaife's multimillion-dollar strategic contributions in this formative decade, see John S. Saloma, *Ominous Politics: The New Conservative Labyrinth* (New York: Hill & Wang, 1984), 27–28, 30–31. For the broader push by right-wing donors to change the debate in this era, see Alice O'Connor, "Financing the Counterrevolution," in *Rightward Bound: Making America Conservative in the 1970s*, ed. Bruce J. Schulman and Julian E. Zelizer (Cambridge, MA: Harvard University Press, 2008).
15. C. E. Ford to Buchanan, March 25, 1971, BHA; Buchanan to Richard M. Larry, January 14, 1972, February 22, 1972, and May 8, 1972, BHA; Buchanan, "Notes for discussion with Richard M. Larry on 4/26/73," April 25, 1973, BHA. For the wider corporate right's recruitment in cash-strapped Sunbelt colleges, see Bethany Moreton and Pamela Voekel, "Learning from the Right: A New Operation Dixie?" in Daniel Katz, ed., *Labor Rising: The Past and Future of Working People in America* (New York: New Press, 2012).
16. Buchanan, "Third Century Movement" document; Buchanan, "Private, Preliminary, and Confidential" document; Buchanan, "Plans, Steps, and Projections" post, March 3, 1973, BHA.
17. Buchanan, "Third Century Movement" document; Buchanan, "Private, Preliminary, and Confidential" document; Buchanan, "Plans, Steps, and Projections" post. Whether from whimsy or knowledge of the original, Buchanan was enlisting John Birch Society language in planning the mission.
18. Buchanan, "Third Century Movement" document.
19. List of attendees, Foundation for Research in Economics and Education Conference, October 4–5, 1973, BHA; Buchanan, "Notes for LA Meeting," October 5, 1973, BHA; see also

Edwin Meese III, *With Reagan: The Inside Story* (Washington, DC: Regnery Gateway, 1992), 32–33.

20. Buchanan, "Notes for LA meeting." Corporations' failure to grasp what the men of the right took to be their real interests was a cause of private anger. "The one thing I am looking forward to in the Communist takeover of America, is the liquidation to the American businessman," the architect of the GOP right said that year, furious at their "timid, herd-like" conduct; William A. Rusher to Jack Kilpatrick, August 3, 1973, box 48, Rusher Papers.
21. Joseph G. Peschek, *Policy-Planning Organizations: Elite Agendas and America's Rightward Turn* (Philadelphia, PA: Temple University Press, 1987), 35. A wealth of ICS material, including participants and activities, can be found in box GO97, Program and Policy Unit, series V, Ronald Reagan: Governor's Papers, Ronald Reagan Presidential Library, Simi Valley, CA.
22. Institute for Contemporary Studies, *Letter* 1, no. 1 (December 1974), a newsletter in box GO97, Reagan Papers, as are all the other items in this note; ICS, introductory brochure, c. 1974; ICS [typescript prospectus, n.d.]; A. Lawrence Chickering to Don Livingston, September 11, 1973; ICS, minutes of special meeting, December 4, 1973; ICS, minutes of special meeting, May 14, 1974. Indeed, a focus on economics enabled the rise of the right, finds Mark A. Smith, *The Right Talk: How Conservatives Transformed the Great Society into the Economic Society* (Princeton, NJ: Princeton University Press, 2007).
23. Peschek, *Policy-Planning Organizations,* 35.
24. Buchanan to Donald A. Collins, April 15, 1970, BHA; Institute for Contemporary Studies, introductory brochure, c. 1974, box GO97, Reagan Papers; ICS, minutes of special meeting, May 14, 1974, box GO97, Reagan Papers. On California Rural Legal Assistance and the wider OEO-backed legal challenge Reagan and his corporate allies faced, see Gourse, "Restraining the Reagan Revolution."
25. The effort was run through the Foundation for Research in Economics and Education (FREE), a nonprofit set up by Buchanan during his brief time at UCLA. On FREE, see Armen A. Alchian, "Well Kept Secrets of Jim's Contributions to Economic Ph.D.s of the University of California, Los Angeles"; http://publicchoice.info/Buchanan/files/alchian.htm; a Buchanan CV from 1980 lists him as an ongoing vice president and board member; BHA.
26. Steven M. Teles, *The Rise of the Conservative Legal Movement: The Battle for Control of the Law* (Princeton, NJ: Princeton University Press, 2008), 90, 102.
27. Buchanan to J. Clayton La Force, May 9, 1973, BHA; Manne to Buchanan, May 17, 1971, BHA.
28. Edwin McDowell, "Bringing Law Profs Up to Date on Economics," *Wall Street Journal,* July 23, 1971, 8.
29. Teles, *Rise of the Conservative Legal Movement,* 106–7, 110–11, 121, 124; Walter Guzzardi Jr., "Judges Discover the World of Economics," *Fortune,* May 21, 1979, 62; O'Connor, "Financing the Counterrevolution," 166–67.
30. Henry G. Manne to Buchanan, March 26, 1976, BHA; Teles, *Rise of the Conservative Legal Movement,* 103–7.
31. Saloma, *Ominous Politics,* 75; Teles, *Rise of the Conservative Legal Movement,* 103–7, 110–15, 121, 124; O'Connor, "Financing the Counterrevolution," 166–67.
32. Teles, *Rise of the Conservative Legal Movement,* 107–8, 114, 116–17. As *Fortune* magazine noted, "the lessons [Manne's program taught] could make a big difference when business cases come to the courtroom"; Guzzardi, "Judges Discover," 58.
33. Saloma, *Ominous Politics,* 75; Henry G. Manne, preface to *The Attack on Corporate America,* by University of Miami Law School, Law and Economics Center (New York: McGraw-Hill, 1978), xi–xv; Teles, *Rise of the Conservative Legal Movement,* 100. "Manne is solely interested in raising money," Buchanan grumbled to Tullock while visiting Manne's program, such that good conversation was rare; Buchanan to Tullock, February 13, 1976, box 11, Tullock Papers.

34. Teles, *Rise of the Conservative Legal Movement,* 104–5.
35. Eugene B. Sydnor Jr. obituary, Virginia House of Delegates, January 14, 2004, http://lis.virginia.gov/cgi-bin/legp604.exe?041+ful+HJ208; "Sydnor Recalls Birth of Constitution Agency," *Richmond News Leader,* February 5, 1966; Kim Phillips-Fein, *Invisible Hands: The Making of the Conservative Movement from the New Deal to Reagan* (New York: W. W. Norton, 2009), 156–62. The memorandum can be found in Powell's papers and online. For Powell's early antiunionism, see Lewis Powell to James J. Kilpatrick, February 14, 1961, Powell Papers. For his delight when Kilpatrick became nationally syndicated, "help[ing] to right the imbalance in national editorial comment which has existed for far too long," see Powell to Kilpatrick, March 7, 1965, Powell Papers.
36. Teles, *Rise of the Conservative Legal Movement,* 3; see also Benjamin C. Waterhouse, *Lobbying America: The Politics of Business from Nixon to NAFTA* (Princeton, NJ: Princeton University Press, 2015).
37. Alliance for Justice, *Justice for Sale: Shortchanging the Public Interest for Private Gain* (Washington, DC: Alliance for Justice, 1993), 6; see also ICS, minutes of special meeting, December 4, 1974, box GO97, Reagan Papers.
38. Project on the Legal Framework of a Free Society, *Law and Liberty* 2, no. 3 (Winter 1976), BHA.
39. McDowell, "Bringing Law Profs Up to Date," 8; Henry G. Manne to Robert LeFevre, May 2, 1974, box 7, LeFevre Papers, University of Oregon. Most "financiers of libertarian causes have been big businessmen" with a deep "personal interest in these ideas," notes an insider's history of the movement. Charles Koch and, later, his brother David became the "biggest financiers"; Brian Doherty, *Radicals for Capitalism: A Freewheeling History of the Modern Libertarian Movement* (Philadelphia, PA: PublicAffairs, 2007), 16.

CHAPTER 9: NEVER COMPROMISE

1. See the discussion of his long quest in Charles G. Koch, *Creating a Science of Liberty* (Fairfax, VA: Institute for Humane Studies, 1997), 2–7.
2. The story of the long legal fight, central to family lore, is best told in Schulman, *Sons of Wichita,* 27–35.
3. Ibid., quote on 33.
4. Gordon Tullock, "The Welfare Costs of Tariffs, Monopolies and Theft," *Western Economic Journal* 5 (1967): 224–32; for elaboration, Tullock, *Rent Seeking* (Brookfield, VT: Edward Elgar, 1993).
5. Ironically, Schulman believes Koch would have lost in a fair trial because he and his partner had learned about the process as employees of Universal Oil before setting off on their own. Schulman, *Sons of Wichita,* 31, 34.
6. Charles G. Koch, *The Science of Success: How Market-Based Management Built the World's Largest Private Company* (Hoboken, NJ: John Wiley & Sons, 2007), 12; Mayer, "Covert Operations"; Schulman, *Sons of Wichita,* 42, 48.
7. Fred C. Koch to James J. Kilpatrick, November 4, 1957, box 29, acc. 6626-b, JJK Papers; Schulman, *Sons of Wichita,* 21–22; J. Allen Broyles, *The John Birch Society: Anatomy of a Protest* (Boston: Beacon Press, 1964), 49, 58.
8. Schulman, *Sons of Wichita,* 21–22; Roy Wenzl and Bill Wilson, "Charles Koch Relentless in Pursuing His Goals," *Wichita Eagle,* October 14, 2012.
9. Koch, *The Science of Success,* 5–12; Wenzl and Wilson, "Charles Koch Relentless"; Mayer, "Covert Operations"; Glassman, "Market-Based Man."
10. "America's Richest Families," *U.S. News & World Report,* August 14, 1978; I came across this clipping because a young libertarian had circled Koch's standing and saved the listing in his papers. He got on the payroll. Roy A. Childs Papers, box 5, Hoover Institution Archives.

11. Charles G. Koch, "Tribute," preface to *The Writings of F. A. Harper*, vol. 1: *The Major Works* (Menlo Park, CA: Institute for Humane Studies, 1978), 1–3; Charles G. Koch, *Creating a Science of Liberty* (Fairfax, VA: Institute for Humane Studies, 1997), 2.
12. F. A. Harper, *Why Wages Rise* (Irvington on Hudson, NY: Foundation for Economic Education, 1957), 6–7, 71, 81–83, 94, 113, 119.
13. F. A. Harper, "Shall the Needy Inherit Our Colleges?" *The Freeman*, July 1957, 31.
14. Harper, *Why Wages Rise*, 6–7, 71, 81–83, 94, 113, 119.
15. F. A. Harper, *Liberty: A Path to Its Recovery* (Irvington on Hudson, NY: Foundation for Economic Education, 1949), 108–10, 124.
16. Koch, "Tribute," 1–3.
17. Robert LeFevre to Jack Kilpatrick, April 23, 1956, with attachments, box 54, LeFevre Papers; Kilpatrick to LeFevre, April 26, 1956, ibid.; LeFevre to Kilpatrick, July 1, 1954, and July 6, 1954, ibid.; LeFevre to Kilpatrick, July 6, 1954, with attachment, ibid. On LeFevre and the school, see Doherty, *Radicals for Capitalism*, 312–22.
18. Doherty, *Radicals for Capitalism*, 318; Schulman, *Sons of Wichita*, 89–96.
19. See "Wichita Collegiate School," Wikipedia, http://en.wikipedia.org/wiki/Wichita_Collegiate_School. On the founder's manifesto, see Robert Love, *How to Start Your Own School: A Guide for the Radical Right, the Radical Left, and Everybody In-Between Who's Fed Up with Public Education* (New York: Macmillan, 1973), especially 9, 31. On Love, see J. Allen Broyles, *The John Birch Society: Anatomy of a Protest* (Boston: Beacon Press, 1964), 40, 49, 59–60. Robert Welch, the Birch Society's founder, argued in 1963, with the Civil Rights Act pending, that segregation was "surely but slowly breaking down" naturally "wherever Negroes *earned the right* by sanitation, education, and a sense of responsibility, to share such facilities" (italics added); Claire Conner, *Wrapped in the Flag: A Personal History of America's Radical* Right (Boston: Beacon Press, 2013), 101.
20. For the bizarre tale, which led to the theocratic Christian right and an early iteration of today's racist and anti-Semitic "alt-right," see Michael McVicar, "Aggressive Philanthropy: Progressivism, Conservatism, and the William Volker Charities Fund," *Missouri Historical Review* 105, no. 4 (2011), 201.
21. Glassman, "Market-Based Man"; Institute for Humane Studies, *The Institute's Story* (Menlo Park, CA: Institute for Humane Studies, n.d., but pre-1975), 7, 15, 23. On the IHS-Volker-Buchanan connection, see John Blundell to Buchanan, October 30, 1986, BHA; and Doherty, *Radicals for Capitalism*, 407. The Koch-funded Center for Independent Education from its start worked with the IHS, formally affiliating in 1973; see Everett Dean Martin, *Liberal Education vs. Propaganda* (Menlo Park, CA: Institute for Humane Studies, n.d.), 17. Documentation of the IHS's work can be found in box 26 of the Hayek Papers, Hoover Institution Archives.
22. Mont Pelerin Society, "By-Laws," rev. ed., February 1966, box 122, Tullock Papers; *Newsletter of the Mont Pelerin Society* 4 (October 1973): 11, also no. 7 (March 1975): 15, and no. 10 (March 1976): 13, all box 122, Tullock Papers. The Charles Koch Foundation's seminars on Austrian economics, the Institute for Humane Studies' conferences on property law and union power, and the Center for Independent Education's cases against public schools, not to mention Henry Manne's Law and Economics program, all built their followings through the society's newsletter's pages.
23. See, for example, Ludwig von Mises, *The Anti-Capitalistic Mentality* (New York: D. Van Nostrand, 1956).
24. Schulman, *Sons of Wichita*, 77, 106. Murray Rothbard explained, in one of his Koch-funded treatises, that some corporations benefited from government-granted privileges and therefore should be considered the enemy as much as organized labor or government itself, but businesses that were crimped by cartels and rejected regulation, "especially those remote from the privileged 'Eastern Establishment,'" were "potentially receptive to free-market and libertarian ideas"; Justin Raimondo, *An Enemy of the State: The Life of Murray N.*

Rothbard (Amherst, NY: Prometheus Books, 2000), 203. Such entrepreneurs were, in fact, remaking America's model of capitalism in this era, as shown in the formative case of Walmart by Bethany E. Moreton, *To Serve God and Wal-Mart: The Making of Christian Free Enterprise* (Cambridge, MA: Harvard University Press, 2009).

25. Koch, *Science of Success*, 80.
26. Schulman, *Sons of Wichita*, 94. Koch's idol, Ludwig von Mises, applauded Ayn Rand for having "the courage to tell the masses what no politician told them: you are inferior and all the improvements in your conditions which you simply take for granted you owe to the efforts of men who are better than you." Jennifer Burns, *Goddess of the Market: Ayn Rand and the American Right* (New York: Oxford University Press, 2009), 177.
27. Wenzl and Wilson, "Charles Koch Relentless."
28. Doherty, *Radicals for Capitalism*, 442–43. James Buchanan likewise complained that Friedman pronounced on policy "as if he has a direct line to God." James Buchanan to Rutledge Vining, March 8, 1974, BHA. He also disassociated himself from the Chicago School under Friedman's leadership. James Buchanan to Warren J. Samuels, December 13, 1974, BHA. Those in the Austrian economics program funded by Koch at George Mason argued that Chicago School economics was incapable of adequately refuting the support for "interventionist policy" coming from such leaders of the discipline as Joseph Stiglitz, Paul Krugman, and Lawrence Summers. Peter J. Boettke and David L. Prychitko, "Introduction: The Present Status of Austrian Economics: Some (Perhaps Biased) Institutional History Behind Market Process Theory," in *The Market Process: Essays in Contemporary Austrian Economics* (Northampton, MA: Edward Elgar, 1994), 16n7.
29. James Glassman, "Market-Based Man," *Philanthropy Roundtable* (2011), www.philanthropyroundtable.org/topic/excellence_in_philanthropy/market_based_man.
30. John Blundell, "IHS and the Rebirth of Austrian Economics: Some Reflections on 1974–1976," *Quarterly Journal of Austrian Economics* 17 (Spring 2014): 93.
31. Ibid., 101–2.
32. There is an excellent literature on the recession of the 1970s as the prompt for a determined corporate mobilization to affect the political process. The works that have most shaped my understanding include Thomas Ferguson and Joel Rogers, *Right Turn: The Decline of the Democrats and the Future of American Politics* (New York: Hill & Wang, 1986); David Vogel, *Fluctuating Fortunes: The Political Power of Business in America* (1989; repr., Washington, DC: Beard Books, 2003); Bruce Schulman, *The Seventies: The Great Shift in American Culture, Society, and Politics* (New York: Free Press, 2001); Kim Phillips-Fein, *Invisible Hands: The Making of the Conservative Movement from the New Deal to Reagan* (New York: W. W. Norton, 2009); Judith Stein, *Pivotal Decade: How the United States Traded Factories for Finance in the Seventies* (New Haven, CT: Yale University Press, 2010); Benjamin C. Waterhouse, *Lobbying America: The Politics of Business from Nixon to NAFTA* (Princeton, NJ: Princeton University Press, 2015); and Meg Jacobs, *Panic at the Pump: The Energy Crisis and the Transformation of American Politics in the 1970s* (New York: Hill & Wang, 2016).
33. On the fracturing of the "business movement" into a state of "every man his own lobbyist," see Waterhouse, *Lobbying America*, quote on 232, also 250–51.
34. Charles Koch, "The Business Community: Resisting Regulation," *Libertarian Review*, August 1978, reprint found in box 5, Roy A. Childs Papers, Hoover Institution Archives, Stanford University.
35. George H. Pearson to Buchanan, December 31, 1975, BHA; "Austrian Economic Theory & Analysis," program, Virginia Seminar, October 18–19, 1975, box 26, Hayek Papers; Buchanan to George H. Pearson, March 22, 1976, BHA, with attached schedule; Buchanan to Edward H. Crane III, November 30, 1977, BHA; Buchanan to Gordon Tullock, February 25, 1971, box 11, Tullock Papers; Tullock to Buchanan, March 2, 1971, box 11, Tullock Papers; George Pearson to Buchanan, October 22, 1975, and March 25, 1976, BHA; James M. Buchanan, *Better than Plowing and Other Personal Essays* (Chicago: University of Chicago Press, 1992), 71–72.

36. George H. Pearson to Buchanan, January 8, 1971, October 22, 1975, and March 25, 1976, BHA. Among the Koch-funded center's other publications on the subject was Murray N. Rothbard, *Education, Free and Compulsory: The Individual's Education* (Wichita, KS: Center for Independent Education, 1972).
37. Charles G. Koch to Buchanan, February 19, 1977, BHA; also Pearson to Buchanan, October 22, 1975, BHA.
38. William E. Simon, *A Time for Truth* (New York: McGraw-Hill, 1978), 230.
39. In his most recent book, Koch includes Lenin among the thinkers who "made tremendous impressions on me." Charles G. Koch, *Good Profit* (New York: Crown Business, 2015), 13.
40. Raimondo, *Enemy of the State*, 23, 28, 179; Doherty, *Radicals for Capitalism*, 45, 59–60, 243–45; Murray N. Rothbard, *The Betrayal of the American Right* (Auburn, AL: Ludwig von Mises Institute, 2007), 69, 73–77.
41. Raimondo, *Enemy of the State*, 211–17.
42. Rothbard, *The Betrayal of the American Right*, 202; also Raimondo, *Enemy of the State*, 224–39.
43. Ibid., 214–17.
44. Koch, "The Business Community."
45. Raimondo, *Enemy of the State*, 217.
46. Doherty, *Radicals for Capitalism*, 392–96; Hazlett, *Libertarian Party*, 84–89.
47. Edward H. Crane III, "Libertarianism," in *Emerging Political Coalitions in American Politics*, ed. Seymour Martin Lipset (San Francisco: Institute for Contemporary Studies, 1978), 353–55.
48. Raimondo, *Enemy of the State*, 218. Buchanan worked with Cato from its founding to his death; see obituary at www.cato.org/people/james-buchanan.
49. Murray N. Rothbard, *Left and Right: The Prospects for Liberty*, Cato Paper No. 1 (Washington, DC: Cato Institute, 1979), 1, 11, 19, 20.
50. Raimondo, *Enemy of the State*, 220–23. "Suddenly," writes Rothbard's devoted biographer, "with the help of one of the wealthiest families in the United States, if not the world, the number and quality of these practically nonexistent creatures would be increased a hundred-fold."
51. Rothbard, *Betrayal of the American Right*, 202; also Raimondo, *Enemy of the State*, 224–39.
52. Raimondo, *Enemy of the State*, 224. That usage of "ruling class" is now common on the Koch-backed right, as a fund-raising letter from the Heritage Foundation illustrates, crediting the 2016 election with "saving the republic from the ruling class," Jim DeMint to mailing list, n.d., but mid-December 2016, copy in author's possession.
53. Rothbard, *Left and Right*, 25.
54. Raimondo, *Enemy of the State*, 224; James Allen Smith, *The Idea Brokers: Think Tanks and the Rise of the New Policy Elite* (New York: New Press, 1991), 221.
55. Doherty, *Radicals for Capitalism*, 16, 394, 409–13; Raimondo, *Enemy of the State*, 218–24.
56. Raimondo, *Enemy of the State*, 239.
57. James M. Buchanan, "The Samaritan's Dilemma," in *Altruism, Morality, and Economic Theory*, ed. Edmund S. Phelps (New York: Russell Sage Foundation, 1975), 71, 74–76, 84.
58. Buchanan, "Samaritan's Dilemma," 71, 74. Without credit to Buchanan, an ally on the libertarian right applied such ideas in a critique of liberal social policy as influential as it was empirically empty and analytically flawed: Charles Murray, *Losing Ground: American Social Policy, 1950–1980* (New York: Basic Books, 1984). Cato brought Buchanan's ethics into policy discussion. See, for example, Doug Brandow, "Right On, Gov. Allen," *Washington Post*, January 29, 1995, C8.
59. Buchanan, "Samaritan's Dilemma," 74–75, 84.
60. Margalit Fox, "Lanny Friedlander, 63, of *Reason* Magazine, Dies," *New York Times*, May 7, 2011.

61. "*Reason* Profile" of editor Robert Poole Jr., *Reason,* October 1972; William Minto and Karen Minto, "Interview with Robert Poole," *Full Context* 11 (May/June 1999), www.fullcontext.info/people/poole_intx.htm.
62. Robert W. Poole Jr., *Cut Local Taxes—Without Reducing Essential Services* (Santa Barbara, CA: Reason Press, 1976); Doherty, *Radicals for Capitalism,* 376–77; Minto and Minto, "Interview with Robert Poole."
63. Poole, *Cut Local Taxes*; Minto and Minto, "Interview with Robert Poole." Proxmire began giving monthly Golden Fleece Awards in 1975 to embarrass government agencies, in one case being successfully sued by a scientist for defamation, though he, unlike Buchanan, often targeted military spending.
64. Doherty, *Radicals for Capitalism,* 441–43; Minto and Minto, "Interview with Robert Poole."
65. Doherty, *Radicals for Capitalism,* 441–43.
66. Smith, *The Idea Brokers,* 221–22.
67. Robert W. Poole Jr. to F. A. Hayek, August 3, 1979, box 101, Hayek Papers, Hoover Institution; Reason Press Release, April 20, 1981; Tibor Machan to F. A. Hayek, September 14, 1981, ibid.; Minto and Minto, "Interview with Robert Poole"; Robert W. Poole, *Cutting Back City Hall* (New York: Universe Books, 1980).
68. The Liberty Fund, kindred to the Institute for Humane Studies, aimed to revive the tradition of the Volker Fund conferences, which had yielded so many hard-core libertarian scholars in the late 1950s, including Buchanan and Nutter. A. Neil McLeod to Buchanan, June 3, 1976, BHA.
69. See, for example, Buchanan to A. Neil McLeod, June 15, 1981, BHA.
70. Buchanan to A. Neil McLeod, July 26, 1976, BHA; the wine listing was in Buchanan's hand. McLeod had been chairman of the Council of Advisors of the IHS in the 1960s.
71. Schulman, *Sons of Wichita,* 107.
72. Ed Clark to Charles G. Koch, February 16, 1978, box 1, Ed Clark Papers, Hoover Institution Archives; Schulman, *Sons of Wichita,* 109.
73. Charles G. Koch to Robert D. Love, March 2, 1978, box 1, Clark Papers. California was indeed promising terrain for an arch-capitalist cause; see Lisa McGirr, *Suburban Warriors: The Origins of the New American Right* (Princeton, NJ: Princeton University Press, 2001).
74. Doherty, *Radicals for Capitalism,* 406, 408. On the tax revolt, see Schulman, *The Seventies,* 205–217, and James M. Buchanan, "The Potential for Taxpayer Revolt in American Democracy," *Social Science Quarterly* 59 (March 1979): 691–96.
75. Doherty, *Radicals for Capitalism,* 414–17, 421; Schulman, *Sons of Wichita,* 114–15.
76. Doherty, *Radicals for Capitalism,* 416, 421; Schulman, *Sons of Wichita,* 116. As it happened, Rothbard was but the first of several loyal players dumped by their patron when they failed to follow his cues; Crane would eventually be shown the door, and others, too, as time went on, usually with enough of a severance to keep them quiet.
77. James M. Buchanan, "Heraclitian Vespers," *American Journal of Economics and Sociology* 63 (January 2004): 269; Buchanan, *Better than Plowing,* 12, 101, 106; James M. Buchanan, *The Limits of Liberty: Between Anarchy and Leviathan* (1975; repr., with new pagination, Indianapolis: Liberty Fund, 2000), 209, 212.
78. Buchanan, *Limits of Liberty,* 5, 220.
79. Ibid., 117, 11, 19–20, also 116. On the antidemocratic impact of these "fortuitous circumstances" on national legislation, see Ira Katznelson, Kim Geiger, and Daniel Kryder, "Limiting Liberalism: The Southern Veto in Congress, 1933–1950," *Political Science Quarterly* 108 (Summer 1993): 283–306.
80. Buchanan, *Limits of Liberty,* 223, 186, also 209.
81. James O'Connor, *The Fiscal Crisis of the State* (New York: St. Martin's, 1973). On the city as an early laboratory for neoliberal policies, see Alice O'Connor, "The Privatized City: The Manhattan Institute, the Urban Crisis, and the Conservative Counterrevolution in New York," *Journal of Urban History* (January 2008); Kimberly K. Phillips-Fein, *Fear City: The*

New York City Fiscal Crisis and the Rise of the Age of Austerity (New York: Metropolitan Books, 2017). Inflation-produced "bracket creep" in tax rates, moreover, led many middle-class taxpayers to see the tax code as unfair.

82. See Holly Sklar, ed., *Trilateralism: The Trilateral Commission and Elite Planning for World Management* (Boston: South End Press, 1980); and Niall Ferguson, et al., *The Shock of the Global: The 1970s in Perspective* (Cambridge, MA: Belknap Press of Harvard University Press, 2010).
83. James M. Buchanan and G. Brennan, "Tax Reform Without Tears: Why Must the Rich Be Made to Suffer?" *The Economics of Taxation,* ed. Henry J. Aaron and Michael Boskin (Washington, DC: Brookings Institution, 1980), 35–54.
84. Buchanan, *Limits of Liberty,* 56, 108, 187.
85. Ibid., 188, 191, 196, 202, 219. See also another version of his case from this era in James M. Buchanan and Richard G. Wagner, *Democracy in Deficit: The Political Legacy of Lord Keynes* (New York: Academic Press, 1977).
86. Buchanan, *Limits of Liberty,* 188, 191, 196, 202, 219. On such coalitions, which many others took to be a sign of progress, see Paul Johnston, *Success While Others Fail: Social Movement Unionism and the Public Workplace* (Ithaca, NY: ILR Press Books, 1994); Marjorie Murphy, *Blackboard Unions: The AFT and the NEA, 1900–1980* (Ithaca, NY: Cornell University Press, 1992), 252–73; and Eileen Boris and Jennifer Klein, *Caring for America: Home Health Care Workers in the Shadow of the Welfare State* (New York: Oxford University Press, 2012), 94–148.
87. Amadae, *Prisoners of Reason,* 175–76, 182, 187, and 191. The entire section she devotes to *Limits of Liberty* deserves close reading (175–92).
88. Buchanan, *Limits of Liberty,* 205.
89. Ibid., 224–25.
90. Ibid., xvi, 208, 212, 215, 220–21.
91. Warren J. Samuels, "The Myths of Economic Liberty and the Realities of the Corporate State: A Review Article," *Journal of Economic Issues* 10 (December 1976), quotes on 937 and 939.
92. "Buchanan Awarded Economic Prize," VPI *News Messenger,* January 27, 1977.
93. George J. Stigler, "Why Have the Socialists Been Winning?" presidential address to the Mont Pelerin Society in Hong Kong, 1978, included in Festschrift for Hayek's eightieth birthday, *Ordo,* Band 30 (Stuttgart, Germany: Gustav Fisher Verlag, 1979), 66–68. I am grateful to Eduardo Canedo for bringing this speech to my attention. Hayek had come to similar conclusions. "So long as the present form of democracy persists," he wrote, "decent government cannot exist." F. A. Hayek, *The Political Order of a Free People,* vol. 3 of *Law, Legislation and Liberty* (Chicago: University of Chicago Press, 1979), 135, 150–51.

CHAPTER 10: A CONSTITUTION WITH LOCKS AND BOLTS

1. Orlando Letelier, "Economic 'Freedom's' Awful Toll: The 'Chicago Boys' in Chile," *The Nation,* August 28, 1976; Naomi Klein, *The Shock Doctrine: The Rise of Disaster Capitalism* (New York: Metropolitan Books, 2007), 98–99. Chile has a complex tradition of naming, with an official second last name not ordinarily used (in Pinochet's case, Ugarte); for the sake of clarity for non-Chilean readers, I have omitted the less used additional name with each Chilean named in this chapter.
2. Chile's tortured history in this period has been the subject of a vast and excellent international literature. Among the English-language works I have found most helpful for this chapter are, in order of publication, Pamela Constable and Arturo Valenzuela, *A Nation of Enemies: Chile Under Pinochet* (New York: W. W. Norton, 1993); Robert Barros, *Constitutionalism and Dictatorship: Pinochet, the Junta, and the 1980 Constitution* (Chicago: University of Chicago Press, 2002); Steve J. Stern, *Battling for Hearts and Minds: Memory Struggles in Pinochet's Chile* (Durham, NC: Duke University Press, 2006); Klein, *Shock Doctrine;* Lois Hecht Oppenheim, *Politics in Chile: Socialism, Authoritarianism and Market Democracy,* 3rd ed. (Boulder, CO: Westview, 2007); and Karin Fischer, "The Influence of Neoliberals in Chile Before, During, and After

Pinochet," in *The Road from Mont Pelerin: The Making of the Neoliberal Thought Collective*, ed. Philip Mirowski and Dieter Plehwe (Cambridge, MA: Harvard University Press, 2009).

3. Jeffrey Rubin, *Sustaining Activism: A Brazilian Women's Movement and a Father-Daughter Collaboration* (Durham, NC: Duke University Press, 2013), 50, 52–53. I am grateful to Rubin for his extremely helpful reading of an early draft, including his pointing out how the Pinochet regime was also abrogating reforms made under the anti-Communist Christian Democrat Frei. For a brief summary, see Lewis H. Diuguid, "Eduardo Frei Dies," *Washington Post*, January 23, 1982.
4. On Friedman's input, see Constable and Valenzuela, *A Nation of Enemies*, 166–67; and Klein, *Shock Doctrine*, 75–128; on Hayek's visit, too, Fischer, "The Influence of Neoliberals in Chile," 310, 316, 328, 339n2. On the human rights campaign in the United States, see Van Gosse, "Unpacking the Vietnam Syndrome: The Coup in Chile and the Rise of Popular Anti-Interventionism," in *The World the Sixties Made*, ed. Van Gosse and Richard Moser (Philadelphia, PA: Temple University Press, 2003).
5. To my knowledge, the only other scholars who have highlighted Buchanan's impact are Alfred Stepan, the distinguished comparative political scientist whose footnote on Buchanan deepened my interest in the Virginia school, and Karin Fischer, now head of the Institute of Sociology at the University of Linz: Stepan, "State Power and the Strength of Civil Society in the Southern Cone of Latin America," in *Bringing the State Back In*, ed. Peter B. Evans, et al. (New York: Oxford University Press, 1985), 341n13; Fischer, "The Influence of Neoliberals in Chile," 321–26. While both wrote with keen insight, neither had the primary sources used in this chapter. Buchanan had explicitly taken issue with Hayek for assuming change in the desired direction could be "evolutionary"; granted, "reform may, indeed, be difficult," Buchanan argued, but it must be tried to achieve their desired world; Buchanan, *The Limits of Liberty: Between Anarchy and Leviathan* (1975; repr., with new pagination, Indianapolis: Liberty Fund, 2000), 211n1.
6. Later president Michelle Bachelet, quoted in Bruno Sommer Catalan, "Chile's Journey Towards a Constituent Assembly," *Equal Times*, November 17, 2014.
7. Klein, *Shock Doctrine*, 78, 133–37.
8. Fischer, "Influence of Neoliberals in Chile," 325–26; Oppenheim, *Politics in Chile*, 133–37.
9. José Piñera, "Chile," in *The Political Economy of Policy Reform*, ed. John Williamson (Washington, DC: Institute for International Economics, 1994), 228–30; Fischer, "Influence of Neoliberals in Chile," 325–26; Klein, *Shock Doctrine*, 78; Oppenheim, *Politics in Chile*, 133–37; Constable and Valenzuela, *A Nation of Enemies*, 155, 191. On Piñera's ongoing Cato position, see www.cato.org/people/jose-pinera.
10. Oppenheim, *Politics in Chile*, 115; Ramon Iván Nuñez Prieto, *Las Transformaciones de la Educación Bajo el Régimen Militar*, vol. 1 (Santiago, Chile: CIAN, 1984), 50–53. I thank Anthony Abata for translating for me.
11. Carlos Francisco Cáceres to James Buchanan, November 27, 1979, BHA.
12. James M. Buchanan, "From Private Preferences to Public Philosophy: The Development of Public Choice," in *The Economics of Politics*, by James Buchanan, et al. (London: Institute of Economic Affairs, 1978), reprinted as "De las Preferencias Privadas a Una Filosofía del Sector Público," *Estudios Públicos* 1 (1980). On CEP, see Sergio de Castro to Buchanan, June 25, 1980, BHA.
13. Juan de Onis, "Purge Is Underway in Chile's Universities," *New York Times*, February 5, 1980, 6. Among those terminated was the director of an economic research center at the University of Chile who headed a group of attorneys and former legislators who opposed the dictatorship's plan to draft a new constitution without involving an "elected constituent assembly."
14. Juan de Onis, "New Crackdown in Chile Greets Appeals for Changes," *New York Times*, July 10, 1980, A2.

15. Vanessa Walker, "At the End of Influence: The Letelier Assassination, Human Rights, and Rethinking Intervention in US-Latin American Relations," *Journal of Contemporary History* 46 (2011); Carlos Francisco Cáceres to Buchanan, November 27, 1979, BHA; "Accomplished U.S. Economist in Chile," *El Mercurio*, May 6, 1980, C4; "Minister de Castro with Economist James Buchanan," *El Mercurio*, May 8, 1980, C3; Constable and Valenzuela, *A Nation of Enemies*, 171, 186. I am grateful to Eladio Bobadilla for translating all the *El Mercurio* articles for me.
16. Carlos Francisco Cáceres to Buchanan, February 12, 1980, BHA; Buchanan to Hernan Cortes Douglas, May 5, 1981, BHA; Jorge Cauas to F. A. Hayek, June 5, 1980, box 15, Hayek Papers; list of attendees, Foundation for Research in Economics and Education conference, October 4–5, 1973, BHA. On Cáceres and Pedro Ibáñez, Buchanan's official hosts, as the most anxious to contain popular power through suffrage restrictions and limits on what elections could control in the new constitution, see Barros, *Constitutionalism and Dictatorship*, 221–22.
17. "Government Interventionism Is Simply Inefficient," *El Mercurio*, May 9, 1980, C1.
18. "Government Interventionism," C1; "Economic Liberty: The Basis for Political Liberty," *El Mercurio*, May 7, 1980, C1.
19. Jorge Cauas to Friedrich Hayek, March 26, 1980, box 15, Hayek Papers.
20. Stern, *Battling for Hearts and Minds*, 170–71.
21. Ibid., 167–78; "Chile's New Constitution: Untying the Knot," *The Economist*, October 21, 2004; "Chile: Democratic at Last—Cleaning Up the Constitution," *The Economist*, September 15, 2005; Carlos Huneeus, "Chile: A System Frozen by Elite Interests," International Institute for Democracy and Electoral Assistance (2005). Link no longer functional, but hard copy in author's possession.
22. Oppenheim, *Politics in Chile*, 118, 137; Constable and Valenzuela, *A Nation of Enemies*, 137–38.
23. Barros, *Constitutionalism and Dictatorship*, 172; Stern, *Battling for Hearts and Minds*, 171–73, 178; Cynthia Gorney, "Pinochet, with Disputed Constitutional Mantle, Moves into Palace," *Washington Post*, March 12, 1981; "Chile's New Constitution: Untying the Knot," *The Economist*, October 21, 2004.
24. Edward Schumacher, "Chile Votes on Charter That Tightens Pinochet's Rule," *New York Times*, September 11, 1980, A2; Heraldo Muñoz, *The Dictator's Shadow: Life Under Augusto Pinochet* (New York: Basic Books, 2008), 128–29; Barros, *Constitutionalism and Dictatorship*, 173n10; Stern, *Battling for Hearts and Minds*, 171–73, 178; Gorney, "Pinochet, with Disputed Constitutional Mantle"; "Chile's New Constitution."
25. Buchanan to Sergio de Castro, May 22, 1980, BHA; similarly, Buchanan to Carlos Francisco Cáceres, May 17, 1980, BHA.
26. Rolf J. Luders, "The Chilean Economic Experiment," paper presented to the 1980 General Meeting of the Mont Pelerin Society, box 24, Mont Pelerin Society Records, Hoover Institution Archives, Stanford University, Palo Alto, CA.
27. Constable and Valenzuela, *A Nation of Enemies*, 311, 313.
28. Hayek, too, was pleased. "A dictatorship which is deliberately restricting itself," he said in defense of the new constitution, "can be more liberal in its policies [presumably, its economic policies] than a democratic society which has no limits"; Fischer, "Influence of Neoliberals in Chile," 328, also 339n2.
29. Center for Study of Public Choice, *Annual Report*, 1980, Virginia Polytechnic Institute and State University, 61–62, BHA.
30. Pedro Ibáñez, Mont Pelerin Society, "Announcement," December 1980, box 88, Hayek Papers; James M. Buchanan, "Democracy: Limited or Unlimited?" paper prepared for 1981 Viña del Mar regional meeting of the Mont Pelerin Society, BHA; Marcus Taylor, *From Pinochet to the 'Third Way': Neoliberalism and Social Transformation in Chile* (London:

Pluto Press, 2006), 199–200. On the grave, see Constable and Valenzuela, *A Nation of Enemies,* 140.

31. Taylor, *From Pinochet to the 'Third Way'*, 199–200.
32. Center for Study of Public Choice, *Annual Report,* 1980, 60–61.
33. William A. Link, *Righteous Warrior: Jesse Helms and the Rise of Modern Conservatism* (New York: St. Martin's Press, 2008), 331.
34. James M. Buchanan, *Politics by Principle, Not Interest: Toward Nondiscriminatory Democracy* (New York: Cambridge University Press, 1998).
35. "Pinochet's Web of Bank Accounts Exposed," *Guardian,* March 16, 2005; Eric Dash, "Pinochet Held 125 Accounts in U.S. Banks, Report Says," *New York Times,* March 16, 2005; Muñoz, *The Dictator's Shadow,* 289, 292; Buchanan, *Economics from the Outside In: "Better than Plowing" and Beyond* (College Station: Texas A&M Press, 2007), 201. I thank my Brazilianist colleague John French for his incisive reading of this chapter and for alerting me to Pinochet's self-enrichment.
36. See, for example, the detailed case by the Union of Radical Economics, *The Economics of Milton Friedman and the Chilean Junta* (New York: URPE, 1997), for distribution at an American Enterprise Institute luncheon to honor his Nobel Prize, copy in box 138, Friedman Papers.
37. Constable and Valenzuela, *A Nation of Enemies,* 194–96.
38. Ibid., 196–98, also 212, on loss of retirement savings.
39. Jorge Contesse, quoted in Alisa Solomon, "Purging the Legacy of Dictatorship from Chile's Constitution," *The Nation,* January 21, 2014; Alfred Stepan, "The Last Days of Pinochet?" *New York Review of Books,* June 2, 1988.
40. Constable and Valenzuela, *A Nation of Enemies,* 310; Barros, *Constitutionalism and Dictatorship,* 306, 310.
41. Oppenheim, *Politics in Chile,* 190.
42. Constable and Valenzuela, *A Nation of Enemies,* 143, 229, 237 (quote), 245; Taylor, *From Pinochet to the 'Third Way,'* 188–89, 237.
43. Ariel Dorfman, "9/11: The Day Everything Changed in Chile," *New York Times,* September 8, 2013, 6–7.
44. Constable and Valenzuela, *A Nation of Enemies,* 312–13; Alfred Stepan, ed., *Democracies in Danger* (Baltimore: Johns Hopkins University Press, 2009), 62–63; Mark Ensalaco, "In with the New, Out with the Old? The Democratizing Impact of Constitutional Reform in Chile," *Journal of Latin American Studies* 26 (May 1994): 418, 420. On the recent push for a constituent assembly to overhaul the constitution, not least by ending the binomial system of representation, see Solomon, "Purging the Legacy."
45. Daniel J. Mitchell and Julia Morriss, "The Remarkable Story of Chile's Economic Renaissance," *Daily Caller,* July 18, 2012, www.cato.org/publications/commentary/remarkable-story-chiles-economic-renaissance; Jonah Goldberg, "Iraq Needs a Pinochet," *Los Angeles Times,* December 14, 2006, cited in Muñoz, *The Dictator's Shadow,* 30; "Chile," 2016 Index of Economic Freedom, Heritage Foundation, www.heritage.org/index/country/chile; Koch, *Good Profit,* 59. For similar trumpeting by Buchanan allies, see Paul Craig Roberts and Karen LaFollette Araujo, *The Capitalist Revolution in Latin America* (New York: Oxford University Press, 1997), especially the preface by his close friend Peter Bauer. It is notable that not one of these glowing accounts acknowledges the U.S. role in "making the economy scream," as Nixon instructed the CIA, under Allende, whom they excoriate for exactly the kinds of problems U.S. policy exacerbated, if it did not wholly cause.
46. Reuters in Santiago, "Chilean Student Leader Camila Vallejo Elected to Congress," *Guardian,* November 18, 2013.
47. Miguel Urquiola, "The Effects of Generalized School Choice on Achievement and Stratification: Evidence from Chile's Voucher Program," *Journal of Public Economics* 90 (2006): 1477, 1479; Pamela Sepúlveda, "Student Protests Spread Throughout Region," Inter Press

Service, November 25, 2011; William Moss Wilson, "Just Don't Call Her Che," *New York Times*, January 29, 2012, 5; Francisco Goldman, "They Made Her an Icon, Which Is Impossible to Live Up To," *New York Times Magazine*, April 8, 2012, 25.

48. Pascale Bonnefoy, "Executives Are Jailed in Chile Finance Scandal," *New York Times*, March 8, 2015, 9: Pascale Bonnefoy, "As Graft Cases in Chile Multiply, a 'Gag Law' Angers Journalists," *New York Times*, April 7, 2016. On the problems of the private pension accounts, see Silvia Borzutsky, "Cooperation or Confrontation Between the State and the Market? Social Security and Health Policies," in *After Pinochet: The Chilean Road to Democracy and the Market*, ed. Silvia Borzutsky and Lois Hecht Oppenheim (Gainesville: University Press of Florida, 2006), 142–66.
49. Linz and Stepan, *Problems of Democratic Transition and Consolidation*, 200.
50. Reuters, "Chile Election Victor Michelle Bachelet Pledges Major Reforms," *Guardian*, December 16, 2013; Muñoz, *The Dictator's Shadow*, 128–29; Barros, *Constitutionalism and Dictatorship*, 298; Bruno Sommer Catalan, "Chile's Journey Towards a Constituent Assembly," *Equal Times*, November 17, 2014.
51. "If the authoritarian features of the Constitution of 1980 are not removed sometime soon, the crisis of representation," worries one leading Chilean constitutional scholar, "could end in another violent struggle"; Javier Couso, "Trying Democracy in the Shadow of an Authoritarian Legality: Chile's Transition to Democracy and Pinochet's Constitution of 1980," *Wisconsin International Law Journal* 29 (2011): 415; also Aldo C. Vacs, "Coping with the General's Long Shadow on Chilean Democracy," in *After Pinochet*, ed. Borzutsky and Oppenheim, 167–73. See also Brianna Lee, "Chile's President Michelle Bachelet Approval Sinks over Economic Malaise, Corruption, and Stalled Reforms," *International Business Times*, September 16, 2015.
52. Center for Study of Public Choice, *Annual Report*, 1980, BHA; James M. Buchanan, "Reform in the Rent-Seeking Society," from *Toward a Theory of the Rent-Seeking Society*, ed. James M. Buchanan, et al. (College Station: Texas A&M University, 1980), 361–62, 367.

CHAPTER 11: DEMOCRACY DEFEATS THE DOCTRINE

1. Leslie Maitland Werner, "George Mason U.: 29 and Growing Fast," *New York Times*, December 31, 1986.
2. The developers commissioned their own storyteller, on whose account my own depends heavily: Russ Banham, *The Fight for Fairfax: A Struggle for a Great American County* (Fairfax, VA: GMU Press, 2009), xiii–xv, 30, 94. On the flagship postwar university-linked metropolitan development strategy and its features, see Margaret Pugh O'Mara, *Cities of Knowledge: Cold War Science and the Search for the Next Silicon Valley* (Princeton, NJ: Princeton University Press, 2004).
3. Banham, *Fight for Fairfax*, 184; see also the discussion of Johnson's "almost daily" conversations with the developers in Paul E. Ceruzzi, *Internet Alley: High Technology in Tysons Corner 1945–2005* (Cambridge, MA: MIT Press, 2008), 125, also 132; notably, federal proximity, defense department contracts, and RAND Corporation connections made it all possible. On Buchanan and RAND, see Amadae, *Rationalizing Capitalist Democracy*, 76, 78, 145. For early local usage of the term "Beltway bandits," see "Fairfax County Bandit Gets 30 Years," *Washington Post*, August 20, 1968, B3.
4. Buchanan, *Better than Plowing and Other Personal Essays* (Chicago: University of Chicago Press, 1992), 45.
5. Ruth S. Intress, "Winner of Nobel Seen As Brilliant but Opinionated," *Richmond Times-Dispatch*, October 1986, reproduction without date or page numbers in Friedman Papers; Eric Randall, "Philosophical Differences Led Nobel Prize Winner Away from Tech," October 22, 1986, *Richmond Times-Dispatch*, clipping in RG 15/8, College of Arts and Sciences Printed Material, Special Collections, Virginia Polytechnic Institute and State University.

6. Intress, "Winner of Nobel"; Randall, "Philosophical Differences."
7. Intress, "Winner of Nobel."
8. Ibid.; Randall, "Philosophical Differences." At Buchanan's memorial service in 2013, friends made references to these explosive rages. For the corporate analogue, see James M. Buchanan and Roger L. Faith, "Secession and the Limits of Taxation: Toward a Theory of Internal Exit," *American Economic Review* 77 (December 1987): 1023–31.
9. Buchanan, *Better than Plowing*, 16; Buchanan and Faith, "Secession and the Limits of Taxation," 1023–31.
10. Leah Y. Latimer, "Nobel Seen as Milestone of Mason's Growing Stature," *Washington Post*, October 17, 1986; Karen I. Vaughn to James Buchanan, August 6, 1978, BHA; Karen I. Vaughn, speech at Buchanan memorial service, September 29, 2013, GMU; D'Vera Cohn, "GMU Raids Faculty Stars from Rivals," *Washington Post*, June 30, 1985; Philip Walzer, "Faculty Stars Seldom Shine for Undergraduates," unidentified AP clipping, n.d., BHA.
11. Vaughn, speech at Buchanan memorial service; Karen I. Vaughn, "How James Buchanan Came to George Mason University," *Journal of Private Enterprise* 30 (2015): 103–9; Karen I. Vaughn, "Remembering Jim Buchanan," *Review of Austrian Economics* 27 (2014), 160.
12. Buchanan to A. Neil McLeod, June 14, 1983, BHA; Latimer, "Nobel Seen as Milestone"; Cohn, "GMU Raids Faculty Stars"; Walzer, "Faculty Stars Seldom Shine." For recognition of the "symbiotic relationship" George Mason built with the business community, in which corporations and right-wing foundations supply it with money and it supplies them with "useful theories" such as those produced by Buchanan, see Michael Kinsley, "How to Succeed in Academia by Really Trying: Viewpoint," *Wall Street Journal*, October 30, 1986, 33.
13. On the changes in public higher education, see the illuminating ethnographic study by Gaye Tuchman, *Wannabe U: Inside the Corporate University* (Chicago: University of Chicago Press, 2009), and the engaging first-person political-economic analysis by Nancy Folbre, *Saving State U: Why We Must Fix Public Higher Education* (New York: New Press, 2010).
14. Wade J. Gilley, "Is GMU Big Enough for Buchanan?" in *Methods and Morals in Constitutional Economics: Essays in Honor of James M. Buchanan*, ed. Geoffrey Brennan, Hartmut Kliemt, and Robert D. Tollison (New York: Springer, 2002), 565–66. Notably, Gilley also took a swipe at the "liberal arts coterie" whose "misconceived" vision of the university emphasized teaching undergraduates "without having to measure up" (564).
15. Buchanan to George Pearson, October 16, 1980, BHA; Peter J. Boettke, David L. Prychitko, "Introduction: The Present Status of Austrian Economics: Some (Perhaps Biased) Institutional History Behind Market Process Theory," in *The Market Process: Essays in Contemporary Austrian Economics Introduction*, ed. Boettke and Prychitko (Northampton, MA: Edward Elgar, 1994), 10; Daniel Schulman, *Sons of Wichita*, 260–62 (also, on Hayek and von Mises, 55, 93, 105); Doherty, *Radicals for Capitalism*, 408. The chair of the American Enterprise Institute's Council of Economic Advisers wrote of Fink's academically undistinguished edited volume on supply-side economics: "It does move the cause along"; Paul W. McCracken, "Taking Supply-Side Economics Seriously," *Wall Street Journal*, January 28, 1983, 30.
16. Brian Doherty, *Radicals for Capitalism: A Freewheeling History of the Modern Libertarian Movement* (Philadelphia, PA: PublicAffairs, 2007), 407, Malcolm X story on 430; James M. Buchanan to Charles Koch, May 24, 1984, BHA; Vaughn, *Remembering Jim Buchanan*, 145.
17. Charles Koch, "The Business Community: Resisting Regulation," *Libertarian Review*, August 1978; Boettke and Prychitko, "Introduction," 11; Paul Craig Roberts quoted in David Warsh, *Economic Principals: Masters and Mavericks of Modern Economics* (New York: New Press), 96.

18. Buchanan to Richard M. Larry, June 14, 1982, BHA (same text sent to Michael S. Joyce, June 14, 1982, BHA); Buchanan to Martin F. Connor, June 15, 1982, BHA; Janet Nelson to Buchanan, September 22, 1983, BHA; Edward H. Crane to Buchanan, September 7, 1983, BHA; James M. Buchanan, "Notes for Heritage Foundation reception," May 23, 1984, BHA; Vaughn, *Remembering Jim Buchanan*," 163.
19. James M. Buchanan, "Notes for Remarks to George Mason Economics Faculty," October 1, 1982.
20. Lawrence Mone, "Thinkers and Their Tanks Move on Washington," *Wall Street Journal*, March 19, 1988, 34.
21. David Shribman, "Academic Climber: University Creates a Niche, Aims to Reach Top Ranks," *Wall Street Journal*, September 30, 1985, 1. The Reason Foundation's head asserted that Buchanan's ideas had become the new "conventional wisdom" in Washington; Robert W. Poole Jr., "The Iron Law of Public Policy," *Wall Street Journal*, August 4, 1986, 13.
22. Miller, known for his advocacy of deregulation on the staff of the American Enterprise Institute, became executive director of the Presidential Task Force on Regulatory Relief, then chair of the Federal Trade Commission and later budget director for Reagan as head of the OMB. Tollison was named director of the Bureau of Economics at the FTC under Miller. Roberts, in the words of a contemporary reporter, "more than any other single player wrote the legislation that brought about the [Reagan-proposed] tax cuts in 1981." Tollison worked under Miller in the FTC. Jane Seaberry, "'Public Choice' Finds Allies in Top Places," *Washington Post*, April 6, 1986, F1; Robert D. Tollison, "Graduate Students in Virginia Political Economy, 1957–1991," occasional paper on Virginia political economy (Fairfax, VA: Center for Study of Public Choice, George Mason University, 1991), 3–4, 21; "Swearing-In Ceremony for Jim Miller," October 8, 1985, box 232, White House Office of Speechwriting, Reagan Library.
23. James M. Buchanan, "Democracy: Limited or Unlimited?" paper prepared for 1981 Viña del Mar regional meeting of the Mont Pelerin Society, BHA. Buchanan voted for Reagan in 1980 and 1984, yet did not himself identify as a Republican, but rather as "an independent"; Ken Singletary, "Nobel Prize Winner Explains Reasons for Leaving Tech," unidentified clipping, November 18, 1986, C1, in T. Marshall Hahn Papers, Virginia Polytechnic Institute and State University, Special Collections, Blacksburg, VA.
24. David A. Stockman, *The Triumph of Politics: Why the Reagan Revolution Failed* (New York: Harper & Row, 1986), quote on 2.
25. See, for example, Thomas Edsall, *Chain Reaction: The Impact of Race, Rights, and Taxes on American Politics* (New York: W. W. Norton, 1991), especially chapter 10, "Coded Language."
26. Stockman, *Triumph of Politics*, 8–9, 11, 92, 125.
27. Ibid., 13, 181, 190–92, 204, 390–92. A recent synthesis by two leading historians bears out Stockman's case on the durability of popular programmatic liberalism; see Meg Jacobs and Julian E. Zelizer, *Conservatives in Power: The Reagan Years, 1981–1989: A Brief History with Documents* (Boston: Bedford/St. Martin's, 2010). For other versions of the same conclusion, see W. Elliot Brownlee and Hugh Davis Graham, eds., *The Reagan Presidency: Pragmatic Conservatism and Its Legacies* (Lawrence: University Press of Kansas, 2003).
28. Stockman, *Triumph of Politics*, 14, 393, 391–92, 394. One full statement bears quoting: "We can afford to be the arsenal of the free world and have our modest welfare state, too. The only thing we cannot afford to do is to continue pretending we do not have to finance it out of current taxation" (292).
29. Ibid., 92, 222. For the chilling tale of "the fateful decision to cover up what we knew to be the true budget numbers" in October 1981, see 329–42, 344–45, 357, 362, 373. For the final tally, see James T. Patterson, *Restless Giant: The United States from Watergate to* Bush v. Gore (New York: Oxford University Press, 2005), 158–59.
30. James M. Buchanan, "Post-Reagan Political Economy," in *Constitutional Economics*, ed. James M. Buchanan (Cambridge, MA: Basil Blackwell, 1991), 1–2, 14; James M. Buchanan,

Why I, Too, Am Not a Conservative: The Normative Vision of Classical Liberalism (Northampton, MA: Edward Elgar, 2005), 60.

31. Buchanan referred to Social Security as a "Bismarckian transplant onto hitherto alien ground" (in a nasty burst of nativism for someone busy importing onto alien ground the ideas of two Austrians). James M. Buchanan, "The Economic Constitution and the New Deal: Lessons for Late Learners," in *Regulatory Change in an Atmosphere of Crisis: Current Implications of the Roosevelt Years,* ed. Gary M. Walton (New York: Academic Press, 1979), 22. On the vast, homegrown, Depression-era struggle for old-age pensions, see Edwin Amenta, *When Movements Matter: The Townsend Plan and the Rise of Social Security* (Princeton, NJ : Princeton University Press, 2006).
32. Social Security was the centerpiece of James M. Buchanan, "Dismantling the Welfare State," notes prepared for presentation at 1981 European Regional Meeting, Mont Pelerin Society, Stockholm, August–September 1981, box 88, Hayek Papers. See also Daniel Orr, "Rent Seeking in an Aging Population," in *Toward a Theory of the Rent-Seeking Society,* ed. James M. Buchanan, et al. (College Station: Texas A&M University, 1980), 222–35.
33. Edward H. Crane to Buchanan, May 6, 1983, BHA; James M. Buchanan, "Social Security Survival: A Public-Choice Perspective," *Cato Journal* 3, no. 2 (Fall 1983): 339–41, 352–53; Mancur Olson, "'Social Security Survival': A Comment," ibid., 355–56. On Cato's move to the capital, criticized by Murray Rothbard as an opportunistic move "toward the State and toward Respectability," see Schulman, *Sons of Wichita,* 116.
34. Buchanan, "'Social Security Survival,'" 339–41, 352–53. Earlier that year, Buchanan had joined the board of advisers for the pro-privatization Family Security Foundation; James M. Wootton to Buchanan, February 28, 1983, BHA.
35. Buchanan, "'Social Security Survival,'" 339–41, 352–53.
36. Ibid.
37. Ibid. For an illuminating discussion of the perceived and enduring differences between social insurance and means-tested programs in America's two-track welfare system, see Linda Gordon, *Pitied but Not Entitled: Single Mothers and the History of Welfare* (New York: Free Press, 1994).
38. Buchanan, "'Social Security Survival.'" On the long campaign that followed, and continues, see Steven M. Teles and Martha Derthick, "Social Security from 1980 to the Present: From Third Rail to Presidential Commitment—and Back?" in *Conservatism and American Political Development,* ed. Brian J. Glenn and Steven M. Teles (New York: Oxford University Press, 2009), 261–90. For the systematic—yet so far failed—efforts of the corporate right to turn young people against Social Security, see Jill Quadagno, "Generational Equity and the Politics of the Welfare State," *Politics and Society* 17 (April 1989): 353–76.
39. Buchanan, "'Social Security Survival.'"
40. Ibid.
41. Stuart Butler and Peter Germanis, "Achieving a 'Leninist' Strategy," *Cato Journal* 3 (Fall 1983): 547–56.
42. Ibid.
43. Ibid.
44. Ibid.
45. Ibid.
46. Ibid. So that no one expected miracles overnight, the authors reminded that "as Lenin well knew, to be a successful revolutionary," the cadre "must be prepared for a long campaign."
47. Koch, *Good Profit,* 41.
48. Jeffrey R. Henig, "Privatization in the United States: Theory and Practice," *Political Science Quarterly* 104 (Winter 1989–90): 649–50; see also Jeffrey R. Henig, Chris Hammett, and Harvey B. Feigenbaum, "The Politics of Privatization: A Comparative Perspective," *Governance: An International Journal of Policy and Administration* 1 (October 1988): 442–68;

and Monica Prasad, *The Politics of Free Markets: The Rise of Neoliberal Economic Policies in Britain, France, Germany, and the United States* (Chicago: University of Chicago Press, 2006), 3, 14, 22, 24, 27.

49. A case in point of underestimation: Jeff Faux, president of the Economic Policy Institute, quoted in Peter T. Kilborn, "Panel Urging Public-to-Private Shift," *New York Times*, March 7, 1988.
50. Butler thus applied Buchanan's approach to produce plans to sharply alter the political dynamics of budget growth in a manner that would be nearly impossible to reverse, becoming so deft at shaping measures that could be pushed by allies in Congress that Heritage promoted him to director of the Center for Policy Innovation. For his earlier career and his interest in public choice, see Richard Crockett, *Thinking the Unthinkable: Think-Tanks and the Economic Counter-Revolution, 1931–1983* (New York: HarperCollins, 1994), 281–82; for his detailed explanation of how privatization would alter the core dynamics of American popular politics, see Stuart M. Butler, *Privatizing Federal Spending: A Strategy to Eliminate the Deficit* (New York: Universe Books, 1985).
51. For Kemp's enthusiasm for the cause from the Goldwater campaign of 1964 onward (save for his belief that collective bargaining was "a sacred right"), see Morton Kondracke and Fred Barnes, *Jack Kemp: The Bleeding-Heart Conservative Who Changed America* (New York: Sentinel, 2015), 25, 27, 119.
52. For staff listing, see front matter of President's Commission on Privatization, *Privatization: Toward a More Effective Government* (Washington, DC: GPO, 1988). For Moore's career history and writing, see: http://premierespeakers.com/stephen_moore/bio; and Zach Beauchamp, "Why the Heritage Foundation Hired an Activist as Its Chief Economist," *ThinkProgress*, January 21, 2014.
53. James M. Buchanan, "Can Democracy Be Tamed?" confidential preliminary draft prepared for presentation at Mont Pelerin Society General Meeting, Cambridge, England, September 1984, in box 58, John Davenport Papers, Hoover Institution Archives, Stanford University, Palo Alto, CA; see also James M. Buchanan, et al., *The Economics of Politics* (London: Institute of Economic Affairs, 1978).
54. Steven M. Teles, *The Rise of the Conservative Legal Movement* (Princeton, NJ: Princeton University Press, 2008), 116, 122, 129–30, 207–16.
55. "A Nobel for James Buchanan" (editorial), *Washington Post*, October 17, 1986; Teles, *Rise of the Conservative Legal Movement*, 116, 122, 129–30, 207–16.
56. Henry G. Manne, "An Intellectual History of the George Mason University School of Law," George Mason University Law and Economics Center (1993), www.law.gmu.edu/about/history.
57. John S. Saloma, *Ominous Politics: The New Conservative Labyrinth* (New York: Hill & Wang, 1984), 75; *The Attack on Corporate America: The Corporate Issues Sourcebook*, ed. M. Bruce Johnson (New York: McGraw-Hill, 1978), xi–xv.
58. Ruth S. Intress, "Winner of Nobel Seen As Brilliant But Opinionated," *Richmond Times-Dispatch*, October 1986, reproduction without date or page numbers in Friedman Papers; Werner, "George Mason U.: 29."
59. Buchanan, *Better than Plowing*, 35–36; James M. Buchanan, "Notes on Nobelity," December 17, 2001, www.nobelprize.org/nobel_prizes/economic-sciences/laureates/1986/buchanan-article.html.
60. Royal Swedish Academy of Sciences, press release for Alfred Nobel Memorial Prize in Economic Sciences, October 16, 1986. The award produced some carping among top economists over the quality of the laureate's work, which irked Buchanan well into retirement, aggravating his bitterness. See Hobart Rowen, "Discreetly Lifted Eyebrows Over Buchanan's Nobel Prize," *Washington Post*, October 26, 1986. Challenged after the award to identify what would be said about public choice two decades hence, the committee's chair replied that it explained "how politicians and public administrators think." Jane Seaberry,

"In Defense of Public Choice: Chairman of Nobel Panel Discusses Economics Winner," *Washington Post*, November 23, 1986.

61. Royal Swedish Academy of Sciences, press release; on Lindbeck, see Avner Offer and Gabriel Söderberg, *The Nobel Factor: The Prize in Economics, Social Democracy, and the Market Turn* (Princeton, NJ: Princeton University Press, 2016), 205–7. On the economics prize's difference from the other, more venerable Nobel Prizes created by Alfred Nobel, not least that it was added six decades after the others, in 1968, on the suggestion of and with funding by the Bank of Sweden, which in the view of some critics created an inbuilt bias, see the illuminating account by Thomas Karier, *Intellectual Capital: Forty Years of the Nobel Prize in Economics* (New York: Cambridge University Press, 2010).
62. "Prize Virginian" (editorial), *Richmond Times-Dispatch*, October 17, 1986. Actually, the shutdown resulted from a clash between the president and the Democratic-controlled House over where to inflict cuts: the armed forces and foreign aid (their choice) or domestic education and welfare programs (his).
63. Robert D. Hershey Jr., "A Bias Toward Bad Government?" *New York Times*, January 19, 1986, F1, 27.
64. See the center's annual reports in BHA.
65. Gordon Tullock, "The Origins of Public Choice," in *The Makers of Modern Economics*, vol. 3, ed. Arnold Heertje (Cheltenham, UK: Edward Elgar, 1999), 127.
66. Buchanan to Gregory R. McDonald, February 25, 1980, BHA; Richard J. Seiden to Buchanan, June 26, 1981, BHA. For sample gatekeeping for Hoover, see Dennis L. Bark to Buchanan, June 5, 1978; for Mont Pelerin, see Buchanan to George J. Stigler, September 21, 1971, BHA; for the Scaife Family Charitable Trusts, see Buchanan to Richard M. Larry, March 16, 1973, BHA. His work with these groups was too abundant for citation, but files of correspondence can be found in BHA.
67. David J. Theroux and M. Bruce Johnson to Buchanan, December 5, 1986, BHA; Buchanan to David J. Theroux and M. Bruce Johnson, December 15, 1986, BHA; Buchanan to Milton Friedman, June 8, 1987, box 171, Friedman Papers.
68. Leonard P. Liggio to Buchanan, May 27, 1985, BHA. For a sense of what a central player Liggio was in linking individuals and organizations in the still-small transnational movement, see the dozens of tributes in *Born on the 5th of July: Letters on the Occasion of Leonard P. Liggio's 65th Birthday* (Fairfax, VA: Atlas Economic Foundation, 1998).
69. Soon after, the Charles G. Koch Foundation gave its first contribution to Buchanan's center. It was a modest gift of $5,000, but a statement of confidence; George Pearson to Robert D. Tollison, December 27, 1985, BHA. Listing of the alumni found on IHS Web site.
70. David R. Henderson, "Buchanan's Prize," *National Review*, December 31, 1986, 20. See also Chamberlain, "Another Nobel for Freedom," 36, 62.
71. Ronald Reagan to David J. Theroux, telegram, October 29, 1987, box 386, Institute of Economic Affairs Records, Hoover Institution Archives.
72. Leonard P. Liggio to Buchanan, December 29, 1986, BHA; Edwin Meese III, "The Attorney General's View of the Supreme Court: Toward a Jurisprudence of Original Intention," *Public Administrative Review* 45 (November 1985): 701–4; Gourse, "Restraining the Reagan Revolution." We need to know much more about the Federalist Society, as about so many other organizations in this story, but for an excellent start, see Jonathan Riehl, "The Federalist Society and Movement Conservatism: How a Fractious Coalition on the Right Is Changing Constitutional Law and the Way We Talk and Think About It" (PhD diss., University of North Carolina at Chapel Hill, 2007).

CHAPTER 12: THE KIND OF FORCE THAT PROPELLED COLUMBUS

1. Brian Doherty, *Radicals for Capitalism: A Freewheeling History of the Modern Libertarian Movement* (Philadelphia, PA: PublicAffairs, 2007), 603.

2. Charles G. Koch, *Creating a Science of Liberty* (Fairfax, VA: Institute for Humane Studies, 1997), 9. Chief among the purists he once admired and subsidized but now deplored as obstacles to exercising the political power to achieve his ends was the prolific Murray Rothbard, who sounded off often about the betrayal of core elements of the libertarian creed after he was pushed out of the Cato Institute, which he had helped design. See, for example, Murray N. Rothbard, "Newt Gingrich Is No Libertarian," *Washington Post*, December 30, 1994, A17.
3. For the contract, see Patterson, *Restless Giant*, 343–45. For the surprising resiliency of the welfare state, owing to its political support and "the critical rules of the game" that had so far stymied the right, no doubt making a bolder plan seem necessary to break through, see Paul Pierson, *Dismantling the Welfare State?: Reagan, Thatcher, and the Politics of Retrenchment* (New York: Cambridge University Press, 1994), quote on 166.
4. Gordon Tullock, "Origins of Public Choice," in *The Makers of Modern Economics*, vol. 3, ed. Arnold Heertje (Cheltenham, UK: Edward Elgar, 1999), 134–36; John J. Fialka, "Cato Institute's Influence Grows in Washington as Republican-Dominated Congress Sets Up Shop," *Wall Street Journal*, December 14, 1994, A16; Luke Mullins, "Armey in Exile," *Washingtonian*, June 26, 2013; Richard Armey, "The Invisible Foot of Government," in *Moral Values in Liberalism and Conservatism*, ed. Andrew R. Cecil and W. Lawson Taitte (Dallas: University of Texas Press, 1995), 119; David Maraniss and Michael Weisskopf, *"Tell Newt to Shut Up!"* (New York: Simon & Schuster, 1996), 7–8, 34, 37, 59, 73–83; Kenneth S. Baer, *Reinventing Government: The Politics of Liberalism from Reagan to Clinton* (Lawrence: University Press of Kansas, 2000), 231, 236–37.
5. John E. Owens, "Taking Power? Institutional Change in the House and Senate," in *The Republican Takeover of Congress*, eds. Dean McSweeney and John E. Owens (New York: St. Martin's Press, 1998), 58; Baer, *Reinventing Government*, 239; Maraniss and Weisskopf, *"Tell Newt to Shut Up!"* 83, 86.
6. Patterson, *Restless Giant*, 343–45.
7. Elizabeth Drew, *Showdown: The Struggle Between the Gingrich Congress and the Clinton White House* (New York: Simon & Schuster, 1996), 97, 175. After a protest led by John L. Lewis, the portrait came down. On Smith's history, see Oberdorfer, "'Judge' Smith Rules with Deliberate Drag"; and Dierenfield, *Keeper of the Rules*.
8. Patterson, *Restless Giant*, 344–45; John Micklethwait and Adrian Wooldridge, *The Right Nation: Conservative Power in America* (New York: Penguin Press, 2004), 115–16. Dubbing Armey "the true ideologue," Elizabeth Drew also notes that he had on his staff Virginia Thomas, the wife of sitting Supreme Court Justice Clarence Thomas; see Elizabeth Drew, *Showdown: The Struggle Between the Gingrich Congress and the Clinton White House*, (New York: Touchstone, 1997), 56.
9. Elizabeth Drew, *Whatever It Takes: The Real Struggle for Power in America* (New York: Viking, 1997), 58; on zealotry, see 35, 121; Owens, "Taking Power?" 58; Baer, *Reinventing Government*, 239; Maraniss and Weisskopf, *"Tell Newt to Shut Up!"* 83, 86.
10. John E. Owens, "The Republican Takeover in Context," in *The Republican Takeover of Congress*, eds. McSweeney and Owens, 1; public-choice-infused allegations of "corruption" proved critical to the campaign for the House; see 2. On the slippage of the House GOP's standing in the polls as it took on middle-class entitlements, see Owens, "Taking Power?," 59. On public choice influence on the Contract with America, see Nigel Ashford, "The Republican Policy Agenda and the Conservative Movement," in *Republican Takeover*, eds. McSweeney and Owens, 103–4.
11. On how Gingrich's ego, Clinton's interpersonal skills, and the talent of the president's team combined to block the attempted revolution, the remainder of *"Tell Newt to Shut Up!"* makes a rollicking good read. For Clinton's triangulation with Gingrich, see Micklethwait and Wooldridge, *The Right Nation*, 117–19. Clinton differed from many in the party on what would be permanently damaging, in particular the "welfare reform" bill he signed, over the objection of the staff most knowledgeable about the issues.

12. James M. Buchanan, *Why I, Too, Am Not a Conservative: The Normative Vision of Classical Liberalism* (Northampton, MA: Edward Elgar, 2005), 4.
13. Doherty, *Radicals for Capitalism*, 603–4.
14. Koch, *Creating a Science of Liberty*. The occasion was a speech at GMU in January 1997, later used in fund-raising for the center; Robert N. Mottice to James Buchanan, August 13, 1998.
15. Ernest Hemingway, *A Moveable Feast* (New York: Scribner, 1964).
16. Koch, *Creating a Science of Liberty*; "James Buchanan Center Funded with $10 Million Gift," *Mason Gazette*, March 1998. The gift came in installments; for the first $3 million, see Richard H. Fink to Alan G. Merten, June 27, 1997, BHA; for Buchanan's gratitude to Koch, see Buchanan to Koch, July 8, 1997, BHA.
17. Koch, *Creating a Science of Liberty*, 12, 13. Koch sounded like John C. Calhoun, who said of his own campaign to overwhelm the majority of his day, "I see with so much apparent clearness as not to leave me a choice to pursue any other course, which has always given me the impression that I acted with the force of destiny"; Richard Hofstadter, *The American Political Tradition and the Men Who Made It* (New York: Random House, 1948), 76.
18. Edwin McDowell, "Bringing Law Profs Up to Date on Economics," *Wall Street Journal*, July 23, 1973; Steven M. Teles, *The Rise of the Conservative Legal Movement* (Princeton, NJ: Princeton University Press, 2008), 122. See also Walter Guzzardi, "Judges Discover the World of Economics," *Fortune*, May 21, 1979, 58–66.
19. Henry Manne to Buchanan, "Draft Program Synopsis for Mont Pelerin Society Meeting in Washington, DC, September 1998," BHA.
20. Ibid. Reporting on the conference by the head of the Heritage Foundation, Ed Feulner, then the society's president, can be found in Lee Edwards, *Leading the Way: The Story of Ed Feulner and the Heritage Foundation* (New York: Crown Forum, 2013), 260–61. Feulner called Social Security "one of the largest barriers to freedom in America" (261).
21. Henry Manne to Buchanan, "Draft Program Synopsis for Mont Pelerin Society Meeting in Washington, DC, September 1998," BHA.
22. Ibid.
23. Ibid.
24. Ibid.
25. Koch would help on that battlefront, too, not only by opportunistic cooperation with the religious right, the veritable antithesis of libertarianism by a dictionary definition, but also by direct funding of and staff support to the Independent Women's Forum. In 2001, Nancy Pfotenhauer, yet another GMU economics product, was appointed its president, after serving as director of the Washington Office of Koch Industries, a senior economist at the Republican National Committee, and executive vice president at Citizens for a Sound Economy (CSE). Biography on the website of the Koch-funded antifeminist organization, http://web.archive.org/web/20041214151602/www.iwf.org/about_iwf/pfotenhauer.asp.
26. James M. Buchanan, "Constitutions, Politics, and Markets," draft prepared for presentation, Porto Alegre, Brazil, April 1993, BHA. See also James M. Buchanan, "Socialism Is Dead; Leviathan Lives," *Wall Street Journal*, July 18, 1990, A8.
27. See, for example, David Rosenbaum, "From Guns to Butter," *New York Times*, December 14, 1989, A1.
28. Alexander Keyssar, *The Right to Vote: The Contested History of Democracy in the United States* (New York: Basic Books, 2000), 314–15. In the lead of the push for the law was ACORN, the community-organizing network later destroyed by two operatives trained by the Koch-funded Leadership Institute. On ACORN's work, see John Atlas, *Seeds of Change: The Story of ACORN, America's Most Controversial Antipoverty Community Organizing Group* (Nashville, TN: Vanderbilt University Press, 2010); and Robert Fisher, ed.,

The People Shall Rule: ACORN, Community Organizing, and the Struggle for Economic Justice (Nashville, TN: Vanderbilt University Press, 2009).

29. James Buchanan, "Notes Prompted by Telephone Conversation with And[rew] Ruttan on 15 February 2001," February 16, 2001, BHA. He was also unnerved at "taxpayer apathy" in the 1990s as compared with the 1970s; James Buchanan, "Taxpayer Apathy, Institutional Inertia, and Economic Growth," March 15, 1999, BHA.
30. Buchanan to Richard H. Fink, July 8, 1997, BHA; Buchanan to Charles G. Koch, July 8, 1997, BHA; James Buchanan Center Affiliation Agreement, effective January 1, 1998, BHA.
31. Fink to Buchanan, August 18, 1998 (italics added). On Mark F. Grady, brought to GMU in 1997, see faculty profile, UCLA School of Law, https://law.ucla.edu/faculty/faculty-profiles/mark-f-grady.
32. Wendy Lee Gramm to Robert E. Weissman, form letter, May 13, 1998, BHA.
33. Ibid.; also, touting the support of Republican Virginia governor Jim Gilmore, Robert N. Mottice to James Buchanan, form letter, August 13, 1998, BHA. On the programs for judges, see also Law and Economics Center, George Mason University School of Law, "The Advanced Institute for Federal Judges," Omni Tucson Golf Resort and Spa, April 25–May 1, 1998, headlined by Buchanan, in a twenty-five-year effort described as the "LEC's most important program."
34. Wendy Lee Gramm to Robert E. Weissman, form letter, May 13, 1998, BHA. In his 1996 reelection bid, Gramm had been Congress's top recipient of campaign contributions from the oil-and-gas industry, garnering more than $800,000 from this sector alone, one in which Koch Industries was the fourth-largest corporate contributor. Alexia Fernandez Campbell, "Koch: 1996 Marks Beginning of National Efforts," July 1, 2013, Investigative Reporting Workshop, American University School of Communication, http://investigativereportingworkshop.org/investigations/the_koch_club/story/Koch-1996_marks_beginning; "Energy Sector Gave $22 Million to Campaigns," *Washington Post*, December 22, 1997.
35. Anonymous note accompanying the envelope containing the Gramm letter, BHA.
36. Robert D. Tollison to Charles Koch, November 23, 1998, BHA. Tollison also suggested putting the economics department into receivership if objections to the program continued to be raised, while leaving in anger for a position at the University of Mississippi.
37. James M. Buchanan to Richard Fink, September 17, 1998, BHA.
38. Buchanan had praised Fink's promise for "a role as an entrepreneur, organizer, and coordinator in the sometimes fuzzy intersections between the academic establishment, the business community, the established think tanks, and the foundations." He added, pointedly, that Fink appreciated "the concerns with the academy" that many in the movement "express (concerns that are, in my opinion, very well founded)." Buchanan to Charles Koch, May 24, 1984, BHA. On CSE, see Asra Q. Nomani, "Critics Say Antitariff Activists in Washington Have Grass-Roots Base That's Made of Astroturf," *Wall Street Journal*, March 17, 1995, A16; David Wessel and Jeanne Saddler, "Foes of Clinton's Tax-Boost Proposals Mislead Public and Firms on the Small-Business Aspects," *Wall Street Journal*., July 20, 1993, A12.
39. Citizens for a Sound Economy (CSE) billed itself as "a grass-roots organization with 200,000 members across the country" (a number soon upped to 250,000, from which it has never deviated) who wanted "to build support for market-oriented policy initiatives and reduce government interference in private decision making." Fink was listed as "Founder, President, Chief Executive Officer"; Mari Maseng to Frederick J. Ryan Jr., January 5, 1987, White House Schedule Proposal, PR007: 471415, White House Office of Records Management, Ronald Reagan Presidential Library; White House press release, September 3, 1987, in Thomas G. Moore Papers, box 10, OA 18900, Ronald Reagan Presidential Library. On Miller, see "The Candidates," *Washington Post*, January 3, 1996, D1.
40. Buchanan to Fink, September 5, 1998, BHA. For his earlier appreciation for Koch's "confidence in my own efforts over the years" and enthusiasm about the effort's prospects and

Fink's "entrepreneurial efforts in guaranteeing that these prospects will, in fact, be realized," see Buchanan to Fink, July 8, 1997, BHA.

41. "Statement by James M. Buchanan to be circulated at meeting on 24 August 1998," BHA; James Buchanan to Tyler Cowen, September 5, 1998, BHA.
42. Tyler Cowen, "A Short Intellectual Autobiography," in *I Chose Liberty: Autobiographies of Contemporary Libertarians,* compiled by Walter Block (Auburn, AL: Ludwig von Mises Institute, 2010), 92–93; Michael S. Rosenwald, "Tyler Cowen's Appetite for Ethnic Food—and Answers About His Life," *Washington Post,* May 13, 2010. Buchanan's longtime collaborator Geoffrey Brennan found Cowen a good choice for the "front-man role" of the new center. He was "totally smooth and presentable" and "smart," to boot, while being "young enough and ambitious enough to make the kind of longer-term investment" the project's success necessitated—rather akin to Buchanan, he noted, at the time of the Thomas Jefferson Center's launch; Geoffrey Brennan to Betty Tillman, August 19, 1998. Cowen's first book, *The Theory of Market Failure: A Critical Examination,* was a collection of essays copublished by the Cato Institute and designed to refute the key argument for government intervention: that markets often fail. Offering tribute to public choice economics, it showcased nonscholars on the payrolls of three different Koch-funded nonprofits. Tyler Cowen, ed., *The Theory of Market Failure: A Critical Examination* (Fairfax, VA: George Mason University Press, 1988). The very season Buchanan was complaining to him, Cowen had published a new book, *In Praise of Commercial Culture,* which elaborated on old shibboleths from Ludwig von Mises. He thanked Richie Fink, Charles Koch, and David Koch for funding his work on it; Tyler Cowen, *In Praise of Commercial Culture* (Cambridge, MA: Harvard University Press, 1998), v; Ludwig von Mises, *The Anti-Capitalistic Mentality* (Princeton, NJ: D. Van Nostrand, 1956).
43. Tyler Cowen, "Memo on Restructuring the James Buchanan Center [n.d., but September 1998], BHA; James Buchanan to David Potter, August 13, 1998, BHA; Walter Williams to Economics Faculty, with Memo on Restructuring the James Buchanan Center, September 30, 1998, BHA; David Nott to Richard Fink, August 19, 1998, with attached "deactivated" Web pages. On Miller's run, see Center for Study of Public Choice, Annual Report, 1994, 2. Earlier, as the John M. Olin Distinguished Fellow at the center, Miller had served as chairman of Koch's Citizens for a Sound Economy; Center for Study of Public Choice, Annual Report, 1992, 2, BHA. Justice Scalia, an alumnus of Henry Manne's Law and Economics training for judges and the founding coeditor of the Cato Institute magazine, *Regulation,* had given the keynote address for the Buchanan Center's 1996 Chief of Staff Winter Retreat in Baltimore, at which the Institute for Justice's president, Chip Mellor, also spoke, as did representatives from Citizens for a Sound Economy, the Cato Institute, and the Reason Foundation, Koch causes all; Jason DeParle, "Debating the Sway of the Federalist Society," *Chicago Daily Law Bulletin,* August 2, 2005; James Buchanan Center, Chief of Staff Winter Retreat Agenda, January 19–21, 1995, BHA.
44. James Buchanan to David Potter, August 13, 1998, BHA; "Statement by James M. Buchanan to be circulated at meeting on 24 August 1998," BHA; Walter Williams to Economics Faculty, with Memo on Restructuring the James Buchanan Center, September 30, 1998, BHA; "Gift to GMU to Be Used for New Center," *Washington Post,* January 13, 1998.
45. David Potter to James Buchanan, August 5, 1998, BHA; see also Potter to Deans and Directors, August 5, 1998, BHA.
46. "Allen Makes Education Appointments," *Washington Post,* June 19, 1997, VAB4; Edwin Meese III to James M. Buchanan, January 24, 2000, BHA. Governor George Allen stacked the Board of Visitors with right-wing figures: in addition to Meese, Ed Feulner of the Heritage Foundation, the journalist William Kristol, and the utility player James Miller. Teles, *Rise of the Conservative Legal Movement,* 212. When Allen had to step down, Richie Fink contributed $50,000 to his Republican successor's campaign and inauguration fund; "A Grand Old Golf Party Rakes in Lots of Green for Republicans," *Washington Post,* August 12, 1998. On Kristol's work to drive the GOP to the right in the 1990s, see Nina Easton, *Gang of Five: Leaders at the Center of the Conservative Crusade* (New York: Simon &

Schuster, 2000), 266–80. As she rightly notes of the late 1990s, "Never before had the Right's activists been so closely tied to the party hierarchy and its professionals" (280).

47. Author's observation at the memorial gathering, September 28–29, 2013.

CONCLUSION: GET READY

1. Charles K. Rowley, "The Calculus of Consent," in *Democracy and Public Choice: Essays in Honor of Gordon Tullock*, ed. Charles K. Rowley (Oxford, UK: Basil Blackwell, 1987), 55. He was no doubt gesturing to Jean-Jacques Rousseau, who had posed the question two centuries earlier.
2. Charles K. Rowley, "James M. Buchanan: A Short Biography," reprinted with permission from Rowley and A. Owens, "Buchanan, James McGill (1919–)," in *The Biographical Dictionary of American Economists*, vol. 1, ed. Ross B. Emmett (New York: Thoemmes Press/Continuum International, 2006), 98–108; distributed in pamphlet form at the George Mason memorial service for Buchanan in September 2013 (in author's possession). Rowley was working on a full-length biography when he died that summer. I expect that it would be as hagiographic as this shorter piece and another like it, but perhaps a bit more critical in light of what unfolded after he wrote it.
3. Charles K. Rowley to Dr. Edwin J. Feulner, November 11, 1997, BHA.
4. He was right about where things were headed. One can find the 2010 roster of this highly exclusive society online, and there the shift in dominance from thinkers to wealthy donors and their operatives is apparent. Alongside the many academic members' names can be found the leading cadre members of the Koch-funded revolution in the making. To mention only those most likely to be familiar to readers, they include, alongside Charles Koch himself: Richard Armey, once House majority leader, later cochair of Citizens for a Sound Economy and by then the chair of FreedomWorks; Edward Crane and David Boaz, then president and executive vice president, respectively, of the Cato Institute; Ed Feulner, then president of the Heritage Foundation; Reed Larson, president of the National Right to Work Committee; William H. Mellor, cofounder of the Institute for Justice; Morton Blackwell, president of the Leadership Institute; David Nott, president of the Reason Foundation; Charles Murray, the libertarian writer on long-term retainer at the American Enterprise Institute; and Edwin Meese III, a veteran of so many arms of the cause, who through his continuing board service connected the Mercatus Center with the Heritage Foundation, the Federalist Society, Judicial Watch, and more; "Mont Pelerin Society Directory—2010," www.desmogblog.com/sites/beta.desmogblog.com/files/Mont%20Pelerin%20Society%20Directory%202010.pdf.
5. "Koch Versus Cato: Unraveling the Riddle," *Charles Rowley's Blog*, March 5, 2012; "Economist's View: Has the 'Kochtupus' Opened Libertarian Eyes?" *Charles Rowley's Blog*, March 6, 2012; Rowley reply, *Charles Rowley's Blog*, March 6, 2012; "Koch Brothers Force Ed Crane Out of Cato," *Charles Rowley's Blog*, June 26, 2012, printouts in author's possession. Since Rowley's death, the blog has come down; interested readers can consult the Wayback Machine archive, https://web.archive.org/web/*/charlesrowley.wordpress.com. See also Schulman, *Sons of Wichita*, 263–64.
6. "Koch Versus Cato."
7. James M. Buchanan, *Economics from the Outside In: "Better than Plowing" and Beyond* (College Station: Texas A&M University Press, 2007).
8. "Koch versus Cato"; "Death of William A. Niskanen Opens Door for Koch Takeover of Cato Institute," *Charles Rowley's Blog*, March 4, 2012; Catherine Probst, "University Mourns Passing of Economics Professor Charles Rowley," *News at Mason*, GMU.edu, August 5, 2013.
9. Dozens of print and online journalists have been following this story, in articles and posts too numerous for individual citation, even with my deep admiration for their work. Among the best book-length studies are Mayer, *Dark Money*; Fang, *The Machine*; Vogel, *Big Money*; and Schulman, *Sons of Wichita*.

10. For orientation to this extraordinary figure, see Jeffrey Rosen, "Why Brandeis Matters," *New Republic*, June 29, 2010, https://newrepublic.com/article/75902/why-brandeis-matters.
11. Theda Skocpol and Vanessa Williamson, *The Tea Party and the Remaking of Republican Conservatism* (New York: Oxford University Press, 2012), 66. As in the civil rights era, arch libertarians show no compunction about exploiting white racial animus to achieve their ends. On the distinctive feelings of lost racial dominance among "real Americans" that animates Tea Party activists, see Christopher S. Parker and Matt A. Barreto, *Change They* Can't *Believe In: The Tea Party and Reactionary Politics in America* (Princeton, NJ: Princeton University Press, 2013).
12. David Boaz, *The Libertarian Mind* (New York: Simon & Schuster, 2015), 252. America is "creating an underclass that votes rather than works for a living," says another in calculated demagogy; Grover G. Norquist, *Leave Us Alone: Getting the Government's Hands Off Our Money, Our Guns, and Our Lives* (New York: HarperCollins, 2008), 119.
13. Romney did not pull this claim from thin air, but from the cause's calculations, based on Buchanan's ideas; see William W. Beach, "An Overview of the Index of Dependency" (Washington, DC: Heritage Foundation, 2002); also Norquist, *Leave Us Alone*, 116–17. Buchanan himself had, of course, depicted modern democratic politics as a criminal conspiracy. "Modern rent seekers are under no delusion about the 'social good,'" he warned. "They do not abide by the precepts of honesty, fairness, respect for the rules of law, etc."; James M. Buchanan, "Hayek and the Forces of History" (typescript), BHA, later published in *Humane Studies Review* 6 (1988–1989). As the new century opened, the people had come to seem beastlike to him. "Adam Smith was presenting his argument in a political setting where the demos had not yet been fully unchained," he mused privately. "With a limited franchise and elite control, governments might have been more readily amenable to rational persuasion" from advocates of economic liberty. The demos must be put back in chains, it seemed, for liberty to prevail. James M. Buchanan, "Notes Prompted by Telephone Conversation with And[rew] Ruttan on 15 February 2001," February 16, 2001, BHA.
14. F. A. Harper, *Liberty: A Path to Its Recovery* (Irvington on Hudson, NY: Foundation for Economic Education, 1949), 113.
15. James M. Buchanan, *Why I, Too, Am Not a Conservative: The Normative Vision of Classical Liberalism* (Northampton, MA: Edward Elgar, 2005), 8. See also James M. Buchanan, "Afraid to Be Free: Dependency as Desideratum," *Public Choice* 124 (July 2005): 19–31.
16. Tyler Cowen, *Average Is Over: Powering America Beyond the Age of the Great Stagnation* (New York: Dutton, 2013), 229–30, 236–39, 241.
17. Ibid., 241–45, 247, 258.
18. Eliana Dockerman, "Paul Ryan Says Free School Lunches Give Kids 'An Empty Soul,'" *Time*, March 6, 2014. And that was after a group of Catholic nuns went on a much-publicized 2,700-mile bus tour to speak out against his contrarian version of Catholic values; Simone Campbell, "We 'Nuns on the Bus' Don't Like Paul Ryan's Idea of Catholic Values," *Guardian*, September 28, 2012.
19. Nicholas Kristof, "Congress to America: Drop Dead," *New York Times*, May 12, 2016, A27.
20. Sam Knight, "Freshman GOP Senator: I'm Okay with Not Forcing Restaurant Workers to Wash Up," *The District Sentinel*, February 2, 2015. See also Rebekah Wilce, "Spending for ALEC Member Tillis Breaks All Records in NC Senate Race," *PR Watch*, posted October, 21, 2014.
21. Gary M. Anderson, "Parasites, Profits, and Politicians: Public Health and Public Choice," *Cato Journal* 9 (Winter 1990): 576. See the Mercatus Web site for more such allegations.
22. Amity Shlaes, "James Buchanan, a Star Economist Who Understood Obamacare," *Bloomberg View*, January 10, 2013.
23. Mason Adams and Jesse Tuel, "They Did Nothing to Deserve This," *Virginia Tech Magazine*, Spring 2016, 41–50; also Elisha Anderson, "Legionnaires'-Associated Deaths Grow to 12 in Flint," *Detroit Free Press*, posted April 11, 2016.

24. For early hiring of the Mackinac Center staff from Koch's offices, see Kelly R. Young to Roy Childs, March 4, 1992, box 5, Roy A. Childs Papers, Hoover Library; Mackinac Center, "Accomplishments: 1988–2013," http://web.archive.org/web/20151013073304/https://www.mackinac.org/18315. For superb investigation and overview of SPN, see Center for Media and Democracy, "Exposed: The State Policy Network," November 2013, www.alecexposed.org/w/images/2/25/SPN_National_Report_FINAL.pdf.
25. Monica Davey, "A State Manager Takes Over and Cuts What a City Can't," *New York Times*, April 26, 2011, 1; Paul Rosenberg, "The Truth About Flint: Kids Drank Poisoned Water Because of the GOP's Radical, Anti-Democratic 'Reforms,'" *Salon*, January 23, 2016. For the deepest explanation, see John Conyers, "Flint Is the Predictable Outcome of Michigan's Long, Dangerous History with 'Emergency Managers,'" *The Nation*, February 17, 2016.
26. Robert D. Tollison and Richard E. Wagner, *The Economics of Smoking* (Boston: Kluwer Academic Publishers, 1992), ix–xi, 140–41, 142, 225. This was just one of several such studies from George Mason's Center for Study of Public Choice. As so often with this cause's allegations, projection seemed to be the order of the day for economists in a public university in a tobacco state whose leading corporations were losing their markets and eager to pay academics to combat well-established research findings.
27. Al Kamen, "Name That Tone," *Washington Post*, March 21, 1997, A25. One historically minded commentator has aptly compared the monetary scale of corporate-sunk investment in fossil fuels to the wealth invested in slaves, the defense of which set off the Civil War; Christopher Hayes, "The New Abolitionism," *The Nation*, April 22, 2014.
28. Donald J. Boudreaux, "The Missing Elements in the 'Science' of Global Warming," *Reason*, September 7, 2006.
29. Naomi Oreskes and Erik M. Conway, *Merchants of Doubt: How a Handful of Scientists Obscured the Truth on Issues from Tobacco Smoke to Global Warming* (New York: Bloomsbury, 2010), 234, 237, 249, quote on 243. More generally, see Naomi Klein, *This Changes Everything: Capitalism vs. the Climate* (New York: Simon & Schuster, 2014); and Jane Mayer, "Covert Operations: The Billionaire Brothers Who Are Waging a War on Obama," *The New Yorker*, August 30, 2010. See also Cato Institute, "Global Warming," www.cato.org/special/climatechange; and Climate Science & Policy Watch, "Americans for Prosperity: Distorting Climate Change Science and Economics in Well-Funded Campaign," www.climatesciencewatch.org/2010/03/18/americans-for-prosperity-distorting-climate-change-science-and-economics-in-well-funded-campaign; on CEI, see Competitive Enterprise Institute, "Cooler Heads Coalition News," https://cei.org/blog/cooler-heads-coalition-news.
30. Iain Murray, "All Aboard the Climate Gravy Train," *National Review*, March 11, 2011; "Christopher C. Horner, Senior Fellow," Competitive Enterprise Institute, https://cei.org/expert/christopher-c-horner. See also Michael S. Greve and Fred L. Smith Jr., eds., *Environmental Politics: Public Costs, Private Rewards* (New York: Praeger, 1992). In a similar vein, see Tollison and Wagner, *Economics of Smoking*, 183–184, 225.
31. Eduardo Porter, "Bringing Republicans to the Talks on Climate," *New York Times*, October 14, 2015, B4.
32. Eric Holmberg and Alexia Fernandez Campbell, "Koch: Climate Pledge Strategy Continues to Grow," Investigative Reporting Workshop, American University School of Communication, July 1, 2013; Paul Krugman, "Climate Denial Denial," *New York Times*, December 4, 2015, A33; Porter, "Bringing Republicans to the Talks," *New York Times*, October 14, 2015, B1, 6.
33. Eric Lipton, "Working So Closely Their Roles Blur," *New York Times*, December 7, 2014, A1, 30–31. By the 1990s, the antienvironmental right was "making slow but steady inroads [in the courts], thanks to a carefully calculated effort to transform the judicial landscape," notes one authoritative study; Judith A. Layzer, *Open for Business: Conservatives' Opposition to Environmental Regulation* (Cambridge, MA: MIT Press, 2012), 185.

34. "Secession is, of course, the most dramatic form of exit," Buchanan noted, but was "only the end of a spectrum of institutional-constitutional rearrangements" the cause should promote, "all of which embody exit as a common element." The spectrum included elements that had become core to Republican practice: "decentralization, devolution, federalism, privatization, deregulation." They were all part of a continuum whereby wealthy minorities could evade "exploitation" by majorities, enlisting "the discipline of competition" to tame them. The core theory was simple. As Buchanan summarized: "If you have exit options, you are free—you have liberty." In constitutional terms, his vision was that "we have to have a genuine competitive federalism" among the states to discipline their policies and national power. Unveiling a major "new initiative on federalism" soon after this, Buchanan's Center invited officers of dozens of corporations, including Amoco, America Online, General Dynamics, Lockheed, and Philip Morris, alongside representatives of such leading right-wing foundations as Heritage, Scaife, Bradley, and, of course, Koch, to learn how to apply it. James M. Buchanan, "The Moral of the Market," typed interview transcript [c. 2004], BHA; James M. Buchanan, "Secession and the Economic Constitution," draft prepared for presentation, Berlin, October 1999, 2, 4, ibid.; John H. Moore to William D. Witter, February 20, 1996, ibid.; Ann Bader to Bob Tollison et al., May 3, 1996, ibid.; Gordon Brady to Bob Tollison et al., February 12, 1997, ibid.; Gordon Brady to Bob Tollison et al., February 5, 1997, ibid. "The only beneficiaries of federalism run amok are large corporations that can use a threat to relocate as leverage in bargaining with state legislatures," notes Michael Lind, *Up from Conservatism: Why the Right Is Wrong for America* (New York: Free Press, 1996), 218.
35. Julie Bosman, "Agency Bans Activism on Climate Change," *New York Times*, April 9, 2015.
36. Every single "environmentally skeptical" book published in the 1990s, one academic study found, was connected to one or more right-wing foundations; Oreskes and Conway, *Merchants of Doubt*, 234, 236.
37. Klein, *This Changes Everything*, 35. For the broader, devastating impact, see Layzer, *Open for Business*, 333–60. On the willful deception, see Ari Rabin-Havt and Media Matters for America, *Lies, Incorporated: The World of Post-Truth Politics* (New York: Anchor Books, 2016), 34–57.
38. Lindsay Wagner, "Starving the Schools," in *Altered State: How Five Years of Conservative Rule Have Redefined North Carolina* (NC Policy Watch, December 2015), 15–18. And for contrast, see Motoko Rich, et al., "In Schools Nationwide, Money Predicts Success," *New York Times*, May 3, 2016, A3.
39. Lindsay Wagner, "Paving the Way Toward Privatization," in *Altered State*, 26–27; see also Valerie Strauss, "The Assault on Public Education in North Carolina Just Keeps on Coming," *Washington Post*, May 18, 2016.
40. Wagner, "Starving the Schools," 15–19; Chris Fitzsimon, "The Wrecking Crew," in *Altered State*, 3.
41. Alexander Tabarrok, ed., *Changing the Guard: Private Prisons and the Control of Crime* (Oakland, CA: Independent Institute, 2003), 1, 6.
42. Stephen Moore and Stuart Butler, *Privatization: A Strategy for Taming the Federal Budget* (Washington, DC: Heritage Foundation, 1987), 1, 8, 10. For a critical empirical view of the impact of privatization, see Elliott D. Sclar, *You Don't Always Get What You Pay For: The Economics of Privatization* (Ithaca, NY: Cornell University Press, 2001).
43. Alex Friedman to Hon. Patrick Leahy, May 9, 2008, BHA. Just as in the days of Buchanan's grandfather, when convict labor helped generate income, so, too, prison corporations have managed to end New Deal–era restrictions that outlawed profiting from incarcerated workers; see Heather Ann Thompson, "Rethinking Working-Class Struggle Through the Lens of the Carceral State: Toward a Labor History of Inmates and Guards," *Labor* 8 (2011): 15–45, on CCA as a pioneer in such profiteering, 34.

44. Silja J. A. Talvi, "Cashing In on Cons," *In These Times*, February 28, 2005, 16–29.
45. Jon Hurdle and Sabrina Tavernise, "Former Judge Is on Trial in 'Cash for Kids' Scheme," *New York Times*, February 8, 2011, A20. See also Charles M. Blow, "Plantations, Prisons and Profits," *New York Times*, May 26, 2012, A17; and Talvi, "Cashing In on Cons," 16–29.
46. Detention Watch Network and Center for Constitutional Rights, "Banking on Detention: 2016 Update," www.detentionwatchnetwork.org/sites/default/files/reports/Banking%20on%20Detention%202016%20Update_DWN,%20CCR.pdf. See also In the Public Interest, "Criminal: How Lockup Quotas and 'Low-Crime Taxes' Guarantee Profits for Private Prison Corporations," September 2013, www.inthepublicinterest.org/wp-content/uploads/Criminal-Lockup-Quota-Report.pdf.
47. Sabrina Dewan and Gregory Randolph, "Unions Are Key to Tackling Inequality, Says Top Global Financial Institution," *Huffington Post*, March 5, 2015. Among the now dozens of scholarly expositions, I have found these to be among the most illuminating: Larry M. Bartels, *Unequal Democracy: The Political Economy of the New Gilded Age* (Princeton, NJ: Princeton University Press, 2008); Jacob S. Hacker and Paul Pierson, *Winner-Take-All Politics: How Washington Made the Rich Richer—and Turned Its Back on the Middle Class* (New York: Simon & Schuster, 2011); Joseph E. Stiglitz, *The Price of Inequality: How Today's Divided Society Endangers Our Future* (New York: W. W. Norton, 2012); Thomas Piketty, *Capital in the Twenty-First Century* (Cambridge, MA: Belknap Press of Harvard University Press, 2014), and, in a more prescriptive mode, Robert B. Reich, *Saving Capitalism: For the Many, Not the Few* (New York: Alfred A. Knopf, 2015); Anthony B. Atkinson, *Inequality: What Can Be Done?* (Cambridge, MA: Harvard University Press, 2015).
48. Lydia DePillis, "West Virginia House Passes Right-to-Work Bill after Harsh Debate," *Washington Post*, February 4, 2016. This made West Virginia the twenty-sixth state with such a law.
49. Michael Cooper and Megan Thee-Brenan, "Majority in Poll Back Employees in Public Unions," *New York Times*, March 1, 2011, A1, 16; "The Hollow Cry of Broke" (editorial), *New York Times*, March 3, 2011, A26; Roger Bybee, "After Proposing Draconian Anti-Union Laws, Wis. Gov. Walker Invokes National Guard," *In These Times*, February 15, 2011. Walker himself notes that his approval rating fell to 37 percent because the act was so unpopular, so he was clearly not acting on the will of most voters; Scott Walker, *Unintimidated: A Governor's Story and a Nation's Challenge* (New York: Sentinel, 2013), 225.
50. Dan Kaufman, "Land of Cheese and Rancor," *New York Times Magazine*, May 27, 2012, 30, 32; Dan Kaufman, "Fate of the Union," *New York Times Magazine*, 55. Walker later bragged that the furor over the bill had enabled his team "to pass a raft of other measures" that usually would have set off "protests and controversy" but "went virtually unnoticed"; Walker, *Unintimidated*, 215.
51. Monica Davey, "Decline in Wisconsin Unions Calls Election Clout into Question," *New York Times*, February 28, 2016, 12, 20.
52. Patricia Cohen, "Public Sector Jobs Vanish, Hitting Blacks Hard," *New York Times*, May 25, 2015, B1, 5; Michael B. Katz, Mark J. Stern, and Jamie J. Fader, "The New African American Inequality," *Journal of American History* 92 (June 2005): 75–108, quote on 77; also Virginia Parks, "Revisiting Shibboleths of Race and Urban Economy: Black Employment in Manufacturing and the Public Sector Compared, Chicago 1950–2000," *International Journal of Urban and Regional Research* 35 (2011): 110–29.
53. Summarizing years of activism and scholarship, Ruth Rosen used that rubric in a lead article, "The Care Crisis: How Women Are Bearing the Burden of a National Emergency," *The Nation*, March 12, 2007, 11–16. For a case study that exposes the multi-sided impact, see Jane Berger, "'There Is Tragedy on Both Sides of the Layoffs': Public Sector Privatization and the Urban Crisis in Baltimore," *International Labor and*

Working-Class History 71 (Spring 2007): 29–49. For a sample of the long tradition of women's activism on these issues, see Dorothy Sue Cobble, *The Other Women's Movement: Workplace Justices and Social Rights in Modern America* (Princeton, NJ: Princeton University Press, 2004); on addressing them in theory, see Nancy Folbre, *The Invisible Heart: Economics and Family Values* (New York: New Press, 2002).

54. Tyler Cowen and Veronique de Rugy, "Reframing the Debate," in *The Occupy Handbook*, ed. Janet Byrne (New York: Little, Brown, 2012), 414–15, 418, 421. See also Norquist, *Leave Us Alone*, 92. To win over young people to such public-choice-derived ideas, the apparatus is funding extensive efforts to organize college youth; see Lee Fang, "Generation Opportunity, New Koch-Funded Front, Says Youth Are Better Off Uninsured," *The Nation*, September 19, 2013.
55. Paul Krugman, "Republicans Against Retirement," *New York Times*, August 17, 2015.
56. Larry Rohter, "Chile Rethinks Its Privatized Pension System," *New York Times*, January 10, 2006; see also Eduardo Gallardo, "Chile's Private Pension System Adds Public Payouts for Poor," *New York Times*, March 10, 2008.
57. Nancy J. Altman and Eric R. Kinston, *Social Security Works: Why Social Security Isn't Going Broke and How Expanding It Will Help Us All* (New York: New Press, 2015), 55, 61, 65, 67; Jacob S. Hacker, *The Great Risk Shift: The New Economic Inequality and the Decline of the American Dream* (New York: Oxford University Press, 2006), 109–38.
58. Koch knew that sooner or later, as his mentor Baldy Harper taught, the day would arrive "when the bubble of illusion on which much of our current affluence floats is finally pricked by some unforeseen event," an event that would enable his team's project to "fill the vacuum"; Institute for Humane Studies, *The Institute's Story* (Menlo Park, CA: n.d., but early 1970s), 25, in box 26, Hayek Papers. There are many excellent books and articles on the Tea Party and the Koch apparatus's role in commandeering the energy on display in the grassroots groups for its own purposes. The most comprehensive and illuminating, to my reading, is Skocpol and Williamson, *The Tea Party and the Remaking of Republican Conservatism*. For Cato's exultation that "libertarians led the way for the tea party," which was pushing the GOP to become "functionally libertarian," see David Kirby and Emily Ekins, "Libertarian Roots of the Tea Party," *Policy Analysis* 705 (August 6, 2012): 1.
59. For research grants to fund the project from the Institute for Humane Studies, see Tyler Cowen and David Nott, memorandum, May 13, 1997, BHA. Charles Koch was initially Cowen's codirector; the CEO remains on the nine-member Mercatus board of directors, joined in that role by Fink and Edwin Meese III.
60. Tyler Cowen, "Why Does Freedom Wax and Wane?: Some Research Questions in Social Change and Big Government," Mercatus Center, George Mason University, 2000 (repr. online, 2015; the original has no page numbers, but all quotes are from this document).
61. Ibid. For Charles Koch's version of the same research agenda, see Charles G. Koch, "Koch Industries, Market Process Analysis, and the Science of Liberty," *Journal of Private Enterprise* 22 (Spring 2007): especially 4–6.
62. Cowen, "Why Does Freedom Wax and Wane?"
63. Ibid.
64. Economic transformation, Piñera earlier explained from his new post at Koch's Cato Institute, had to be done rapidly and "on all fronts simultaneously"; José Piñera, "Chile," in *The Political Economy of Policy Reform*, ed. John Williamson (Washington, DC: Institute for International Economics, 1994), 228. Although she was unaware of Buchanan and his writing before the Koch brothers were in the news, Naomi Klein brilliantly identified how neoliberal actors have exploited crisis situations in which public oversight is paralyzed in order to achieve their ends. See her groundbreaking work *The Shock Doctrine: The Rise of Disaster Capitalism* (New York: Metropolitan Books, 2007). Cowen was drawing out the lessons of such practice for application in the United States and other democracies, where change could not be imposed by brute force.

65. Cowen, "Why Does Freedom Wax and Wane?"
66. His own economics colleague at George Mason, the John M. Olin Distinguished Professor Walter E. Williams, became a fixture on right-wing radio. A mentee of Buchanan during the latter's brief sojourn at UCLA and a syndicated columnist, Williams has for more than twenty years been acting as a guest host for Rush Limbaugh's radio show; Colleen Kearney Rich, "The Wonderful World of Masonomics," *Mason Spirit,* November 1, 2010.
67. David Waldstreicher, *Slavery's Constitution: From Revolution to Ratification* (New York: Hill & Wang, 2009); Waldstreicher notes the design "favoring people who owned people" (5). For the Koch project's plan here, see the chilling report by Michael Wines, "Push to Alter Constitution, via the States," *New York Times,* August 23, 2016, A1. The opening reads: "Taking advantage of almost a decade of political victories in state legislatures across the country, conservative advocacy groups are quietly marshaling support for an event unprecedented in the nation's history, a convention of the fifty states, summoned to consider amending the Constitution." Wines notes that the planning "is playing out largely beyond public notice" and, with control over more state legislatures, is gaining "a plausible chance of success." For a taste of the changes the cause would like, see the summary by Koch grantee Mark R. Levin, *The Liberty Amendments: Restoring the American Republic* (New York: Threshold Editions, 2013).
68. Alfred Stepan and Juan J. Linz, "Comparative Perspectives on Inequality and the Quality of Democracy in the United States," *Perspectives on Politics* 9 (December 2011): 844. Thanks to Jill Lepore for drawing public attention to this piece with her usual brilliance in her "Richer and Poorer: Accounting for Inequality," *The New Yorker,* March 16, 2015.
69. The U.S. Constitution appears so incapacitating to emerging nations with fully enfranchised adult populations that it no longer attracts emulators as it once did. Supreme Court Justice Ruth Bader Ginsburg rued, "I would not look to the United States Constitution if I were drafting a Constitution in the year 2012"; "'We the People' Loses Followers," *New York Times,* February 7, 2012, A1. See also Sanford Levinson, *Our Undemocratic Constitution: Where the Constitution Goes Wrong (and How We the People Can Correct It)* (New York: Oxford University Press, 2006).
70. Stepan and Linz, "Comparative Perspectives," 841–56, quote on 844.
71. Unless political means are found to serve as the equivalent of global war in righting inequality, the leading systemic account concludes, it will only get worse; Thomas Piketty, *Capital in the Twenty-First Century* (Cambridge, MA: Belknap Press of Harvard University Press, 2014). Summarizing the situation with stark accuracy, a leading philosopher concludes that capitalism is, again, destroying the social and political conditions for its own perpetuation; Nancy Fraser, "Legitimation Crisis: On the Political Contradictions of Financialized Capitalism," *Critical Historical Studies* 2, no. 2 (Fall 2015): 157–89. On the fiscal straitjacket that bodes ill for democracy, see Armin Schäfer and Wolfgang Streeck, eds., *Politics in the Age of Austerity* (Cambridge, UK: Polity, 2013), especially authors' essays.
72. Jessica Silver-Greenberg and Robert Gebeloff, "Arbitration Everywhere, Stacking the Deck of Justice," *New York Times,* November 1, 2015, A1, 22–23. See also Katherine V. W. Stone, "Signing Away Our Rights," *American Prospect,* April 2011, 20–22. Here is some relevant GMU context: Near the time of Charles Koch's first big gift to George Mason, Citizens for a Sound Economy (CSE) "launched a grass-roots lobbying drive supporting a package of bills aimed at overhauling the U.S. civil litigation system." That multimillion-dollar effort was led by C. Boyden Gray, who had worked with Ed Meese to transform the judiciary, served on the board of CSE as its chair, and was a founding co-chair, with Dick Armey and Jack Kemp, of FreedomWorks. Gray has since been appointed a distinguished faculty member at GMU's Scalia School of Law. The circumstantial trail leaves many open questions, of course. But the ten-plus years of work that went into producing this outcome signal, at minimum, the patient and ambitious reach

of the strategic thinking that is transforming governance in America. Indeed, one of the early litigators who sought Supreme Court blessing for such practices was John G. Roberts Jr. Then a private attorney representing Discover Bank, he was appointed chief justice in 2005. See Silver-Greenberg and Gebeloff, "Arbitration Everywhere"; Jessica Silver-Greenberg and Michael Corkery, "In Arbitration, a 'Privatization of the Justice System,'" *New York Times*, November 2, 2015, A1, B4; Peter H. Stone, "Grass-Roots Group Rakes in the Green," *National Journal* 27 (March 11, 1995): 521; David D. Kirkpatrick, "Conservatives See Court Shift as Culmination," *New York Times*, January 30, 2006, A1, 18; FreedomWorks, "Citizens for a Sound Economy (CSE) and Empower America Merge to Form FreedomWorks," undated 2004 press release, http://web.archive.org/web/20040725031033/http://www.freedomworks.org/release.php.

73. Silver-Greenberg and Gebeloff, "Arbitration Everywhere"; Greenberg and Corkery, "In Arbitration, a 'Privatization of the Justice System,'" A1, B4. See also Noam Scheiber, "As Americans Take Up Populism, the Supreme Court Embraces Business," *New York Times*, March 11, 2016.
74. See, for example, Charles Murray, *By the People: Rebuilding Liberty Without Permission* (New York: Crown Forum, 2015).
75. James M. Buchanan and Gordon Tullock, *The Calculus of Consent: Logical Foundations of Constitutional Democracy* (Ann Arbor: University of Michigan Press, 1962), 289. One could also trace the cause's distorted notions further back, to the Anti-Federalists who opposed the Constitution; see Garry Wills, *A Necessary Evil: A History of American Distrust of Government* (New York: Doubleday, 2000).
76. Barry Friedman, *The Will of the People: How Public Opinion Has Influenced the Supreme Court and Shaped the Meaning of the Constitution* (New York: Farrar, Straus and Giroux, 2009), 168; Jane Dailey, *Before Jim Crow: The Politics of Race in Postemancipation Virginia* (Chapel Hill: University of North Carolina Press, 2000), 163; Nell Irvin Painter, *Standing at Armageddon: The United States, 1877–1919* (New York: W. W. Norton, 1987), Tarbell quote on 72. Painter's title captures the consensus of several generations of historians on the explosive divisions of this era; if the Koch cause continues to advance, we may again find ourselves "Standing at Armageddon."
77. Ira Katznelson, *Fear Itself: The New Deal and the Origins of Our Time* (New York: Liveright, 2013). For a stark contrast to Katznelson's cogent comparative analysis, see the Buchanan-influenced account by libertarian journalist Amity Shlaes, *The Forgotten Man: A New History of the Great Depression* (New York: HarperCollins, 2007). For the internal evolution of legal doctrine on the court, see Alan Brinkley, et al., "AHR Forum: The Debate over the Constitutional Revolution of 1937," *American Historical Review* 110 (October 2005): 1047. As the brilliant refugee economist Karl Polanyi observed in 1944, looking out on a world in flames, a self-adjusting market "could not exist for any length of time without annihilating the human and natural substance of society"; Karl Polanyi, *The Great Transformation: The Political and Economic Origins of Our Time* (Boston: Beacon Press, 1944), 3.
78. Clint Bolick, *David's Hammer: The Case for an Activist Judiciary* (Washington, DC: Cato Institute, 2007). For an apt description of the overall project and the headway it had made by 2005, see Jeffrey Rosen, "The Unregulated Offensive," *New York Times Magazine*, April 17, 2005.
79. Monica Davey, "Concerns Grow as Court Races Draw Big Cash," *New York Times*, March 28, 2015, A1, 15; Sharon McCloskey, "Win the Courts, Win the War," in *Altered State*, 51. Koch grantee Clint Bolick offered another reason: "state constitutions . . . can be amended more easily than the U.S. Constitution"; Bolick, *Two-Fer: Electing a President and a Supreme Court* (Stanford, CA: Hoover Institution Press, 2012), 88–91. In January 2016, in what one smart journalist dubbed "the most chilling political appointment that you've probably

never heard of," Arizona's Tea Party governor named Bolick to the state supreme court, after Bolick himself had advised that the cause required "judges willing to enforce [the new] constitutional provisions" coming from "skilled advocates" (Bolick, *Two-Fer*, 95, also 96). Bolick is no longer a bit player on the margins. Jeb Bush, then the expected establishment "moderate" frontrunner, who had just coauthored a book with Bolick, pronounced it a "fantastic" appointment. Ian Millhiser, "The Most Chilling Political Appointment That You've Probably Never Heard Of," *ThinkProgress*, January 6, 2016.

80. Jeffrey Toobin, "To Your Health," *The New Yorker*, July 9 and 16, 2012, 29–30. For deeper context, see Adam Liptak, "The Most Conservative Court in Decades," *New York Times*, July 25, 2010, A1, 20–21; and Adam Liptak, "Justices Offer Receptive Ear to Business Interests," *New York Times*, December 19, 2010, A1, 32.
81. Pamela S. Karlan, "No Respite for Liberals," *New York Times Sunday Review*, June 30, 2012.
82. Nicholas Fando, "University in Turmoil Over Scalia Tribute and Koch Role," *New York Times*, April 28, 2016; David E. Bernstein, *Rehabilitating Lochner: Defending Individual Rights Against Progressive Reform* (Chicago: University of Chicago Press); Michael S. Greve, *The Upside-Down Constitution* (Cambridge, MA: Harvard University Press, 2012). Also see the works of two Koch grantees not at the Scalia School of Law: Clint Bolick's *Death Grip: Loosening the Law's Stranglehold over Economic Liberty* (Stanford, CA: Hoover Institution Press, 2011); and Levin, *The Liberty Amendments*, which conveys the impression that altering the Constitution is the ultimate reason for the push to control a supermajority of states.
83. For the rationale today, see Clint Bolick, *Leviathan: The Growth of Local Government and the Erosion of Liberty* (Stanford, CA: Hoover Institution Press, 2004). North Carolina's General Assembly, for its part, has altered the rules of representation in specific local bodies; as one Democratic critic aptly noted, they aimed "to reshape the rules to dictate the outcomes so that they win at every level of government, whether or not the voters want them to win"; Richard Fausset, "With State Control, North Carolina Republicans Pursue Some Smaller Prizes," *New York Times*, April 7, 2015, A12.
84. Editorial, "G.O.P. Statehouse Shows the Locals Who's Boss," *New York Times*, February 21, 2017, A22; Alan Blinder, "When a State Balks at a City's Minimum Wage," *New York Times*, February 22, 2016; Kate Scanlon, "In Texas, State Leaders Attack Local Governments for Going Big on Regulations," *Daily Signal*, March 15, 2015; Shaila Dewan, "States Are Overturning Local Laws, Often at Behest of Industry," *New York Times*, February 24, 1915, A1.
85. Even such an architect of the GOP right as the Reagan kingmaker William A. Rusher knew this. Taking issue with the endorsement by his colleagues at *National Review* of measures to turn over federal revenue to the states, he reminded them in private, as the magazine's publisher, of "the indisputable fact that state and local governments in this country are, commonly, far more corrupt and corruptible than the federal government." Rusher went on to explain that "the Washington bureaucrats may be snakes in the grass, but ordinarily they are honest snakes in the grass." So, he pushed, was the right's answer to be that "at least the state and local bureaucrats are our snakes in the grass"? William Rusher to William F. Buckley, Priscilla Buckley, James Burnham, Jeffrey Hart, and Frank Meyer, February 3, 1971, box 121, Rusher Papers. For an incisive social science analysis of how state governments became sites "in which the foes of liberalism could consolidate their power, refine their appeals, and develop their evolving justifications for restricting the scope of federal activism," see Margaret Weir, "States, Race, and the Decline of New Deal Liberalism," *Studies in American Political Development* 19 (Fall 2005): 157–72.
86. "States Get a Poor Report Card" (editorial), *New York Times*, March 20, 2012, A22. For the full report, see Caitlin Ginley, "Grading the Nation: How Accountable Is Your State?"

Center for Public Integrity, March 19, 2012, www.publicintegrity.org/2012/03/19/8423/grading-nation-how-accountable-your-state, and later editions.

87. Andrew Young to the Editor, *New York Times,* June 11, 2015. Calling voters who do not share the cause's economics "a public nuisance," one Mercatus economist said it would be wise "to reduce or eliminate efforts to increase voter turnout"; Bryan Caplan, *The Myth of the Rational Voter: Why Democracies Choose Bad Policies* (Princeton, NJ: Princeton University Press, 2007), 197, 199.
88. Lori C. Minnite, *The Myth of Voter Fraud* (Ithaca, NY: Cornell University Press, 2010), 154–57; "The Success of the Voter Fraud Myth" (editorial), *New York Times,* September 20, 2016, A22.
89. Ari Berman, *Give Us the Ballot: The Modern Struggle for Voting Rights in America* (New York: Farrar, Straus and Giroux, 2015), 260, 263. For Walker's earlier efforts to hold down the vote as Milwaukee County executive, see Minnite, *Myth of Voter Fraud,* 103–8.
90. Wendy Weiser, "Voter Suppression: How Bad?" *American Prospect,* Fall 2014, 12–16.
91. Jane Mayer, "State for Sale," *The New Yorker,* October 10, 2011; Mayer, *Dark Money,* 240–67, quote on 263. Mayer emphasizes the partisan and policy motives for the gerrymandering; I believe another goal is to line up states for a constitutional convention to amend the Constitution. See, for hints of this endgame, Wines, "Push to Alter Constitution, via the States."
92. David Daley, *Ratf**ked: The True Story Behind the Secret Plan to Steal America's Democracy* (New York: Liveright, 2016), xxvi, 110, 181–84, 187, 199–200. A colleague of Buchanan's going back to the Virginia Tech days, W. Mark Crain, had led in thinking about how to redistrict while on the GMU economics faculty and won recognition from the two Virginia Republican governors associated with the Koch base camp at George Mason; CV at https://policystudies.lafayette.edu/wp-content/uploads/sites/41/2016/02/Mark-Crain-CV.pdf. Apparently wanting still more power, the cause is seeking additional ways to underrepresent the urban and suburban voters from whom it expects opposition. In a rule-rigging scheme worthy of the Constitution's three-fifths clause and Harry Byrd's midcentury Organization, cadre attorneys have litigated to require that those ineligible to vote (such as noncitizen immigrants, disenfranchised felons, and children) go uncounted for purposes of apportioning representation and funding. The Supreme Court rejected such a bid in early 2016, but, as *The American Prospect* rightly prophesied, the new-style "'one person, one vote' battle [is] just starting." One voting expert and court watcher warns that the outcome would be "an enormous transfer of political power"; Scott Lemieux, et al., "'One Person, One Vote' Battle Just Starting," *American Prospect,* April 18, 2016; Eliza Newlin Carney, "How Scalia's Absence Impacts Democracy Rulings," *American Prospect,* February 18, 2016.
93. Norquist, *Leave Us Alone,* 217, 222.
94. Kenneth P. Vogel, "The Koch Intelligence Agency," *Politico,* November 18, 2015, www.politico.com/story/2015/11/the-koch-brothers-intelligence-agency-215943#ixzz47cZ8Bqci. Koch employees claim to have disbanded that particular operation, but such methods have become central to the operation's functioning. Members of the State Policy Network, for example, have initiated "Mapping the Left" projects that, like their massive-resistance-era predecessors, try to create the appearance of a single, coherent, unified enemy to rally their base against, as they also enable assessment of their targets' defense capabilities, and seek to smear and intimidate individuals; see, for example, Susan Myrick, "Mapping the Left in NC: Roots of Radicalism," *NC Capitol Connection* 7, no. 2 (February 2015): 1, 10; Paul Krugman, "American Thought Police," *New York Times,* March 28, 2011, A27. For the best-documented state inquisitionary body of the civil rights era, see Yasuhiro Katagiri, *The Mississippi State Sovereignty Commission: Civil Rights and States' Rights* (Jackson: University Press of Mississippi, 2001); and Rick Bowers, *Spies of Mississippi: The True Story of the Spy Network That Tried to Destroy the Civil Rights Movement* (Washington, DC: National Geographic, 2010).

95. Shulman, *Sons of Wichita,* 285–86.
96. John Hope Franklin, "History: Weapon of War and Peace," *Phylon* 5 (1944): 258. I thank Evelyn Brooks Higginbotham for this reference.
97. The author notes, too, how Buchanan's ideas "threaten to become self-fulfilling" by discrediting the aspirational behavioral norm of public spirit; Steven Kelman, "'Public Choice' and Public Spirit," *The Public Interest* 87 (March 1987): 80–94, quotes on 81, 93. See also the extended close analysis of how Buchanan's theory, in effect, makes a case for the supremacy of property rights backed by brute force, by Amadae, *Prisoners of Reason,* 175–203.
98. For recognition of how much jurisprudential ground the cause has conquered, see Brian Beutler, "The Rehabilitationists," *New Republic,* Fall 2015.
99. Norquist, *Leave Us Alone,* xv; Daniel Fisher, "Inside the Koch Empire: How the Brothers Plan to Reshape America," *Forbes,* December 5, 2012.

BIBLIOGRAPHY

Author's note: This bibliography includes only works cited, not all those from which I have learned. To keep the book inviting for general readers, a full listing of all the sources that have informed my understanding was not possible. I ask the forbearance of the scholars and journalists who do not see their relevant works listed here. I deeply appreciate the rich literature on which I was able to draw for so many areas, even if citations had to be limited to particular points in the text.

ARCHIVAL COLLECTIONS

AFL-CIO George Meany Memorial Archives, Special Collections, University of Maryland, College Park, MD
    Civil Rights Department Records
American Friends Service Committee Archives, Philadelphia
    Community Relations Department
    Southern Program Project
    Southside Virginia School Desegregation
Buchanan House Archives, Center for Study of Public Choice, George Mason University, Fairfax, VA
David R. Rubenstein Rare Book and Manuscript Library, Duke University, Durham, NC
    William Volker Fund Records, 1953–1961
Ford Foundation Records, Projects, Ford Foundation Archives, Rockefeller Archive Center, Sleepy Hollow, NY
    Educational Program of Thomas Jefferson Center for Studies in Political Economy, University of Virginia
George Mason University Special Collections and Archives, Fairfax, VA
    C. Harrison Mann Papers
Hoover Institution Archives, Stanford University, Stanford, CA
    Roy A. Childs Papers
    Ed Clark Papers
    John Davenport Papers
    Roger Freeman Papers
    Milton Friedman Papers, 1931–2006
    Friedrich A. von Hayek Papers
    Institute of Economic Affairs Records
    Mont Pelerin Society Records
    Henry Regnery Papers
    Gordon Tullock Papers
James Branch Cabell Library, Special Collections and Archives, Virginia Commonwealth University, Richmond, VA

Edward H. Peeples Jr. Collection
Richmond Crusade for Voters Archive
Jean and Alexander Heard Library, Special Collections, Vanderbilt University, Nashville, TN
Donald Grady Davidson Papers
Lewis F. Powell Jr. Archives, Washington and Lee University School of Law, Lexington, VA
Lewis F. Powell Jr. Papers
Library of Congress, Manuscript Division, Washington, DC
William J. Baroody Papers
William A. Rusher Papers, 1940–1989
Robert Russa Moton Museum, Farmville, VA
Barbara Rose Johns Manuscript Memoir
Ronald Reagan Presidential Library, Simi Valley, CA
Thomas G. Moore Papers
Office of Domestic Affairs
Ronald Reagan Governor's Papers
White House Office of Records Management
White House Office of Speechwriting
University of Chicago Library, Special Collections Research Center, Chicago
Frank Hyneman Knight Papers
University of Oregon, Special Collections & University Archives, Eugene, OR
T. Coleman Andrews Papers
Robert LeFevre Collection
University of Virginia Library, Special Collections Department, Charlottesville, VA
Harry Flood Byrd Sr. Papers
Leon Dure Papers
John Segar Gravatt Papers
James J. Kilpatrick Papers
Papers of the President of the University of Virginia
Louise O. Wensel Papers
Virginia Polytechnic Institute and State University, Special Collections, Blacksburg, VA
T. Marshall Hahn Papers
William E. Lavery Records
Yale University, Manuscripts and Archives, New Haven, CT
William F. Buckley Jr. Papers

NEWSPAPERS, MAGAZINES, AND ONLINE PUBLICATIONS

American Prospect
Atlantic
Bloomberg News
Carolina Israelite
Cavalier Daily
Charles Rowley's Blog
Christian Century
Commentary
Daily Caller (Cato Institute)
Daily Progress (Charlottesville, VA)
Daily Signal (Heritage Foundation)
Dissent
The Economist
Equal Times
Farmville Herald
Forbes

Fortune
The Freeman
Guardian
Huffington Post
Human Events
In These Times
International Business Times
Investigative Reporting Workshop (American University School of Communication)
Jet
Lew Rockwell.com
Los Angeles Times
Lynchburg News
Mason Gazette
El Mercurio
The Nation
National Journal
National Review
New Republic
The New Yorker
New York Times
News & Observer (Raleigh, NC)
Politico
Potomac Magazine
The Public Interest
Reason
Richmond News Leader
Richmond Times-Dispatch
Salon
Saturday Evening Post
Staunton (VA) *Daily News*
ThinkProgress
Time
U.S. News & World Report
Virginian-Pilot
Wall Street Journal
Washington Post
Yahoo News

DISSERTATIONS AND THESES

Corley, Robert Gaines. "James Jackson Kilpatrick: The Evolution of a Southern Conservative, 1955–1965." Master's thesis, University of Virginia, 1970.

Currin, Scovill. "An Army of the Willing: Fayette'Nam, Soldier Dissent, and the Untold Story of the All-Volunteer Force." PhD diss., Duke University, 2015.

Glickman, Andrew Ziet. "Virginia Desegregation and the Freedom of Choice Plan: The Role of Leon Dure and the Freedom of Association." Master's thesis, University of Virginia, 1991.

Gourse, Alexander. "Restraining the Reagan Revolution: The Lawyers' War on Poverty and the Durable Liberal State, 1964–1989." PhD diss., Northwestern University, 2015.

Hershman, James H., Jr. "A Rumbling in the Museum: The Opponents of Virginia's Massive Resistance." PhD diss., University of Virginia, 1978.

Kay, Bryan. "The History of Desegregation at the University of Virginia, 1950–1969. Master's thesis, University of Virginia, 1979.

Mound, Joshua M. "Inflated Hopes, Taxing Times: The Fiscal Crisis, the Pocketbook Squeeze, and the Roots of the Tax Revolt." PhD diss., University of Michigan, 2015.

Owen, Jan Gaylord. "Shannon's University: A History of the University of Virginia, 1959 to 1974." PhD diss., Columbia University, 1993.

Rasche, Pamela Jane. "Leon Dure and the 'Freedom of Association.'" Master's thesis, University of Virginia, 1977.

Riehl, Jonathan. "The Federalist Society and Movement Conservatism: How a Fractious Coalition on the Right Is Changing Constitutional Law and the Way We Talk and Think About It." PhD diss., University of North Carolina at Chapel Hill, 2007.

Turner, Kara Miles. "'It Is Not at Present a Very Successful School': Prince Edward County and the Black Educational Struggle, 1865–1995." PhD diss., Duke University, 2001.

JOURNAL ARTICLES

Aranson, Peter H. "Calhoun's Constitutional Economics." *Constitutional Political Economy* 2 (1991).

Berger, Jane. "'There Is Tragedy on Both Sides of the Layoffs': Public Sector Privatization and the Urban Crisis in Baltimore." *International Labor and Working-Class History* 71 (Spring 2007).

Blackford, Staige. "Free Choice and Tuition Grants in Five Southern States." *New South* 19, no. 14 (April 1964).

Breit, William. "Creating the 'Virginia School': Charlottesville as an Academic Environment in the 1960s." *Economic Inquiry* 25 (October 1987).

Brennan, Geoffrey. "Life in the Putty-Knife Factory." *American Journal of Economics and Sociology* 63 (January 2004).

Brinkley, Alan, et al. "AHR Forum: The Debate over the Constitutional Revolution of 1937." *American Historical Review* 110, no. 4 (2005).

Buchanan, James M. "Afraid to Be Free: Dependency as Desideratum." *Public Choice* 124 (July 2005).

———. "America's Third Century." *Atlantic Economic Journal* 1 (November 1973).

———. "Constitutional Imperatives for the 1990s: The Legal Order for a Free and Productive Economy." Hoover Institution, Stanford University (1988).

———. "DICTA: Some Remarks on Privatization." *Virginia Law Weekly* (October 23, 1987).

———. "Heraclitian Vespers." *American Journal of Economics and Sociology*, no. 63 (January 2004).

———. "The Potential for Taxpayer Revolt in American Democracy." *Social Science Quarterly* 59 (March 1979).

———. "Saving the Soul of Classical Liberalism." *Cato Policy Report*, March/April 2013.

———. "The Sayer of Truth: A Personal Tribute to Peter Bauer." *Public Choice*, no. 112 (September 2002).

———. "Social Insurance in a Growing Economy: A Proposal for Radical Reform." *National Tax Journal*, December 1968.

———. "Social Security Survival: A Public-Choice Perspective." *Cato Journal* 3 (Fall 1983).

———. "The Thomas Jefferson Center for Studies in Political Economy." *University of Virginia News Letter* 35, no. 2 (October 15, 1958).

Buchanan, James M., and R. L. Faith. "Secession and the Limits of Taxation: Toward a Theory of Internal Exit." *American Economic Review* 77 (1987).

Butler, Henry N. "The Manne Programs in Economics for Federal Judges." *Case Western Reserve Law Review* 50 (Fall 1999).

Butler, Stuart, and Peter Germanis. "Achieving a 'Leninist' Strategy." *Cato Journal* 3 (Fall 1983).

Couso, Javier. "Trying Democracy in the Shadow of an Authoritarian Legality: Chile's Transition to Democracy and Pinochet's Constitution of 1980." *Wisconsin International Law Journal* 29 (2011).

Current, Richard N. "John C. Calhoun, Philosopher of Reaction." *Antioch Review* 3 (June 1943).
Desai, Meghnad. "Economics v. Anarchy." *Higher Education Review* 3 (Summer 1971).
Einhorn, Robin L. "Slavery." *Journal of Business History* (2008).
Ensalaco, Mark. "In with the New, Out with the Old? The Democratizing Impact of Constitutional Reform in Chile." *Journal of Latin American Studies* 26 (May 1994).
Epps, Garrett. "The Littlest Rebel: James J. Kilpatrick and the Second Civil War." *Constitutional Commentary* 10, no. 1 (1993).
Feigenbaum, Harvey B. "The Politics of Privatization: A Comparative Perspective." *Governance: An International Journal of Policy and Administration* 1 (October 1988).
Ford, Charles H., and Jeffrey L. Littlejohn. "Reconstructing the Old Dominion: Lewis F. Powell, Stuart T. Saunders, and the Virginia Industrialization Group, 1958–1965." *Virginia Magazine of History & Biography* 121, no. 2 (2013).
Ford, Lacy, Jr. "Inventing the Concurrent Majority: Madison, Calhoun, and the Problem of Majoritarianism in American Political Thought." *Journal of Southern History* 60 (February 1994).
Fraser, Nancy. "Legitimation Crisis: On the Political Contradictions of Financialized Capitalism." *Critical Historical Studies* 2, no. 2 (Fall 2015).
Friedman, Murray. "One Episode in Southern Jewry's Response to Desegregation: An Historical Memoir." *American Jewish Archives* 30 (November 1981).
Greenberg, David. "The Idea of 'the Liberal Media' and Its Roots in the Civil Rights Movement." *The Sixties* (Winter 2008–2009).
Haddigan, Lee. "How Anticommonism 'Cemented' the American Conservative Movement in a Liberal Age of Conformity." *Libertarian Papers* 2 (2010).
Henig, Jeffrey R. "Privatization in the United States: Theory and Practice." *Political Science Quarterly* 104, no. 4 (Winter 1989–90).
Henig, Jeffrey R., Chris Hammett, and Harvey B. Feigenbaum. "The Politics of Privatization: A Comparative Perspective." *Governance: An International Journal of Policy and Administration* 1, no. 4 (October 1988).
Katz, Michael B., Mark J. Stern, and Jamie J. Fader. "The New African American Inequality." *Journal of American History* 92, no. 1 (June 2005).
Katznelson, Ira, Kim Geiger, and Daniel Kryder. "Limiting Liberalism: The Southern Veto in Congress, 1933–1950." *Political Science Quarterly* 108 (Summer 1993).
Kelman, Steven. "'Public Choice' and Public Spirit." *The Public Interest* 87 (March 1987): 80–94.
Kirby, David, and Emily Ekins. "Libertarian Roots of the Tea Party." *Policy Analysis* 705 (August 6, 2012).
Koch, Charles G. "The Business Community: Resisting Regulation." *Libertarian Review*, August 1978.
———. "Koch Industries, Market Process Analysis, and the Science of Liberty." *Journal of Private Enterprise* 22 (Spring 2007).
Lee, Dwight R. "*The Calculus of Consent* and the Constitution of Capitalism." *Cato Journal* 7 (Fall 1987).
Leidholdt, Alexander S. "Showdown on Mr. Jefferson's Lawn: Contesting Jim Crow During the University of Virginia's Protodesegregation." *Virginia Magazine of History and Biography* 122 (2014).
Lemieux, Pierre. "The Public Choice Revolution." *Regulation* 27, no. 3 (Fall 2004).
Lewis, George. "'Any Old Joe Named Zilch'? The Senatorial Campaign of Dr. Louise Oftedal Wensel." *Virginia Magazine of History and Biography* 107 (Summer 1999).
———. "Virginia's Northern Strategy: Southern Segregationists and the Route to National Conservatism." *Journal of Southern History* 72 (February 2006).
Lomasky, Loren. "When Hard Heads Collide: A Philosopher Encounters Public Choice." *American Journal of Economics and Sociology* 63 (January 2004).

Mack, Kenneth W. "Law and Mass Politics in the Making of the Civil Rights Lawyer, 1931–1941." *Journal of American History* 93 (June 2006).

Manne, Henry G. "An Intellectual History of the George Mason University School of Law." George Mason University Law and Economics Center, 1993. www.law.gmu.edu/about/history.

———. "A New Perspective for Public Interest Law Firms." Washington Legal Foundation, Critical Legal Issue Working Paper Series, no. 3 (November 1985).

McVicar, Michael J. "Aggressive Philanthropy: Progressivism, Conservatism, and the William Volker Charities Fund." *Missouri Historical Review* 105 (2011).

Medema, Steven G. "'Related Disciplines': The Professionalization of Public Choice Analysis." *History of Political Economy* 32, suppl. 1 (2000).

Meese, Edwin III. "The Attorney General's View of the Supreme Court: Toward a Jurisprudence of Original Intention." *Public Administrative Review* 45 (November 1985).

O'Connor, Alice. "The Privatized City: The Manhattan Institute, the Urban Crisis, and the Conservative Counterrevolution in New York." *Journal of Urban History* 34, (January 2008).

Olson, Mancur, and Christopher K. Clague. "Dissent in Economics: The Convergence of Extremes." *Social Research* 38 (Winter 1971).

Quadagno, Jill. "Generational Equity and the Politics of the Welfare State." *Politics and Society* 17 (April 1989).

Rothbard, Murray N. "Rothbard's Confidential Memorandum to the Volker Fund, 'What Is to Be Done?'" *Libertarian Papers* 1, no. 3 (2009).

Skocpol, Theda, and Alexander Hertel-Fernandez. "The Koch Effect: The Impact of a Cadre-Led Network on American Politics." Paper prepared for the Inequality Mini-Conference, Southern Political Science Association, San Juan, Puerto Rico, January 8, 2016. https://www.scholarsstrategynetwork.org/sites/default/files/the_koch_effect_for_spsa_w_apps_skocpol_and_hertel-fernandez-corrected_1-4-16_1.pdf.

Stepan, Alfred, and Juan J. Linz. "Comparative Perspectives on Inequality and the Quality of Democracy in the United States." *Perspectives on Politics* 9 (December 2011).

Stigler, George J. "Why Have the Socialists Been Winning?" *Ordo*, Band 30. Stuttgart: Gustav Fisher Verlag, 1979.

Sweeney, R. "A Postscript to Massive Resistance: The Decline and Fall of the Virginia Commission on Constitutional Government." *Virginia Magazine of History and Biography* 121 (2013).

Tabarrok, Alexander, and Tyler Cowen. "The Public Choice Theory of John C. Calhoun." *Journal of Institutional and Theoretical Economics* 148 (1992).

Tullock, Gordon. "Problems of Majority Voting." *Journal of Political Economy* 68 (1959).

———. "The Welfare Costs of Tariffs, Monopolies and Theft." *Western Economic Journal* 5 (1967).

Urquiola, Miguel. "The Effects of Generalized School Choice on Achievement and Stratification: Evidence from Chile's Voucher Program." *Journal of Public Economics* 90 (2006).

Vaughn, Karen I. "Remembering Jim Buchanan," *Review of Austrian Economics* 27 (2014).

———. "How James Buchanan Came to George Mason University." *Journal of Private Enterprise* 30 (2015).

Wagner, Richard E. "Public Choice as Academic Enterprise." *American Journal of Economics and Sociology* 63 (January 2004).

Walker, Vanessa. "At the End of Influence: The Letelier Assassination, Human Rights, and Rethinking Intervention in US–Latin American Relations." *Journal of Contemporary History* 46 (2011).

BOOKS, BOOK CHAPTERS, AND OTHER PUBLICATIONS

Alliance for Justice. *Justice for Sale: Shortchanging the Public Interest for Private Gain*. Washington, DC: Alliance for Justice, 1993.

Altman, Nancy J., and Eric R. Kinston. *Social Security Works: Why Social Security Isn't Going Broke and How Expanding It Will Help Us All*. New York: New Press, 2015.

Amadae, S. M. *Prisoners of Reason: Game Theory and Neoliberal Political Economy.* New York: Cambridge University Press, 2016.

———. *Rationalizing Capitalist Democracy: The Cold War Origins of Rational Choice Liberalism.* Chicago: University of Chicago Press, 2003.

Amenta, Edwin. *When Movements Matter: The Townsend Plan and the Rise of Social Security.* Princeton, NJ : Princeton University Press, 2006.

American Jewish Congress. *Assault upon Freedom of Association: A Study of the Southern Attack on the National Association for the Advancement of Colored People.* New York: American Jewish Congress, 1957.

Andrew, John A., III. *The Other Side of the Sixties: Young Americans for Freedom and the Rise of Conservative Politics.* New Brunswick, NJ: Rutgers University Press, 1997.

Applebome, Peter. *Dixie Rising: How the South Is Shaping American Values, Politics, and Culture.* New York: Harcourt Brace, 1996.

Armey, Dick, and Matt Kibbe. *Give Us Liberty: A Tea Party Manifesto.* New York: HarperCollins, 2010.

Atkinson, Frank B. *The Dynamic Dominion: Realignment and the Rise of Virginia's Republican Party Since 1945.* Fairfax, VA: George Mason University Press, 1992.

Atlas, John. *Seeds of Change: The Story of ACORN, America's Most Controversial Antipoverty Community Organizing Group.* Nashville, TN: Vanderbilt University Press, 2010.

Austin, Curtis J. *Up Against the Wall: Violence in the Making and Unmaking of the Black Panther Party.* Fayetteville: University of Arkansas Press, 2006.

Baer, Kenneth S. *Reinventing Government: The Politics of Liberalism from Reagan to Clinton.* Lawrence: University Press of Kansas, 2000.

Balogh, Brian. *A Government Out of Sight: The Mystery of National Authority in Nineteenth-Century America.* Cambridge, UK: Cambridge University Press, 2009.

Banham, Russ. *The Fight for Fairfax: A Struggle for a Great American County.* Fairfax, VA: George Mason University Press, 2009.

Baptist, Edward. *The Half Has Never Been Told: Slavery and the Making of American Capitalism.* New York: Basic Books, 2014.

Barnard, Hollinger F., ed. *Outside the Magic Circle: The Autobiography of Virginia Foster Durr.* Tuscaloosa: University of Alabama Press, 1985.

Barros, Robert. *Constitutionalism and Dictatorship: Pinochet, the Junta, and the 1980 Constitution.* Chicago: University of Chicago Press, 2002.

Bartels, Larry M. *Unequal Democracy: The Political Economy of the New Gilded Age.* Princeton, NJ: Princeton University Press and Russell Sage, 2008.

Bartley, Numan V. *The Rise of Massive Resistance: Race and Politics During the 1950s.* Rev. ed. Baton Rouge: Louisiana State University Press, 1997.

Beckert, Sven. *Empire of Cotton: A Global History.* New York: Alfred A. Knopf, 2014.

Berman, Ari. *Give Us the Ballot: The Modern Struggle for Voting Rights in America.* New York: Farrar, Straus and Giroux, 2015.

Bernstein, David E. *Rehabilitating Lochner: Defending Individual Rights Against Progressive Reform.* Chicago: University of Chicago Press, 2011.

Biondi, Martha. *The Black Revolution on Campus.* Berkeley: University of California Press, 2012.

Block, Walter, compiler. *I Chose Liberty: Autobiographies of Contemporary Libertarians.* Auburn, AL: Ludwig von Mises Institute, 2010.

Bloom, Joshua, and Waldo E. Martin Jr. *Black Against Empire: The History and Politics of the Black Panther Party.* Berkeley: University of California Press, 2013.

Blumenthal, Sidney. *The Rise of the Counter-Establishment: The Conservative Ascent to Political Power.* New York: Times Books, 1986.

Boaz, David. *The Libertarian Mind.* New York: Simon & Schuster, 2015.

Boettke, Peter J. and David L. Prychitko. "Introduction: The Present Status of Austrian Economics: Some (Perhaps Biased) Institutional History behind Market Process Theory."

In *The Market Process: Essays in Contemporary Austrian Economics*, ed. Boettke and Prychitko. Northampton, MA: Edward Elgar, 1994.

Bolick, Clint. *David's Hammer: The Case for an Activist Judiciary*. Washington, DC: Cato Institute, 2007.

———. *Death Grip: Loosening the Law's Stranglehold over Economic Liberty*. Stanford, CA: Hoover Institution Press, 2011.

———. *Leviathan: The Growth of Local Government and the Erosion of Liberty*. Stanford, CA: Hoover Institution Press, 2004.

———. *Two-Fer: Electing a President and a Supreme Court*. Stanford, CA: Hoover Institution Press, 2012.

———. *Unfinished Business: A Civil Rights Strategy for America's Third Century*. San Francisco: Pacific Research Institute for Public Policy, 1991.

———. *Voucher Wars: Waging the Legal Battle over School Choice*. Washington, DC: Cato Institute, 2003.

Boris, Eileen, and Jennifer Klein. *Caring for America: Home Health Care Workers in the Shadow of the Welfare State*. New York: Oxford University Press, 2012.

Borzutsky, Silvia. "Cooperation or Confrontation Between the State and the Market? Social Security and Health Policies." In *After Pinochet: The Chilean Road to Democracy and the Market*, ed. Silvia Borzutsky and Lois Hecht Oppenheim. Gainesville: University Press of Florida, 2006.

Bradley, Philip D., ed. *The Public Stake in Union Power*. Charlottesville: University of Virginia Press, 1959.

Branch, Taylor. *Parting the Waters: America in the King Years, 1954–1963*. New York: Simon & Schuster, 1988.

Breit, William, and Barry T. Hirsch, eds. *Lives of the Laureates: Twenty-Three Nobel Economists*. Cambridge, MA: MIT Press, 2009.

Brown, Wendy. *Undoing the Demos: Neoliberalism's Stealth Revolution* (New York: Zone Books, 2015).

Browne, Elaine. *A Taste of Power: A Black Woman's Story*. New York: Pantheon, 1992.

Brownlee, W. Elliot, and Hugh Davis Graham, eds. *The Reagan Presidency: Pragmatic Conservatism and Its Legacies*. Lawrence: University Press of Kansas, 2003.

Broyles, J. Allen. *The John Birch Society: Anatomy of a Protest*. Boston: Beacon, 1964.

Buchanan, James M. *Better than Plowing and Other Personal Essays*. Chicago: University of Chicago Press, 1992.

———. "The Economic Constitution and the New Deal: Lessons for Late Learners." In *Regulatory Change in an Atmosphere of Crisis: Current Implications of the Roosevelt Years*, ed. Gary M. Walton. New York: Academic Press, 1979.

———. *Economics from the Outside In: "Better than Plowing" and Beyond*. College Station: Texas A&M University Press, 2007.

———. "From Private Preferences to Public Philosophy: The Development of Public Choice." In *The Economics of Politics*. London: Institute of Economic Affairs, 1978.

———. *The Limits of Liberty: Between Anarchy and Leviathan*. Indianapolis: Liberty Fund, 2000. First published 1975.

———, ed. *Political Economy, 1957–1982: The G. Warren Nutter Lectures in Political Economy*. Washington, DC: American Enterprise Institute for Public Policy Research, 1982.

———. *Politics by Principle, Not Interest: Toward Nondiscriminatory Democracy*. New York: Cambridge University Press, 1998.

———. "Post-Reagan Political Economy." In *Constitutional Economics*, ed. James Buchanan. Cambridge, MA: Basil Blackwell, 1991.

———. *Public Principles of Public Debt: A Defense and Restatement*. Homewood, IL: Richard D. Irwin, 1958.

———. "The Samaritan's Dilemma." In *Altruism, Morality and Economic Theory*, ed. Edmund S. Phelps. New York: Russell Sage Foundation, 1975.

———. *The Thomas Jefferson Center for Studies in Political Economy.* Charlottesville: University of Virginia Press, 1957.

———. "The Virginia Renaissance in Political Economy: The 1960s Revisited." In *Money and Markets: Essays in Honor of Leland B. Yeager*, ed. Roger Koppl. New York: Routledge, 2006.

———. *Why I, Too, Am Not a Conservative: The Normative Vision of Classical Liberalism.* Northampton, MA: Edward Elgar, 2005.

Buchanan, James M. and G. Brennan. "Tax Reform Without Tears: Why Must the Rich Be Made to Suffer?" *The Economics of Taxation*, ed. Henry J. Aaron and Michael Boskin. Washington, DC: Brookings Institution, 1980.

Buchanan, James M., and Nicos E. Devletoglou. *Academia in Anarchy: An Economic Diagnosis.* New York: Basic Books, 1970.

Buchanan, James M., and Gordon Tullock. *The Calculus of Consent: Logical Foundations of Constitutional Democracy.* Ann Arbor: University of Michigan Press, 1962.

Buchanan, James M., and Richard E. Wagner. *Democracy in Deficit: The Political Legacy of Lord Keynes.* New York: Academic Press, 1977.

———. et al. *The Economics of Politics.* London: Institute of Economic Affairs, 1978.

———. et al., eds. *Toward a Theory of the Rent-Seeking Society.* College Station: Texas A&M University Press, 1980.

Burgin, Angus. *The Great Persuasion: Reinventing Free Markets Since the Depression.* Cambridge, MA: Harvard University Press, 2012.

Burns, Jennifer. *Goddess of the Market: Ayn Rand and the American Right.* New York: Oxford University Press, 2009.

Caplan, Bryan. *The Myth of the Rational Voter: Why Democracies Choose Bad Policies.* Princeton, NJ: Princeton University Press, 2007.

Caro, Robert. *The Passage of Power.* New York: Alfred A. Knopf, 2012.

Chappell, David L. *Inside Agitators: White Southerners in the Civil Rights Movement.* Baltimore: Johns Hopkins University Press, 1994.

Chappell, Marisa. *The War on Welfare: Family, Poverty, and Politics in Modern America.* Philadelphia: University of Pennsylvania Press, 2009.

Cheek, H. Lee, Jr., ed. *John C. Calhoun: Selected Writings and Speeches.* Washington, DC: Regnery, 2003.

Conner, Claire. *Wrapped in the Flag: A Personal History of America's Radical Right.* Boston: Beacon, 2013.

Constable, Pamela, and Arturo Valenzuela. *A Nation of Enemies: Chile Under Pinochet.* New York: W. W. Norton, 1993.

Conway, Erik M. *Merchants of Doubt: How a Handful of Scientists Obscured the Truth on Issues from Tobacco Smoke to Global Warming.* New York: Bloomsbury Press, 2010.

Cosman, Bernard, and Robert J. Huckshorn, eds. *Republican Politics: The 1964 Campaign and Its Aftermath for the Party.* Westport, CT: Praeger, 1968.

Cowen, Tyler. *Average Is Over: Powering America Beyond the Age of the Great Stagnation.* New York: Dutton, 2013.

———. *The Theory of Market Failure: A Critical Examination.* Fairfax, VA: George Mason University Press, 1988.

Cowen, Tyler, and Veronique de Rugy. "Reframing the Debate." In *The Occupy Handbook*, ed. Janet Byrne. New York: Little, Brown, 2012.

Crane, Edward H., III. "Libertarianism." In *Emerging Political Coalitions in American Politics*, ed. Seymour Martin Lipset. San Francisco: Institute for Contemporary Studies, 1978.

Crespino, Joseph. *In Search of Another Country: Mississippi and the Conservative Counterrevolution.* Princeton, NJ: Princeton University Press, 2007.

———. *Strom Thurmond's America.* New York: Hill & Wang, 2012.

Crockett, Richard. *Thinking the Unthinkable: Think Tanks and the Economic Counter-Revolution, 1931–1983.* New York: HarperCollins, 1994.

Dabney, Virginius. *Mr. Jefferson's University: A History.* Charlottesville: University of Virginia Press, 1981.

Dailey, Jane. *Before Jim Crow: The Politics of Race in Postemancipation Virginia.* Chapel Hill: University of North Carolina Press, 2000.

Daley, David. *Ratf**ked: The True Story Behind the Secret Plan to Steal America's Democracy.* New York: Liveright, 2016.

Davidson, Donald. *The Attack on Leviathan: Regionalism and Nationalism in the United States.* Gloucester, MA: Peter Smith, 1962. First published 1938.

Davis, Angela, et al. *If They Come in the Morning: Voices of Resistance.* New York: New American Library, 1971.

Dierenfield, Bruce J. *Keeper of the Rules: Congressman Howard W. Smith of Virginia.* Charlottesville: University of Virginia Press, 1987.

Dionne, E. J. *Why the Right Went Wrong: Conservatism—from Goldwater to Trump.* New York: Simon & Schuster, 2016.

Doherty, Brian. *Radicals for Capitalism.* New York: Public Affairs, 2009.

Drew, Elizabeth. *Showdown: The Struggle Between the Gingrich Congress and the Clinton White House.* New York: Simon & Schuster, 1996.

———. *Whatever It Takes: The Real Struggle for Power in America.* New York: Viking, 1997.

Du Bois, William Edward Burghardt. *Black Reconstruction in America: An Essay toward a History of the Part which Black Folk Played in the Attempt to Reconstruct Democracy in America, 1860–1880.* New York: Oxford University Press, 1935.

Dykeman, Wilma. *Tennessee: A Bicentennial History.* New York: W. W. Norton, 1975.

Easton, Nina. *Gang of Five: Leaders at the Center of the Conservative Crusade.* New York: Simon & Schuster, 2000.

Ebenstein, Alan O. *Chicagonomics: The Evolution of Chicago Free Market Economics.* New York: St. Martin's, 2015.

———. *Friedrich Hayek: A Biography.* New York: Palgrave Macmillan, 2001.

———. *Milton Friedman: A Biography.* New York: Palgrave Macmillan, 2007.

Edsall, Thomas Byrne, with Mary D. Edsall. *Chain Reaction: The Impact of Race, Rights, and Taxes on American Politics.* New York: W. W. Norton, 1992.

Edwards, Laura F. *A Legal History of the Civil War and Reconstruction: A Nation of Rights.* New York: Cambridge University Press, 2015.

———. *The People and Their Peace: Legal Culture and the Transformation of Inequality in the Post-Revolutionary South.* Chapel Hill: University of North Carolina Press, 2009.

Edwards, Lee. *Leading the Way: The Story of Ed Feulner and the Heritage Foundation.* New York: Crown Forum, 2013.

Einhorn, Robin L. *American Slavery, American Taxation.* Chicago: University of Chicago Press, 2006.

Fang, Lee. *The Machine: A Field Guide to the Resurgent Right.* New York: New Press, 2013.

Federal Writers' Project. *The WPA Guide to Tennessee.* Knoxville: University of Tennessee Press, 1986.

Ferguson, Niall, et al. *The Shock of the Global: The 1970s in Perspective.* Cambridge, MA: Belknap Press of Harvard University Press, 2010.

Ferguson, Thomas, and Joel Rogers. *Right Turn: The Decline of the Democrats and the Future of American Politics.* New York: Hill & Wang, 1986.

Fields, Karen E., and Barbara J. Fields. *Racecraft: The Soul of Inequality in American Life.* New York: Verso, 2014.

Fink, Richard H., and Jack C. High, eds. *A Nation in Debt: Economists Debate the Federal Budget Deficit.* Frederick, MD: University Publications of America, 1987.

Fisher, Robert, ed., *The People Shall Rule: ACORN, Community Organizing, and the Struggle for Economic Justice.* Nashville, TN: Vanderbilt University Press, 2009.

Fitzpatrick, Ellen. *Endless Crusade: Women Social Scientists and Progressive Reform*. New York: Oxford University Press, 1990.

Fones-Wolf, Elizabeth. *Selling Free Enterprise: The Business Assault on Labor and Liberalism, 1945–1960*. Urbana: University of Illinois Press, 1994.

Frank, Thomas. *The Wrecking Crew: How Conservatives Ruined Government, Enriched Themselves, and Beggared the Nation*. New York: Metropolitan Books, 2008.

Freehling, William W. *Secessionists at Bay, 1776–1854*. Vol. 1 of *The Road to Disunion*. New York: Oxford University Press, 1991.

Freeman, Roger A. *Federal Aid to Education—Boon or Bane?* Washington, DC: American Enterprise Association, 1955.

Friddell, Guy. *Colgate Darden: Conversations with Guy Friddell*. Charlottesville: University of Virginia Press, 1978.

Friedman, Barry. *The Will of the People: How Public Opinion Has Influenced the Supreme Court and Shaped the Meaning of the Constitution*. New York: Farrar, Straus and Giroux, 2009.

Friedman, Milton. *Capitalism and Freedom*. Chicago: University of Chicago Press, 1962.

———. "The Role of Government in Education." In *Economics and the Public Interest*, ed. Robert A. Solo. New Brunswick, NJ: Rutgers University Press, 1955.

Friedman, Milton, and Rose D. Friedman. *Two Lucky People: Memoirs*. Chicago: University of Chicago Press, 1998.

Frohnen, Bruce, et al., eds. *American Conservatism: An Encyclopedia*. Wilmington, DE: Intercollegiate Studies Institute, 2006.

Gaston, Paul M. *Coming of Age in Utopia: The Odyssey of an Idea*. Montgomery, AL: NewSouth Books, 2010.

Gilmore, Glenda Elizabeth. *Defying Dixie: The Radical Roots of Civil Rights, 1919–1950*. New York: W. W. Norton, 2009.

Gilpin, R. Blakeslee. *John Brown Still Lives! America's Long Reckoning with Violence, Equality, & Change*. Chapel Hill: University of North Carolina Press, 2011.

Goldberg, Robert Alan. *Barry Goldwater*. New Haven, CT: Yale University Press, 1995.

Gordon, Linda. *Pitied but Not Entitled: Single Mothers and the History of Welfare*. New York: Free Press, 1994.

Gosse, Van. "Unpacking the Vietnam Syndrome: The Coup in Chile and the Rise of Popular Anti-Interventionism." *The World the Sixties Made*, ed. Van Gosse and Richard Moser. Philadelphia, PA: Temple University Press, 2003.

Green, Kristen. *Something Must Be Done About Prince Edward County: A Family, a Virginia Town, a Civil Rights Battle*. New York: HarperCollins, 2015.

Greve, Michael S., and Fred L. Smith Jr., eds. *Environmental Politics: Public Costs, Private Rewards*. Westport, CT: Praeger, 1992.

———. *The Upside-Down Constitution*. Cambridge, MA: Harvard University Press, 2012.

Hacker, Jacob S. *The Great Risk Shift: The New Economic Inequality and the Decline of the American Dream*. New York: Oxford University Press, 2006.

Hacker, Jacob S., and Paul Pierson. *American Amnesia: How the War on Government Led Us to Forget What Made America Prosper*. New York: Simon & Schuster, 2016.

———. *Winner-Take-All Politics: How Washington Made the Rich Richer—and Turned Its Back on the Middle Class*. New York: Simon & Schuster, 2011.

Hahamovich, Cindy. *No Man's Land: Jamaican Guestworkers in America and the Global History of Deportable Labor*. Princeton, NJ: Princeton University Press, 2011.

Harper, F. A. *Liberty: A Path to Its Recovery*. Irvington on Hudson, NY: Foundation for Economic Education, 1949.

———. *Why Wages Rise*. Irvington on Hudson, NY: Foundation for Economic Education, 1957.

Hartwell, R. M. *History of the Mont Pelerin Society*. Indianapolis: Liberty Fund, 1995.

Hartz, Louis. *The Liberal Tradition in America*. New York: Harcourt, Brace, 1955.

Hayek, F. A. "Postscript: Why I Am Not a Conservative." *The Constitution of Liberty*. 1960; repr., Chicago: Regnery, 1972.

———. *The Mirage of Social Justice*. Vol. 2 of *Law, Legislation and Liberty*. Chicago: University of Chicago Press, 1978.

———. *The Political Order of a Free People*. Vol. 3 of *Law, Legislation and Liberty*. Chicago: University of Chicago Press, 1979.

———. *The Road to Serfdom*. Chicago: University of Chicago Press, 1944.

Hazlett, Joseph M., II. *The Libertarian Party and Other Minor Parties in the United States*. Jefferson, NC: McFarland & Co., 1992.

Heinemann, Ronald L. *Harry Byrd of Virginia*. Charlottesville: University Press of Virginia, 1996.

Hetherington, Marc J. *Why Trust Matters: Declining Political Trust and the Demise of American Liberalism*. Princeton, NJ: Princeton University Press, 2005.

Hofstadter, Richard. *The American Political Tradition and the Men Who Made It*. New York: Random House, 1948.

———. *Social Darwinism in American Thought*. Boston: Beacon Press, 1955.

Holloway, Jonathan Scott. *Confronting the Veil: Abram Harris, Jr., E. Franklin Frazier, and Ralph Bunche, 1919–1941*. Chapel Hill: University of North Carolina Press, 2002.

Horwitz, Morton J. *The Transformation of American Law, 1870–1960: The Crisis of Legal Orthodoxy*. New York: Oxford University Press, 1992.

———. *The Warren Court and the Pursuit of Justice*. New York: Hill & Wang, 1998.

Hustwit, William P. *James K. Kilpatrick: Salesman for Segregation*. Chapel Hill: University of North Carolina Press, 2013.

Hutt, W. H. *The Theory of Collective Bargaining*. Glencoe, IL: Free Press, 1954.

Jacobs, Meg. *Panic at the Pump: The Energy Crisis and the Transformation of American Politics in the 1970s*. New York: Hill & Wang, 2016.

———. *Pocketbook Politics: Economic Citizenship in Twentieth-Century America*. Princeton, NJ: Princeton University Press, 2005.

———. "The Politics of Environmental Regulation: Business-Governmental Relations in the 1970s and Beyond." In *What's Good for American Business*, ed. Kimberly Phillips-Fein and Julian E. Zelizer. New York: Oxford University Press, 2012.

Jacobs, Meg, and Julian E. Zelizer. *Conservatives in Power: The Reagan Years, 1981–1989: A Brief History with Documents*. Boston: Bedford/St. Martin's, 2010.

Johnson, Dennis W. *The Laws That Shaped America: Fifteen Acts of Congress and Their Lasting Impact*. New York: Routledge, 2009.

Johnson, M. Bruce, ed. *The Attack on Corporate America: The Corporate Issues Sourcebook*. New York: McGraw-Hill, 1978.

Johnson, Walter. *River of Dark Dreams: Slavery and Empire in the Cotton Kingdom*. Cambridge, MA: Belknap Press of Harvard University Press, 2013.

Jones, Daniel Stedman. *Masters of the Universe: Hayek, Friedman, and the Birth of Neoliberal Economics*. Princeton, NJ: Princeton University Press, 2012.

Kabaservice, Geoffrey. *Rule and Ruin: The Downfall of Moderation and the Destruction of the Republican Party, from Eisenhower to the Tea Party*. New York: Oxford University Press, 2012.

Kahn, Si, and Elizabeth Minnich. *The Fox in the Henhouse: How Privatization Threatens Democracy*. San Francisco: Berrett-Koehler, 2005.

Katznelson, Ira. *Fear Itself: The New Deal and the Origins of Our Time*. New York: Liveright, 2013.

Key, V. O., Jr. *Southern Politics, in State and Nation*. New York: Random House, 1949.

Keyssar, Alexander. *The Right to Vote: The Contested History of Democracy in the United States*. New York: Basic Books, 2000.

Kibbe, Matt. *Hostile Takeover: Resisting Centralized Government's Stranglehold on America*. New York: HarperCollins, 2012.

Kilpatrick, James J. *Interposition: Editorials and Editorial Page Presentations, 1955–1956*. Richmond, VA: Richmond News Leader, 1956.

———. *The Southern Case for School Segregation*. New York: Crowell-Collier Press, 1962.

———. *The Sovereign States: Notes of a Citizen of Virginia*. Chicago: Henry Regnery, 1957.

———. "The States Are Being Extorted into Ratifying the Twenty-Sixth Amendment." In *Amendment XXVI: Lowering the Voting Age*, ed. Sylvia Engdahl. New York: Greenhaven Press, 2010.

Kintz, Linda. *Between Jesus and the Market: The Emotions That Matter in Right-Wing America*. Durham, NC: Duke University Press, 1997.

Klein, Naomi. *The Shock Doctrine: The Rise of Disaster Capitalism*. New York: Metropolitan Books, 2007.

———. *This Changes Everything: Capitalism vs. the Climate*. New York: Simon & Schuster, 2014.

Klingaman, William K. *J. Harvie Wilkinson, Jr.: Banker, Visionary*. Richmond, VA: Crestar Financial Corporation, 1994.

Kluger, Richard. *Simple Justice: The History of* Brown v. Board of Education *and Black America's Struggle for Equality*. New York: Random House, 1975.

Koch, Charles G. *Creating a Science of Liberty*. Fairfax, VA: Institute for Humane Studies at George Mason University, 1997.

———. *Good Profit: How Creating Value for Others Built One of the World's Most Successful Companies*. New York: Crown Business, 2015.

———. *The Science of Success: How Market-Based Management Built the World's Largest Private Company*. Hoboken, NJ: John Wiley & Sons, 2007.

———. "Tribute." Preface to *The Writings of F. A. Harper*, vol. 1: *The Major Works*. Menlo Park, CA: Institute for Humane Studies, 1978.

Koch, Fred C. *A Business Man Looks at Communism*. Farmville, VA: Farmville Herald, n.d.

Kondracke, Morton, and Fred Barnes. *Jack Kemp: The Bleeding-Heart Conservative Who Changed America*. New York: Sentinel, 2015.

Korstad, Robert Rodgers. *Civil Rights Unionism: Tobacco Workers and the Struggle for Democracy in the Mid-Twentieth-Century South*. Chapel Hill: University of North Carolina Press, 2004.

Kotz, Nick. *Judgment Days: Lyndon Baines Johnson, Martin Luther King, Jr., and the Laws That Changed America*. New York: Houghton Mifflin, 2003.

Kousser, J. Morgan. *The Shaping of Southern Politics: Suffrage Restriction and the Establishment of the One-Party South*. New Haven, CT: Yale University Press, 1974.

Kruse, Kevin M. *White Flight: Atlanta and the Making of Modern Conservatism*. Princeton, NJ: Princeton University Press, 2005.

Lassiter, Matthew D. *The Silent Majority: Suburban Politics in the Sunbelt South*. Princeton, NJ: Princeton University Press, 2006.

Lassiter, Matthew D., and Andrew B. Lewis, eds. *The Moderates' Dilemma: Massive Resistance to School Desegregation in Virginia*. Charlottesville: University Press of Virginia, 1998.

Lawson, Steven F. *Black Ballots: Voting Rights in the South, 1944–1969*. Lanham, MD: Lexington Books, 1999. First published 1976.

Layzer, Judith A. *Open for Business: Conservatives' Opposition to Environmental Regulation*. Boston: MIT Press, 2012.

Lee, Sophia Z. *The Workplace Constitution, from the New Deal to the New Right*. New York: Cambridge University Press, 2014.

Levin, Mark R. *The Liberty Amendments: Restoring the American Republic*. New York: Threshold Editions, 2013.

Levinson, Sanford. *Our Undemocratic Constitution: Where the Constitution Goes Wrong (and How We the People Can Correct It)*. New York: Oxford University Press, 2006.

Levenstein, Lisa. *A Movement Without Marches: African American Women and the Politics of Poverty in Postwar Philadelphia*. Chapel Hill: University of North Carolina Press, 2009.

Lienesch, Michael. *Redeeming America: Piety and Politics in the New Christian Right*. Chapel Hill: University of North Carolina Press, 1993.

Light, Jessica. "Public Choice: A Critical Reassessment." In *Government and Markets: Toward a New Theory of Regulation*, ed. Edward J. Balleisen and David A. Moss. New York: Cambridge University Press, 2010.

Lightner, David L. *Slavery and the Commerce Power: How the Struggle Against the Interstate Slave Trade Led to the Civil War*. New Haven, CT: Yale University Press, 2006.

Lind, Michael. *Up from Conservatism: Why the Right Is Wrong for America*. New York: Free Press, 1996.

Link, William A. *Righteous Warrior: Jesse Helms and the Rise of Modern Conservatism*. New York: St. Martin's, 2008.

Linz, Juan J., and Alfred Stepan. *Problems of Democratic Transition and Consolidation: Southern Europe, South America, and Post-Communist Europe*. Baltimore: Johns Hopkins University Press, 1996.

Love, Robert. *How to Start Your Own School: A Guide for the Radical Right, the Radical Left, and Everybody In-Between Who's Fed Up with Public Education*. New York: Macmillan, 1973.

Lowndes, Joseph E. *From the New Deal to the New Right: Race and the Southern Origins of Modern Conservatism*. New Haven, CT: Yale University Press, 2008.

Lynn, Susan. *Progressive Women in Conservative Times: Racial Justice, Peace, and Feminism, 1945 to the 1960s*. New Brunswick, NJ: Rutgers University Press.

MacKenzie, G. Calvin, and Robert Weisbrot. *The Liberal Hour: Washington and the Politics of Change in the 1960s*. New York: Penguin, 2008.

MacLean, Nancy. *Freedom Is Not Enough: The Opening of the American Workplace*. Cambridge, MA: Harvard University Press, 2006.

Mann, Thomas E., and Norman Ornstein. *It's Even Worse than It Looks: How the American Constitutional System Collided with the New Politics of Extremism*. New York: Basic Books, 2012.

Manne, Henry G., and James A. Dorn, eds. *Economic Liberties and the Judiciary*. Fairfax, VA, and Washington, DC: George Mason University Press and the Cato Institute, 1987.

Maraniss, David, and Michael Weisskopf. *"Tell Newt to Shut Up!"* New York: Simon & Schuster, 1996.

Martin, Everett Dean. *Liberal Education vs. Propaganda*. Menlo Park, CA: Institute for Humane Studies, n.d.

Martin, Isaac William. *Rich People's Movements: Grassroots Campaigns to Untax the One Percent*. New York: Oxford University Press, 2013.

Mayer, Jane. *Dark Money: The Hidden History of the Billionaires Behind the Rise of the Radical Right*. New York: Doubleday, 2016.

Mayer, Jane, and Jill Abramson. *Strange Justice: The Selling of Clarence Thomas*. New York: Houghton Mifflin, 1994.

McEnaney, Laura. *World War II's "Postwar": A Social and Policy History of Peace, 1944–1953*. Philadelphia: University of Pennsylvania Press, forthcoming 2017.

McGirr, Lisa. *Suburban Warriors: The Origins of the New American Right*. Princeton, NJ: Princeton University Press, 2001.

McNeil, Genna Rae. *Groundwork: Charles Hamilton Houston and the Struggle for Civil Rights*. Philadelphia: University of Pennsylvania Press, 1983.

McSweeney, Dean, and John E. Owens, eds. *The Republican Takeover of Congress*. New York: St. Martin's, 1998.

Medvetz, Thomas. *Think Tanks in America*. Chapel Hill: University of North Carolina Press, 2012.

Meese, Edwin, III. "Speech by Attorney General Edwin Meese, III, Before the American Bar Association." In *The Great Debate: Interpreting Our Written Constitution*. Occasional Paper. Washington, DC: Federalist Society, 1986.

———. *With Reagan: The Inside* Story. Washington, DC: Regnery Gateway, 1992.

Micklethwait, John, and Adrian Wooldridge. *The Right Nation: Conservative Power in America*. New York: Penguin Press, 2004.

Mills, Charles. *The Racial Contract*. Ithaca, NY: Cornell University Press, 1997.

Minchin, Timothy J. *What Do We Need a Union For? The TWUA in the South, 1945–1955*. Chapel Hill: University of North Carolina Press, 2000.

Minnite, Lori C. *The Myth of Voter Fraud*. Ithaca, NY: Cornell University Press, 2010.

Mirowski, Philip, and Dieter Plehwe, eds. *The Road from Mont Pelerin: The Making of the Neoliberal Thought Collective*. Cambridge, MA: Harvard University Press, 2009.

Mises, Ludwig von. *The Anti-Capitalistic Mentality*. New York: D. Van Nostrand, 1956.

Moreton, Bethany E. *To Serve God and Wal-Mart: The Making of Christian Free Enterprise*. Cambridge, MA: Harvard University Press, 2009.

Moreton, Bethany, and Pamela Voekel. "Learning from the Right: A New Operation Dixie?" In *Labor Rising: The Past and Future of Working People in America*, ed. Richard Greenwald and Daniel Katz. New York: New Press, 2012.

Muñoz, Heraldo. *The Dictator's Shadow: Life Under Augusto Pinochet*. New York: Basic Books, 2008.

Murphy, Paul V. *The Rebuke of History: The Southern Agrarians and American Conservative Thought*. Chapel Hill: University of North Carolina Press, 2001.

Murray, Charles. *By the People: Rebuilding Liberty Without Permission*. New York: Crown Forum, 2015.

Muse, Benjamin. *Virginia's Massive Resistance*. Bloomington: Indiana University Press, 1961.

Nash, George H. *The Conservative Intellectual Movement in America, Since 1945*. Wilmington, DE: Intercollegiate Studies Institute, 1998. First published 1976.

Norquist, Grover G. *Leave Us Alone: Getting the Government's Hands Off Our Money, Our Guns, and Our Lives*. New York: HarperCollins, 2008.

Novak, Robert D. *The Agony of the G.O.P., 1964*. New York: Macmillan, 1965.

Novak, William J. *The People's Welfare: Law and Regulation in Nineteenth-Century America*. Chapel Hill: University of North Carolina Press, 1996.

O'Connor, Alice. "Financing the Counterrevolution." In *Rightward Bound: Making America Conservative in the 1970s*, ed. Bruce J. Schulman and Julian E. Zelizer. Cambridge, MA: Harvard University Press, 2008.

O'Connor, James. *The Fiscal Crisis of the State*. New York: St. Martin's, 1973.

Oppenheim, Lois Hecht. *Politics in Chile: Socialism, Authoritarianism and Market Democracy*. Boulder, CO: Westview, 2007.

Orr, Daniel. "Rent Seeking in an Aging Population." In *Toward a Theory of the Rent-Seeking Society*, ed. James M. Buchanan, et al. College Station: Texas A&M University Press, 1980.

Painter, Nell Irvin. *Standing at Armageddon: The United States, 1877–1919*. New York: W. W. Norton, 1987.

Palmer, Bruce. *"Man over Money": The Southern Populist Critique of American Capitalism*. Chapel Hill: University of North Carolina Press, 1980.

Parker, Christopher S., and Matt A. Barreto. *Change They* Can't *Believe In: The Tea Party and Reactionary Politics in America*. Princeton, NJ: Princeton University Press, 2013.

Patterson, James T. *Restless Giant: The United States from Watergate to* Bush v. Gore. New York: Oxford University Press, 2005.

Peeples, Edward H., with Nancy MacLean. *Scalawag: A White Southerner's Journey Through Segregation to Human Rights Activism*. Charlottesville: University of Virginia Press, 2014.

Perlstein, Rick. *Before the Storm: Barry Goldwater and the Unmaking of the American Consensus*. New York: Nation Books, 2001.

Peschek, Joseph G. *Policy-Planning Organizations: Elite Agendas and America's Right Turn*. Philadelphia, PA: Temple University Press, 1987.

Phillips-Fein, Kim. *Invisible Hands: The Making of the Conservative Movement from the New Deal to Reagan*. New York: W. W. Norton, 2009.

Pierson, Paul. *Dismantling the Welfare State?: Reagan, Thatcher, and the Politics of Retrenchment*. New York: Cambridge University Press, 1994.

Piketty, Thomas. *Capital in the Twenty-First Century*. Cambridge, MA: Belknap Press of Harvard University Press, 2014.

Piñera, José. "Chile." In *The Political Economy of Policy Reform*, ed. John Williamson. Washington, DC: Institute for International Economics, 1994.

Polanyi, Karl. *The Great Transformation: The Political and Economic Origins of Our Time*. Boston: Beacon, 1957. First published 1944.

Poole, Robert W. *Cut Local Taxes Without Reducing Essential Services*. Santa Barbara, CA: Reason Press, 1976.

———. *Cutting Back City Hall*. New York: Universe Books, 1980.

Postel, Charles. *The Populist Vision*. New York: Oxford University Press, 2007.

Potter, David M. *The South and the Concurrent Majority*. Baton Rouge: Louisiana State University Press, 1972.

Prasad, Monica. *The Politics of Free Markets: The Rise of Neoliberal Economic Policies in Britain, France, Germany and the United States*. Chicago: University of Chicago Press, 2006.

Prieto, Ramon Iván Nuñez. *Las Transformaciones de la Educación Bajo el Régimen Militar*, vol. 1. Santiago: CIAN, 1984.

Rabin-Havt, Ari, and Media Matters for America. *Lies, Incorporated: The World of Post-Truth Politics*. New York: Anchor Books, 2016.

Rae, Nicol C. *The Decline and Fall of the Liberal Republicans: From 1952 to the Present*. New York: Oxford University Press, 1989.

Raimondo, Justin. *An Enemy of the State: The Life of Murray N. Rothbard*. Amherst, NY: Prometheus, 2000.

Reinhard, David. *The Republican Right Since 1945*. Lexington: University Press of Kentucky, 1983.

Ribuffo, Leo P. *The Old Christian Right: The Protestant Far Right from the Great Depression to the Cold War*. Philadelphia, PA: Temple University Press, 1983.

Roberts, Gene, and Hank Klibanoff. *The Race Beat: The Press, the Civil Rights Struggle, and the Awakening of a Nation*. New York: Alfred A. Knopf, 2006.

Roberts, Paul Craig, and Karen LaFollette Araujo. *The Capitalist Revolution in Latin America*. New York: Oxford University Press, 1997.

Robin, Corey. *The Reactionary Mind: From Edmund Burke to Sarah Palin*. New York: Oxford University Press, 2011.

Rodgers, Daniel T. *The Age of Fracture*. Cambridge, MA: Belknap Press of Harvard University Press, 2011.

———. *Atlantic Crossings: Social Politics in a Progressive Era*. Cambridge, MA: Belknap Press of Harvard University Press, 1998.

Rothbard, Murray N. *Power & Market: Government and the Economy*. Menlo Park, CA: Institute for Humane Studies, 1970.

———. *The Betrayal of the American Right*. Auburn, AL: Ludwig von Mises Institute, 2007.

Rowan, Carl T. *South of Freedom*. New York: Alfred A. Knopf, 1952.

Rowley, Charles K., ed. *Democracy and Public Choice: Essays in Honor of Gordon Tullock*. Oxford, UK: Basil Blackwell, 1987.

Rubin, Jeffrey, and Vivienne Bennett, eds. *Enduring Reform: Progressive Activism and Private Sector Responses in Latin America's Democracies*. Pittsburgh: University of Pittsburgh Press.

Rubin, Jeffrey W., and Emma Sokoloff-Rubin. *Sustaining Activism: A Brazilian Women's Movement and a Father-Daughter Collaboration*. Durham, NC: Duke University Press, 2013.

Saloma, John S. *Ominous Politics: The New Conservative Labyrinth*. New York: Hill & Wang, 1984.

Sanders, Elizabeth. *Roots of Reform: Farmers, Workers, and the American State, 1877–1917.* Chicago: University of Chicago Press, 1999.
Schäfer, Armin and Wolfgang Streeck, eds., *Politics in the Age of Austerity.* Cambridge, UK: Polity, 2013.
Schoenwald, Jonathan M. *A Time for Choosing: The Rise of Modern American Conservatism.* New York: Oxford University Press, 2002.
Schulman, Bruce J. *From Cotton Belt to Sunbelt: Federal Policy, Economic Development, and the Transformation of the South, 1938–1980.* New York: Oxford University Press, 1991.
———. *The Seventies: The Great Shift in American Culture, Society, and Politics.* New York: Free Press, 2001.
Schulman, Daniel. *Sons of Wichita: How the Koch Brothers Became America's Most Powerful and Private Dynasty.* New York: Grand Central, 2014.
Sclar, Elliott D. *You Don't Always Get What You Pay For: The Economics of Privatization.* Ithaca, NY: Cornell University Press, 2001.
Shapiro, Karin A. *A New South Rebellion: The Battle Against Convict Labor in the Tennessee Coalfields, 1871–1896.* Chapel Hill: University of North Carolina Press, 1998.
Shlaes, Amity. *The Forgotten Man: A New History of the Great Depression.* New York: Harper, 2007.
Simon, William E. *A Time for Truth.* New York: McGraw-Hill, 1978.
Sinha, Minisha. *The Counter-Revolution of Slavery: Politics and Ideology in Antebellum South Carolina.* Chapel Hill: University of North Carolina Press, 2000.
Sklar, Holly, ed. *Trilateralism: The Trilateral Commission and Elite Planning for World Management.* Boston: South End Press, 1980.
Skocpol, Theda, and Vanessa Williamson. *The Tea Party and the Remaking of Republican Conservatism.* New York: Oxford University Press, 2012.
Smith, J. Douglas. *Managing White Supremacy: Race, Politics, and Citizenship in Jim Crow Virginia.* Chapel Hill: University of North Carolina Press, 2002.
———. *On Democracy's Doorstep: The Inside Story of How the Supreme Court Brought "One Person, One Vote" to the United States.* New York: Hill & Wang, 2014.
Smith, James Allen. *The Idea Brokers: Think Tanks and the Rise of the New Policy Elite.* New York: New Press, 1991.
Smith, Mark A. *The Right Talk: How Conservatives Transformed the Great Society into the Economic Society.* Princeton, NJ: Princeton University Press, 2007.
Smith, Robert C. *They Closed Our Schools: Prince Edward County, Virginia 1951–1964.* Chapel Hill: University of North Carolina Press, 1965.
Specter, Arlen. *Life Among the Cannibals: A Political Career, a Tea Party Uprising, and the End of Governing as We Know It.* New York: Thomas Dunne, 2012.
Stein, Judith. *Pivotal Decade: How the United States Traded Factories for Finance in the Seventies.* New Haven, CT: Yale University Press, 2010.
Stepan, Alfred. "State Power and the Strength of Civil Society in the Southern Cone of Latin America." In *Bringing the State Back In,* ed. Peter B. Evans, et al. New York: Oxford University Press, 1985.
Stepan, Alfred, ed. *Democracies in Danger.* Baltimore: Johns Hopkins University Press, 2009.
Stern, Steve. *Battling for Hearts and Minds: Memory Struggles in Pinochet's Chile, 1973–1988.* Durham, NC: Duke University Press, 2006.
———. *Reckoning with Pinochet: The Memory Question in Democratic Chile, 1989–2006.* Durham, NC: Duke University Press, 2010.
Stiglitz, Joseph E. *The Price of Inequality: How Today's Divided Society Endangers Our Future.* New York: W. W. Norton, 2012.
Stockman, David A. *The Triumph of Politics: Why the Reagan Revolution Failed.* New York: Harper & Row, 1986.
Stokes, John, with Lois Wolfe and Herman J. Viola. *Students on Strike: Jim Crow, Civil Rights,* Brown, *and Me: A Memoir.* Washington, DC: National Geographic, 2008.

Sullivan, Patricia. *Days of Hope: Race and Democracy in the New Deal Era.* Chapel Hill: University of North Carolina Press, 1996.

Sunstein, Cass R. *Why Nudge? The Politics of Libertarian Paternalism.* New Haven, CT: Yale University Press, 2014.

Sweeney, James R., ed. *Race, Reason, and Massive Resistance: The Diary of David J. Mays, 1954–1959.* Athens: University of Georgia Press, 2008.

Tabarrok, Alexander, ed. *Changing the Guard: Private Prisons and the Control of Crime.* Oakland, CA: Independent Institute, 2003.

Tarter, Brent. *The Grandees of Government: The Origins and Persistence of Undemocratic Politics in Virginia.* Charlottesville: University of Virginia Press, 2013.

Taylor, Marcus. *From Pinochet to the "Third Way": Neoliberalism and Social Transformation in Chile.* London: Pluto Press, 2006.

Teles, Steven M. *The Rise of the Conservative Legal Movement: The Battle for Control of the Law.* Princeton, NJ: Princeton University Press, 2008.

Teles, Steven M., and Brian J. Glenn, eds. *Conservatism and American Political Development.* New York: Oxford University Press, 2009.

Teles, Steven, and Daniel A. Kenney, "Spreading the Word: The Diffusion of American Conservatism in Europe and Beyond." In *Growing Apart? America and Europe in the Twenty-First Century,* eds. Jeffrey Kopstein and Sven Steinmo. Cambridge, UK: Cambridge University Press, 2008.

Thaler, Richard H., and Cass R. Sunstein. *Nudge: Improving Decisions About Health, Wealth, and Happiness.* New York: Penguin, 2009.

Thorndike, Joseph J. " 'The Sometimes Sordid Level of Race and Segregation': James J. Kilpatrick and the Virginia Campaign Against *Brown.*" In *The Moderates' Dilemma: Massive Resistance to School Desegregation in Virginia,* ed. Matthew D. Lassiter and Andrew B. Lewis. Charlottesville: University Press of Virginia, 1998.

Tollison, Robert D., and Richard E. Wagner. *The Economics of Smoking.* Boston: Kluwer Academic Publishers, 1992.

Tullock, Gordon. "Origins of Public Choice." In *The Makers of Modern Economics,* vol. 3, ed. Arnold Heertje. Cheltenham, UK: Edward Elgar, 1999.

———. *The Politics of Bureaucracy.* Washington, DC: Public Affairs, 1965.

———. *Rent Seeking.* Brookfield, VT: Edward Elgar, 1993.

———. *Toward a Mathematics of Politics.* Ann Arbor: University of Michigan Press, 1967.

Turner, Kara Miles. "'Liberating Lifescripts': Prince Edward County, Virginia, and the Roots of *Brown v. Board of Education.*" In *From the Grassroots to the Supreme Court: Prince Edward County, Virginia, and the Roots of* Brown v. Board of Education, ed. Peter F. Lau. Durham. NC: Duke University Press, 2004.

Twelve Southerners. *I'll Take My Stand: The South and the Agrarian Tradition.* Baton Rouge: Louisiana State University Press, 1977. First published 1930.

Vacs, Aldo C. "Coping with the General's Long Shadow on Chilean Democracy." In *After Pinochet: The Chilean Road to Democracy and the Market,* ed. Silvia Borzutsky and Lois Hecht Oppenheim. Gainesville: University Press of Florida, 2006.

van Horn, Robert, Philip Mirowski, and Thomas A. Stapleford. *Building Chicago Economics: New Perspectives on the History of America's Most Powerful Economics Program.* New York: Cambridge University Press, 2011.

Vogel, David. *Fluctuating Fortunes: The Political Power of Business in America.* Washington, DC: Beard Books, 2003. First published 1989.

Vogel, Kenneth P. *Big Money: 2.5 Billion Dollars, One Suspicious Vehicle, and a Pimp—on the Trail of the Ultra-Rich Hijacking American Politics.* New York: Public Affairs, 2014.

Waldstreicher, David. *Slavery's Constitution, from Revolution to Ratification.* New York: Hill & Wang, 2009.

Walker, Scott. *Unintimidated: A Governor's Story and a Nation's Challenge*. New York: Sentinel, 2013.

Waterhouse, Benjamin C. *Lobbying America: The Politics of Business from Nixon to NAFTA*. Princeton, NJ: Princeton University Press, 2015.

White, Morton. *Social Thought in America: The Revolt Against Formalism*. Boston: Beacon Press, 1947.

Whitman, Mark. Brown v. Board of Education*: A Documentary History*. Princeton, NJ: Markus Wiener, 2004.

Wilentz, Sean. *The Age of Reagan: A History, 1974–2008*. New York: HarperCollins, 2008.

Wilkinson, J. Harvie. *Harry Byrd and the Changing Face of Virginia Politics, 1945–1966*. Charlottesville: University Press of Virginia, 1968.

Wills, Garry. *A Necessary Evil: A History of American Distrust of Government*. New York: Doubleday, 2000.

Woodward, C. Vann. *Origins of the New South, 1877–1913*. Baton Rouge: Louisiana State University Press, 1951.

Zernike, Kate. *Boiling Mad: Behind the Lines in Tea Party America*. New York: St. Martin's Griffin, 2011.

INDEX